Visualization
Analysis & Design

A K PETERS VISUALIZATION SERIES

Series Editor: Tamara Munzner

Visualization Analysis and Design
Tamara Munzner
2014

Visualization
Analysis & Design

Tamara Munzner
Department of Computer Science
University of British Columbia

Illustrations by Eamonn Maguire

CRC Press
Taylor & Francis Group
Boca Raton London New York

CRC Press is an imprint of the
Taylor & Francis Group, an **informa** business

AN A K PETERS BOOK

CRC Press
Taylor & Francis Group
6000 Broken Sound Parkway NW, Suite 300
Boca Raton, FL 33487-2742

Printed on acid-free paper
Version Date: 20140909
Printed in Canada

International Standard Book Number-13: 978-1-4665-0891-0 (Pack - Book and Ebook)

Library of Congress Cataloging-in-Publication Data

Munzner, Tamara.
   Visualization analysis and design / Tamara Munzner, Department of Computer Science, University of British Columbia.
      pages cm -- (A K Peters visualization series)
   Includes bibliographical references and index.
   ISBN 978-1-4665-0891-0 (alk. paper)
      1. Information visualization. I. Title.

   QA76.9.I52M86 2015
   001.4'226--dc23   2014020715

Visit the Taylor & Francis Web site at
http://www.taylorandfrancis.com

and the CRC Press Web site at
http://www.crcpress.com

Contents

Preface

Why a New Book?

I wrote this book to scratch my own itch: the book I wanted to teach out of for my graduate visualization (vis) course did not exist. The itch grew through the years of teaching my own course at the University of British Columbia eight times, co-teaching a course at Stanford in 2001, and helping with the design of an early vis course at Stanford in 1996 as a teaching assistant.

I was dissatisfied with teaching primarily from original research papers. While it is very useful for graduate students to learn to read papers, what was missing was a synthesis view and a framework to guide thinking. The principles and design choices that I intended a particular paper to illustrate were often only indirectly alluded to in the paper itself. Even after assigning many papers or book chapters as preparatory reading before each lecture, I was frustrated by the many major gaps in the ideas discussed. Moreover, the reading load was so heavy that it was impossible to fit in any design exercises along the way, so the students only gained direct experience as designers in a single monolithic final project.

I was also dissatisfied with the lecture structure of my own course because of a problem shared by nearly every other course in the field: an incoherent approach to crosscutting the subject matter. Courses that lurch from one set of crosscuts to another are intellectually unsatisfying in that they make vis seem like a grab-bag of assorted topics rather than a field with a unifying theoretical framework. There are several major ways to crosscut vis material. One is by the field from which we draw techniques: cognitive science for perception and color, human–computer interaction for user studies and user-centered design, computer graphics for rendering, and so on. Another is by the problem domain addressed: for example, biology, software engineering, computer networking, medicine, casual use, and so on. Yet another is by the families of techniques: focus+context, overview/detail, volume rendering, and statistical graphics. Finally, evaluation is an important and central topic that should be interwoven throughout, but it did not fit into the standard pipelines and models. It was typically relegated to a single lecture, usually near the end, so that it felt like an afterthought.

Existing Books

Vis is a young field, and there are not many books that provide a synthesis view of the field. I saw a need for a next step on this front.

Tufte is a curator of glorious examples [Tufte 83, Tufte 91, Tufte 97], but he focuses on what can be done on the static printed page for purposes of exposition. The hallmarks of the last 20 years of computer-based vis are interactivity rather than simply static presentation and the use of vis for exploration of the unknown in addition to exposition of the known. Tufte's books do not address these topics, so while I use them as supplementary material, I find they cannot serve as the backbone for my own vis course. However, any or all of them would work well as supplementary reading for a course structured around this book; my own favorite for this role is *Envisioning Information* [Tufte 91].

Some instructors use *Readings in Information Visualization* [Card et al. 99]. The first chapter provides a useful synthesis view of the field, but it is only one chapter. The rest of the book is a collection of seminal papers, and thus it shares the same problem as directly reading original papers. Here I provide a book-length synthesis, and one that is informed by the wealth of progress in our field in the past 15 years.

Ware's book *Information Visualization: Perception for Design* [Ware 13] is a thorough book on vis design as seen through the lens of perception, and I have used it as the backbone for my own course for many years. While it discusses many issues on how one could design a vis, it does not cover what has been done in this field for the past 14 years from a synthesis point of view. I wanted a book that allows a beginning student to learn from this collective experience rather than starting from scratch. This book does not attempt to teach the very useful topic of perception per se; it covers only the aspects directly needed to get started with vis and leaves the rest as further reading. Ware's shorter book, *Visual Thinking for Design* [Ware 08], would be excellent supplemental reading for a course structured around this book.

This book offers a considerably more extensive model and framework than Spence's *Information Visualization* [Spence 07]. Wilkinson's *The Grammar of Graphics* [Wilkinson 05] is a deep and thoughtful work, but it is dense enough that it is more suitable for vis insiders than for beginners. Conversely, Few's *Show Me The Numbers* [Few 12] is extremely approachable and has been used at the undergraduate level, but the scope is much more limited than the coverage of this book.

The recent book *Interactive Data Visualization* [Ward et al. 10] works from the bottom up with algorithms as the base, whereas I work from the top down and stop one level above algorithmic considerations; our approaches are complementary. Like this book, it covers both nonspatial and spatial data. Similarly, the *Data Visualization* [Telea 07] book focuses on the algorithm level. The book on *The Visualization Toolkit* [Schroeder et al. 06] has a scope far beyond the vtk software, with considerable synthesis coverage of the concerns of visualizing spatial data. It has been used in many scientific visualization courses, but it does not cover nonspatial data. The voluminous *Visualization Handbook* [Hansen and Johnson 05] is an edited collection that contains a mix of synthesis material and research specifics; I refer to some specific chapters as good resources in my Further Reading sections at the end of each chapter in this book.

Audience

The primary audience of this book is students in a first vis course, particularly at the graduate level but also at the advanced undergraduate level. While admittedly written from a computer scientist's point of view, the book aims to be accessible to a broad audience including students in geography, library science, and design. It does not assume any experience with programming, mathematics, human–computer interaction, cartography, or graphic design; for those who do have such a background, some of the terms that I define in this book are connected with the specialized vocabulary from these areas through notes in the margins. Other audiences are people from other fields with an interest in vis, who would like to understand the principles and design choices of this field, and practitioners in the field who might use it as a reference for a more formal analysis and improvements of production vis applications.

I wrote this book for people with an interest in the design and analysis of vis idioms and systems. That is, this book is aimed at vis designers, both nascent and experienced. This book is not directly aimed at vis end users, although they may well find some of this material informative.

The book is aimed at both those who take a problem-driven approach and those who take a technique-driven approach. Its focus is on broad synthesis of the general underpinnings of vis in terms of principles and design choices to provide a framework for the design and analysis of techniques, rather than the algorithms to instantiate those techniques.

The book features a unified approach encompassing information visualization techniques for abstract data, scientific visualization techniques for spatial data, and visual analytics techniques for interleaving data transformation and analysis with interactive visual exploration.

Who's Who

I use pronouns in a deliberate way in this book, to indicate roles. I am the author of this book. I cover many ideas that have a long and rich history in the field, but I also advocate opinions that are not necessarily shared by all visualization researchers and practitioners. The pronoun **you** means the reader of this book; I address you as if you're designing or analyzing a visualization system. The pronoun **they** refers to the intended users, the target audience for whom a visualization system is designed. The pronoun **we** refers to all humans, especially in terms of our shared perceptual and cognitive responses.

I'll also use the abbreviation **vis** throughout this book, since *visualization* is quite a mouthful!

Structure: What's in This Book

The book begins with a definition of vis and walks through its many implications in Chapter 1, which ends with a high-level introduction to an analysis framework of breaking down vis design according *what–why–how* questions that have *data–task–idiom* answers. Chapter 2 addresses the *what* question with answers about data abstractions, and Chapter 3 addresses the *why* question with task abstractions, including an extensive discussion of deriving new data, a preview of the framework of design choices for *how* idioms can be designed, and several examples of analysis through this framework.

Chapter 4 extends the analysis framework to two additional levels: the domain situation level on top and the algorithm level on the bottom, with the what/why level of data and task abstraction and the how level of visual encoding and interaction idiom design in between the two. This chapter encourages using methods to validate your design in a way that matches up with these four levels.

Chapter 5 covers the principles of marks and channels for encoding information. Chapter 6 presents eight rules of thumb for design.

The core of the book is the framework for analyzing how vis idioms can be constructed out of design choices. Three chapters cover choices of how to visually encode data by arranging space: Chapter 7 for tables, Chapter 8 for spatial data, and Chapter 9 for networks. Chapter 10 continues with the choices for mapping color and other channels in visual encoding. Chapter 11 discusses ways to manipulate and change a view. Chapter 12 covers ways to facet data between multiple views. Choices for how to reduce the amount of data shown in each view are covered in Chapter 13, and Chapter 14 covers embedding information about a focus set within the context of overview data. Chapter 15 wraps up the book with six case studies that are analyzed in detail with the full framework.

Each design choice is illustrated with concrete examples of specific idioms that use it. Each example is analyzed by decomposing its design with respect to the design choices that have been presented so far, so these analyses become more extensive as the chapters progress; each ends with a table summarizing the analysis. The book's intent is to get you familiar with analyzing existing idioms as a springboard for designing new ones.

I chose the particular set of concrete examples in this book as evocative illustrations of the space of vis idioms and my way to approach vis analysis. Although this set of examples does cover many of the more popular idioms, it is certainly not intended to be a complete enumeration of all useful idioms; there are many more that have been proposed that aren't in here. These examples also aren't intended to be a historical record of who first proposed which ideas: I often pick more recent examples rather than the very first use of a particular idiom.

All of the chapters start with a short section called **The Big Picture** that summarizes their contents, to help you quickly determine whether a chapter covers material that you care about. They all end with a **Further Reading** section that points you to more information about their topics. Throughout the book are boxes in the margins: vocabulary notes in purple starting with a star, and cross-reference notes in blue starting with a triangle. Terms are highlighted in purple where they are defined for the first time.

The book has an accompanying web page at http://www.cs.ubc.ca/~tmm/vadbook with errata, pointers to courses that use the book in different ways, example lecture slides covering the material, and downloadable versions of the diagram figures.

What's Not in This Book

This book focuses on the abstraction and idiom levels of design and doesn't cover the domain situation level or the algorithm levels.

I have left out algorithms for reasons of space and time, not of interest. The book would need to be much longer if it covered algorithms at any reasonable depth; the middle two levels provide more than enough material for a single volume of readable size. Also, many good resources already exist to learn about algorithms, including original papers and some of the previous books discussed above. Some points of entry for this level are covered in Further Reading sections at the end of each chapter. Moreover, this book is intended to be accessible to people without a computer science background, a decision that precludes algorithmic detail. A final consideration is that the state of the art in algorithms changes quickly; this book aims to provide a framework for thinking about design that will age more gracefully. The book includes many concrete examples of previous vis tools to illustrate points in the design space of possible idioms, not as the final answer for the very latest and greatest way to solve a particular design problem.

The domain situation level is not as well studied in the vis literature as the algorithm level, but there are many relevant resources from other literatures including human–computer interaction. Some points of entry for this level are also covered in Further Reading.

Acknowledgments

My thoughts on visualization in general have been influenced by many people, but especially Pat Hanrahan and the students in the vis group while I was at Stanford: Robert Bosch, Chris Stolte, Diane Tang, and especially François Guimbretiére.

This book has benefited from the comments and thoughts of many readers at different stages.

I thank the recent members of my research group for their incisive comments on chapter drafts and their patience with my sometimes-obsessive focus on this book over the past six years: Matt Brehmer, Jessica Dawson, Joel Ferstay, Stephen Ingram, Miriah Meyer, and especially Michael Sedlmair. I also thank the previous members of my group for their collaboration and discussions that have helped shape my thinking: Daniel Archambault, Aaron Barsky, Adam Bodnar, Kristian Hildebrand, Qiang Kong, Heidi Lam, Peter McLachlan, Dmitry Nekrasovski, James Slack, Melanie Tory, and Matt Williams.

I thank several people who gave me useful feedback on my *Visualization* book chapter [Munzner 09b] in the *Fundamentals of Computer Graphics* textbook [Shirley and Marschner 09]: TJ Jankun-Kelly, Robert Kincaid, Hanspeter Pfister, Chris North, Stephen North, John Stasko, Frank van Ham, Jarke van Wijk, and Martin Wattenberg. I used that chapter as a test run of my initial structure for this book, so their feedback has carried forward into this book as well.

I also thank early readers Jan Hardenburgh, Jon Steinhart, and Maureen Stone. Later reader Michael McGuffin contributed many thoughtful comments in addition to several great illustrations.

Many thanks to the instructors who have test-taught out of draft versions of this book, including Enrico Bertini, Remco Chang, Heike Jänicke Leitte, Raghu Machiragu, and Melanie Tory. I especially thank Michael Laszlo, Chris North, Hanspeter Pfister, Miriah Meyer, and Torsten Möller for detailed and thoughtful feedback.

I also thank all of the students who have used draft versions of this book in a course. Some of these courses were structured to provide me with a great deal of commentary from the students on the drafts, and I particularly thank these students for their contributions.

From my own 2011 course: Anna Flagg, Niels Hanson, Jingxian Li, Louise Oram, Shama Rashid, Junhao (Ellsworth) Shi, Jillian Slind, Mashid ZeinalyBaraghoush, Anton Zoubarev, and Chuan Zhu.

From North's 2011 course: Ankit Ahuja, S.M. (Arif) Arifuzzaman, Sharon Lynn Chu, Andre Esakia, Anurodh Joshi, Chiranjeeb Kataki, Jacob Moore, Ann Paul, Xiaohui Shu, Ankit Singh, Hamilton Turner, Ji Wang, Sharon Chu Yew Yee, Jessica Zeitz, and especially Lauren Bradel.

From Pfister's 2012 course: Pankaj Ahire, Rabeea Ahmed, Salen Almansoori, Ayindri Banerjee, Varun Bansal, Antony Bett, Madelaine Boyd, Katryna Cadle, Caitline Carey, Cecelia Wenting Cao, Zamyla Chan, Gillian Chang, Tommy Chen, Michael Cherkassky, Kevin Chin, Patrick Coats, Christopher Coey, John Connolly, Daniel Crookston Charles Deck, Luis Duarte, Michael Edenfield, Jeffrey Ericson, Eileen Evans, Daniel Feusse, Gabriela Fitz, Dave Fobert, James Garfield, Shana Golden, Anna Gommerstadt, Bo Han, William Herbert, Robert Hero, Louise Hindal, Kenneth Ho, Ran Hou, Sowmyan Jegatheesan, Todd Kawakita, Rick Lee, Natalya Levitan, Angela Li, Eric Liao, Oscar Liu, Milady Jiminez Lopez, Valeria Espinosa Mateos, Alex Mazure, Ben Metcalf, Sarah Ngo, Pat Njolstad, Dimitris Papnikolaou, Roshni Patel, Sachin Patel, Yogesh Rana, Anuv Ratan, Pamela Reid, Phoebe Robinson, Joseph Rose, Kishleen Saini, Ed Santora, Konlin Shen, Austin Silva, Samuel Q. Singer, Syed Sobhan, Jonathan Sogg, Paul Stravropoulos, Lila Bjorg Strominger, Young Sul, Will Sun, Michael Daniel Tam, Man Yee Tang, Mark Theilmann, Gabriel Trevino, Blake Thomas Walsh, Patrick Walsh, Nancy Wei, Karisma Williams, Chelsea Yah, Amy Yin, and Chi Zeng.

From Möller's 2014 course: Tamás Birkner, Nikola Dichev, Eike Jens Gnadt, Michael Gruber, Martina Kapf, Manfred Klaffenböck, Sümeyye Kocaman, Lea Maria Joseffa Koinig, Jasmin Kuric, Mladen Magic, Dana Markovic, Christine Mayer, Anita Moser, Magdalena Pöhl, Michael Prater, Johannes Preisinger, Stefan Rammer, Philipp Sturmlechner, Himzo Tahic, Michael Tögel, and Kyriakoula Tsafou.

I thank all of the people connected with A K Peters who contributed to this book. Alice Peters and Klaus Peters steadfastedly kept asking me if I was ready to write a book yet for well over a decade and helped me get it off the ground. Sarah Chow, Charlotte Byrnes, Randi Cohen, and Sunil Nair helped me get it out the door with patience and care.

I am delighted with and thankful for the graphic design talents of Eamonn Maguire of Antarctic Design, an accomplished vis researcher in his own right, who tirelessly worked with me to turn my hand-drawn Sharpie drafts into polished and expressive diagrams.

I am grateful for the friends who saw me through the days, through the nights, and through the years: Jen Archer, Kirsten Cameron, Jenny Gregg, Bridget Hardy, Jane Henderson, Yuri Hoffman, Eric Hughes, Kevin Leyton-Brown, Max Read, Shevek, Anila Srivastava, Aimée Sturley, Jude Walker, Dave Whalen, and Betsy Zeller.

I thank my family for their decades of love and support: Naomi Munzner, Sheila Oehrlein, Joan Munzner, and Ari Munzner. I also thank Ari for the painting featured on the cover and for the way that his artwork has shaped me over my lifetime; see http://www. aribertmunzner.com.

Chapter 1

What's Vis, and Why Do It?

1.1 The Big Picture

This book is built around the following definition of visualization—
vis, for short:

> Computer-based **visualization** systems provide visual representations of datasets designed to help people carry out tasks more effectively.
>
> Visualization is suitable when there is a need to augment human capabilities rather than replace people with computational decision-making methods. The design space of possible vis idioms is huge, and includes the considerations of both how to create and how to interact with visual representations. Vis design is full of trade-offs, and most possibilities in the design space are ineffective for a particular task, so validating the effectiveness of a design is both necessary and difficult. Vis designers must take into account three very different kinds of resource limitations: those of computers, of humans, and of displays. Vis usage can be analyzed in terms of why the user needs it, what data is shown, and how the idiom is designed.

I'll discuss the rationale behind many aspects of this definition as a way of getting you to think about the scope of this book, and about visualization itself:

- Why have a human in the decision-making loop?

- Why have a computer in the loop?

- Why use an external representation?

- Why depend on vision?

- Why show the data in detail?

- Why use interactivity?

- Why is the vis idiom design space huge?

- Why focus on tasks?

- Why are most designs ineffective?

- Why care about effectiveness?

- Why is validation difficult?

- Why are there resource limitations?

- Why analyze vis?

1.2 Why Have a Human in the Loop?

Vis allows people to analyze data when they don't know exactly what questions they need to ask in advance.

The modern era is characterized by the promise of better decision making through access to more data than ever before. When people have well-defined questions to ask about data, they can use purely computational techniques from fields such as statistics and machine learning.* Some jobs that were once done by humans can now be completely automated with a computer-based solution. If a fully automatic solution has been deemed to be acceptable, then there is no need for human judgement, and thus no need for you to design a vis tool. For example, consider the domain of stock market trading. Currently, there are many deployed systems for high-frequency trading that make decisions about buying and selling stocks when certain market conditions hold, when a specific price is reached, for example, with no need at all for a time-consuming check from a human in the loop. You would not want to design a vis tool to help a person make that check faster, because even an augmented human will not be able to reason about millions of stocks every second.

However, many analysis problems are ill specified: people don't know how to approach the problem. There are many possible questions to ask—anywhere from dozens to thousands or more—and people don't know which of these many questions are the right ones in advance. In such cases, the best path forward is an analysis process with a human in the loop, where you can exploit the

★ The field of **machine learning** is a branch of artificial intelligence where computers can handle a wide variety of new situations in response to data-driven training, rather than by being programmed with explicit instructions in advance.

powerful pattern detection properties of the human visual system in your design. Vis systems are appropriate for use when your goal is to augment human capabilities, rather than completely replace the human in the loop.

You can design vis tools for many kinds of uses. You can make a tool intended for transitional use where the goal is to "work itself out of a job", by helping the designers of future solutions that are purely computational. You can also make a tool intended for long-term use, in a situation where there is no intention of replacing the human any time soon.

For example, you can create a vis tool that's a stepping stone to gaining a clearer understanding of analysis requirements before developing formal mathematical or computational models. This kind of tool would be used very early in the transition process in a highly exploratory way, before even starting to develop any kind of automatic solution. The outcome of designing vis tools targeted at specific real-world domain problems is often a much crisper understanding of the user's task, in addition to the tool itself.

In the middle stages of a transition, you can build a vis tool aimed at the designers of a purely computational solution, to help them refine, debug, or extend that system's algorithms or understand how the algorithms are affected by changes of parameters. In this case, your tool is aimed at a very different audience than the end users of that eventual system; if the end users need visualization at all, it might be with a very different interface. Returning to the stock market example, a higher-level system that determines which of multiple trading algorithms to use in varying circumstances might require careful tuning. A vis tool to help the algorithm developers analyze its performance might be useful to these developers, but not to people who eventually buy the software.

You can also design a vis tool for end users in conjunction with other computational decision making to illuminate whether the automatic system is doing the right thing according to human judgement. The tool might be intended for interim use when making deployment decisions in the late stages of a transition, for example, to see if the result of a machine learning system seems to be trustworthy before entrusting it to spend millions of dollars trading stocks. In some cases vis tools are abandoned after that decision is made; in other cases vis tools continue to be in play with long-term use to monitor a system, so that people can take action if they spot unreasonable behavior.

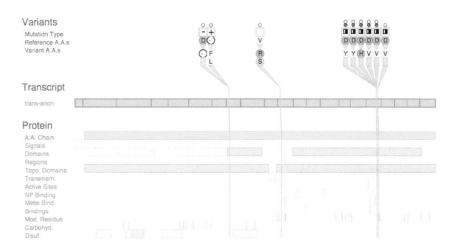

Figure 1.1. The Variant View vis tool supports biologists in assessing the impact of genetic variants by speeding up the exploratory analysis process. From [Ferstay et al. 13, Figure 1].

In contrast to these transitional uses, you can also design vis tools for long-term use, where a person will stay in the loop indefinitely. A common case is exploratory analysis for scientific discovery, where the goal is to speed up and improve a user's ability to generate and check hypotheses. Figure 1.1 shows a vis tool designed to help biologists studying the genetic basis of disease through analyzing DNA sequence variation. Although these scientists make heavy use of computation as part of their larger workflow, there's no hope of completely automating the process of cancer research any time soon.

You can also design vis tools for presentation. In this case, you're supporting people who want to explain something that they already know to others, rather than to explore and analyze the unknown. For example, *The New York Times* has deployed sophisticated interactive visualizations in conjunction with news stories.

1.3   Why Have a Computer in the Loop?

By enlisting computation, you can build tools that allow people to explore or present large datasets that would be completely infeasible to draw by hand, thus opening up the possibility of seeing how datasets change over time.

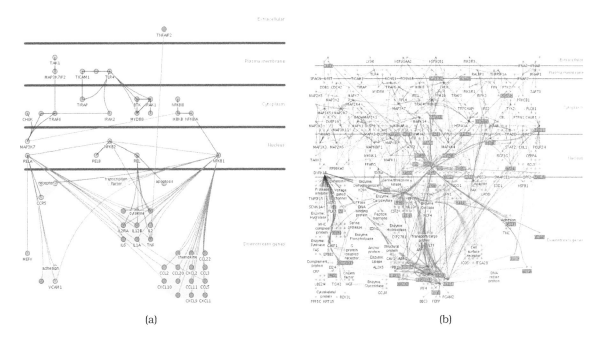

(a)   (b)

Figure 1.2. The Cerebral vis tool captures the style of hand-drawn diagrams in biology textbooks with vertical layers that correspond to places within a cell where interactions between genes occur. (a) A small network of 57 nodes and 74 edges might be possible to lay out by hand with enough patience. (b) Automatic layout handles this large network of 760 nodes and 1269 edges and provides a substrate for interactive exploration: the user has moved the mouse over the MSK1 gene, so all of its immmediate neighbors in the network are highlighted in red. From [Barsky et al. 07, Figures 1 and 2].

People could create visual representations of datasets manually, either completely by hand with pencil and paper, or with computerized drawing tools where they individually arrange and color each item. The scope of what people are willing and able to do manually is strongly limited by their attention span; they are unlikely to move beyond tiny static datasets. Arranging even small datasets of hundreds of items might take hours or days. Most real-world datasets are much larger, ranging from thousands to millions to even more. Moreover, many datasets change dynamically over time. Having a computer-based tool generate the visual representation automatically obviously saves human effort compared to manual creation.

As a designer, you can think about what aspects of hand-drawn diagrams are important in order to automatically create drawings that retain the hand-drawn spirit. For example, Figure 1.2 shows an example of a vis tool designed to show interactions between genes in a way similar to stylized drawings that appear in biology textbooks, with vertical layers that correspond to the location within the cell where the interaction occurs [Barsky et al. 07]. Figure 1.2(a) could be done by hand, while Figure 1.2(b) could not.

1.4 Why Use an External Representation?

External representations augment human capacity by allowing us to surpass the limitations of our own internal cognition and memory.

Vis allows people to offload internal cognition and memory usage to the perceptual system, using carefully designed images as a form of **external representations**, sometimes also called *external memory*. External representations can take many forms, including touchable physical objects like an abacus or a knotted string, but in this book I focus on what can be shown on the two-dimensional display surface of a computer screen.

Diagrams can be designed to support perceptual inferences, which are very easy for humans to make. The advantages of diagrams as external memory is that information can be organized by spatial location, offering the possibility of accelerating both search and recognition. Search can be sped up by grouping all the items needed for a specific problem-solving inference together at the same location. Recognition can also be facilitated by grouping all the relevant information about one item in the same location, avoiding the need for matching remembered symbolic labels. However, a nonoptimal diagram may group irrelevant information together, or support perceptual inferences that aren't useful for the intended problem-solving process.

1.5 Why Depend on Vision?

Visualization, as the name implies, is based on exploiting the human visual system as a means of communication. I focus exclusively on the visual system rather than other sensory modalities because it is both well characterized and suitable for transmitting information.

The visual system provides a very high-bandwidth channel to our brains. A significant amount of visual information processing occurs in parallel at the preconscious level. One example is visual popout, such as when one red item is immediately noticed from a sea of gray ones. The popout occurs whether the field of other objects is large or small because of processing done in parallel across the entire field of vision. Of course, our visual systems also feed into higher-level processes that involve the conscious control of attention.

Sound is poorly suited for providing overviews of large information spaces compared with vision. An enormous amount of background visual information processing in our brains underlies our ability to think and act as if we see a huge amount of information at once, even though technically we see only a tiny part of our visual field in high resolution at any given instant. In contrast, we experience the perceptual channel of sound as a sequential stream, rather than as a simultaneous experience where what we hear over a long period of time is automatically merged together. This crucial difference may explain why *sonification* has never taken off despite many independent attempts at experimentation.

The other senses can be immediately ruled out as communication channels because of technological limitations. The perceptual channels of taste and smell don't yet have viable recording and reproduction technology at all. Haptic input and feedback devices exist to exploit the touch and kinesthetic perceptual channels, but they cover only a very limited part of the dynamic range of what we can sense. Exploration of their effectiveness for communicating abstract information is still at a very early stage.

▶ Chapter 5 covers implications of visual perception that are relevant for vis design.

1.6 Why Show the Data in Detail?

Vis tools help people in situations where seeing the dataset structure in detail is better than seeing only a brief summary of it. One of these situations occurs when exploring the data to find patterns, both to confirm expected ones and find unexpected ones. Another occurs when assessing the validity of a statistical model, to judge whether the model in fact fits the data.

Statistical characterization of datasets is a very powerful approach, but it has the intrinsic limitation of losing information through summarization. Figure 1.3 shows Anscombe's Quartet, a suite of four small datasets designed by a statistician to illustrate how datasets that have identical descriptive statistics can have very different structures that are immediately obvious when the dataset is shown graphically [Anscombe 73]. All four have identical mean, variance, correlation, and linear regression lines. If you

Anscombe's Quartet: Raw Data

	1		2		3		4	
	X	Y	X	Y	X	Y	X	Y
	10.0	8.04	10.0	9.14	10.0	7.46	8.0	6.58
	8.0	6.95	8.0	8.14	8.0	6.77	8.0	5.76
	13.0	7.58	13.0	8.74	13.0	12.74	8.0	7.71
	9.0	8.81	9.0	8.77	9.0	7.11	8.0	8.84
	11.0	8.33	11.0	9.26	11.0	7.81	8.0	8.47
	14.0	9.96	14.0	8.10	14.0	8.84	8.0	7.04
	6.0	7.24	6.0	6.13	6.0	6.08	8.0	5.25
	4.0	4.26	4.0	3.10	4.0	5.39	19.0	12.50
	12.0	10.84	12.0	9.13	12.0	8.15	8.0	5.56
	7.0	4.82	7.0	7.26	7.0	6.42	8.0	7.91
	5.0	5.68	5.0	4.74	5.0	5.73	8.0	6.89
Mean	9.0	7.5	9.0	7.5	9.0	7.5	9.0	7.5
Variance	10.0	3.75	10.0	3.75	10.0	3.75	10.0	3.75
Correlation	0.816		0.816		0.816		0.816	

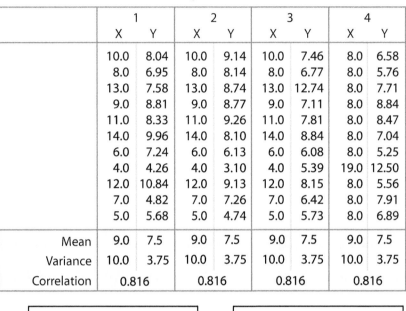

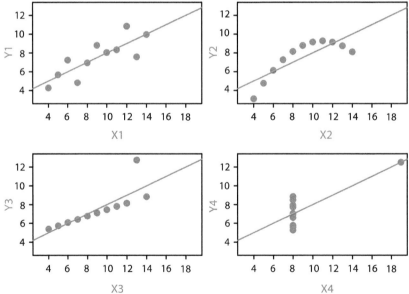

Figure 1.3. Anscombe's Quartet is four datasets with identical simple statistical properties: mean, variance, correlation, and linear regression line. However, visual inspection immediately shows how their structures are quite different. After [Anscombe 73, Figures 1–4].

are familiar with these statistical measures, then the scatterplot of the first dataset probably isn't surprising, and matches your intuition. The second scatterplot shows a clear nonlinear pattern in the data, showing that summarizing with linear regression doesn't adequately capture what's really happening. The third dataset shows how a single outlier can lead to a regression line that's misleading in a different way because its slope doesn't quite match the line that our eyes pick up clearly from the rest of the data. Finally, the fourth dataset shows a truly pernicious case where these measures dramatically mislead, with a regression line that's almost perpendicular to the true pattern we immediately see in the data.

The basic principle illustrated by Anscombe's Quartet, that a single summary is often an oversimplification that hides the true structure of the dataset, applies even more to large and complex datasets.

1.7 Why Use Interactivity?

Interactivity is crucial for building vis tools that handle complexity. When datasets are large enough, the limitations of both people and displays preclude just showing everything at once; **interaction** where user actions cause the view to change is the way forward. Moreover, a single static view can show only one aspect of a dataset. For some combinations of simple datasets and tasks, the user may only need to see a single visual encoding. In contrast, an interactively changing display supports many possible queries.

In all of these cases, interaction is crucial. For example, an interactive vis tool can support investigation at multiple levels of detail, ranging from a very high-level overview down through multiple levels of summarization to a fully detailed view of a small part of it. It can also present different ways of representing and summarizing the data in a way that supports understanding the connections between these alternatives.

Before the widespread deployment of fast computer graphics, visualization was limited to the use of static images on paper. With computer-based vis, interactivity becomes possible, vastly increasing the scope and capabilities of vis tools. Although static representations are indeed within the scope of this book, interaction is an intrinsic part of many idioms.

1.8 Why Is the Vis Idiom Design Space Huge?

A vis **idiom** is a distinct approach to creating and manipulating visual representations. There are many ways to create a **visual encoding** of data as a single picture. The design space of possibilities gets even bigger when you consider how to manipulate one or more of these pictures with **interaction**.

Many vis idioms have been proposed. Simple static idioms include many chart types that have deep historical roots, such as scatterplots, bar charts, and line charts. A more complicated idiom can link together multiple simple charts through interaction. For example, selecting one bar in a bar chart could also result in highlighting associated items in a scatterplot that shows a different view of the same data. Figure 1.4 shows an even more complex idiom that supports incremental layout of a multilevel network through interactive navigation. Data from Internet Movie Database showing all movies connected to Sharon Stone is shown, where actors are represented as grey square nodes and links between them

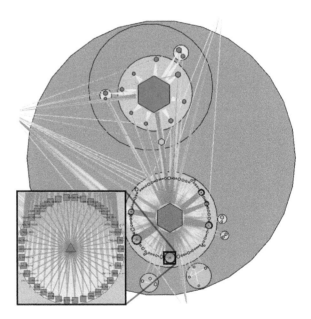

Figure 1.4. The Grouse vis tool features a complex idiom that combines visual encoding and interaction, supporting incremental layout of a network through interactive navigation. From [Archambault et al. 07a, Figure 5].

mean appearance in the same movie. The user has navigated by opening up several metanodes, shown as discs, to see structure at many levels of the hierarchy simultaneously; metanode color encodes the topological structure of the network features it contains, and hexagons indicate metanodes that are still closed. The inset shows the details of the opened-up clique of actors who all appear in the movie *Anything but Here*, with name labels turned on.

▶ Compound networks are discussed further in Section 9.5.

This book provides a framework for thinking about the space of vis design idioms systematically by considering a set of design choices, including how to encode information with spatial position, how to facet data between multiple views, and how to reduce the amount of data shown by filtering and aggregation.

1.9   Why Focus on Tasks?

A tool that serves well for one task can be poorly suited for another, for exactly the same dataset. The task of the users is an equally important constraint for a vis designer as the kind of data that the users have.

Reframing the users' task from domain-specific form into abstract form allows you to consider the similarities and differences between what people need across many real-world usage contexts. For example, a vis tool can support presentation, or discovery, or enjoyment of information; it can also support producing more information for subsequent use. For discovery, vis can be used to generate new hypotheses, as when exploring a completely unfamiliar dataset, or to confirm existing hypotheses about some dataset that is already partially understood.

▶ The space of task abstractions is discussed in detail in Chapter 3.

1.10   Why Focus on Effectiveness?

The focus on effectiveness is a corollary of defining vis to have the goal of supporting user tasks. This goal leads to concerns about correctness, accuracy, and truth playing a very central role in vis. The emphasis in vis is different from other fields that also involve making images: for example, art emphasizes conveying emotion, achieving beauty, or provoking thought; movies and comics emphasize telling a narrative story; advertising emphasizes setting a mood or selling. For the goals of emotional engagement, storytelling, or allurement, the deliberate distortion and even fabrication of facts is often entirely appropriate, and of course fiction is as

respectable as nonfiction. In contrast, a vis designer does not typically have artistic license. Moreover, the phrase "it's not just about
making pretty pictures" is a common and vehement assertion in
vis, meaning that the goals of the designer are not met if the result
is beautiful but not effective.

However, no picture can communicate the truth, the whole truth,
and nothing but the truth. The correctness concerns of a vis designer are complicated by the fact that *any* depiction of data is
an abstraction where choices are made about which aspects to
emphasize. Cartographers have thousands of years of experience
with articulating the difference between the abstraction of a map
and the terrain that it represents. Even photographing a real-world
scene involves choices of abstraction and emphasis; for example,
the photographer chooses what to include in the frame.

▶ Abstraction is discussed
in more detail in Chapters 3
and 4.

1.11   Why Are Most Designs Ineffective?

The most fundamental reason that vis design is a difficult enter-
prise is that the vast majority of the possibilities in the design space
will be ineffective for any specific usage context. In some cases, a
possible design is a poor match with the properties of the human
perceptual and cognitive systems. In other cases, the design would
be comprehensible by a human in some other setting, but it's a bad
match with the intended task. Only a very small number of possibilities are in the set of reasonable choices, and of those only
an even smaller fraction are excellent choices. Randomly choosing
possibilities is a bad idea because the odds of finding a very good
solution are very low.

Figure 1.5 contrasts two ways to think about design in terms of
traversing a search space. In addressing design problems, it's not
a very useful goal to **optimize**; that is, to find the very best choice. A
more appropriate goal when you design is to **satisfy**; that is, to find
one of the many possible good solutions rather than one of the even
larger number of bad ones. The diagram shows five spaces, each
of which is progressively smaller than the previous. First, there
is the space of all possible solutions, including potential solutions
that nobody has ever thought of before. Next, there is the set of
possibilities that are *known* to you, the vis designer. Of course,
this set might be small if you are a novice designer who is not
aware of the full array of methods that have been proposed in the
past. If you're in that situation, one of the goals of this book is to
enlarge the set of methods that you know about. The next set is the

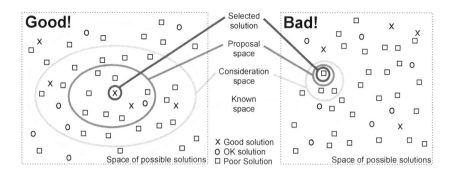

Figure 1.5. A search space metaphor for vis design.

consideration space, which contains the solutions that you actively consider. This set is necessarily smaller than the known space, because you can't consider what you don't know. An even smaller set is the *proposal* space of possibilities that you investigate in detail. Finally, one of these becomes the *selected* solution.

Figure 1.5 contrasts a good strategy on the left, where the known and consideration spaces are large, with a bad strategy on the right, where these spaces are small. The problem of a small consideration space is the higher probability of only considering ok or poor solutions and missing a good one. A fundamental principle of design is to consider multiple alternatives and then choose the best, rather than to immediately fixate on one solution without considering any alternatives. One way to ensure that more than one possibility is considered is to explicitly generate multiple ideas in parallel. This book is intended to help you, the designer, entertain a broad consideration space by systematically considering many alternatives and to help you rule out some parts of the space by noting when there are mismatches of possibilities with human capabilities or the intended task.

As with all design problems, vis design cannot be easily handled as a simple process of optimization because trade-offs abound. A design that does well by one measure will rate poorly on another. The characterization of trade-offs in the vis design space is a very open problem at the frontier of vis research. This book provides several guidelines and suggested processes, based on my synthesis of what is currently known, but it contains few absolute truths.

> ▶ Chapter 4 introduces a model for thinking about the design process at four different levels; the model is intended to guide your thinking through these trade-offs in a systematic way.

1.12 Why Is Validation Difficult?

The problem of **validation** for a vis design is difficult because there are so many questions that you could ask when considering whether a vis tool has met your design goals.

How do you know if it works? How do you argue that one design is better or worse than another for the intended users? For one thing, what does *better* mean? Do users get something done faster? Do they have more fun doing it? Can they work more effectively? What does *effectively* mean? How do you measure *insight* or *engagement*? What is the design better than? Is it better than another vis system? Is it better than doing the same things manually, without visual support? Is it better than doing the same things completely automatically? And what sort of thing does it do better? That is, how do you decide what sort of task the users should do when testing the system? And who is this *user*? An expert who has done this task for decades, or a novice who needs the task to be explained before they begin? Are they familiar with how the system works from using it for a long time, or are they seeing it for the first time? A concept like *faster* might seem straightforward, but tricky questions still remain. Are the users limited by the speed of their own thought process, or their ability to move the mouse, or simply the speed of the computer in drawing each picture?

How do you decide what sort of *benchmark* data you should use when testing the system? Can you characterize what classes of data the system is suitable for? How might you measure the *quality* of an image generated by a vis tool? How well do any of the automatically computed quantitative metrics of quality match up with human judgements? Even once you limit your considerations to purely computational issues, questions remain. Does the complexity of the algorithm depend on the number of data items to show or the number of pixels to draw? Is there a trade-off between computer speed and computer memory usage?

> ▶ Chapter 4 answers these questions by providing a framework that addresses when to use what methods for validating vis designs.

1.13 Why Are There Resource Limitations?

When designing or analyzing a vis system, you must consider at least three different kinds of limitations: computational capacity, human perceptual and cognitive capacity, and display capacity.

Vis systems are inevitably used for larger datasets than those they were designed for. Thus, **scalability** is a central concern: designing systems to handle large amounts of data gracefully. The continuing increase in dataset size is driven by many factors: improvements in data acquisition and sensor technology, bringing real-world data into a computational context; improvements in computer capacity, leading to ever-more generation of data from within computational environments including simulation and logging; and the increasing reach of computational infrastructure into every aspect of life.

As with any application of computer science, computer time and memory are limited resources, and there are often soft and hard constraints on the availability of these resources. For instance, if your vis system needs to interactively deliver a response to user input, then when drawing each frame you must use algorithms that can run in a fraction of a second rather than minutes or hours. In some scenarios, users are unwilling or unable to wait a long time for the system to preprocess the data before they can interact with it. A soft constraint is that the vis system should be parsimonious in its use of computer memory because the user needs to run other programs simultaneously. A hard constraint is that even if the vis system can use nearly all available memory in the computer, dataset size can easily outstrip that finite capacity. Designing systems that gracefully handle larger datasets that do not fit into core memory requires significantly more complex algorithms. Thus, the computational complexity of algorithms for dataset preprocessing, transformation, layout, and rendering is a major concern. However, computational issues are by no means the only concern!

On the human side, memory and attention are finite resources. Chapter 5 will discuss some of the power and limitations of the low-level visual preattentive mechanisms that carry out massively parallel processing of our current visual field. However, human memory for things that are not directly visible is notoriously limited. These limits come into play not only for long-term recall but also for shorter-term working memory, both visual and nonvisual. We store surprisingly little information internally in visual working memory, leaving us vulnerable to **change blindness**: the phenomenon where even very large changes are not noticed if we are attending to something else in our view [Simons 00].

▶ More aspects of memory and attention are covered in Section 6.5.

Display capacity is a third kind of limitation to consider. Vis designers often run out of pixels; that is, the resolution of the screen is not enough to show all desired information simultaneously. The **information density** of a single image is a measure of the amount of information encoded versus the amount of unused space.* Figure 1.6 shows the same tree dataset visually encoded three differ-

★ Synonyms for *information density* include **graphic density** and **data–ink ratio**.

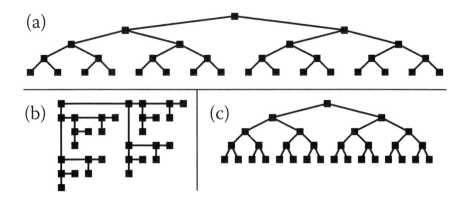

Figure 1.6. Low and high information density visual encodings of the same small tree dataset; nodes are the same size in each. (a) Low information density. (b) Higher information density, but depth in tree cannot be read from spatial position. (c) High information density, while maintaining property that depth is encoded with position. From [McGuffin and Robert 10, Figure 3].

ent ways. The layout in Figure 1.6(a) encodes the depth from root to leaves in the tree with vertical spatial position. However, the information density is low. In contrast, the layout in Figure 1.6(b) uses nodes of the same size but is drawn more compactly, so it has higher information density; that is, the ratio between the size of each node and the area required to display the entire tree is larger. However, the depth cannot be easily read off from spatial position. Figure 1.6(c) shows a very good alternative that combines the benefits of both previous approaches, with both high information density from a compact view and position coding for depth.

There is a trade-off between the benefits of showing as much as possible at once, to minimize the need for navigation and exploration, and the costs of showing too much at once, where the user is overwhelmed by visual clutter. The goal of idiom design choices is to find an appropriate balance between these two ends of the information density continuum.

1.14 Why Analyze?

This book is built around the premise that analyzing existing systems is a good stepping stone to designing new ones. When you're confronted with a vis problem as a designer, it can be hard to decide what to do. Many computer-based vis idioms and tools have

Figure 1.7. Three-part analysis framework for a vis instance: *why* is the task being performed, *what* data is shown in the views, and *how* is the vis idiom constructed in terms of design choices.

been created in the past several decades, and considering them one by one leaves you faced with a big collection of different possibilities. There are so many possible combinations of data, tasks, and idioms that it's unlikely that you'll find exactly what you need to know just by reading papers about previous vis tools. Moreover, even if you find a likely candidate, you might need to dig even deeper into the literature to understand whether there's any evidence that the tool was a success.

This book features an analysis framework that imposes a structure on this enormous design space, intended as a scaffold to help you think about design choices systematically. It's offered as a guide to get you started, not as a straitjacket: there are certainly many other possible ways to think about these problems!

Figure 1.7 shows the high-level framework for analyzing vis use according to three questions: **what** data the user sees, **why** the user intends to use a vis tool, and **how** the visual encoding and interaction idioms are constructed in terms of design choices. Each three-fold **what–why–how** question has a corresponding *data–task–idiom* answer trio. One of these analysis trios is called an **instance**.

Simple vis tools can be fully described as an isolated analysis instance, but complex vis tool usage often requires analysis in terms of a sequence of instances that are chained together. In these cases, the chained sequences are a way to express dependencies. All analysis instances have the **input** of *what* data is shown; in some cases, **output** data is produced as a result of using the vis tool. Figure 1.8 shows an abstract example of a chained sequence, where the output of a prior instance serves as the input to a subsequent one.

The combination of distinguishing why from how and chained sequences allows you to distinguish between means and ends in

▶ Chapter 2 discusses data and the question of *what*. Chapter 3 covers tasks and the question of *why*. Chapters 7 through 14 answer the question of *how* idioms can be designed in detail.

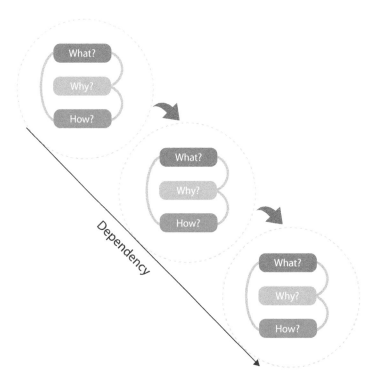

Figure 1.8. Analyzing vis usage as chained sequences of instances, where the output of one instance is the input to another.

your analysis. For example, a user could *sort* the items shown within the vis. That operation could be an end in itself, if the user's goal is to produce a list of items ranked according to a particular criterion as a result of an analysis session. Or, the sorting could be the means to another end, for example, finding outliers that do not match the main trend of the data; in this case, it is simply done along the way as one of many different operations.

1.15   Further Reading

Each Further Reading section provides suggestions for further reading about some of the ideas presented in the chapter and acknowledges key sources that influenced the discussion.

Why Use an External Representation? The role and use of external representations are analyzed in papers on the nature of external representations in problem solving [Zhang 97] and a representational analysis of number systems [Zhang and Norman 95]. The influential paper *Why A Diagram Is (Sometimes) Worth Ten Thousand Words* is the basis for my discussion of diagrams in this chapter [Larkin and Simon 87].

Why Show the Data in Detail? Anscombe proposed his quartet of illustrative examples in a lovely, concise paper [Anscombe 73]. An early paper on the many faces of the scatterplot includes a cogent discussion of why to show as much of the data as possible [Cleveland and McGill 84b].

What Is the Vis Design Space? My discussion of the vis design space is based on our paper on the methodology of design studies that covers the question of progressing from a loose to a crisp understanding of the user's requirements [Sedlmair et al. 12].

What Resource Limitations Matter? Ware's textbook provides a very thorough discussion of human limitations in terms of perception, memory, and cognition [Ware 13]. A survey paper provides a good overview of the change blindness literature [Simons 00].

The idea of information density dates back to Bertin's discussion of *graphic density* [Bertin 67], and Tufte has discussed the *data–ink ratio* at length [Tufte 83].

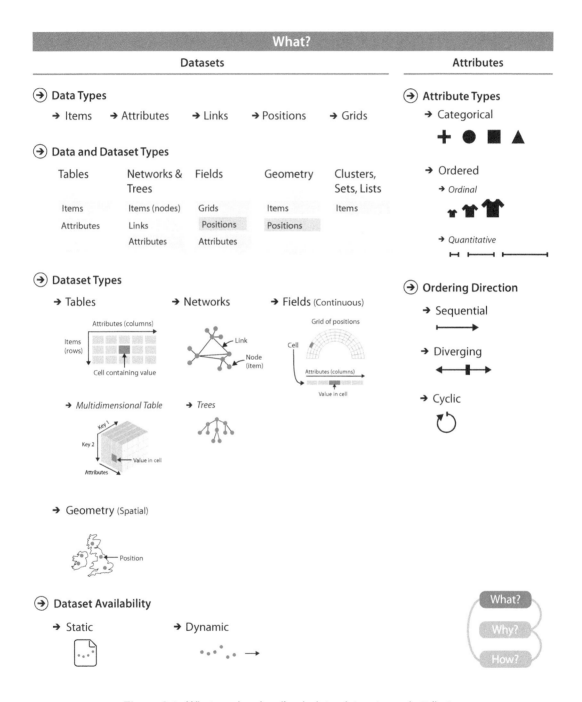

Figure 2.1. *What* can be visualized: data, datasets, and attributes.

Chapter 2

What: Data Abstraction

2.1   The Big Picture

Figure 2.1 shows the abstract types of *what* can be visualized. The four basic dataset types are tables, networks, fields, and geometry; other possible collections of items include clusters, sets, and lists. These datasets are made up of different combinations of the five data types: items, attributes, links, positions, and grids. For any of these dataset types, the full dataset could be available immediately in the form of a static file, or it might be dynamic data processed gradually in the form of a stream. The type of an attribute can be categorical or ordered, with a further split into ordinal and quantitative. The ordering direction of attributes can be sequential, diverging, or cyclic.

2.2   Why Do Data Semantics and Types Matter?

Many aspects of vis design are driven by the kind of data that you have at your disposal. What kind of data are you given? What information can you figure out from the data, versus the meanings that you must be told explicitly? What high-level concepts will allow you to split datasets apart into general and useful pieces?

Suppose that you see the following data:

```
14, 2.6, 30, 30, 15, 100001
```

What does this sequence of six numbers mean? You can't possibly know yet, without more information about how to interpret each number. Is it locations for two points far from each other in three-dimensional space, $14, 2.6, 30$ and $30, 15, 100001$? Is it two points closer to each other in two-dimensional space, $14, 2.6$ and

30, 30, with the fifth number meaning that there are 15 links between these two points, and the sixth number assigning the weight
of '100001' to that link?

Similarly, suppose that you see the following data:

```
Basil, 7, S, Pear
```

These numbers and words could have many possible meanings.
Maybe a food shipment of produce has arrived in satisfactory condition on the 7th day of the month, containing basil and pears.
Maybe the Basil Point neighborhood of the city has had 7 inches
of snow cleared by the Pear Creek Limited snow removal service.
Maybe the lab rat named Basil has made seven attempts to find
his way through the south section of the maze, lured by scent of
the reward food for this trial, a pear.

To move beyond guesses, you need to know two crosscutting
pieces of information about these terms: their semantics and their
types. The **semantics** of the data is its real-world meaning. For
instance, does a word represent a human first name, or is it the
shortened version of a company name where the full name can be
looked up in an external list, or is it a city, or is it a fruit? Does a
number represent a day of the month, or an age, or a measurement
of height, or a unique code for a specific person, or a postal code
for a neighborhood, or a position in space?

The **type** of the data is its structural or mathematical interpretation. At the data level, what kind of thing is it: an item, a link, an
attribute? At the dataset level, how are these data types combined
into a larger structure: a table, a tree, a field of sampled values?
At the attribute level, what kinds of mathematical operations are
meaningful for it? For example, if a number represents a count of
boxes of detergent, then its type is a quantity, and adding two such
numbers together makes sense. If the number represents a postal
code, then its type is a *code* rather than a *quantity*—it is simply
the name for a *category* that happens to be a number rather than
a textual name. Adding two of these numbers together does not
make sense.

Table 2.1 shows several more lines of the same dataset. This
simple example table is tiny, with only nine rows and four columns.
The exact semantics should be provided by the creator of the dataset; I give it with the column titles. In this case, each person has a
unique identifier, a name, an age, a shirt size, and a favorite fruit.

Sometimes types and semantics can be correctly inferred simply
by observing the syntax of a data file or the names of variables

ID	Name	Age	Shirt Size	Favorite Fruit
1	Amy	8	S	Apple
2	Basil	7	S	Pear
3	Clara	9	M	Durian
4	Desmond	13	L	Elderberry
5	Ernest	12	L	Peach
6	Fanny	10	S	Lychee
7	George	9	M	Orange
8	Hector	8	L	Loquat
9	Ida	10	M	Pear
10	Amy	12	M	Orange

Table 2.1. A full table with column titles that provide the intended semantics of the attributes.

within it, but often they must be provided along with the dataset in order for it to be interpreted correctly. Sometimes this kind of additional information is called **metadata**; the line between data and metadata is not clear, especially given that the original data is often derived and transformed. In this book, I don't distinguish between them, and refer to everything as *data*.

▶ Deriving data is discussed in Section 3.4.2.3.

The classification below presents a way to think about dataset and attribute types and semantics in a way that is general enough to cover the cases interesting in vis, yet specific enough to be helpful for guiding design choices at the abstraction and idiom levels.

2.3 Data Types

Figure 2.2 shows the five basic **data types** discussed in this book: items, attributes, links, positions, and grids. An **attribute** is some specific property that can be measured, observed, or logged.* For example, attributes could be salary, price, number of sales, protein expression levels, or temperature. An **item** is an individual entity that is discrete, such as a row in a simple table or a node

★ Synonyms for *attribute* are **variable** and **data dimension**, or just **dimension** for short. Since *dimension* has many meanings, in this book it is reserved for the visual channels of spatial position as discussed in Section 6.3.

→ **Data Types**

→ Items   → Attributes   → Links   → Positions   → Grids

Figure 2.2. The five basic data types: items, attributes, links, positions, and grids.

in a network. For example, items may be people, stocks, coffee shops, genes, or cities. A **link** is a relationship between items, typically within a network. A **grid** specifies the strategy for sampling continuous data in terms of both geometric and topological relationships between its cells. A **position** is spatial data, providing a location in two-dimensional (2D) or three-dimensional (3D) space. For example, a position might be a latitude–longitude pair describing a location on the Earth's surface or three numbers specifying a location within the region of space measured by a medical scanner.

2.4   Dataset Types

★ The word *dataset* is singular. In vis the word **data** is commonly used as a singular mass noun as well, in contrast to the traditional usage in the natural sciences where *data* is plural.

A **dataset** is any collection of information that is the target of analysis.* The four basic **dataset types** are tables, networks, fields, and geometry. Other ways to group items together include clusters, sets, and lists. In real-world situations, complex combinations of these basic types are common.

Figure 2.3 shows that these basic dataset types arise from combinations of the data types of items, attributes, links, positions, and grids.

Figure 2.4 shows the internal structure of the four basic dataset types in detail. Tables have cells indexed by items and attributes, for either the simple flat case or the more complex multidimensional case. In a network, items are usually called nodes, and they are connected with links; a special case of networks is trees. Continuous fields have grids based on spatial positions where cells contain attributes. Spatial geometry has only position information.

➔ **Data and Dataset Types**

Tables	Networks & Trees	Fields	Geometry	Clusters, Sets, Lists
Items	Items (nodes)	Grids	Items	Items
Attributes	Links	Positions	Positions	
	Attributes	Attributes		

Figure 2.3. The four basic dataset types are tables, networks, fields, and geometry; other possible collections of items are clusters, sets, and lists. These datasets are made up of five core data types: items, attributes, links, positions, and grids.

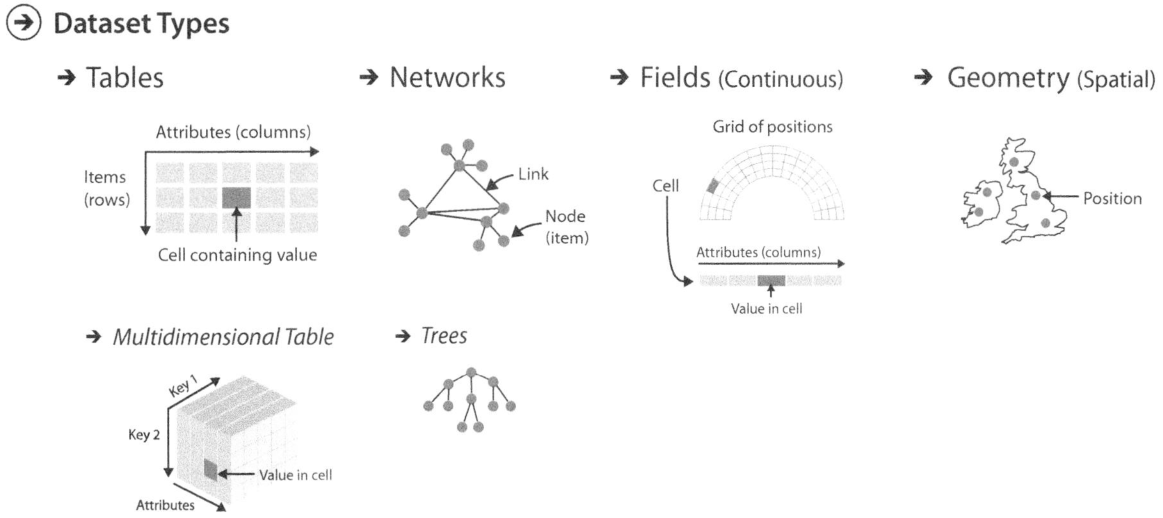

➔ **Dataset Types**

→ Tables   → Networks   → Fields (Continuous)   → Geometry (Spatial)

→ *Multidimensional Table*   → *Trees*

Figure 2.4. The detailed structure of the four basic dataset types.

2.4.1   Tables

Many datasets come in the form of **tables** that are made up of
rows and columns, a familiar form to anybody who has used a
spreadsheet. In this chapter, I focus on the concept of a table as
simply a type of dataset that is independent of any particular visual
representation; later chapters address the question of what visual
representations are appropriate for the different types of datasets.

▶ Chapter 7 covers how to arrange tables spatially.

For a simple **flat table**, the terms used in this book are that each
row represents an **item** of data, and each column is an **attribute** of
the dataset. Each **cell** in the table is fully specified by the combination of a row and a column—an item and an attribute—and
contains a **value** for that pair. Figure 2.5 shows an example of
the first few dozen items in a table of orders, where the attributes
are order ID, order date, order priority, product container, product
base margin, and ship date.

A **multidimensional table** has a more complex structure for in-
dexing into a cell, with multiple keys.

▶ Keys and values are discussed further in Section 2.6.1.

A	B	C	S	T	U
Order ID	Order Date	Order Priority	Product Container	Product Base Margin	Ship Date
3	10/14/06	5-Low	Large Box	0.8	10/21/06
6	2/21/08	4-Not Specified	Small Pack	0.55	2/22/08
32	7/16/07	2-High	Small Pack	0.79	7/17/07
32	7/16/07	2-High	Jumbo Box		7/17/07
32	7/16/07	2-High	Medium Box	attribute	7/18/07
32	7/16/07	2-High	Medium Box	0.65	7/18/07
35	10/23/07	4-Not Specified	Wrap Bag	0.52	10/24/07
35	10/23/07	4-Not Specified	Small Box	0.58	10/25/07
36	11/3/07	1-Urgent	Small Box	0.55	11/3/07
65	3/18/07	1-Urgent	Small Pack	0.49	3/19/07
66	1/20/05	5-Low	Wrap Bag	0.56	1/20/05
69	item	5 4-Not Specified	Small Pack	cell	6/6/05
69		5 4-Not Specified	Wrap Bag	0.6	6/6/05
70	12/18/06	5-Low	Small Box	0.59	12/23/06
70	12/18/06	5-Low	Wrap Bag	0.82	12/23/06
96	4/17/05	2-High	Small Box	0.55	4/19/05
97	1/29/06	3-Medium	Small Box	0.38	1/30/06
129	11/19/08	5-Low	Small Box	0.37	11/28/08
130	5/8/08	2-High	Small Box	0.37	5/9/08
130	5/8/08	2-High	Medium Box	0.38	5/10/08
130	5/8/08	2-High	Small Box	0.6	5/11/08
132	6/11/06	3-Medium	Medium Box	0.6	6/12/06
132	6/11/06	3-Medium	Jumbo Box	0.69	6/14/06
134	5/1/08	4-Not Specified	Large Box	0.82	5/3/08
135	10/21/07	4-Not Specified	Small Pack	0.64	10/23/07
166	9/12/07	2-High	Small Box	0.55	9/14/07
193	8/8/06	1-Urgent	Medium Box	0.57	8/10/06
194	4/5/08	3-Medium	Wrap Bag	0.42	4/7/08

Figure 2.5. In a simple table of orders, a row represents an *item*, a column represents an *attribute*, and their intersection is the *cell* containing the value for that pairwise combination.

2.4.2 Networks and Trees

★ A synonym for *networks* is **graphs**. The word *graph* is also deeply overloaded in vis. Sometimes it is used to mean *network* as we discuss here, for instance in the vis subfield called *graph drawing* or the mathematical subfield called *graph theory*. Sometimes it is used in the field of statistical graphics to mean **chart**, as in bar graphs and line graphs.

★ A synonym for *node* is **vertex**.

★ A synonym for *link* is **edge**.

The dataset type of **networks** is well suited for specifying that there is some kind of relationship between two or more items.★ An item in a network is often called a **node**.★ A **link** is a relation between two items.★ For example, in an articulated social network the nodes are people, and links mean friendship. In a gene interaction network, the nodes are genes, and links between them mean that these genes have been observed to interact with each other. In a computer network, the nodes are computers, and the links represent the ability to send messages directly between two computers using physical cables or a wireless connection.

Network nodes can have associated attributes, just like items in a table. In addition, the links themselves could also be considered to have attributes associated with them; these may be partly or wholly disjoint from the node attributes.

It is again important to distinguish between the abstract con-cept of a network and any particular visual layout of that network where the nodes and edges have particular spatial positions. This chapter concentrates on the former.

▶ The spatial arrangement of networks is covered in Chapter 9.

2.4.2.1   Trees

Networks with hierarchical structure are more specifically called **trees**. In contrast to a general network, trees do not have cycles: each child node has only one parent node pointing to it. One exam-ple of a tree is the organization chart of a company, showing who reports to whom; another example is a tree showing the evolu-tionary relationships between species in the biological tree of life, where the child nodes of humans and monkeys both share the same parent node of primates.

2.4.3   Fields

The **field** dataset type also contains attribute values associated with cells.[1] Each **cell** in a field contains measurements or calcula-tions from a **continuous** domain: there are conceptually infinitely many values that you might measure, so you could always take a new measurement between any two existing ones. Continuous phenomena that might be measured in the physical world or simu-lated in software include temperature, pressure, speed, force, and density; mathematical functions can also be continuous.

For example, consider a field dataset representing a medical scan of a human body containing measurements indicating the density of tissue at many sample points, spread regularly through-out a volume of 3D space. A low-resolution scan would have 262,144 cells, providing information about a cubical volume of space with 64 bins in each direction. Each cell is associated with a specific region in 3D space. The density measurements could be taken closer together with a higher resolution grid of cells, or further apart for a coarser grid.

Continuous data requires careful treatment that takes into ac-count the mathematical questions of **sampling**, how frequently to

---

[1]My use of the term *field* is related to but not identical to its use in the math-ematics literature, where it denotes a mapping from a domain to a range. In this case, the domain is a Euclidean space of one, two, or three dimensions, and the ad-jective modifying *field* is a statement about the range: **scalars**, **vectors**, or **tensors**. Although the term *field* by itself is not commonly found in the literature, when I use it without an adjective I'm emphasizing the continuous nature of the domain, rather than specifics of the ranges of scalars, vectors, or tensors.

take the measurements, and interpolation, how to show values in between the sampled points in a way that does not mislead. Interpolating appropriately between the measurements allows you to reconstruct a new view of the data from an arbitrary viewpoint that's faithful to what you measured. These general mathematical problems are studied in areas such as signal processing and statistics. Visualizing fields requires grappling extensively with these concerns.

In contrast, the table and network datatypes discussed above are an example of discrete data where a finite number of individual items exist, and interpolation between them is not a meaningful concept. In the cases where a mathematical framework is necessary, areas such as graph theory and combinatorics provide relevant ideas.[2]

2.4.3.1   Spatial Fields

Continuous data is often found in the form of a spatial field, where the cell structure of the field is based on sampling at spatial positions. Most datasets that contain inherently spatial data occur in the context of tasks that require understanding aspects of its spatial structure, especially shape.

For example, with a spatial field dataset that is generated with a medical imaging instrument, the user's task could be to locate suspected tumors that can be recognized through distinctive shapes or densities. An obvious choice for visual encoding would be to show something that spatially looks like an X-ray image of the human body and to use color coding to highlight suspected tumors. Another example is measurements made in a real or simulated wind tunnel of the temperature and pressure of air flowing over airplane wings at many points in 3D space, where the task is to compare the flow patterns in different regions. One possible visual encoding would use the geometry of the wing as the spatial substrate, showing the temperature and pressure using size-coded arrows.

The likely tasks faced by users who have spatial field data constrains many of the choices about the use of space when designing visual encoding idioms. Many of the choices for nonspatial data, where no information about spatial position is provided with the dataset, are unsuitable in this case.*

★ A synonym for *nonspatial data* is **abstract data**.

---

[2]Technically, all data stored within a computer is discrete rather than continuous; however, the interesting question is whether the underlying semantics of the bits that are stored represents samples of a continuous phenomenon or intrinsically discrete data.

Thus, the question of whether a dataset has the type of a spatial field or a nonspatial table has extensive and far-reaching implications for idiom design. Historically, vis diverged into areas of specialization based on this very differentiation. The subfield of **scientific visualization**, or **scivis** for short, is concerned with situations where spatial position is *given* with the dataset. A central concern in scivis is handling continuous data appropriately within the mathematical framework of signal processing. The subfield of **information visualization**, or **infovis** for short, is concerned with situations where the use of space in a visual encoding is *chosen* by the designer. A central concern in infovis is determining whether the chosen idiom is suitable for the combination of data and task, leading to the use of methods from human–computer interaction and design.

2.4.3.2 Grid Types

When a field contains data created by sampling at completely regular intervals, as in the previous example, the cells form a **uniform grid**. There is no need to explicitly store the **grid geometry** in terms of its location in space, or the **grid topology** in terms of how each cell connects with its neighboring cells. More complicated examples require storing different amounts of geometric and topological information about the underlying grid. A **rectilinear grid** supports nonuniform sampling, allowing efficient storage of information that has high complexity in some areas and low complexity in others, at the cost of storing some information about the geometric location of each each row. A **structured grid** allows curvilinear shapes, where the geometric location of each cell needs to be specified. Finally, **unstructured grids** provide complete flexibility, but the topological information about how the cells connect to each other must be stored explicitly in addition to their spatial positions.

2.4.4 Geometry

The **geometry** dataset type specifies information about the shape of items with explicit spatial positions. The items could be points, or one-dimensional lines or curves, or 2D surfaces or regions, or 3D volumes.

Geometry datasets are intrinsically spatial, and like spatial fields they typically occur in the context of tasks that require shape understanding. Spatial data often includes hierarchical structure at multiple scales. Sometimes this structure is provided intrinsically with the dataset, or a hierarchy may be derived from the original data.

Geometry datasets do not necessarily have attributes, in contrast to the other three basic dataset types. Many of the design issues in vis pertain to questions about how to encode attributes. Purely geometric data is interesting in a vis context only when it is derived or transformed in a way that requires consideration of design choices. One classic example is when contours are derived from a spatial field. Another is when shapes are generated at an appropriate level of detail for the task at hand from raw geographic data, such as the boundaries of a forest or a city or a country, or the curve of a road. The problem of how to create images from a geometric description of a scene falls into another domain: computer graphics. While vis draws on algorithms from computer graphics, it has different concerns from that domain. Simply showing a geometric dataset is not an interesting problem from the point of view of a vis designer.

> ▶ Section 3.4.2.3 covers deriving data.

> ▶ Section 8.4 covers generating contours from scalar fields.

Geometric data is sometimes shown alone, particularly when shape understanding is the primary task. In other cases, it is the backdrop against which additional information is overlaid.

2.4.5 Other Combinations

Beyond tables, there are many ways to group multiple *items* together, including sets, lists, and clusters. A **set** is simply an unordered group of items. A group of items with a specified ordering could be called a **list**.* A **cluster** is a grouping based on attribute similarity, where items within a cluster are more similar to each other than to ones in another cluster.

> ★ In computer science, **array** is often used as a synonym for *list*.

There are also more complex structures built on top of the basic network type. A **path** through a network is an ordered set of segments formed by links connecting nodes. A **compound network** is a network with an associated tree: all of the nodes in the network are the leaves of the tree, and interior nodes in the tree provide a hierarchical structure for the nodes that is different from network links between them.

Many other kinds of data either fit into one of the previous categories or do so after transformations to create derived attributes. Complex and hybrid combinations, where the complete dataset contains multiple basic types, are common in real-world applications.

The set of basic types presented above is a starting point for describing the *what* part of an analysis instance that pertains to

Figure 2.6. Dataset availability can be either static or dynamic, for any dataset type.

data; that is, the **data abstraction**. In simple cases, it may be possible to describe your data abstraction using only that set of terms. In complex cases, you may need additional description as well. If so, your goal should be to translate domain-specific terms into words that are as generic as possible.

2.4.6 Dataset Availability

Figure 2.6 shows the two kinds of dataset availability: *static* or *dynamic*.

The default approach to vis assumes that the entire dataset is available all at once, as a **static file**. However, some datasets are instead **dynamic streams**, where the dataset information trickles in over the course of the vis session.* One kind of dynamic change is to add new items or delete previous items. Another is to change the values of existing items.

★ A synonym for *dynamic* is **online**, and a synonym for *static* is **offline**.

This distinction in availability crosscuts the basic dataset types: any of them can be static or dynamic. Designing for streaming data adds complexity to many aspects of the vis process that are straightforward when there is complete dataset availability up front.

2.5 Attribute Types

Figure 2.7 shows the attribute types. The major disinction is between categorical versus ordered. Within the ordered type is a further differentiation between ordinal versus quantitative. Ordered data might range sequentially from a minimum to a maximum value, or it might diverge in both directions from a zero point in the middle of a range, or the values may wrap around in a cycle. Also, attributes may have hierarchical structure.

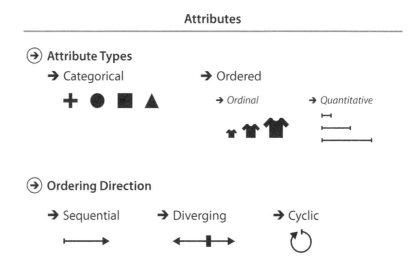

Figure 2.7. Attribute types are categorical, ordinal, or quantitative. The direction of attribute ordering can be sequential, diverging, or cyclic.

2.5.1 Categorical

The first distinction is between categorical and ordered data. The type of **categorical** data, such as favorite fruit or names, does not have an implicit ordering, but it often has hierarchical structure.*
Categories can only distinguish whether two things are the same (apples) or different (apples versus oranges). Of course, any arbitrary external ordering can be imposed upon categorical data. Fruit could be ordered alphabetically according to its name, or by its price—but only if that auxiliary information were available. However, these orderings are not implicit in the attribute itself, the way they are with quantitative or ordered data. Other examples of categorical attributes are movie genres, file types, and city names.

★ A synonym for *categorical* is **nominal**.

2.5.2 Ordered: Ordinal and Quantitative

All **ordered** data does have an implicit ordering, as opposed to unordered *categorical* data. This type can be further subdivided. With **ordinal** data, such as shirt size, we cannot do full-fledged arithmetic, but there is a well-defined ordering. For example, large minus medium is not a meaningful concept, but we know that medium falls between small and large. Rankings are another kind of ordinal data; some examples of ordered data are top-ten lists of movies or initial lineups for sports tournaments depending on past performance.

A subset of ordered data is **quantitative** data, namely, a measurement of magnitude that supports arithmetic comparison. For example, the quantity of 68 inches minus 42 inches is a meaningful concept, and the answer of 26 inches can be calculated. Other examples of quantitative data are height, weight, temperature, stock price, number of calling functions in a program, and number of drinks sold at a coffee shop in a day. Both integers and real numbers are quantitative data.[3]

In this book, the *ordered* type is used often; the ordinal type is only occasionally mentioned, when the distinction between it and the quantitative type matters.

2.5.2.1 Sequential versus Diverging

Ordered data can be either **sequential**, where there is a homogeneous range from a minimum to a maximum value, or **diverging**, which can be deconstructed into two sequences pointing in opposite directions that meet at a common zero point. For instance, a mountain *height* dataset is sequential, when measured from a minimum point of sea level to a maximum point of Mount Everest. A *bathymetric* dataset is also sequential, with sea level on one end and the lowest point on the ocean floor at the other. A full *elevation* dataset would be diverging, where the values go up for mountains on land and down for undersea valleys, with the zero value of sea level being the common point joining the two sequential datasets.

2.5.2.2 Cyclic

Ordered data may be **cyclic**, where the values wrap around back to a starting point rather than continuing to increase indefinitely. Many kinds of time measurements are cyclic, including the hour of the day, the day of the week, and the month of the year.

2.5.3 Hierarchical Attributes

There may be hierarchical structure within an attribute or between multiple attributes. The daily stock prices of companies collected

---

[3]In some domains the quantitative category is further split into **interval** versus **ratio** data [Stevens 46]; this distinction is typically not useful when designing a visual encoding, so in this book these types remain collapsed together into this single category.

over the course of a decade is an example of a time-series dataset, where one of the attributes is time. In this case, time can be aggregated hierarchically, from individual days up to weeks, up to months, up to years. There may be interesting patterns at multiple temporal scales, such as very strong weekly variations for weekday versus weekend, or more subtle yearly patterns showing seasonal variations in summer versus winter. Many kinds of attributes might have this sort of hierarchical structure: for example, the geographic attribute of a postal code can be aggregated up to the level of cities or states or entire countries.

▶ Section 13.4 covers hierarchical aggregation in more detail, and Section 7.5 covers the visual encoding of attribute hierarchies.

2.6 Semantics

Knowing the type of an attribute does not tell us about its semantics, because these two questions are crosscutting: one does not dictate the other. Different approaches to considering the semantics of attributes that have been proposed across the many fields where these semantics are studied. The classification in this book is heavily focused on the semantics of keys versus values, and the related questions of spatial and continuous data versus nonspatial and discrete data, to match up with the idiom design choice analysis framework. One additional consideration is whether an attribute is temporal.

2.6.1 Key versus Value Semantics

★ A synonym for *key attribute* is **independent attribute**. A synonym for *value attribute* is **dependent attribute**. The language of independent and dependent is common in statistics. In the language of data warehouses, a synonym for *independent* is **dimension**, and a synonym for *dependent* is **measure**.

A **key** attribute acts as an index that is used to look up **value** attributes.* The distinction between key and value attributes is important for the dataset types of tables and fields, as shown in Figure 2.8.

2.6.1.1 Flat Tables

A simple **flat table** has only one key, where each item corresponds to a row in the table, and any number of value attributes. In this case, the key might be completely implicit, where it's simply the index of the row. It might be explicit, where it is contained within the table as an attribute. In this case, there must not be any duplicate values within that attribute. In tables, keys may be categorical or ordinal attributes, but quantititive attributes are typically unsuitable as keys because there is nothing to prevent them from having the same values for multiple items.

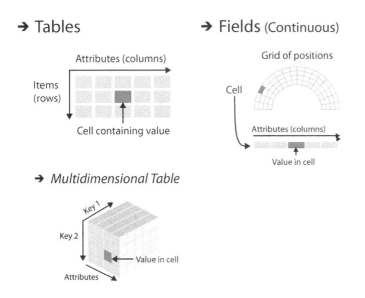

Figure 2.8. Key and value semantics for tables and fields.

For example, in Table 2.1, *Name* is a categorical attribute that might appear to be a reasonable key at first, but the last line shows that two people have the same name, so it is not a good choice. *Favorite Fruit* is clearly not a key, despite being categorical, because *Pear* appears in two different rows. The quantitative attribute of *Age* has many duplicate values, as does the ordinal attribute of *Shirt Size*. The first attribute in this flat table has an explicit unique identifier that acts as the key.[4] This key attribute could either be ordinal, for example if the order that the rows were entered into the table captures interesting temporal information, or categorical, if it's simply treated as a unique code.

Figure 2.9 shows the order table from Figure 2.5 where each attribute is colored according to its type. There is no explicit key: even the *Order ID* attribute has duplicates, because orders consist of multiple items with different container sizes, so it does not act as a unique identifier. This table is an example of using an implicit key that is the row number within the table.

---

[4]It's common to store the key attribute in the first column, for understandability by people and ease of building data structures by computers.

A	B	C	S	T	U
Order ID	Order Date	Order Priority	Product Container	Product Base Margin	Ship Date
3	10/14/06	5-Low	Large Box	0.8	10/21/06
6	2/21/08	4-Not Specified	Small Pack	0.55	2/22/08
32	7/16/07	2-High	Small Pack	0.79	7/17/07
32	7/16/07	2-High	Jumbo Box	0.72	7/17/07
32	7/16/07	2-High	Medium Box	0.6	7/18/07
32	7/16/07	2-High	Medium Box	0.65	7/18/07
35	10/23/07	4-Not Specified	Wrap Bag	0.52	10/24/07
35	10/23/07	4-Not Specified	Small Box	0.58	10/25/07
36	11/3/07	1-Urgent	Small Box	0.55	11/3/07
65	3/18/07	1-Urgent	Small Pack	0.49	3/19/07
66	1/20/05	5-Low	Wrap Bag	0.56	1/20/05
69	6/4/05	4-Not Specified	Small Pack	0.44	6/6/05
69	6/4/05	4-Not Spec		0.6	6/6/05
70	12/18/06	5-Low		0.59	12/23/06
70	12/18/06	5-Low		0.82	12/23/06
96	4/17/05	2-High		0.55	4/19/05
97	1/29/06	3-Medium		0.38	1/30/06
129	11/19/08	5-Low		0.37	11/28/08
130	5/8/08	2-High	Small Box	0.37	5/9/08
130	5/8/08	2-High	Medium Box	0.38	5/10/08
130	5/8/08	2-High	Small Box	0.6	5/11/08
132	6/11/06	3-Medium	Medium Box	0.6	6/12/06
132	6/11/06	3-Medium	Jumbo Box	0.69	6/14/06
134	5/1/08	4-Not Specified	Large Box	0.82	5/3/08
135	10/21/07	4-Not Specified	Small Pack	0.64	10/23/07
166	9/12/07	2-High	Small Box	0.55	9/14/07
193	8/8/06	1-Urgent	Medium Box	0.57	8/10/06
194	4/5/08	3-Medium	Wrap Bag	0.42	4/7/08

quantitative
ordinal
categorical

Figure 2.9. The order table with the attribute columns colored by their type; none of them is a key.

2.6.1.2   Multidimensional Tables

The more complex case is a **multidimensional table**, where multiple keys are required to look up an item. The combination of all keys must be unique for each item, even though an individual key attribute may contain duplicates. For example, a common multidimensional table from the biology domain has a gene as one key and time as another key, so that the value in each cell is the activity level of a gene at a particular time.

The information about which attributes are keys and which are values may not be available; in many instances determining which attributes are independent keys versus dependent values is the goal of the vis process, rather than its starting point. In this case, the successful outcome of analysis using vis might be to recast a flat table into a more semantically meaningful multidimensional table.

2.6.1.3   Fields

Although fields differ from tables a fundamental way because they represent continuous rather than discrete data, keys and values are still central concerns. (Different vocabulary for the same basic idea is more common with spatial field data, where the term *independent variable* is used instead of *key*, and *dependent variable* instead of *value*.)

Fields are structured by sampling in a systematic way so that each grid cell is spanned by a unique range from a continuous domain. In spatial fields, spatial position acts as a quantitative key, in contrast to a nonspatial attribute in the case of a table that is categorical or ordinal. The crucial difference between fields and tables is that useful answers for attribute values are returned for locations throughout the sampled range, not just the exact points where data was recorded.

Fields are typically characterized in terms of the number of keys versus values. Their **multivariate** structure depends on the number of value attributes, and their **multidimensional** structure depends on the number of keys. The standard multidimensional cases are 2D and 3D fields for static measurements taken in two or three spatial dimensions,[5] and fields with three or four keys, in the case where these measurements are time-varying. A field can be both multidimensional and multivariate if it has multiple keys and multiple values. The standard classification according to multivariate structure is that a **scalar field** has one attribute per cell, a **vector field** has two or more attributes per cell, and a **tensor field** has many attributes per cell.*

2.6.1.4   Scalar Fields

A **scalar field** is univariate, with a single value attribute at each point in space. One example of a 3D scalar field is the time-varying medical scan above; another is the temperature in a room at each point in 3D space. The geometric intuition is that each point in a scalar field has a single value. A point in space can have several different numbers associated with it; if there is no underlying connection between them then they are simply multiple separate scalar fields.

2.6.1.5   Vector Fields

A **vector field** is multivariate, with a list of multiple attribute values at each point. The geometric intuition is that each point in a vector

★ These definitions of *scalar*, *vector*, and *tensor* follow the common usage in vis. In a strict mathematical sense, these distinctions are not technically correct, since scalars and vectors are included as a degenerate case of tensors. Mapping the mathematical usage to the vis usage, **scalars** mean mathematical tensors of order 0, **vectors** mean mathematical tensors of order 1, and **tensors** mean mathematical tensors of order 2 or more.

---

[5]It's also possible for a spatial field to have just one key.

field has a direction and magnitude, like an arrow that can point in any direction and that can be any length. The length might mean the speed of a motion or the strength of a force. A concrete example of a 3D vector field is the velocity of air in the room at a specific time point, where there is a direction and speed for each item. The dimensionality of the field determines the number of components in the direction vector; its length can be computed directly from these components, using the standard Euclidean distance formula. The standard cases are two, three, or four components, as above.

2.6.1.6 Tensor Fields

A **tensor field** has an array of attributes at each point, representing a more complex multivariate mathematical structure than the list of numbers in a vector. A physical example is stress, which in the case of a 3D field can be defined by nine numbers that represent forces acting in three orthogonal directions. The geometric intution is that the full information at each point in a tensor field cannot be represented by just an arrow and would require a more complex shape such as an ellipsoid.

2.6.1.7 Field Semantics

This categorization of spatial fields requires knowledge of the attribute semantics and cannot be determined from type information alone. If you are given a field with multiple measured values at each point and no further information, there is no sure way to know its structure. For example, nine values could represent many things: nine separate scalar fields, or a mix of multiple vector fields and scalar fields, or a single tensor field.

2.6.2 Temporal Semantics

A **temporal** attribute is simply any kind of information that relates to time. Data about time is complicated to handle because of the rich hierarchical structure that we use to reason about time, and the potential for periodic structure. The time hierarchy is deeply multiscale: the scale of interest could range anywhere from nanoseconds to hours to decades to millennia. Even the common words *time* and *date* are a way to partially specify the scale of temporal interest. Temporal analysis tasks often involve finding or verifying periodicity either at a predetermined scale or at some scale not known in advance. Moreover, the temporal scales of interest do not all fit into a strict hierarchy; for instance, weeks do not fit

cleanly into months. Thus, the generic vis problems of transformation and aggregation are often particularly complex when dealing
with temporal data. One important idea is that even though the
dataset semantics involves change over time, there are many approaches to visually encoding that data—and only one of them is
to show it changing over time in the form of an animation.

> Section 3.4.2.3 intro-
> duces the problem of
> data transformation. Sec-
> tion 13.4 discusses the
> question of aggregation in
> detail.

Temporal attributes can have either value or key semantics. Examples of temporal attributes with dependent value semantics are
a duration of elapsed time or the date on which a transaction occurred. In both spatial fields and abstract tables, time can be an
independent key. For example, a time-varying medical scan can
have the independent keys of x, y, z, t to cover spatial position and
time, with the dependent value attribute of density for each combination of four indices to look up position and time. A temporal
key attribute is usually considered to have a quantitative type, although it's possible to consider it as ordinal data if the duration
between events is not interesting.

> Vision versus memory is
> discussed further in Sec-
> tion 6.5.

2.6.2.1   Time-Varying Data

A dataset has **time-varying** semantics when time is one of the key
attributes, as opposed to when the temporal attribute is a value
rather than a key. As with other decisions about semantics, the
question of whether time has key or value semantics requires external knowledge about the nature of the dataset and cannot be
made purely from type information. An example of a dataset with
time-varying semantics is one created with a sensor network that
tracks the location of each animal within a herd by taking new
measurements every second. Each animal will have new location
data at every time point, so the temporal attribute is an independent key and is likely to be a central aspect of understanding the
dataset. In contrast, a horse-racing dataset covering a year's worth
of races could have temporal value attributes such as the race start
time and the duration of each horse's run. These attributes do indeed deal with temporal information, but the dataset is not time-
varying.

A common case of temporal data occurs in a **time-series** dataset,
namely, an ordered sequence of time–value pairs. These datasets
are a special case of tables, where time is the key. These time-
value pairs are often but not always spaced at uniform temporal
intervals. Typical time-series analysis tasks involve finding trends,
correlations, and variations at multiple time scales such as hourly,
daily, weekly, and seasonal.

▶ The dataset types of dynamic streams versus static
files are discussed in Section 2.4.6.

The word **dynamic** is often used ambiguously to mean one of two very different things. Some use it to mean a dataset has *time-varying* semantics, in contrast to a dataset where time is not a key attribute, as discussed here. Others use it to mean a dataset has *stream* type, in contrast to an unchanging file that can be loaded all at once. In this latter sense, items and attributes can be added or deleted and their values may change during a running session of a vis tool. I carefully distinguish between these two meanings here.

2.7 Further Reading

The Big Picture The framework presented here was inspired in part by the many taxonomies of data that have been previously proposed, including the synthesis chapter at the beginning of an early collection of infovis readings [Card et al. 99], a taxonomy that emphasizes the division between continuous and discrete data [Tory and Möller 04a], and one that emphasizes both data and tasks [Shneiderman 96].

Field Datasets Several books discuss the spatial field dataset type in far more detail, including two textbooks [Telea 07, Ward et al. 10], a voluminous handbook [Hansen and Johnson 05], and the *vtk* book [Schroeder et al. 06].

Attribute Types The attribute types of categorical, ordered, and quantitative were proposed in the seminal work on scales of measurement from the psychophysics literature [Stevens 46]. Scales of measurement are also discussed extensively in the book *The Grammar of Graphics* [Wilkinson 05] and are used as the foundational axes of an influential vis design space taxonomy [Card and Mackinlay 97].

Key and Value Semantics The Polaris vis system, which has been commercialized as Tableau, is built around the distinction between key attributes (independent dimensions) and value attributes (dependent measures) [Stolte et al. 02].

Temporal Semantics A good resource for time-oriented data vis is a recent book, *Visualization of Time-Oriented Data* [Aigner et al. 11].

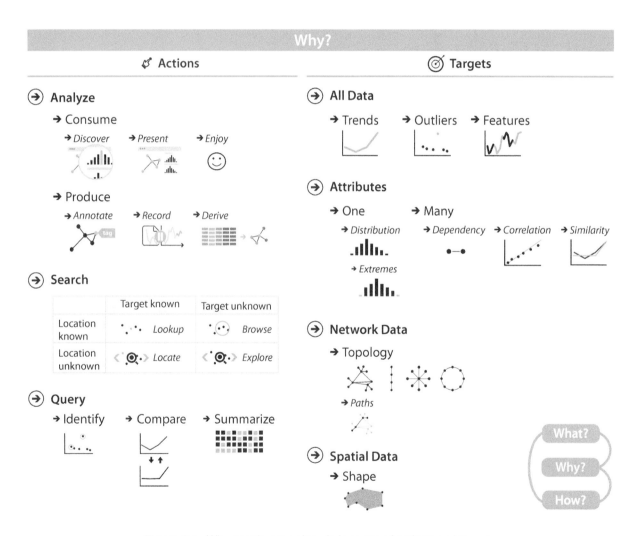

Figure 3.1. *Why* people are using vis in terms of actions and targets.

Chapter 3

Why: Task Abstraction

3.1 The Big Picture

Figure 3.1 breaks down into actions and targets the reasons *why* a vis tool is being used. The highest-level actions are to use vis to consume or produce information. The cases for consuming are to present, to discover, and to enjoy; discovery may involve generating or verifying a hypothesis. At the middle level, search can be classified according to whether the identity and location of targets are known or not: both are known with lookup, the target is known but its location is not for locate, the location is known but the target is not for browse, and neither the target nor the location are known for explore. At the low level, queries can have three scopes: identify one target, compare some targets, and summarize all targets. Targets for all kinds of data are finding trends and outliers. For one attribute, the target can be one value, the extremes of minimum and maximum values, or the distribution of all values across the entire attribute. For multiple attributes, the target can be dependencies, correlations, or similarities between them. The target with network data can be topology in general or paths in particular, and with spatial data the target can be shape.

3.2 Why Analyze Tasks Abstractly?

This framework encourages you to consider tasks in abstract form, rather than the domain-specific way that users typically think about them.

Transforming task descriptions from domain-specific language into abstract form allows you to reason about similarities and differences between them. Otherwise, it's hard to make useful comparisons between domain situations, because if you don't do this kind of translation then everything just appears to be different. That apparent difference is misleading: there are a lot of similarities in what people want to do once you strip away the surface language differences.

For example, an epidimiologist studying the spread of a new strain of influenza might initially describe her task as "contrast the prognosis of patients who were intubated in the ICU more than one month after exposure to patients hospitalized within the first week", while a biologist studying immune system response might use language such as "see if the results for the tissue samples treated with LL-37 match up with the ones without the peptide". Even if you know what all the specialized vocabulary means, it's still hard to think about what these two descriptions have in common because they're using different words: "contrast" versus "match up". If you transform these into descriptions using a consistent set of generic terms, then you can spot that these two tasks are just two instances of the same thing: "compare values between two groups".

The analysis framework has a small set of carefully chosen words to describe *why* people are using vis, designed to help you crisply and concisely distinguish between different goals. This set has verbs describing *actions*, and nouns describing *targets*. It's possible that you might decide to use additional terms to completely and precisely describe the user's goals; if so, strive to translate domain-specific terms into words that are as generic as possible.

The same vis tool might be usable for many different goals. It is often useful to consider only one of the user's goals at a time, in order to more easily consider the question of *how* a particular idiom supports that goal. To describe complex activities, you can specify a chained sequence of tasks, where the output of one becomes the input to the next.

Another important reason to analyze the task is to understand whether and how to transform the user's original data into different forms by deriving new data. That is, the task abstraction can and should guide the data abstraction.

3.3   Who: Designer or User

It's sometimes useful to augment an analysis instance specification by indicating *who* has a goal or makes a design choice: the designer of the vis or the end user of the vis. Both cases are common.

Vis tools fall somewhere along a continuum from specific to general. On the specific side, tools are narrow: the designer has built many choices into the design of the tool itself in a way that the user cannot override. These tools are limited in the kinds of data and tasks that they can address, but their strength is that users are not faced with an overwhelming array of design choices. On the general side, tools are flexible and users have many choices to make. The breadth of choices is both a strength and a limitation: users have a lot of power, but they also may make ineffective choices if they do not have a deep understanding of many vis design issues.

Specialized vis tools are designed for specific contexts with a narrow range of data configurations, especially those created through a problem-driven process. These specialized datasets are often an interesting mix of complex combinations of and special cases of the basic data types. They also are a mix of original and derived data. In contrast, general vis tools are designed to handle a wide range of data in a flexible way, for example, by accepting any dataset of a particular type as input: tables, or fields, or networks. Some particularly broad tools handle multiple dataset types, for instance, supporting transformations between tables and networks.

> ▶ Dataset types are covered in Section 2.4.

3.4 Actions

Figure 3.2 shows three levels of **actions** that define user goals. The high-level choices describe how the vis is being used to *analyze*, either to consume existing data or to also produce additional data. The mid-level choices cover what kind of *search* is involved, in terms of whether the target and location are known or not. The low-level choices pertain to the kind of *query*: does the user need to identify one target, compare some targets, or summarize all of the targets? The choices at each of these three levels are independent from each other, and it's usually useful to describe actions at all three of them.

3.4.1 Analyze

At the highest level, the framework distinguishes between two possible goals of people who want to **analyze** data using a vis tool: users might want only to *consume* existing information or also to actively *produce* new information.

The most common use case for vis is for the user to **consume** information that has already been generated as data stored in a

Figure 3.2. Three levels of actions: analyze, search, and query.

format amenable to computation. The framework has three further distinctions within that case: whether the goal is to present
something that the user already understands to a third party, or
for the user to discover something new or analyze information that

is not already completely understood, or for users to enjoy a vis to indulge their casual interests in a topic.

3.4.1.1   Discover

The **discover** goal refers to using vis to find new knowledge that was not previously known. Discovery may arise from the serendipitous observation of unexpected phenomena, but investigation may be motivated by existing theories, models, hypotheses, or hunches. This usage includes the goal of finding completely new things; that is, the outcome is to **generate** a new hypothesis. It also includes the goal of figuring out whether a conjecture is true or false; that is, to **verify**—or disconfirm—an existing hypothesis.

While vis for discovery is often associated with modes of scientific inquiry, it is not restricted to domain situations that are formally considered branches of science. The discover goal is often discussed as the classic motivation for sophisticated interactive idioms, because the vis designer doesn't know in advance what the user will need to see.* The fundamental motivation of this analysis framework is to help you separate out the questions of *why* the vis is being used from *how* the vis idiom is designed to achieve those goals, so I will repeatedly emphasize that *why* doesn't dictate *how*.

★ This distinction between the goals of presentation of the known and discovery of the unknown is very common in the vis literature, but other sources may use different terms, such as **explain** versus **explore**.

3.4.1.2   Present

The **present** goal refers to the use of vis for the succinct communication of information, for telling a story with data, or guiding an audience through a series of cognitive operations. Presentation using vis may take place within the context of decision making, planning, forecasting, and instructional processes. The crucial point about the *present* goal is that vis is being used by somebody to communicate something specific and already understood to an audience.

Presentation may involve collaborative or pedagogical contexts, and the means by which a presentation is given may vary according to the size of the audience, whether the presentation is live or prerecorded, and whether the audience is in the same place as the presenter. One classic example of a *present* vis is static information graphics, such as a diagram in a newspaper or an image in a blog. However, the *present* goal is not intrinsically limited to a static visual encoding idiom; it's very possible to pursue this goal with dynamic vis idioms that include interaction and animation. Once again, the decision about *why* is separable from *how* the idiom is designed: presentation can be supported through a wide variety of idiom design choices.

A crucial aspect of presentation is that the knowledge communicated is already known to the presenter in advance. Sometimes the presenter knows it before using vis at all and uses the vis only for communication. In other cases, the knowledge arose from the presenter's previous use of vis with the goal of discovery, and it's useful to think about a chained sequence of tasks where the output of a discover session becomes the input to a present session.

3.4.1.3 Enjoy

The **enjoy** goal refers to casual encounters with vis. In these contexts, the user is not driven by a previously pressing need to verify or generate a hypothesis but by curiosity that might be both stimulated and satisfied by the vis. Casual encounters with vis for enjoyment can be fleeting, such as when looking at an infographic while reading a blog post. However, users can become sufficiently engaged with an enjoyable vis tool that they use it intensively for a more extended period of time.

One aspect of this classification that's tricky is that the goals of the eventual vis user might not be a match with the user goals conjectured by the vis designer. For example, a vis tool may have been intended by the designer for the goal of discovery with a particular audience, but it might be used for pure enjoyment by a different group of people. In the analyses presented in this book I'll assume that these goals are aligned, but in your own experience as a designer you might need to consider how they might diverge.

Figure 3.3 shows the Name Voyager, which was created for expectant parents deciding what to name their new baby. When the user types characters of a name, the vis shows data for the popularity of names in the United States since 1900 that start with that sequence of characters. The tool uses the visual encoding idiom where each name has a stripe whose height corresponds to popularity at a given time. Currently popular names are brighter, and gender is encoded by color. The Name Voyager appealed to many people with no interest in having children, who analyzed many different historical trends and posted extensively about their findings in their personal blogs, motivated by their own enjoyment rather than a pressing need [Wattenberg 05].

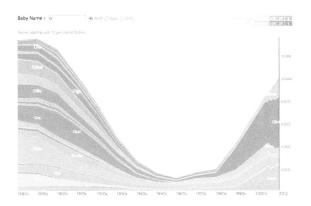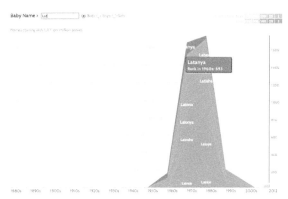

Figure 3.3. Name Voyager, a vis tool originally intended for parents focused deciding on what to name their expected baby, ended up being used by many nonparents to analyze historical trends for their own enjoyment. Left: Names starting with 'O' had a notable dip in popularity in the middle of the century. Right: Names starting with 'LAT' show a trend of the 1970s. After [Wattenberg 05, Figures 2 and 3], using http://www.babynamewizard.com.

3.4.2 Produce

In contrast to using vis only for consuming existing information, in the **produce** case the intent of the user is to generate new material. Often the goal with *produce* is to produce output that is used immediately, as input to a next instance. Sometimes the user intends to use this new material for some other vis-related task later on, such as discovery or presentation. Sometimes the intended use of the new material is for some other purpose that does not require vis, such as downstream analysis using nonvisual tools. There are three kinds of produce goals: *annotate*, *record*, and *derive*.

3.4.2.1 Annotate

The **annotate** goal refers to the addition of graphical or textual annotations associated with one or more preexisting visualization elements, typically as a manual action by the user. When an annotation is associated with data items, the annotation could be thought of as a new attribute for them. For example, the user could annotate all of the points within a cluster with a text label.

▶ Attributes are covered in Chapter 2.

3.4.2.2 Record

The **record** goal saves or captures visualization elements as persistent artifacts. These artifacts include screen shots, lists of book-

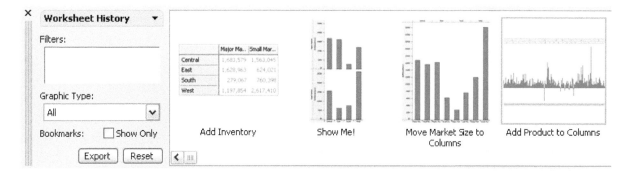

Figure 3.4. Graphical history recorded during an analysis session with Tableau. From [Heer et al. 08, Figure 1].

marked elements or locations, parameter settings, interaction logs, or annotations. The *record* choice saves a persistent artifact, in contrast to the *annotate*, which attaches information temporarily to existing elements; an annotation made by a user can subsequently be recorded. One interesting example of a *record* goal is to assemble a *graphical history*, in which the output of each task includes a static snapshot of the view showing its current state, and these snapshots accumulate in a branching meta-visualization showing what occurred during the user's entire session of using the vis tool. Figure 3.4 shows an example from the Tableau vis tool [Heer et al. 08]. Recording and retaining artifacts such as these are often desirable for maintaining a sense of analytical provenance, allowing users to revisit earlier states or parameter settings.

3.4.2.3 Derive

The **derive** goal is to produce new data elements based on existing data elements. New attributes can be derived from information contained within existing ones, or data can be transformed from one type into another. Deriving new data is a critical part of the vis design process. The common case is that deriving new data is a choice made by vis designers, but this choice could also be driven by a user of a vis tool.

When you are faced with a dataset, you should always consider whether to simply use it as is, or to transform it to another form: you could create newly derived attributes from the original ones, or even transform the dataset from the original type to another one.

There is a strong relationship between the form of the data—the attribute and dataset types—and what kinds of vis idioms are effective at displaying it. The good news is that your hands are not tied as a designer because you can transform the data into a form more useful for the task at hand. Don't just draw what you're given; decide what the right thing to show is, create it with a series of transformations from the original dataset, and draw that!

The ability to derive new data is why the data abstraction used in a vis tool is an active choice on the part of the designer, rather than simply being dictated by what the user provides. Changing the dataset to another form by deriving new attributes and types greatly expands the design space of possible vis idioms that you can use to display it. The final data abstraction that you choose might simply be the dataset in its original form, but more complex data abstractions based on deriving new attributes and types are frequently necessary if you're designing a vis tool for a complex, real-world use case. Similarly, when you consider the design of an existing vis system, understanding how the original designer chose to transform the given dataset should be a cornerstone of your analysis.

A dataset often needs to be transformed beyond its original state in order to create a visual encoding that can solve the desired problem. To do so, we can create **derived attributes** that extend the dataset beyond the original set of attributes that it contains.*

★ A synonym for *derive* is **transform**.

In some cases, the derived attribute encodes the same data as the original, but with a change of type. For example, a dataset might have an original attribute that is quantitative data: for instance, floating point numbers that represent temperature. For some tasks, like finding anomalies in local weather patterns, that raw data might be used directly. For another task, like deciding whether water is an appropriate temperature for a shower, that quantitative attribute might be transformed into a new derived attribute that is ordered: hot, warm, or cold. In this transformation, most of the detail is aggregated away. In a third example, when making toast, an even more lossy transformation into a binary categorical attribute might suffice: burned or not burned.

In other cases, creating the derived attribute requires access to additional information. For a geographic example, a categorical attribute of city name could be transformed into two derived quantitative attributes containing the latitude and longitude of the city. This transformation could be accomplished through a lookup to a separate, external database.

A new derived attribute may be created using arithmetic, logical, or statistical operations ranging from simple to complex. A common simple operation is subtracting two quantitative attributes

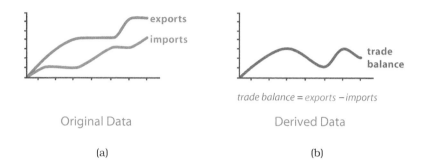

Original Data   Derived Data

(a)   (b)

Figure 3.5. Derived attributes can be directly visually encoded. (a) Two original data attributes are plotted, imports and exports. (b) The quantitative derived attribute of trade balance, the difference between the two originals, can be plotted directly.

to create a new quantitative difference attribute, which can then be directly visually encoded. Figure 3.5 shows an example of encoding two attributes directly, versus encoding the derived variable of the difference between them. For tasks that require understanding this difference, Figure 3.5(b) is preferable because it encodes the difference directly. The user can interpret the information by judging position along a common frame. In contrast, in Figure 3.5(a) the user must judge the difference in heights between the two original curves at each step, a perceptual operation that is more difficult and demanding. This operation is simple because it is localized to a pair of attribute values; a more complex operation would require global computations across all values for an attribute, such as averaging for a single attribute or the correlation between two of them.

Datasets can be transformed into new ones of a different type, just as new attributes can be derived from existing ones. The full process of creating derived data may involve multiple stages of transformation.

For example, the VxInsight system transforms a table of genomics data into a network through a multistage derivation process by first creating a quantitative derived attribute of similarity, and then creating a derived network with links only between the most similar items [Davidson et al. 01]. The table had 6000 rows of yeast genes, and 18 columns containing measurements of the gene activity level in a specific experimental condition. The values in the columns were used to derive a new attribute, the similarity score, defined between each pair of genes. The similarity score was computed using sophisticated statistical processing to be robust in the presence of nonlinear and noisy data, as occurs in this sort of biological application. This derived attribute was then used to create a derived network, where the nodes in the network were genes. A link was established between two genes when the similarity score was high; specifically, links were created only for the top 20 similarity scores.

3.4.3 Search

All of the high-level *analyze* cases require the user to **search** for elements of interest within the vis as a mid-level goal.* The classification of search into four alternatives is broken down according to whether the identity and location of the search target is already known or not.

★ The verb **find** is often used as a synonym in descriptions of *search* tasks, implying a successful outcome.

3.4.3.1 Lookup

If users already know both what they're looking for and where it is, then the search type is simply **lookup**. For example, a user of a tree vis showing the ancestral relationships between mammal species might want to look up humans, and can get to the right spot quickly by remembering how humans are classified: they're in the group that has live young rather than laying eggs like a platypus or having a pouch like kangaroos, and within that group humans fall into the category of primates.

3.4.3.2 Locate

To find a known target at an unknown location, the search type is **locate**: that is, find out where the specific object is. In a similar example, the same user might not know where to find rabbits, and would have to look around in a number of places before locating them as lagomorphs (not rodents)!

3.4.3.3 Browse

In contrast, the exact identity of a search target might not be known in advance; rather, it might be specified based on characteristics. In this case, users are searching for one or more items that fit some kind of specification, such as matching up with a particular range of attribute values. When users don't know exactly what they're looking for, but they do have a location in mind of where to look for it, the search type is **browse**. For instance, if a user of a tree vis is searching within a particular subtree for leaf nodes having few siblings, it would be an instance of *browse* because the location is known in advance, even though the exact identity of the search target isn't. Another example of browsing is a user of a vis tool with the visual encoding idiom of a line graph displaying the share price of multiple companies over the past month, who examines the share price of each line on June 15.

3.4.3.4 Explore

When users are not even sure of the location, the search type is **explore**. It entails searching for characteristics without regard to their location, often beginning from an overview of everything. Examples include searching for outliers in a scatterplot, for anomalous spikes or periodic patterns in a line graph of time-series data, or for unanticipated spatially dependent patterns in a choropleth map.

3.4.4 Query

Once a target or set of targets for a search has been found, a low-level user goal is to **query** these targets at one of three scopes: *identify*, *compare*, or *summarize*. The progression of these three corresponds to an increase in the amount of search targets under consideration: one, some, or all. That is, **identify** refers to a single target, **compare** refers to multiple targets, and **summarize** refers to the full set of possible targets.

For a concrete example, consider different uses of a choropleth map of US election results, where each state is color-coded by the party that won. A user can *identify* the election results for one state, *compare* the election results of one state to another, or *summarize* the election results across all states to determine how many favored one candidate or the other or to determine the overall distribution of margin of victory values.

3.4.4.1 Identify

The scope of **identify** is a single target. If a search returns known targets, either by *lookup* or *locate*, then *identify* returns their characteristics. For example, a user of a static map that represents US election results by color coding each state red or blue, with the saturation level of either hue showing the proportion, can *identify* the winning party and margin of victory for the state of California. Conversely, if a search returns targets matching particular characteristics, either by *browse* or *explore*, then *identify* returns specific references. For instance, the election map user can *identify* the state having the highest margin of victory.

3.4.4.2   Compare

The scope of **compare** is multiple targets. Comparison tasks are typically more difficult than identify tasks and require more sophisticated idioms to support the user. For example, the capability of inspecting a single target in detail is often necessary, but not sufficient, for comparison.

3.4.4.3   Summarize

The scope of **summarize** task is all possible targets. A synonym for *summarize* is **overview**, a term is frequently used in the vis literature both as a verb, where it means to provide a comprehensive view of everything, and as a noun, where it means a summary display of everything. The goal of providing an overview is extremely common in visualization.

▶ Section 6.7 discusses the question of how and when to provide overviews.

3.5   Targets

Figure 3.6 shows four kinds of abstract targets. The actions discussed above refer to a **target**, meaning some aspect of the data that is of interest to the user. Targets are nouns, whereas actions are verbs. The idea of a target is explicit with search and query actions. It is more implicit with the use actions, but still relevant: for example, the thing that the user presents or discovers.

Three high-level targets are very broadly relevant, for all kinds of data: *trends*, *outliers*, and *features*. A **trend** is a high-level characterization of a pattern in the data.* Simple examples of trends include increases, decreases, peaks, troughs, and plateaus. Almost inevitably, some data doesn't fit well with that backdrop; those elements are the **outliers**.* The exact definition of **features** is task dependent, meaning any particular structures of interest.

★ Indeed, a synonym for *trend* is simply **pattern**.

★ There are many other synonyms for *outliers*, including **anomalies**, **novelties**, **deviants**, and **surprises**.

Attributes are specific properties that are visually encoded. The lowest-level target for an attribute is to find an individual value. Another frequent target of interest is to find the extremes: the minimum or maximum value across the range. A very common

▶ Attributes are discussed in detail in Chapter 2.

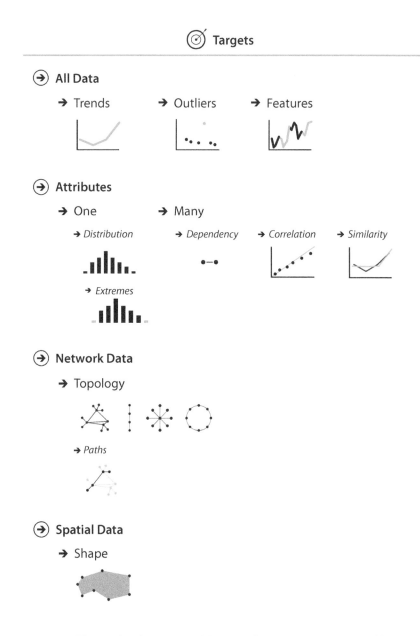

Figure 3.6. The goals of the user might be to find or understand specific aspects of the data: trends and outliers for all kinds of data; individual values, the minimum or maximum extremes of the range, or the entire distribution of a single attribute; or the dependencies, correlations, or similarities between multiple attributes; topology or paths for network data, and shape for spatial data.

target that has high-level scope is the distribution of all values for an attribute.

Some targets encompass the scope of multiple attributes: *dependencies*, *correlations*, and *similarities* between attributes. A first attribute can have a **dependency** on a second, where the values for the first directly depend on those of the second. There is a **correlation** between one attribute and another if there is a tendency for the values of second to be tied to those of the first. The **similarity** between two attributes can be defined as a quantitative measurement calculated on all of their values, allowing attributes to be ranked with respect to how similar, or different, they are from each other.

The abstract tasks of understanding trends, outliers, distributions, and correlations are extremely common reasons to use vis. Each of them can be expressed in very diverse terms using domain-specific language, but you should be on the lookout to recognize these abstractions.

Some targets pertain to specific types of datasets. Network data specifies relationships between nodes as links. The fundamental target with network data is to understand the structure of these interconnections; that is, the network's **topology**. A more specific topological target is a **path** of one or more links that connects two nodes. For spatial data, understanding and comparing the geometric **shape** is the common target of user actions.

▶ The network datatype is covered in Section 2.4.2, and choices for how arrange networks are covered in Chapter 9.

3.6   How: A Preview

The third part of an analysis instance trio is *how* a vis idiom can be constructed out of a set of design choices. Figure 3.7 provides a preview of these choices, with a high-level breakdown into four major classes.

The family of how to encode data within a view has five choices for how to arrange data spatially: express values; separate, order, and align regions; and use given spatial data. This family also includes how to map data with all of the nonspatial visual channels including color, size, angle, shape, and many more. The manipulate family has the choices of change any aspect of the view, select elements from within the view, and navigate to change the viewpoint within the view—an aspect of change with a rich enough set of choices to merit its own category. The family of how to facet data between views has choices for how to juxtapose and coordinate multiple views, how to partition data between views, and how to superimpose layers on top of each other. The family of how to

▶ Section 2.4.3.1 covers the dataset type of spatial fields, and Section 2.4.4 covers geometry. Choices for arranging spatial data are covered in Chapter 8.

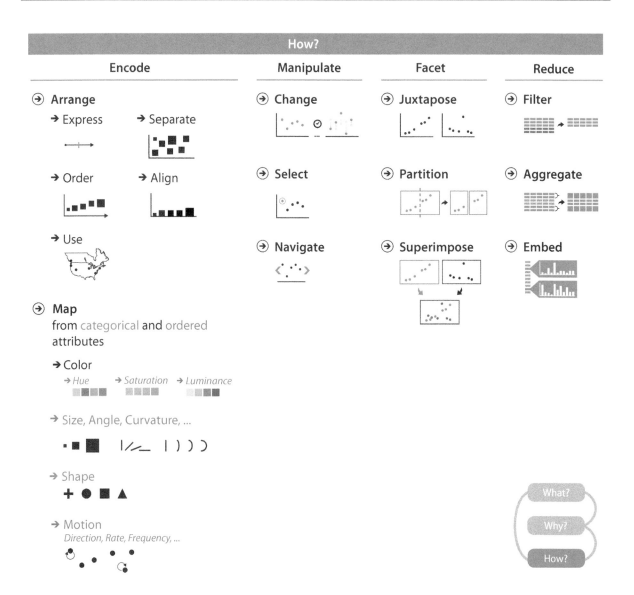

Figure 3.7. *How* to design vis idioms: encode, manipulate, facet, and reduce.

reduce the data shown has the options of filter data away, aggregate many data elements together, and embed focus and context information together within a single view.

The rest of this book defines, describes, and discusses these choices in depth.

3.7   Analyzing and Deriving: Examples

The three analysis and derivation examples below give a taste of how this what–why–how framework can be used right away. The first example covers comparative analysis between two vis tools. The second example discusses deriving a single attribute, an importance measure for trees to decide which branches to show to summarize its topological structure. The third example covers deriving many new attributes and augmenting a spatial fluid dynamics dataset by creating derived spaces in which features of interest are easy to find.

3.7.1   Comparing Two Idioms

The what–why–how analysis framework is useful for comparative analysis, for example, to examine two different vis tools that have different answers for the question of *how* the idiom is designed when used for exactly the same context of *why* and *what* at the abstraction level.

SpaceTree [Plaisant et al. 02], shown in Figure 3.8(a), and Tree-Juxtaposer [Munzner et al. 03], shown in Figure 3.8(b), are tree vis

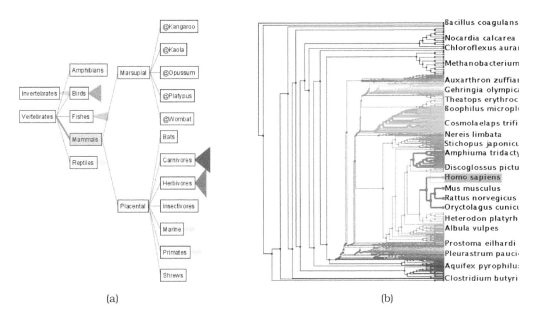

(a)   (b)

Figure 3.8. Comparing two idioms. (a) SpaceTree [Plaisant et al. 02]. (b) TreeJuxtaposer. From http://www.cs.umd.edu/hcil/spacetree and [Munzner et al. 03, Figure 1].

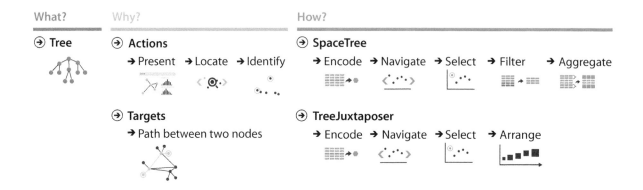

Figure 3.9. Analyzing what–why–how comparatively for the SpaceTree and TreeJuxtaposer idioms.

tools that use somewhat different idioms. What these tools take as input data is the same: a large tree composed of nodes and links. Why these tools are being used is for the same goal in this scenario: to present a path traced between two nodes of interest to a colleague. In more detail, both tools can be used to locate paths between nodes and identify them.

Some aspects of idioms are the same: both systems allow the user to navigate and to select a path, with the result that it's encoded differently from the nonselected paths through highlighting. The systems differ in how elements of the visualization are manipulated and arranged. SpaceTree ties the act of selection to a change of what is shown by automatically aggregating and filtering the unselected items. In contrast, TreeJuxtaposer allows the user to arrange areas of the tree to ensure visibility for areas of interest. Figure 3.9 summarizes this what–why–how analyis.

3.7.2   Deriving One Attribute

In a vis showing a complex network or tree, it is useful to be able to filter out most of the complexity by drawing a simpler picture that communicates the key aspects of its topological structure. One way to support this kind of summarization is to calculate a new derived attribute that measures the importance of each node in the graph and filter based on that attribute. Many different approaches to calculating importance have been proposed; **centrality metrics** do so in a way that takes into account network topology. The Strahler number is a measure of node importance originally

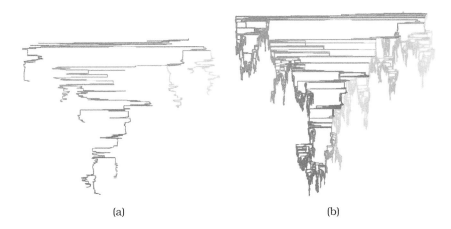

(a)   (b)

Figure 3.10. The derived quantitative attribute of Strahler numbers is used to filter the tree in order to create a recognizable summary. (a) The important skeleton of a large tree is visible when only 5000 of the highest-ranked nodes are drawn. (b) The full tree has over a half million nodes. From [Auber 02, Figures 10 and 13].

developed in hydrogeology to characterize the branching structure of rivers that has been adapted and extended for use visualizing trees and networks [Auber 02]. Very central nodes have large Strahler numbers, whereas peripheral nodes have low values. The Strahler number is an example of a derived attribute for network data that is the result of a complex and global computation, rather than simply a local calculation on a small neighborhood around a node.

Figure 3.10 shows an example of filtering according to the Strahler derived attribute to summarize a tree effectively. The result of drawing only the top-ranked 5000 nodes and the links that connect them is a recognizable skeleton of the full tree, shown in Figure 3.10(a), while over a half million nodes are shown in Figure 3.10(b). In contrast, if the 5000 nodes to draw were picked randomly, the structure would not be understandable. Both versions of the network are also colored according to the Strahler number, to show how the centrality measure varies within the network.

To summarize this example concisely in terms of a what–why–how analysis, as shown in Figure 3.11, a new quantitative attribute is derived and used to filter away the peripheral parts of a tree, in support of the task of summarizing the tree's overall topology. As in the previous example, the tree is encoded as a node–link diagram, the most common choice for tree and network arrangment.

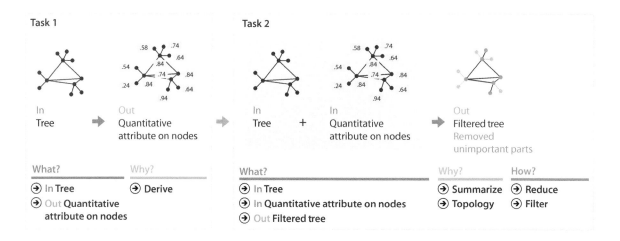

Figure 3.11. Analyzing a chained sequence of two instances where an attribute is derived in order to summarize a tree by filtering away the unimportant parts.

3.7.3   Deriving Many New Attributes

> ▶ Multiple views are discussed further in Chapter 12.

Data transformations can shed light into spatial data as well. In an example from computational fluid dynamics, linked derived spaces are used for feature detection [Henze 98]. The vis system shown in Figure 3.12 allows the user to quickly create plots of any two original or derived variables from the palette of variables shown in the upper left *derived fields* pane. The views are linked together with color highlighting. The power of this idiom lies in seeing where regions that are contiguous in one view fall in the other views.

The original dataset is a time-varying spatial field with measurements along a curvilinear mesh fitted to an airfoil. The plot in the *physical space* pane on the upper right of Figure 3.12 shows the data in this physical space, using the two spatial field variables. Undisturbed airflow enters the physical space from the left, and the back tip of the airfoil is on the right. Two important regions in back of the airfoil are distinguished with color: a red recirculation region and a yellow wake region. While these regions are not easy to distinguish in this physical view, they can be understood and selected more easily by interaction with the four other derived views. For example, in the derived space of *vorticity vs enthalpy* in the upper middle of Figure 3.12, the recirculation zone is distinguishable as a coherent spatial structure at the top, with the yellow wake also distinguishable beneath it. As the white box shows, the

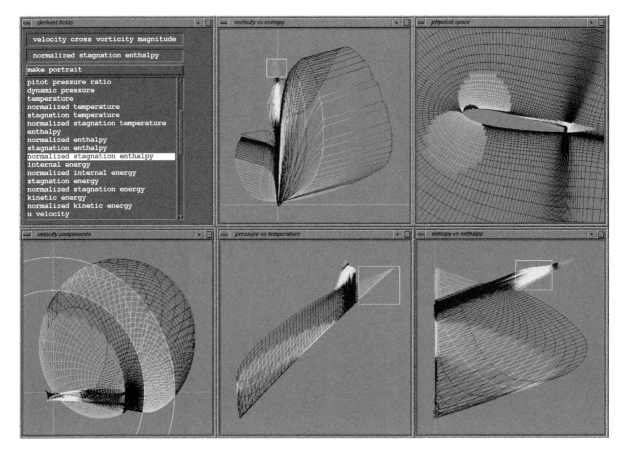

Figure 3.12. Computational fluid dynamics vis showing the list of many derived attributes (top left), one view of the original spatial field (top right), and four other views showing pairs of selected derived attributes. The multiple juxtaposed views are coordinated with shared colored highlights. From [Henze 98, Figure 5].

recirculation zone can easily be selected in this view. The *pressure vs temperature* pane in the bottom middle of Figure 3.12 shows another derived space made by plotting the pressure versus the temperature. In this view, the red recirculation zone and the yellow wake appear where both the pressure and temperature variables are high, in the upper right. Without getting into the exact technical meaning of the derived variables as used in fluid dynamics (vorticity, entropy, enthalpy, and so on), the point of this example is that many structures of interest in fluid dynamics can be seen more easily from layouts in the derived spaces.

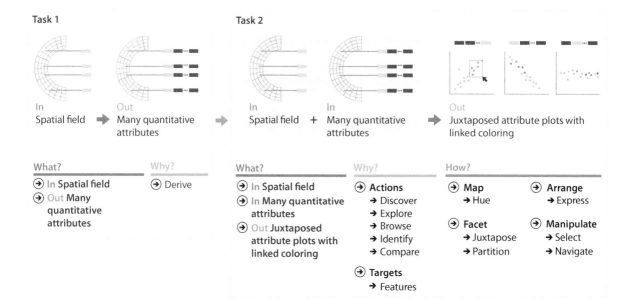

Figure 3.13. Analyzing a chained sequence, where many attributes are derived and visually encoded.

To summarize this example in terms of a what–why–how analysis, as shown in Figure 3.13, many new quantitative attributes are derived from an original spatial field dataset. Each pair of them is visually encoded into a view, as is the original spatial data, and the multiple juxtaposed views are coordinated with shared color coding and highlighting.

3.8   Further Reading

The Big Picture An earlier version of the what–why–how framework was first presented as a paper [Brehmer and Munzner 13], which includes a very detailed discussion of its relationship to the extensive previous work in classifications of tasks and interaction idioms. That discussion covers 30 previous classifications and 20 relevant references, ranging from a characterization of the scientific data analysis process [Springmeyer et al. 92], to an influential low-level task classification [Amar et al. 05], to a taxonomy of tasks for network datasets [Lee et al. 06], to a recent taxonomy of interaction dynamics [Heer and Shneiderman 12].

Who: Designers versus Users Some of the challenges inherent in bridging the gaps between vis designers and users are discussed in an influential paper [van Wijk 06].

Derive Many vis pipeline models discuss the idea of data transformation as a critical early step [Card et al. 99, Chi and Riedl 98], and others also point out the need to transform between different attribute types [Velleman and Wilkinson 93]. A later taxonomy of vis explicitly discusses the idea that data types can change as the result of the transformation [Tory and Möller 04b].

Examples The analysis examples are SpaceTree [Plaisant et al. 02], TreeJuxtaposer [Munzner et al. 03], Strahler numbers for tree simplification [Auber 02], and linked derived spaces for feature detection [Henze 98].

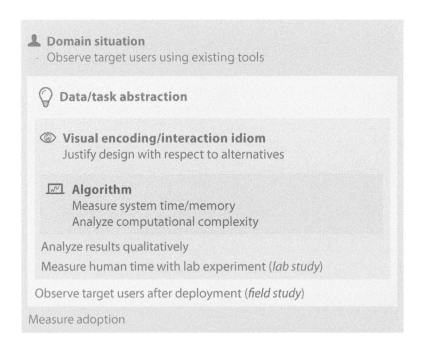

Figure 4.1. The four nested levels of vis design have different threats to validity at each level, and validation approaches should be chosen accordingly.

Chapter 4

Analysis: Four Levels for Validation

4.1 The Big Picture

Figure 4.1 shows four nested levels of design: domain situation, task and data abstraction, visual encoding and interaction idiom, and algorithm. The task and data abstraction level addresses the *why* and *what* questions, and the idiom level addresses the question of *how*. Each of these levels has different threats to validity, so it's a good idea to choose your validation method with these levels in mind.

4.2 Why Validate?

Validation is important for the reasons discussed in Chapter 1: the vis design space is huge, and most designs are ineffective. In that chapter, I also discuss the many reasons that validation is a tricky problem that is difficult to get right. It's valuable to think about how you might validate your choices from the very beginning of the design process, rather than leaving these considerations for the end as an afterthought.

This chapter introduces two more levels of design to consider, one above the *why–what* abstraction level and one below the *how* idiom level. While this book focuses on the two middle levels, considering all four is helpful when thinking about how to validate whether a given design has succeeded.

4.3 Four Levels of Design

Splitting the complex problem of vis design into four cascading levels provides an analysis framework that lets you address different concerns separately. Figure 4.2 shows these four levels.

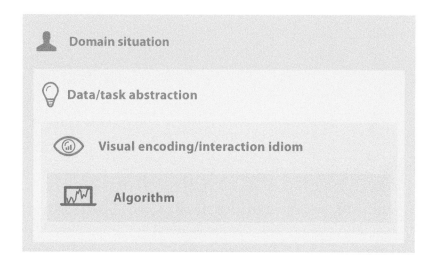

Figure 4.2. The four nested levels of vis design.

At the top is the situation level, where you consider the details of a particular application domain for vis. Next is the *what–why* abstraction level, where you map those domain-specific problems and data into forms that are independent of the domain. The following *how* level is the design of idioms that specify the approach to visual encoding and interaction. Finally, the last level is the design of algorithms to instantiate those idioms computationally.

These levels are nested; the output from an **upstream** level above is input to the **downstream** level below. A **block** is the outcome of the design process at that level. The challenge of this nesting is that choosing the wrong block at an upstream level inevitably cascades to all downstream levels. If you make a poor choice in the abstraction stage, then even perfect choices at the idiom and algorithm levels will not result in a vis system that solves the intended problem.

The value of separating these concerns into four levels is that you can separately analyze the question of whether each level has been addressed correctly, independently of whatever order design decisions were made in the process of building the vis tool. Although I encourage you to consider these four levels separately for analysis, in practice you wouldn't finalize design decisions at one level before moving on to the next. Vis design is usually a highly iterative refinement process, where a better understanding of the blocks at one level will feed back and forward into refining the blocks at the other levels. Thus, it is one of many examples of the principle of *design as redesign* [Green 89].

4.3.1   Domain Situation

Blocks at this top level describe a specific **domain situation**, which encompasses a group of target users, their domain of interest, their questions, and their data. The term **domain** is frequently used in the vis literature to mean a particular field of interest of the target users of a vis tool, for example microbiology or high-energy physics or e-commerce. Each domain usually has its own vocabulary for describing its data and problems, and there is usually some existing workflow of how the data is used to solve their problems. The group of target users might be as narrowly defined as a handful of people working at a specific company, or as broadly defined as anybody who does scientific research.

One example of a situation block is a computational biologist working in the field of comparative genomics, using genomic sequence data to ask questions about the genetic source of adaptivity in a species [Meyer et al. 09]. While one kind of situation is a specific set of users whose questions about their data arise from their work, situations arise in other contexts. For example, another situation is members of the general public making medical decisions about their healthcare in the presence of uncertainty [Micallef et al. 12].

At this level, situation blocks are *identified*: the outcome of the design process is an understanding that the designer reaches about the needs of the user. The methods typically used by designers to identify domain situation blocks include interviews, observations, or careful research about target users within a specific domain.

Developing a clear understanding of the requirements of a particular target audience is a tricky problem for a designer.* While it might seem obvious to you that it would be a good idea to understand requirements, it's a common pitfall for designers to cut corners by making assumptions rather than actually engaging with any target users.

In most cases users know they need to somehow view their data, but they typically cannot directly articulate their analysis needs in a clear-cut way. Eliciting system requirements is not easy, even when you have unfettered access to target users fluent in the vocabulary of the domain and immersed in its workflow. Asking

★ Working closely with a specific target audience to iteratively refine a design is called **user-centered design** or **human-centered design** in the human–computer interaction literature.

users to simply introspect about their actions and needs is notoriously insufficient: what users say they do when reflecting on their past behavior gives you an incomplete picture compared with what they actually do if you observe them.

The outcome of identifying a situation block is a detailed set of questions asked about or actions carried out by the target users, about a possibly heterogeneous collection of data that's also understood in detail. Two of the questions that may have been asked by the computational biologist working in comparative genomics working above were "What are the differences between individual nucleotides of feature pairs?" and "What is the density of coverage and where are the gaps across a chromosome?" [Meyer et al. 09]. In contrast, a very general question such as "What is the genetic basis of disease?" is not specific enough to be useful as input to the next design level.

4.3.2   Task and Data Abstraction

Design at the next level requires abstracting the specific domain questions and data from the domain-specific form that they have at the top level into a generic representation. Abstracting into the domain-independent vocabulary allows you to realize how domain situation blocks that are described using very different language might have similar reasons why the user needs the vis tool and what data it shows.

Questions from very different domain situations can map to the same abstract vis tasks. Examples of abstract tasks include browsing, comparing, and summarizing. Task blocks are identified by the designer as being suitable for a particular domain situation block, just as the situation blocks themselves are identified at the level above.

▶ Chapter 3 covers abstract tasks in detail.

Abstract data blocks, however, are *designed*. Selecting a data block is a creative design step rather than simply an act of identification. While in some cases you may decide to use the data in exactly the way that it was identified in the domain situation, you will often choose to transform the original data from its upstream form to something quite different. The data abstraction level requires you to consider whether and how the same dataset provided by a user should be transformed into another form. Many vis idioms are specific to a particular data type, such as a table of numbers where the columns contain quantitative, ordered, or categorical data; a node–link graph or tree; or a field of values at every point in space. Your goal is to determine which data type would support a visual representation of it that addresses the user's problem. Although sometimes the original form of the dataset is a good match for a visual encoding that solves the problem, often a transformation to another data type provides a better solution.

▶ Chapter 2 covers abstract data types, and Section 3.4.2.3 discusses transforming and deriving data.

Explicitly considering the choices made in abstracting from domain-specific to generic tasks and data can be very useful in the vis design process. The unfortunate alternative is to do this abstraction implicitly and without justification. For example, many early web vis papers implicitly posited that solving the "lost in hyperspace" problem should be done by showing the searcher a visual representation of the topological structure of the web's hyperlink connectivity graph. In fact, people do not need an internal mental representation of this extremely complex structure to find a page of interest. Thus, no matter how cleverly the information was visually encoded at the idiom design level, the resulting vis tools all incurred additional cognitive load for the user rather than reducing it.

4.3.3 Visual Encoding and Interaction Idiom

At the third level, you decide on the specific way to create and manipulate the visual representation of the abstract data block that you chose at the previous level, guided by the abstract tasks that you also identified at that level. I call each distinct possible approach an **idiom**. There are two major concerns at play with idiom design. One set of design choices covers how to create a single picture of the data: the **visual encoding** idiom controls exactly what users see. Another set of questions involves how to manipulate that representation dynamically: the **interaction** idiom controls how users change what they see. For example, the Word Tree system [Wattenberg and Viegas 08] shown in Figure 4.3 combines the visual encoding idiom of a hierarchical tree representation of keywords laid out horizontally, preserving information about the context of their use within the original text, and the interaction idiom of navigation based on keyword selection. While it's often possible to analyze encoding and interaction idioms as separable decisions, in some cases these decisions are so intertwined that it's best to consider the outcome of these choices to be a single combined idiom.

Idiom blocks are designed: they are the outcome of decisions that you make. The design space of static visual encoding idioms is already enormous, and when you consider how to manipulate them dynamically that space of possibilities is even bigger. The

▶ Chapters 7 through 14 feature a thorough look at the design space of vis idioms.

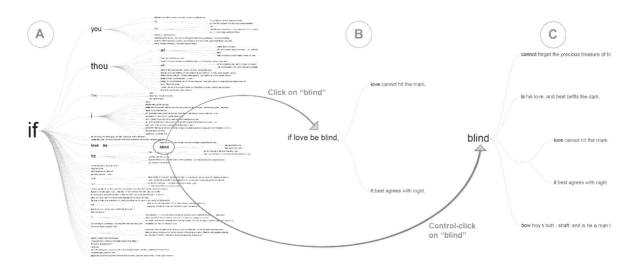

Figure 4.3. Word Tree combines the visual encoding idiom of a hierarchical tree of keywords laid out horizontally and the interaction idiom of navigation based on keyword selection. From [Wattenberg and Viegas 08, Figure 3].

> ► Chapters 5 and 6 cover principles of human perception and memory that are relevant for making idiom design choices.

nested model emphasizes identifying task abstractions and deciding on data abstractions in the previous level exactly so that you can use them to rule out many of the options as being a bad match for the goals of the users. You should make decisions about good and bad matches based on understanding human abilities, especially in terms of visual perception and memory.

While it's common for vis tools to provide multiple idioms that users might choose between, some vis tools are designed to be very narrow in scope, supporting only a few or even just a single idiom.

4.3.4 Algorithm

The innermost level involves all of the design choices involved in creating an **algorithm**: a detailed procedure that allows a computer to automatically carry out a desired goal. In this case, the goal is to efficiently handle the visual encoding and interaction idioms that you chose in the previous level. Algorithm blocks are also designed, rather than just identified.

You could design many different algorithms to instantiate the same idiom. For example, one visual encoding idiom for creating images from a three-dimensional field of measurements, such as scans created for medical purposes with magnetic resonance imaging, is direct volume rendering. Many different algorithms have been proposed as ways to achieve the requirements of this idiom, including ray casting, splatting, and texture mapping. You might determine that some of these are better than others according to measures such as the speed of the computation, how much computer memory is required, and whether the resulting image is an exact match with the specified visual encoding idiom or just an approximation.

The nested model emphasizes separating algorithm design, where your primary concerns are about computational issues, from idiom design, where your primary concerns are about human perceptual issues.

Of course, there is an interplay between these levels. For example, a design that requires something to change dynamically when the user moves the mouse may not be feasible if computing that would take minutes or hours instead of a fraction of a second. However, clever algorithm design could save the day if you come up with a way to precompute data that supports a fast enough response.

4.4 Angles of Attack

There are two common angles of attack for vis design: top down or bottom up. With **problem-driven** work, you start at the top domain situation level and work your way down through abstraction, idiom, and algorithm decisions. In **technique-driven** work, you work at one of the bottom two levels, idiom or algorithm design, where your goal is to invent new idioms that better support existing abstractions, or new algorithms that better support existing idioms.

In problem-driven vis, you begin by grappling with the problems of some real-world user and attempt to design a solution that helps them work more effectively. In this vis literature, this kind of work is often called a **design study**. Often the problem can be solved using existing visual encoding and interaction idioms rather than designing new ones, and much of the challenge lies at the abstraction level. However, sometimes the problem motivates the design of new idioms, if you decide that no existing ones will adequately solve the abstracted design problem.

Considering the four levels of nested model explicitly can help you avoid the pitfall of skipping important steps in problem-driven work. Some designers skip over the domain situation level completely, short-circuit the abstraction level by assuming that the first abstraction that comes to mind is the correct one, and jump immediately into the third level of visual encoding and interaction idiom design. I argue against this approach; the abstraction stage is often the hardest to get right. A designer struggling to find the right abstraction may end up realizing that the domain situation has not yet been adequately characterized and jump back up to work at that level before returning to this one. As mentioned above, the design process for problem-driven work is almost never strictly linear; it involves iterative refinement at all of the levels.

In technique-driven work, your starting point is an idea for a new visual encoding or interaction idiom, or a new algorithm. In this style of work, you start directly at one of the two lower levels and immediately focus design at that level. Considering the nested model can help you articulate your assumptions at the level just above your primary focus: either to articulate the abstraction requirements for your new idiom, or to articulate the idiom requirements for your algorithm.

The analysis framework of this book is focused on the *what–why* abstraction and *how* idiom levels and is intended to help you work in either direction. For problem-driven work, it allows you to work downward when searching for existing idioms by analyzing what design choices are appropriate for task abstraction that you have identified and data abstraction that you have chosen. For technique-driven work, it allows you to work upward by classifying your proposed idiom within the framework of design choices, giving you a clear framework in which to discuss its relationship with previously proposed idioms. Similarly, it is helpful to explicitly analyze a new algorithm with respect to the idioms that it supports. Although in some cases this analysis is very straightforward, it can sometimes be tricky to untangle connections between algorithms and idioms. Can your new algorithm simply be switched for a previous one, providing a faster way to compute the same visual encoding? Or does your new algorithm result in a visual encoding different enough to constitutes a new idiom that requires justification to show it's a good match for human capabilities and the intended task?

4.5 Threats to Validity

▶ Section 1.12 presented many questions to consider when validating a vis design.

Validating the effectiveness of a vis design is difficult because there are so many possible questions on the table. Considering the validity of your decisions at each level of the nested model separately

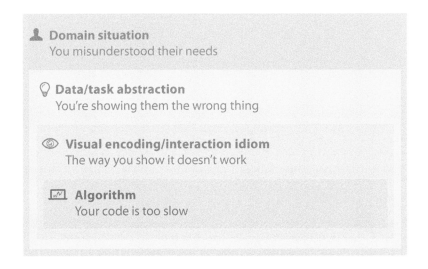

Figure 4.4. The four nested levels of vis design have different threats to validity at each level.

can help you find your way through this thicket of questions about validating your decisions, in the same way that the levels also constrain the decision-making process itself.

Each of the four levels has a different set of **threats to validity**: that is, different fundamental reasons why you might have made the wrong choices.* Figure 4.4 summarizes the four classes of threats, where **they** means the target users and **you** means the vis designer:

- Wrong problem: You misunderstood their needs.

- Wrong abstraction: You're showing them the wrong thing.

- Wrong idiom: The way you show it doesn't work.

- Wrong algorithm: Your code is too slow.

4.6   Validation Approaches

Different threats require very different approaches to validation. Figure 4.5 shows a summary of the threats and validation approaches possible at each level. The rest of this section explains

★ I have borrowed the evocative phrase *threats to validity* from the computer security domain, by way of the software engineering literature. I use the word **validation** rather than **evaluation** to underscore the idea that validation is required for every level and extends beyond user studies and ethnographic observation to include complexity analysis and benchmark timings. In software engineering, **validation** is about whether you have built the right product, and **verification** is about whether you have built the product right. Similarly, in the simulation community, **validation** of the scientific model with respect to real-world observations is similarly considered separately from **verification** of the implementation, and connotes a level of rigor beyond the methods discussed here. My use of **validation** includes both of these questions.

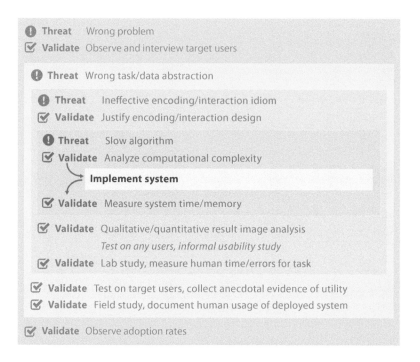

Figure 4.5. Threats and validation at each of the four levels. Many threats at the outer levels require downstream validation, which cannot be carried out until the inner levels within them are addressed, as shown by the red lines. Any single project would only address a subset of these levels, not all of them at once.

these ideas in more detail. I give only a brief outline of each validation method here; the Further Reading section at the end of this chapter has pointers to more thorough discussions of their use.

The analysis below distinguishes between **immediate** and **downstream** validation approaches. An important corollary of the model having nested levels is that most kinds of validation for the outer levels are not immediate because they require results from the downstream levels nested within them. These downstream dependencies add to the difficulty of validation: a poor showing of a test may misdirect attention upstream, when in fact the problem results from a poor choice at the current level. For example, a poor visual encoding choice may cast doubt when testing a legitimate abstraction choice, or poor algorithm design may cast doubt when testing an interaction technique. Despite their difficulties, the downstream validations are necessary. The immediate validations only offer partial evidence of success; none of them are sufficient to demonstrate that the threat to validity at that level has been addressed.

This model uses the language of *immediate* and *downstream* in order to make the discussion of the issues at each level easier to understand—but it is not always necessary to carry out the full process of design and implementation at each level before doing any downstream validation. There are many rapid prototyping methodologies for accelerating this process by creating low-fidelity stand-ins exactly so that downstream validation can occur sooner. For example, paper prototypes and Wizard of Oz testing [Dow et al. 05] can be used to get feedback from target users about abstraction and encoding designs before diving into designing or implementing any algorithms.

4.6.1 Domain Validation

At the top level, when characterizing the domain situation, a vis designer is asserting that particular problems of the target audience would benefit from vis tool support. The primary threat is that the problem is mischaracterized: the target users do not in fact have these problems. An immediate form of validation is to interview and observe the target audience to verify the characterization, as opposed to relying on assumptions or conjectures. A common approach for this case is a **field study**, where the investigator observes how people act in real-world settings, rather than by bringing them into a laboratory setting. Field studies for domain situation assessment often involve gathering qualitative data through semi-structured interviews. The method of contextual inquiry [Holtzblatt and Jones 93], where the researcher observes users working in their real-world context and interrupts to ask questions when clarification is needed, is typically better suited for vis designers than silent observation because of the complex cognitive tasks that are targeted.

One downstream form of validation is to report the rate at which the tool has been adopted by the target audience. Of course, adoption rates do not tell the whole story: many well-designed tools fail to be adopted, and some poorly designed tools win in the marketplace. Nevertheless, the important aspect of this signal is that it reports what the target users do of their own accord, as opposed to the approaches below where target users are implicitly or explicitly asked to use a tool. In particular, a tool that is actually used by its intended users has reached a different level of success than one that has only been used by its designers.

4.6.2 Abstraction Validation

At the abstraction level, the threat is that the identified task abstraction blocks and designed data abstraction blocks do not solve the characterized problems of the target audience. The key aspect of validation against this threat is that the system must be tested by target users doing their own work, rather than doing an abstract task specified by the designers of the vis system.

A common downstream form of validation is to have a member of the target user community try the tool, in hopes of collecting anecdotal evidence that the tool is in fact useful. These anecdotes may have the form of insights found or hypotheses confirmed. Of course, this observation cannot be made until after all three of the other levels have been fully addressed, after the algorithm designed at the innermost level is implemented. Although this form of validation is usually qualitative, some influential work toward quantifying insight has been done [Saraiya et al. 05]. As with the level above, it's important to distinguish between a discovery made by a target user and one that you've make yourself; the former is a more compelling argument for the utility of the vis tool.

A more rigorous validation approach for this level is to conduct a field study to observe and document how the target audience uses the deployed system, again as part of their real-world workflow. The key difference between field studies at this level and those just described for assessing domain situations is that you're observing how their behavior changes after intervening with the deployment of a vis tool, as opposed to documenting their existing work practices.

4.6.3 Idiom Validation

▶ Perceptual and cognitive principles will be covered in Chapters 5 and 6.

At the visual encoding and interaction idiom level, the threat is that the chosen idioms are not effective at communicating the desired abstraction to the person using the system. One immediate validation approach is to carefully justify the design of the idiom with respect to known perceptual and cognitive principles. Evaluation methods such as heuristic evaluation [Zuk et al. 08] and expert review [Tory and Möller 05] are a way to systematically ensure that no known guidelines are being violated by the design.

A downstream approach to validate against this threat is to carry out a **lab study**: a controlled experiment in a laboratory setting.* This method is appropriate for teasing out the impact of specific idiom design choices by measuring human performance on abstract tasks that were chosen by the study designers. Many experimental designs include both quantitative and qualitative measurements. It's extremely common to collect the objective measurements of the time spent and errors made by the study participants; subjective measurements such as their preferences are also popular. Other kinds of quantitative data that are sometimes gathered include logging actions such as mouse moves and clicks by instrumenting the vis tool, or tracking the eye movements of the participants with external gear. Qualitative data gathering often includes asking participants to reflect about their strategies through questionnaires. In this context, the expected variation in human behavior is small enough that it is feasible to design experiments where the number of participants is sufficient to allow testing for statistical significance during the analysis process.

Another downstream validation approach is the presentation of and qualitative discussion of results in the form of still images or video. This approach is downstream because it requires an implemented system to carry out the visual encoding and interaction specifications designed at this level. This validation approach is strongest when there is an explicit discussion pointing out the desirable properties in the results, rather than assuming that every reader will make the desired inferences by unassisted inspection of the images or video footage. These qualitative discussions of images sometimes occur as usage scenarios, supporting an argument that the tool is useful for a particular task–dataset combination.

A third appropriate form of downstream validation is the quantitative measurement of result images created by the implemented system; these are often called **quality metrics**. For example, many measurable layout metrics such as number of edge crossings and edge bends have been proposed to assess drawings of node–link networks. Some of these metrics have been empirically tested against human judgement, while others remains unproved conjectures.

Informal usability studies do appear in Figure 4.5, but I specifically refrain from calling them a validation method. As Andrews eloquently states: "Formative methods [including usability studies] lead to better and more usable systems, but neither offer validation of an approach nor provide evidence of the superiority of an approach for a particular context" [Andrews 08]. They are listed

★ The term **user study** is common in the vis literature, but it's used ambiguously: sometimes it's narrowly used to mean only a **lab study**, whereas other times it might also be applied to a **field study**. I use it broadly, to mean both of these.

at this level because it is a very good idea to do them upstream of attempting a validating laboratory or field study. If the system is unusable, no useful conclusions about its utility can be drawn from a user study. I distinguish usability studies from informal testing with users in the target domain, as described for the level above. Although the informal testing with target users described at the level above may uncover usability problems, the goal is to collect anecdotal evidence that the system meets its design goals. Such anecdotes are much less convincing when they come from a random person rather than a member of the target audience. In contrast, in an informal usability study, the person using the system does not need to be in the target audience; the only constraint is that the user is not the system designer.

4.6.4   Algorithm Validation

At the algorithm level, the primary threat is that the algorithm is suboptimal in terms of time or memory performance, either to a theoretical minimum or in comparison with previously proposed algorithms. Obviously, poor time performance is a problem if the user expects the system to respond in milliseconds but instead the operation takes hours or days.

> ▶ The issue of matching system latency to user expectations is discussed in more detail in Section 6.8.

An immediate form of validation is to analyze the computational complexity of the algorithm, using the standard approaches from the computer science literature. While many designers analyze algorithm complexity in terms of the number of items in the dataset, in some cases it will be more appropriate to consider the number of pixels in the display.

The downstream form of validation is to measure the wall-clock time and memory performance of the implemented algorithm. This type of measurement is so common that it's nearly mandatory for papers claiming a contribution at the algorithm level. The primary consideration is typically scalability in terms of how dataset size affects algorithm speed. One of the trickier questions is to determine what data you should use to test the algorithm. Considerations include matching up with standard **benchmarks**, which are used in previous papers, and incorporating a sufficiently broad set of data.

Another threat is incorrectness at the algorithm level, where the implementation does not meet the specification from the idiom level above. The problem could come from poor algorithm design, or the implementation of the algorithm could have bugs like any computer program. Establishing the correctness of a computer program is a notoriously difficult problem, whether through careful testing or formal methods.

The threat of algorithm incorrectness is often addressed implicitly rather than explicitly within the vis literature. Presenting still images or videos created by the implemented algorithm is one form of implicit validation against this threat, where the reader of a paper can directly see that the algorithm correctness objectives have been met. Explicit qualitative discussion of why these images show that the algorithm is in fact correct is not as common.

4.6.5   Mismatches

A common problem in weak vis projects is a mismatch between the level at which the benefit is claimed and the validation methodologies chosen. For example, the benefit of a new visual encoding idiom cannot be validated by wall-clock timings of the algorithm, which addresses a level downstream of the claim. Similarly, the threat of a mischaracterized task cannot be addressed through a formal laboratory study, where the task carried out by the participants is dictated by the study designers, so again the validation method is at a different level than the threat against the claim. The nested model explicitly separates the vis design problem into levels in order to guide validation according to the unique threats at each level.

However, it would be impossible for any single research paper to address all four levels in detail, because of limitations on space and time—such a paper would require hundreds of pages and might take a decade to finish! Instead, any individual research paper would use only a small subset of these validation methods, where careful consideration is made of which methods match the levels of design where research contributions are being claimed.

4.7   Validation Examples

This section presents examples of several vis research papers, analyzed according to the levels of vis design that they target and the methods used to validate their benefits. These projects also provide a preview of many approaches to vis that are discussed in more detail later in the book.

4.7.1   Genealogical Graphs

McGuffin and Balakrishnan present a system for the visualization of genealogical graphs [McGuffin and Balakrishnan 05]. They pro-

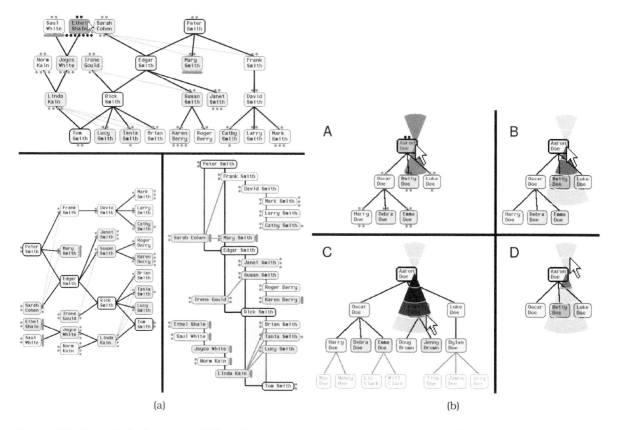

Figure 4.6. Genealogical graphs. (a) Three layouts for the dual-tree: classical node–link top-to-bottom at the top, classical left-to-right on the left, and the new indented outline algorithm on the right. (b) Widget for subtree collapsing and expanding with ballistic drags. From [McGuffin and Balakrishnan 05, Figures 13 and 14].

pose multiple new visual encoding idioms, including one based on the *dual-tree*, a subgraph formed by the union of two trees, as shown in Figure 4.6(a). Their prototype features sophisticated interaction idioms, including automatic camera framing, animated transitions, and a new widget for ballistically dragging out subtrees to arbitrary depths as shown in Figure 4.6(b).

This exemplary paper explicitly covers all four levels. The first domain situation level is handled concisely but clearly: their domain is genealogy, and they briefly discuss the needs of and current tools available for genealogical hobbyists. The paper particularly shines in the analysis at the second abstraction level. They point out that the very term *family tree* is highly misleading, be-

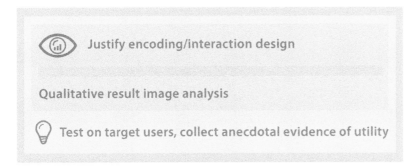

Figure 4.7. Genealogical graphs [McGuffin and Balakrishnan 05] validation levels.

cause the data type in fact is a more general graph with specialized constraints on its structure. They discuss conditions for which the data type is a true tree, a multitree, or a directed acyclic graph. They map the domain problem of recognizing nuclear family structure into an abstract task of determining subgraph structure. At the third level of the model, they discuss the strengths and weaknesses of several visual encoding idiom design choices, including using connection, containment, adjacency and alignment, and indentation. They present in passing two more specialized encoding idioms, fractal node–link and containment for free trees, before presenting in detail their main proposal for visual encoding. They also carefully address interaction idiom design, which also falls into the third level of the model. At the fourth level of algorithm design, they concisely cover the algorithmic details of dual-tree layout.

▶ Design choices for visual encoding idioms for network data are discussed in Chapter 9.

Three validation methods are used in this paper, shown in Figure 4.7. There is the immediate justification of encoding and interaction idiom design decisions in terms of established principles, and the downstream method of a qualitative discussion of result images and videos. At the abstraction level, there is the downstream informal testing of a system prototype with a target user to collect anecdotal evidence.

4.7.2   MatrixExplorer

Henry and Fekete present the MatrixExplorer system for social network analysis [Henry and Fekete 06], shown in Figure 4.8. Its design comes from requirements formalized by interviews and partic-

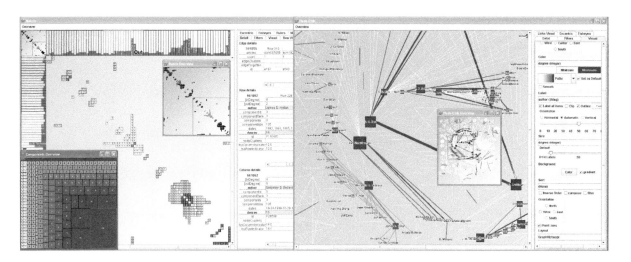

Figure 4.8. MatrixExplorer features both node–link and matrix representations in an interface designed for sociologists and historians to explore social networks. From [Henry and Fekete 06, Figure 1].

▶ The strengths and weaknesses of matrix and node–link representations of networks are discussed in Section 9.4.

ipatory design sessions with social science researchers. They use both matrix representations to minimize clutter for large and dense graphs and the more intuitive node–link representations of graphs for smaller networks.

All four levels of the model are addressed, with validation at three of the levels, shown in Figure 4.9. At the domain situation level, there is explicit characterization of the social network analysis domain, which is validated with the qualitative techniques of interviews and an exploratory study using participatory design methods with social scientists and other researchers who use social network data. At the abstraction level, the paper includes a detailed list of requirements of the target user needs discussed in terms of abstract tasks and data. There is a thorough discussion of the primary encoding idiom design decision to use both node–link and matrix views to show the data, and also of many secondary encoding issues. There is also a discussion of both basic interaction idioms and more complex interaction via interactive reordering and clustering. In both cases the authors use the immediate validation method of justifying these design decisions. There is also an extensive downstream validation of this level using qualitative discussion of result images. At the algorithm level, the focus is on the reordering algorithm. Downstream benchmark timings are mentioned very briefly.

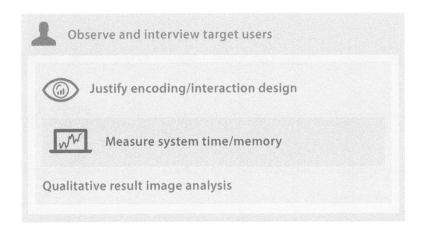

Figure 4.9. MatrixExplorer [Henry and Fekete 06] validation methods.

4.7.3 Flow Maps

Phan et al. propose a system for creating **flow maps** that show the movement of objects from one location to another, and demonstrate it on network traffic, census data, and trade data [Phan et al. 05]. Flow maps reduce visual clutter by merging edges, but most previous instances were hand drawn. They present automatic techniques inspired by graph layout algorithms to minimize edge crossings and distort node positions while maintaining relative positions, as shown in Figure 4.10. Figure 4.10(a) shows migration to California, while Figure 4.10(b) shows the top ten states sending migrants to California and New York.

> ▶ The visual encoding of geographic data is discussed in Section 8.3.1.

In their paper, Phan et al. focus on the innermost algorithm design level, but the idiom and abstraction levels are also covered. Their analysis of the useful characteristics of hand-drawn flow maps falls into the abstraction level. At the idiom level, they have a brief but explicit description of the goals of their layout algorithm, namely, intelligent distortion of positions to ensure that the separation distance between nodes is greater than the maximum thickness of the flow lines while maintaining left–right and up–down ordering relationships. The domain situation level is addressed more implicitly than explicitly: there is no actual discussion of who uses flow maps and why. However, the analysis of hand-drawn flow maps could be construed as an implicit claim of longstanding usage needs.

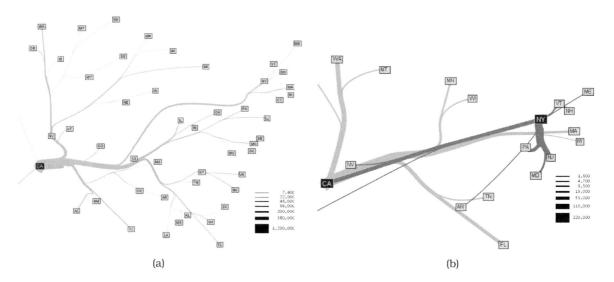

(a)   (b)

Figure 4.10. Flow maps showing migration patterns from 1995 to 2000 US Census data. (a) Migration from California. (b) The top ten states that sent migrants to California shown in green, and to New York in blue. From [Phan et al. 05, Figures 1c and 10].

Four validation methods were used in this paper, shown in Figure 4.11. At the algorithm level, there is an immediate complexity analysis. There is also a brief downstream report of system timing, saying that all images were computed in a few seconds. There is also a more involved downstream validation through the qualita-

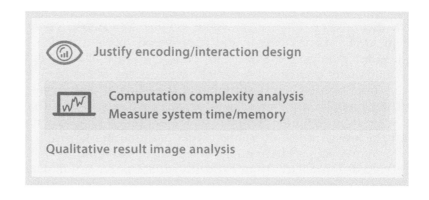

Figure 4.11. Flow map [Phan et al. 05] validation methods.

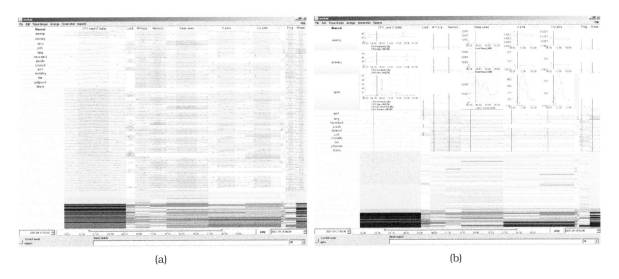

Figure 4.12. LiveRAC supports exploration of system management time-series data with a reorderable matrix and semantic zooming. (a) The first several dozen rows have been stretched out to show sparklines for the devices. (b) The top three rows have been enlarged more, so the charts appear in full detail. From [McLachlan et al. 08, Figure 3].

tive discussion of result images generated by their system. In this case, the intent was mainly to discuss algorithm correctness issues at the innermost algorithm level, as opposed to addressing the visual encoding idiom level. At the idiom level, the authors justify their three fundamental requirements as the outcome of analyzing hand-drawn diagrams: intelligent distortion of positions, merging of edges that share destinations, and intelligent edge routing.

4.7.4 LiveRAC

McLachlan et al. present the LiveRAC system for exploring system management time-series data [McLachlan et al. 08]. LiveRAC uses a reorderable matrix of charts with stretch and squish navigation combined with semantic zooming, so that the chart's visual representation adapts to the available space. Figure 4.12(a) shows a mix of small boxes showing only a single attribute encoded with color and somewhat larger boxes showing concise line charts. The top three rows have been enlarged in Figure 4.12(b), providing enough room that the representation switches to detailed charts with axes and labels. The paper reports on an informal longitudinal field study of its deployment to operators of a large corporate

▶ Reorderable matrix alignments are covered in Section 7.5.2, semantic zooming is covered in Section 11.5.2, and stretch and squish navigation is covered in Section 14.5.

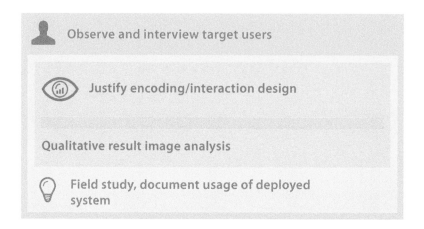

Figure 4.13. LiveRAC [McLachlan et al. 08] validation methods.

web hosting service. Four validation methods were used in this paper, shown in Figure 4.13.

At the domain situation level, the paper explains the roles and activities of system management professionals and their existing workflow and tools. The validation approach was interviews with the target audience. The phased design methodology, where management approval was necessary for access to the true target users, led to a mix of immediate and downstream timing for this validation: many of these interviews occurred after a working prototype was developed. This project is a good example of the iterative process alluded to in Section 4.3.

At the abstraction level, the choice of a collection of time-series data for data type is discussed early in the paper. The rationale is presented in the opposite manner from the discussion above: rather than justifying that time-series data is the correct choice for the system management domain, the authors justify that this domain is an appropriate one for studying this data type. The paper also contains a set of explicit design requirements, which includes abstract tasks like search, sort, and filter. The downstream validation for the abstraction level is a longitudinal field study of the system deployed to the target users, life cycle engineers for managed hosting services inside a large corporation.

At the visual encoding and interaction level, there is an extensive discussion of design choices, with immediate validation by justification in terms of design principles and downstream validation through a qualitative discussion of the results. Algorithms are not discussed.

4.7.5 LinLog

Noack's LinLog paper introduces an energy model for graph drawing designed to reveal clusters in the data, where clusters are defined as a set of nodes with many internal edges and few edges to nodes outside the set [Noack 03]. Energy-based and force-directed methods are related approaches to network layout and have been heavily used in information visualization. Previous models strove to enforce a layout metric of uniform edge lengths, but Noack points out that creating visually distinguishable clusters requires long edges between them. Figure 4.14(a) shows the success of this approach, in contrast to the indifferentiated blob created by a previously proposed method shown in Figure 4.14(b).

▶ Force-directed placement is discussed in Section 9.2.

Although a quick glance might lead to an assumption that this graph drawing paper has a focus on algorithms, the primary contribution is in fact at the visual encoding idiom level. The two validation methods used in the paper are qualitative and quantitative result image analysis, shown in Figure 4.15.

Noack clearly distinguishes between the two aspects of energy-based methods for force-directed graph layout: the energy model itself versus the algorithm that searches for a state with minimum total energy. In the vocabulary of my model, his LinLog energy model is a visual encoding idiom. Requiring that the edges between clusters are longer than those within clusters is a visual encoding

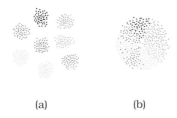

(a) (b)

Figure 4.14. The LinLog energy model reveals clusters in node–link graphs. (a) LinLog clearly shows clusters with spatial separation. (b) The popular Fructerman-Reingold model for force-directed placement does not separate the clusters. From [Noack 03, Figure 1].

Figure 4.15. LinLog [Noack 03] validation methods.

using the visual channel of spatial position. One downstream validation approach in this paper is a qualitative discussion of result images, which is appropriate for a contribution at the encoding level. This paper also contains a validation method not listed in the model, because it is relatively rare in vis: mathematical proof. These proofs are about the optimality of the model results when measured by quantitative metrics involving edge lengths and node distances. Thus, this model classifies it in the quantitative image analysis category, another appropriate method to validate at the idiom level.

This paper does not in fact address the innermost algorithm level. Noack explicitly leaves the problem of designing better energy-minimization algorithms as future work, using previously proposed algorithms to showcase the results of his model. The domain situation level is handled concisely but adequately by referencing previous work about application domains with graph data where there is a need to see clusters. For the abstraction level, although the paper does not directly use the vocabulary of *task* and *data abstraction*, it clearly states that the abstract task is finding clusters and that the data abstraction is a network.

4.7.6 Sizing the Horizon

▶ Line charts are discussed in Section 9.2.

Heer et al. compare line charts to the more space-efficient **horizon graphs** [Heer et al. 09], as Figure 4.16 shows. They identify transition points at which reducing the chart height results in significantly differing drops in estimation accuracy across the compared chart types, and they find optimal positions in the speed–accuracy trade-off curve at which viewers performed quickly without attendant drops in accuracy. This paper features lab studies that are designed to validate (or invalidate) specific design choices at the

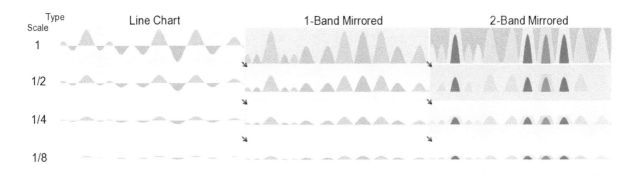

Figure 4.16. Experiment 2 of Sizing the Horizon compared filled line charts, one-band horizon graphs, and two-band horizon graphs of different sizes to find transition points where reducing chart height results in major drops in estimation accuracy across chart types. From [Heer et al. 09, Figure 7].

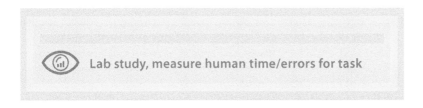

Figure 4.17. Lab studies as a validation method.

visual encoding and interaction idiom level by measuring time and error rates of people carrying out abstracted tasks, as shown in Figure 4.17.

4.8 Further Reading

The Big Picture I first presented the four-level nested model of vis design as a paper [Munzner 09a], with a discussion of blocks and guidelines between them in a follow-up paper [Meyer et al. 13]; both of these contain many more references to previous and related work. McGrath's analysis of the strengths and limitations of different experimental methods is well worth reading [McGrath 94], and it influenced my partition of validation techniques according to levels.

Problem-Driven Work A good entry point for problem-driven vis work is a detailed discussion of design study methodology, with a nine-stage framework for conducting them and suggestions for how to avoid 32 pitfalls [Sedlmair et al. 12]. Another framework for problem-driven work is the Multidimensional In-depth Long-term Case studies (MILC) approach, which also advocates working closely with domain users [Shneiderman and Plaisant 06].

Abstraction Level A recent paper argues that both data and task abstractions are important points of departure for vis designers [Pretorius and van Wijk 09]. The problems at the abstraction level fall into the realm of requirements elicitation and analysis in software engineering; a good starting point for that literature is a recent book chapter [Maalej and Thurimella 13].

Algorithm Level There are several existing books with a heavy focus on the algorithm level, including two textbooks [Telea 07, Ward et al. 10] and a large handbook [Hansen and Johnson 05]. Other options are recent survey papers on a particular topic, or specific research papers for very detailed discussion about a given algorithm. The larger issues of algorithm design are certainly not unique to vis; an excellent general reference for algorithms is a popular textbook that also covers complexity analysis [Cormen et al. 90].

Human–Computer Interaction A comprehensive textbook is a good starting point for the academic human–computer interaction literature [Sharp et al. 07]. A very accessible book is a good starting point for the large literature aimed at practitioners [Kuniavsky 03].

Evaluation Methods A book chapter provides an excellent survey and overview of evaluation and validation methods for vis, including an extensive discussion of qualitative methods [Carpendale 08]. Another discussion of evaluation challenges includes a call for more repositories of data and tasks [Plaisant 04]. A viewpoint article contains the thoughts of several researchers on why, how, and when to do user studies [Kosara et al. 03].

Field Studies For field studies, contextual inquiry is a particularly important method and is covered well in a book by one of its pioneers [Holtzblatt and Jones 93].

Experiment Design For lab studies, my current favorite references for experiment design and analysis are a cogent and accessible recent monograph [Hornbaek 13], a remarkably witty book [Field and Hole 03], and a new textbook with many examples featuring visualization [Purchase 12].

Channels: Expressiveness Types and Effectiveness Ranks

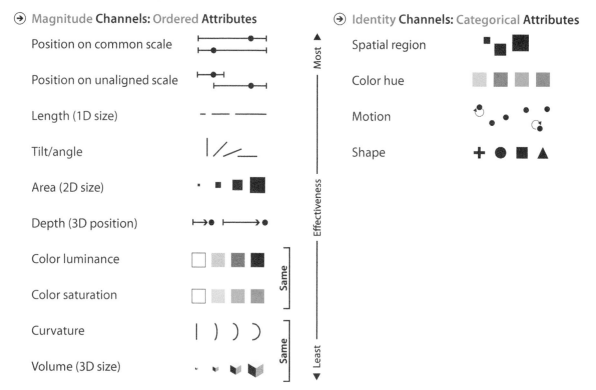

Figure 5.1. The effectiveness of channels that modify the appearance of marks depends on matching the expressiveness of channels with the attributes being encoded.

Chapter 5

Marks and Channels

5.1 The Big Picture

Marks are basic geometric elements that depict items or links, and channels control their appearance. The effectiveness of a channel for encoding data depends on its type: the channels that perceptually convey magnitude information are a good match for ordered data, and those that convey identity information with categorical data. Figure 5.1 summarizes the channel rankings.

5.2 Why Marks and Channels?

Learning to reason about marks and channels gives you the building blocks for analyzing visual encodings. The core of the design space of visual encodings can be described as an orthogonal combination of two aspects: graphical elements called marks, and visual channels to control their appearance. Even complex visual encodings can be broken down into components that can be analyzed in terms of their marks and channel structure.

5.3 Defining Marks and Channels

A **mark** is a basic graphical element in an image. Marks are geometric primitive objects classified according to the number of spatial dimensions they require. Figure 5.2 shows examples: a zero-dimensional (**0D**) mark is a point, a one-dimensional (**1D**) mark is a line, and a two-dimensional (**2D**) mark is an area. A three-dimensional (**3D**) volume mark is possible, but they are not frequently used.

Figure 5.2. Marks are geometric primitives.

★ The term *channel* is popular in the vis literature and is not meant to imply any particular theory about the underlying mechanisms of human visual perception. There are many, many synonyms for **visual channel**: nearly any combination of *visual*, *graphical*, *perceptual*, *retinal* for the first word, and *channel*, *attribute*, *dimension*, *variable*, *feature*, and *carrier* for the second word.

A visual **channel** is a way to control the appearance of marks, independent of the dimensionality of the geometric primitive.* Figure 5.3 shows a few of the many visual channels that can encode information as properties of a mark. Some pertain to spatial position, including aligned planar position, unaligned planar position, depth (3D position), and spatial region. Others pertain to color, which has three distinct aspects: hue, saturation, and luminance. There are three size channels, one for each added dimension: length is 1D size, area is 2D size, and volume is 3D size. The motion-oriented channels include the motion pattern, for instance, oscillating circles versus straight jumps, the direction of motion, and the velocity. Angle is also a channel, sometimes called tilt. Curvature is also a visual channel. Shape is a complex phenomenon, but it is treated as a channel in this framework.

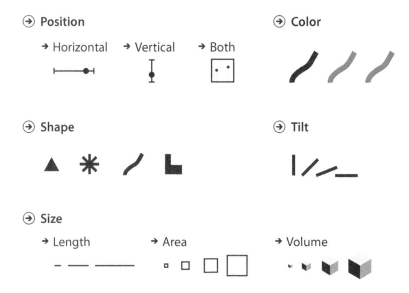

Figure 5.3. Visual channels control the appearance of marks.

(a)   (b)   (c)   (d)

Figure 5.4. Using marks and channels. (a) Bar charts encode two attributes using a line mark with the vertical spatial position channel for the quantitative attribute, and the horizontal spatial position channel for the categorical attribute. (b) Scatterplots encode two quantitative attributes using point marks and both vertical and horizontal spatial position. (c) A third categorical attribute is encoded by adding color to the scatterplot. (d) Adding the visual channel of size encodes a fourth quantitative attribute as well.

Figure 5.4 shows a progression of chart types, with each showing one more quantitative data attribute by using one more visual channel. A single quantitative attribute can be encoded with vertical spatial position. Bar charts are a common example of this encoding: the height of the bar conveys a quantitative value for that attribute, as in Figure 5.4(a). Bar charts show two attributes, but only one is quantitative: the other is the categorical attribute used to spread out the bars along the axis (in this case, the horizontal axis). A second, independent quantitative attribute can be encoded by using the visual channel of horizontal spatial position to directly encode information. It doesn't make sense any more to use a line for the mark in this case, so the mark type needs to be a point. This visual encoding, shown in Figure 5.4(b), is a scatterplot. You cannot continue to add more spatial position channels when creating drawings in two-dimensional space, but many visual channels are nonspatial. An additional categorical data attribute can be encoded in a scatterplot format using the visual channel of hue (one aspect of color), as in Figure 5.4(c). Figure 5.4(d) shows the addition of a fourth quantitative attribute encoded with the visual channel of size.

In these examples, each attribute is encoded with a single channel. Multiple channels can be combined to redundantly encode the same attribute. The limitation of this approach is that more channels are "used up" so that not as many attributes can be encoded in total, but the benefit is that the attributes that are shown will be very easily perceived.

The size and shape channels cannot be used on all types of marks: the higher-dimensional mark types usually have built-in constraints that arise from the way that they are defined. An area mark has both dimensions of its size constrained intrinsically as part of its shape, so area marks typically are not size coded or shape coded. For example, an area mark denoting a state or province within a country on a geographic map already has a certain size, and thus attempting to size code the mark with an additional attribute usually doesn't make sense.[1] Similarly, the treemap visual encoding idiom shows the hierarchical structure of a tree using nested area marks; Figure 9.8 shows an example. The size of these marks is determined by an existing attribute that was used in construction of the treemap, as is their shape and position. Changing the size of a mark according to an additional attribute would destroy the meaning of the visual encoding.

A line mark that encodes a quantitative attribute using length in one direction can be size coded in the other dimension by changing the width of the line to make it fatter. However, it can't be size coded in the first direction to make it longer because its length is already "taken" with the length coding and can't be co-opted by a second attribute. For example, the bars in Figure 5.4(a) can't be size coded vertically. Thus, even though lines are often considered to be infinitely thin objects in mathematical contexts, line marks used in visual encoding do take up a nonzero amount of area. They can be made wider on an individual basis to encode an additional attribute, or an entire set of bars can simply be made wider in a uniform way to be more visible.

Point marks can indeed be size coded and shape coded because their area is completely unconstrained. For instance, the circles of varying size in the Figure 5.4(d) scatterplot are point marks that have been size coded, encoding information in terms of their area. An additional categorical attribute could be encoded by changing the shape of the point as well, for example, to a cross or a triangle instead of a circle. This meaning of the term *point* is different than the mathematical context where it implies something that is infinitely small in area and cannot have a shape. In the context of visual encoding, point marks intrinsically convey information only about position and are exactly the vehicle for conveying additional information through area and shape.

---

[1]The cartogram visual encoding idiom, where exactly this kind of size coding of an additional attribute on a set of geographic regions is carried out, is an exception. This idiom carefully alters the boundaries with a unified calculation that guarantees that the borders remain contiguous while attempting to preserve each area's shape as much as possible.

5.3.1 Channel Types

The human perceptual system has two fundamentally different kinds of sensory modalities. The **identity** channels tell us information about *what* something is or *where* it is. In contrast, the **magnitude** channels tell us *how much* of something there is.*

For instance, we can tell *what* shape we see: a circle, a triangle, or a cross. It does not make much sense to ask magnitude questions for shape. Other *what* visual channels are shape, the color channel of hue, and motion pattern. We can tell *what* spatial region marks are within, and *where* the region is.

In contrast, we can ask about magnitudes with line length: how much longer is this line than that line? And identity is not a productive question, since both objects are lines. Similarly, we can ask luminance questions about how much darker one mark is than another, or angle questions about how much space is between a pair of lines, or size questions about how much bigger one mark is than another. Many channels give us magnitude information, including the size channels of length, area, and volume; two of the three color channels, namely, luminance and saturation; and tilt.

> ★ In the psychophysics literature, the *identity* channels are called **metathetic** or **what–where**, and the *magnitude* channels are called **prothetic** or **how much**.

5.3.2 Mark Types

The discussion so far has been focused on table datasets, where a mark always represents an item. For network datasets, a mark might represent either an item—also known as a node—or a link. Link marks represent a relationship between items. The two link mark types are connection and containment. A **connection** mark shows a pairwise relationship between two items, using a line. A **containment** mark shows hierarchical relationships using areas, and to do so connection marks can be nested within each other at multiple levels.* While the visual representation of the area mark might be with a line that depicts its boundary, containment is fundamentally about the use of area. Links cannot be represented by points, even though individual items can be. Figure 5.5 summarizes the possibilities.

> ★ Synonyms for *containment* are **enclosure** and **nesting**.

5.4 Using Marks and Channels

All channels are not equal: the same data attribute encoded with two different visual channels will result in different information

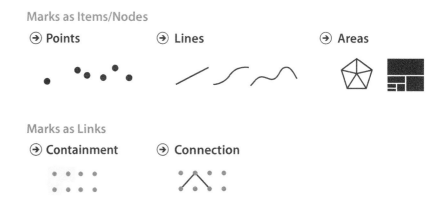

Figure 5.5. Marks can represent individual items, or links between them.

content in our heads after it has passed through the perceptual and cognitive processing pathways of the human visual system.

The use of marks and channels in vis idiom design should be guided by the principles of expressiveness and effectiveness. These ideas can be combined to create a ranking of channels according to the type of data that is being visually encoded. If you have identified the most important attributes as part of developing your task and data abstraction, you can ensure that they are encoded with the highest ranked channels.

5.4.1 Expressiveness and Effectiveness

Two principles guide the use of visual channels in visual encoding: expressiveness and effectiveness.

The **expressiveness principle** dictates that the visual encoding should express all of, and only, the information in the dataset attributes. The most fundamental expression of this principle is that ordered data should be shown in a way that our perceptual system intrinsically senses as ordered. Conversely, unordered data should not be shown in a way that perceptually implies an ordering that does not exist. Violating this principle is a common beginner's mistake in vis.

It's no coincidence that the classification of data attributes in Chapter 2 has a central split along this very same line. This split of channel types into two major categories is so fundamental to visual encoding design that this distinction is built into the classification at the ground level. The identity channels are the correct match for the categorical attributes that have no intrinsic order. The magnitude channels are the correct match for the ordered attributes, both ordinal and quantitative.

The **effectiveness principle** dictates that the importance of the attribute should match the **salience** of the channel; that is, its noticeability. In other words, the most important attributes should be encoded with the most effective channels in order to be most noticeable, and then decreasingly important attributes can be matched with less effective channels.

The rest of this chapter is devoted to the question of what the word *effectiveness* means in the context of visual encoding.

5.4.2 Channel Rankings

Figure 5.6 presents effectiveness rankings for the visual channels broken down according to the two expressiveness types of ordered and categorical data. The rankings range from the most effective channels at the top to the least effective at the bottom.

Ordered attributes should be shown with the magnitude channels. The most effective is **aligned spatial position**, followed by **unaligned spatial position**. Next is **length**, which is one-dimensional size, and then **angle**, and then **area**, which is two-dimensional size. Position in 3D, namely, **depth**, is next. The next two channels are roughly equally effective: **luminance** and **saturation**. The final two channels, **curvature** and **volume** (3D size), are also roughly equivalent in terms of accuracy.

▶ Luminance and saturation are aspects of color discussed in Chapter 10.

Categorical attributes should be shown with the identity channels. The most effective channel for categorical data is spatial **region**, with color **hue** as the next best one. The **motion** channel is also effective, particularly for a single set of moving items against a sea of static ones. The final identity channel appropriate for categorical attributes is **shape**.

▶ Hue is an aspect of color discussed in Chapter 10.

While it is possible in theory to use a magnitude channel for categorical data or a identity channel for ordered data, that choice would be a poor one because the expressiveness principle would be violated.

The two ranked lists of channels in Figure 5.6 both have channels related to spatial position at the top in the most effective spot. Aligned and unaligned spatial position are at the top of the list for ordered data, and spatial region is at the top of the list for categorical data. Moreover, the spatial channels are the only ones that appear on both lists; none of the others are effective for both data

Channels: Expressiveness Types and Effectiveness Ranks

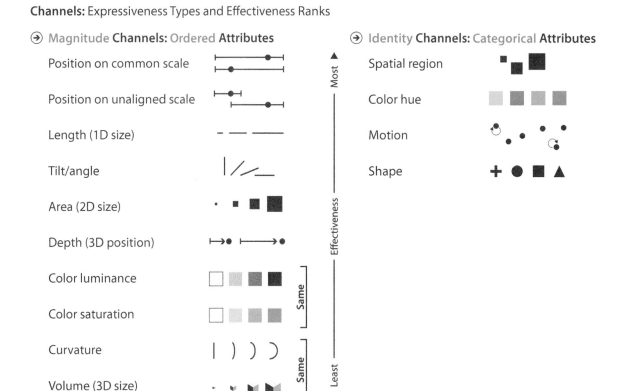

Figure 5.6. Channels ranked by effectiveness according to data and channel type. Ordered data should be shown with the magnitude channels, and categorical data with the identity channels.

> ▶ The limitations and benefits of 3D are covered in Section 6.3.

types. This primacy of spatial position applies only to 2D positions in the plane; 3D depth is a much lower-ranked channel. These fundamental observations have motivated many of the vis idioms illustrated in this book, and underlie the framework of idiom design choices. The choice of which attributes to encode with position is the most central choice in visual encoding. The attributes encoded with position will dominate the user's **mental model**—their internal mental representation used for thinking and reasoning—compared with those encoded with any other visual channel.

These rankings are my own synthesis of information drawn from many sources, including several previous frameworks, experimental evidence from a large body of empirical studies, and my own analysis. The further reading section at the end of this chapter contains pointers to the previous work. The following sections of this chapter discuss the reasons for these rankings at length.

5.5   Channel Effectiveness

To analyze the space of visual encoding possibilities you need to understand the characteristics of these visual channels, because many questions remain unanswered: How are these rankings justified? Why did the designer decide to use those particular visual channels? How many more visual channels are there? What kinds of information and how much information can each channel encode? Why are some channels better than others? Can all of the channels be used independently or do they interfere with each other?

This section addresses these questions by introducing the analysis of channels according to the criteria of accuracy, discriminability, separability, the ability to provide visual popout, and the ability to provide perceptual groupings.

5.5.1   Accuracy

The obvious way to quantify effectiveness is **accuracy**: how close is human perceptual judgement to some objective measurement of the stimulus? Some answers come to us from **psychophysics**, the subfield of psychology devoted to the systematic measurement of general human perception. We perceive different visual channels with different levels of accuracy; they are not all equally distinguishable. Our responses to the sensory experience of magnitude are characterizable by power laws, where the exponent depends on the exact sensory modality: most stimuli are magnified or compressed, with few remaining unchanged.

Figure 5.7 shows the psychophysical power law of Stevens [Stevens 75]. The apparent magnitude of all sensory channels follows a power function based on the stimulus intensity:

$$S = I^n, \qquad\qquad (5.1)$$

where S is the perceived sensation and I is the physical intensity. The power law exponent n ranges from the sublinear 0.5 for brightness to the superlinear 3.5 for electric current. That is, the sublinear phenomena are compressed, so doubling the physical

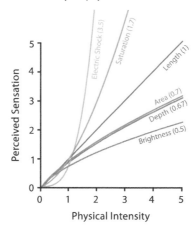

Figure 5.7. Stevens showed that the apparent magnitude of all sensory channels follows a power law $S = I^n$, where some sensations are perceptually magnified compared with their objective intensity (when $n > 1$) and some compressed (when $n < 1$). Length perception is completely accurate, whereas area is compressed and saturation is magnified. Data from Stevens [Stevens 75, p. 15].

brightness results in a perception that is considerably less than twice as bright. The superlinear phenomena are magnified: doubling the amount of electric current applied to the fingertips results is a sensation that is much more than twice as great. Figure 5.7 shows that length has an exponent of $n = 1.0$, so our perception of length is a very close match to the true value. Here *length* means the length of a line segment on a 2D plane perpendicular to the observer. The other visual channels are not perceived as accurately: area and brightness are compressed, while red–gray saturation is magnified.

Another set of answers to the question of accuracy comes from controlled experiments that directly map human response to visually encoded abstract information, giving us explicit rankings of perceptual accuracy for each channel type. For example, Cleveland and McGill's experiments on the magnitude channels [Cleveland and McGill 84a] showed that aligned position against a common scale is most accurately perceived, followed by unaligned position against an identical scale, followed by length, followed by angle. Area judgements are notably less accurate than all of these. They also propose rankings for channels that they did not directly test: after area is an equivalence class of volume, curvature, and lumi-

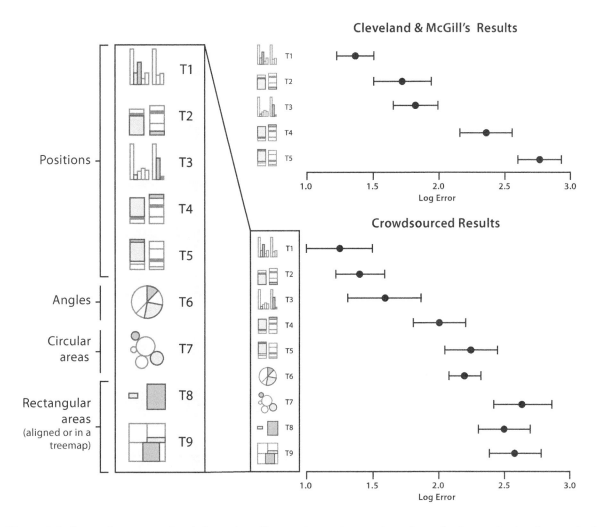

Figure 5.8. Error rates across visual channels, with recent crowdsourced results replicating and extending seminal work from Cleveland and McGill [Cleveland and McGill 84a]. After [Heer and Bostock 10, Figure 4].

nance; that class is followed by hue in last place. (This last place ranking is for hue as a magnitude channel, a very different matter than its second-place rank as a identity channel.) These accuracy results for visual encodings dovetail nicely with the psychophysical channel measurements in Figure 5.7. Heer and Bostock confirmed and extended this work using crowdsourcing, summarized in Figure 5.8 [Heer and Bostock 10]. The only discrepancy is that the later work found length and angle judgements roughly equivalent.

The rankings in Figure 5.6 are primarily based on accuracy, which differs according to the type of the attribute that is being encoded, but also take into account the other four considerations.

5.5.2 Discriminability

The question of **discriminability** is: if you encode data using a particular visual channel, are the differences between items perceptible to the human as intended? The characterization of visual channel thus should quantify the number of **bins** that are available for use within a visual channel, where each bin is a distinguishable step or level from the other.

For instance, some channels have a very limited number of bins. Consider line width: changing the line size only works for a fairly small number of steps. Increasing the width past that limit will result in a mark that is perceived as a polygon area rather than a line mark. A small number of bins is not a problem if the number of values to encode is also small. For example, Figure 5.9 shows an example of effective linewidth use. Linewidth can work very well to show three or four different values for a data attribute, but it would be a poor choice for dozens or hundreds of values. The key factor is matching the ranges: the number of different values that need to be shown for the attribute being encoded must not be greater than the number of bins available for the visual channel used to encode it. If these do not match, then the vis designer should either explicitly aggregate the attribute into meaningful bins or use a different visual channel.

5.5.3 Separability

You cannot treat all visual channels as completely independent from each other, because some have dependencies and interactions with others. You must consider a continuum of potential interactions between channels for each pair, ranging from the orthogonal and independent **separable** channels to the inextricably combined **integral** channels. Visual encoding is straightforward with separable channels, but attempts to encode different information in integral channels will fail. People will not be able to access the desired information about each attribute; instead, an unanticipated combination will be perceived.

Clearly, you cannot separately encode two attributes of information using vertical and horizontal spatial position and then expect to encode a third attribute using planar proximity. In this case it

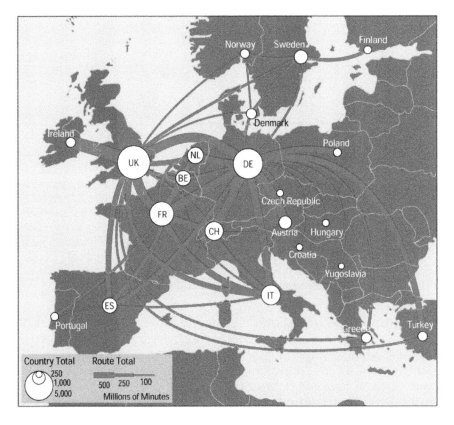

Figure 5.9. Linewidth has a limited number of discriminable bins.

is obvious that the third channel precludes the use of the first two. However, some of the interchannel interference is less obvious.

Figure 5.10 shows pairs of visual channels at four points along this continuum. On the left is a pair of channels that are completely separable: position and hue. We can easily see that the points fall into two categories for spatial position, left and right. We can also separately attend to their hue and distinguish the red from the blue. It is easy to see that roughly half the points fall into each of these categories for each of the two channels.

Next is an example of interference between channels, showing that size is not fully separable from color hue. We can easily distinguish the large half from the small half, but within the small half discriminating between the two colors is much more difficult. Size interacts with many visual channels, including shape.

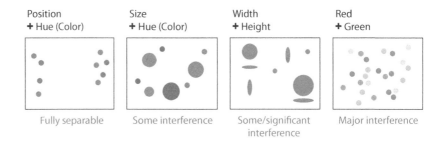

Position   Size   Width   Red
+ Hue (Color)   + Hue (Color)   + Height   + Green

Fully separable   Some interference   Some/significant   Major interference
                                      interference

Figure 5.10. Pairs of visual channels fall along a continuum from fully separable to intrinsically integral. Color and location are separable channels well suited to encode different data attributes for two different groupings that can be selectively attended to. However, size interacts with hue, which is harder to perceive for small objects. The horizontal size and and vertical size channels are automatically fused into an integrated perception of area, yielding three groups. Attempts to code separate information along the red and green axes of the RGB color space fail, because we simply perceive four different hues. After [Ware 13, Figure 5.23].

The third example shows an integral pair. Encoding one variable with horizontal size and another with vertical size is ineffective because what we directly perceive is the planar size of the circles, namely, their area. We cannot easily distinguish groupings of wide from narrow, and short from tall. Rather, the most obvious perceptual grouping is into three sets: small, medium, and large. The medium category includes the horizontally flattened as well as the vertically flattened.

The far right on Figure 5.10 shows the most inseparable channel pair, where the red and green channels of the RGB color space are used. These channels are not perceived separately, but integrated into a combined perception of color. While we can tell that there are four colors, even with intensive cognitive effort it is very difficult to try to recover the original information about high and low values for each axis. The RGB color system used to specify information to computers is a very different model than the color

▶ Color is discussed in detail in Section 10.2.

processing systems of our perceptual system, so the three channels are not perceptually separable.

Integrality versus separability is not good or bad; the important idea is to match the characteristics of the channels to the information that is encoded. If the goal is to show the user two different data attributes, either of which can be attended to selectively, then a separable channel pair of position and color hue is a good choice. If the goal is to show a single data attribute with three categories, then the integral channel pair of horizontal and vertical size is a reasonable choice because it yields the three groups of small, flattened, and large.

Finally, integrality and separability are two endpoints of a continuum, not strictly binary categories. As with all of the other perceptual issues discussed in this chapter, many open questions remain. I do not present a definitive list with a categorization for each channel pair, but it's wise to keep this consideration in mind as you design with channels.

5.5.4 Popout

Many visual channels provide visual **popout**, where a distinct item stands out from many others immediately.* Figure 5.11 shows two examples of popout: spotting a red object from a sea of blue ones, or spotting one circle from a sea of squares. The great value of popout is that the time it takes us to spot the different object does not depend on the number of distractor objects. Our low-level visual system does massively parallel processing on these visual channels, without the need for the viewer to consciously directly attention to items one by one. The time it takes for the red circle to pop out of the sea of blue ones is roughly equal when there are 15 blue ones as in Figure 5.11(a) or 50 as in Figure 5.11(b).

Popout is not an all-or-nothing phenomenon. It depends on both the channel itself and how different the target item is from its surroundings. While the red circle pops out from the seas of 15 and 50 red squares in Figures 5.11(c) and 5.11(d) at roughly

> ★ Visual *popout* is often called **preattentive processing** or **tunable detection**.

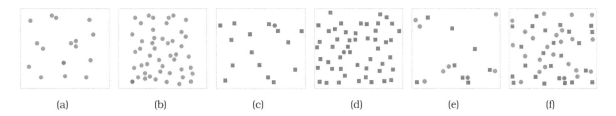

(a) (b) (c) (d) (e) (f)

Figure 5.11. Visual popout. (a) The red circle pops out from a small set of blue circles. (b) The red circle pops out from a large set of blue circles just as quickly. (c) The red circle also pops out from a small set of square shapes, although a bit slower than with color. (d) The red circle also pops out of a large set of red squares. (e) The red circle does not take long to find from a small set of mixed shapes and colors. (f) The red circle does not pop out from a large set of red squares and blue circles, and it can only be found by searching one by one through all the objects. After http://www.csc.ncsu.edu/faculty/healey/PP by Christopher G. Healey.

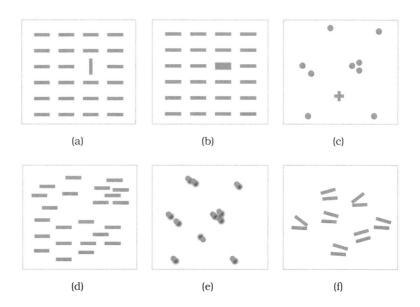

Figure 5.12. Many channels support visual popout, including (a) tilt, (b) size, (c) shape, (d) proximity, and (e) shadow direction. (f) However, parallel line pairs do not pop out from a sea of slightly tilted distractor object pairs and can only be detected through serial search. After http://www.csc.ncsu.edu/faculty/healey/PP by Christopher G. Healey.

the same time, this popout effect is slower than with the color difference versions in Figures 5.11(a) and 5.11(b). The difference between red and blue on the color hue channel is larger than the difference in shape between filled-in circles and filled-in squares.

Although many different visual channels provide popout on their own, they cannot simply be combined. A red circle does not pop out automatically from a sea of objects that can be red or blue and circles or squares: the speed of finding the red circle is much faster in Figures 5.11(e) with few distracting objects than in Figure 5.11(f) with many distractors. The red circle can only be detected with serial search: checking each item, one by one. The amount of time it takes to find the target depends linearly on the number of distractor objects.

Most pairs of channels do not support popout, but a few pairs do: one example is space and color, and another is motion and shape. Popout is definitely not possible with three or more channels. As a general rule, vis designers should only count on using popout for a single channel at a time.

Popout occurs for many channels, not just color hue and shape. Figures 5.12(a) through 5.12(e) show several examples: tilt, size, shape, proximity, and even shadow direction. Many other channels support popout, including several different kinds of motion such as flicker, motion direction, and motion velocity. All of the major channels commonly used in visual encoding that are shown in Figure 5.6 do support popout individually, although not in combination with each other. However, a small number of potential channels do not support popout. Figure 5.12(f) shows that parallelism is not preattentively detected; the exactly parallel pair of lines does not pop out from the slightly angled pairs but requires serial search to detect.

5.5.5 Grouping

The effect of perceptual grouping can arises from either the use of link marks, as shown in Figure 5.5, or from the use of identity channels to encode categorical attributes, as shown in Figure 5.6.

Encoding link marks using areas of containment or lines of connection conveys the information that the linked objects form a group with a very strong perceptual cue. Containment is the strongest cue for grouping, with connection coming in second.

Another way to convey that items form a group is to encode categorical data appropriately with the identity channels. All of the items that share the same level of the categorical attribute can be perceived as a group by simply directing attention to that level selectively. The perceptual grouping cue of the identity channels is not as strong as the use of connection or containment marks, but a benefit of this lightweight approach is that it does not add additional clutter in the form of extra link marks. The third strongest grouping approach is **proximity**; that is, placing items within the same spatial region. This perceptual grouping phenomenon is the reason that the top-ranked channel for encoding categorical data is spatial region. The final grouping channel is **similarity** with the other categorical channels of hue and motion, and also shape if chosen carefully. Logically, proximity is like similarity for spatial position; however, from a perceptual point of view the effect of the spatial channels is so much stronger than the effect of the others that it is is useful to consider them separately.

For example, the categorical attribute of animal type with the three levels of *cat*, *dog*, and *wombat* can be encoded with the three hue bins of *red*, *green*, and *blue* respectively. A user who chooses to attend to the blue hue will automatically see all of the wombats as a perceptual group globally, across the entire scene.

The shape channel needs to be used with care: it is possible to encode categorical data with shape in a way that does not automatically create perceptual groupings. For example, the shapes of a forward 'C' and a backward 'C' do not automatically form globally selectable groups, whereas the shapes of a circle versus a star do. Similarly, motion also needs to be used with care. Although a set of objects moving together against a background of static objects is a very salient cue, multiple levels of motion all happening at once may overwhelm the user's capacity for selective attention.

5.6 Relative versus Absolute Judgements

The human perceptual system is fundamentally based on relative judgements, not absolute ones; this principle is known as **Weber's Law**.* For instance, the amount of length difference we can detect is a percentage of the object's length.

★ More formally, Weber's Law is typically stated as the detectable difference in stimulus intensity I as a fixed percentage K of the object magnitude: $\delta I / I = K$.

This principle holds true for all sensory modalities. The fact that our senses work through relative rather than absolute judgements has far-ranging implications. When considering questions such as the accuracy and discriminability of our perceptions, we must distinguish between relative and absolute judgements. For example, when two objects are directly next to each other and aligned, we can make much more precise judgements than when they are not aligned and when they are separated with many other objects between them.

An example based on Weber's Law illuminates why position along a scale can be more accurately perceived than a pure length judgement of position without a scale. The length judgement in Figure 5.13(a) is difficult to make with unaligned and unframed bars. It is easier with framing, as in Figure 5.13(b), or alignment, as in Figure 5.13(c), so that the bars can be judged against a common scale. When making a judgement without a common scale, the only information is the length of the bars themselves. Placing a common frame around the bars provides another way to estimate magnitude: we can check the length of the unfilled bar. Bar B is only about 15% longer than Bar A, approaching the range where length differences are difficult to judge. But the unfilled part of the frame for Bar B is about 50% smaller than the one for Bar A, an easily discriminable difference. Aligning the bars achieves the same effect without the use of a frame.

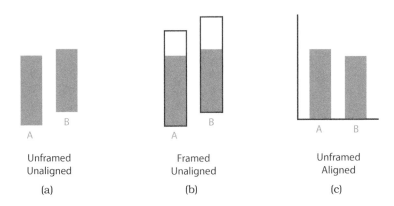

Figure 5.13. Weber's Law states that we judge based on relative, not absolute differences. (a) The lengths of unframed, unaligned rectangles of slightly different sizes are hard to compare. (b) Adding a frame allows us to compare the very different sizes of the unfilled rectangles between the bar and frame tops. (c) Aligning the bars also makes the judgement easy. Redrawn and extended after [Cleveland and McGill 84a, Figure 12].

Another example shows that our perception of color and luminance is completely contextual, based on the contrast with surrounding colors. In Figure 5.14(a), the two labeled squares in a checkerboard appear to be quite different shades of gray. In Figure 5.14(b), superimposing a solid gray mask that touches both squares shows that they are identical. Conversely, Figure 5.15

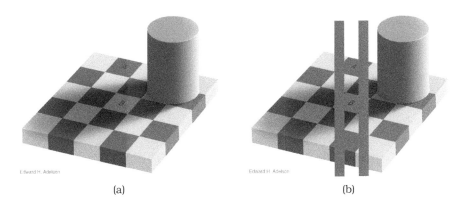

Figure 5.14. Luminance perception is based on relative, not absolute, judgements. (a) The two squares A and B appear quite different. (b) Superimposing a gray mask on the image shows that they are in fact identical.

(a)   (b)

Figure 5.15. Color perception is also relative to surrounding colors and depends on context. (a) Both cubes have tiles that appear to be red. (b) Masking the intervening context shows that the colors are very different: with yellow apparent lighting, they are orange; with blue apparent lighting, they are purple.

shows two colorful cubes. In Figure 5.15(a) corresponding squares both appear to be red. In Figure 5.15(b), masks show that the tile color in the image apparently illuminated by a yellowish light source is actually orange, and for the bluish light the tiles are actually purple. Our visual system evolved to provide **color constancy** so that the same surface is identifiable across a broad set of illumination conditions, even though a physical light meter would yield very different readings. While the visual system works very well in natural environments, many of its mechanisms work against simple approaches to visually encoding information with color.

5.7   Further Reading

The Big Picture The highly influential theory of visual marks and channels was proposed by Bertin in the 1960s [Bertin 67]. The ranking of channel effectiveness proposed in this chapter is my synthesis across the ideas of many previous authors and does not come directly from any specific source. It was influenced by the foundational work on ranking of visual channels through measured-response experiments [Cleveland and McGill 84a], models [Cleveland 93a], design guidelines for matching visual channels to data type [Mackinlay 86], and books on visualization [Ware 13] and cartography [MacEachren 95]. It was also affected by the more recent work on crowdsourced judgements [Heer and Bostock 10], taxonomy-based glyph design [Maguire et al. 12], and glyph design in general [Borgo et al. 13].

Psychophysical Measurement The foundational work on the variable distinguishability of different visual channels, the categorization of channels as metathetic identity and prothetic magnitude, and scales of measurement was done by a pioneer in psychophysics [Stevens 57, Stevens 75].

Effectiveness and Expressiveness Principles The principles of expressiveness for matching channel to data type and effectiveness for choosing the channels by importance ordering appeared in a foundational paper [Mackinlay 86].

Perception This chapter touches on many perceptual and cognitive phenomena, but I make no attempt to explain the mechanisms that underlie them. I have distilled an enormous literature down to the bare minimum of what a beginning vis designer needs to get started. The rich literature on perception and cognitive phenomena is absolutely worth a closer look, because this chapter only scratches the surface; for example, the Gestalt principles are not covered.

Ware offers a broad, thorough, and highly recommended introduction to perception for vis in his two books [Ware 08, Ware 13]. His discussion includes more details from nearly all of the topics in this chapter, including separability and popout. An overview of the literature on popout and other perceptual phenomena appears on a very useful page that includes interactive demos http://www.csc.ncsu.edu/faculty/healey/PP [Healey 07]; one of the core papers in this literature begins to untangle what low-level features are detected in early visual processing [Treisman and Gormican 88].

- No Unjustified 3D

  - The Power of the Plane
  - The Disparity of Depth
  - Occlusion Hides Information
  - Perspective Distortion Dangers
  - Tilted Text Isn't Legible

- No Unjustified 2D

- Eyes Beat Memory

- Resolution over Immersion

- Overview First, Zoom and Filter, Detail on Demand

- Responsiveness Is Required

- Get It Right in Black and White

- Function First, Form Next

Figure 6.1. Eight rules of thumb.

Chapter 6

Rules of Thumb

6.1 The Big Picture

This chapter contains **rules of thumb**: advice and guidelines. Each of them has a catchy title in hopes that you'll remember it as a slogan. Figure 6.1 lists these eight rules of thumb.

6.2 Why and When to Follow Rules of Thumb?

These rules of thumb are my current attempt to synthesize the current state of knowledge into a more unified whole. In some cases I refer to empirical studies, in others I make arguments based on my own experience, and some have been proposed in previous work. They are not set in stone; indeed, they are deeply incomplete. The characterization of what idioms are appropriate for which task and data abstractions is still an ongoing research frontier, and there are many open questions.

6.3 No Unjustified 3D

Many people have the intuition that if two dimensions are good, three dimensions must be better—after all, we live in a three-dimensional world. However, there are many difficulties in visually encoding information with the third spatial dimension, depth, which has important differences from the two planar dimensions.

In brief, 3D vis is easy to justify when the user's task involves shape understanding of inherently three-dimensional structures. In this case, which frequently occurs with inherently spatial data, the benefits of 3D absolutely outweigh the costs, and designers can use the many interaction idioms designed to mitigate those costs.

In all other contexts, the use of 3D needs to be carefully justified. In most cases, rather than choosing a visual encoding using three dimensions of spatial position, a better answer is to visually encode using only two dimensions of spatial position. Often an appropriate 2D encoding follows from a different choice of data abstraction, where the original dataset is transformed by computing derived data.

The cues that convey depth information to our visual system include occlusion, perspective distortion, shadows and lighting, familiar size, stereoscopic disparity, and others. This section discusses the costs of these **depth cues** in a visual encoding context and the challenges of text legibility given current display technology. It then discusses situations where the benefits of showing depth information could outweigh these costs and the need for justification that the situation has been correctly analyzed.

6.3.1 The Power of the Plane

A crucial point when interpreting the channel rankings in Figure 5.6 is that the spatial position channels apply only to planar spatial position, not arbitrary 3D position.

Vertical and horizontal position are combined into the shared category of *planar* because the differences between the up–down and side-to-side axes are relatively subtle. We do perceive height differences along the up–down axis as more important than horizontal position differences, no doubt due to the physical effects of gravity in real life. While the vertical spatial channel thus has a slight priority over the horizontal one, the aspect ratio of standard displays gives more horizontal pixels than vertical ones, so information density considerations sometimes override this concern. For the perceived importance of items ordered within the axes, reading conventions probably dominate. Most Western languages go from left to right and from top to bottom, but Arabic and Hebrew are read from right to left, and some Asian languages are read vertically.

6.3.2 The Disparity of Depth

The psychophysical power law exponents for accuracy shown in Figure 5.7 are different for depth position judgements in 3D than for planar position judgements in 2D. Our highly accurate length perception capability, with the linear n value of 1.0, only holds for planar spatial position. For depth judgements of visual distance, n was measured as 0.67 [Stevens 57]; that exponent is even worse than the value of 0.7 for area judgements. This phenomenon is

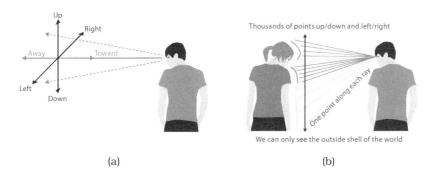

(a)   (b)

Figure 6.2. Seeing planar position versus depth. (a) The sideways and up–down axes are fundamentally different from the toward–away depth axis. (b) Along the depth axis we can see only one point for each ray, as opposed to millions of rays for the other two axes. After [Ware 08, page 44].

not surprising when considered mathematically, because as shown in Figure 6.2 the length of a line that extends into the scene is scaled nonlinearly in depth, whereas a line that traverses the picture plane horizontally or vertically is scaled linearly, so distances and angles are distorted [St. John et al. 01].

Considered perceptually, the inaccuracy of depth judgements is also not surprising; the common intuition that we experience the world in 3D is misleading. We do not really live in 3D, or even 2.5D: to quote Colin Ware, we *see* in 2.05D [Ware 08]. That is, most of the visual information that we have is about a two-dimensional *image plane*, as defined below, whereas the information that we have about a third depth dimension is only a tiny additional fraction beyond it. The number of 0.05 is chosen somewhat arbitrarily to represent this tiny fraction.

Consider what we see when we look out at the world along a ray from some fixed viewpoint, as in Figure 6.2(a). There is a major difference between the toward–away depth axis and the other two axes, sideways and up–down. There are millions of rays that we can see along these two axes by simply moving our eyes, to get information about the nearest opaque object. This information is like a two-dimensional picture, often called the image plane. In contrast, we can only get information at one point along the depth axis for each ray away from us toward the world, as in Figure 6.2(b). This phenomenon is called line-of-sight ambiguity [St. John et al. 01]. In order to get more information about what is hidden behind the closest objects shown in the image plane, we would need to move our viewpoint or the objects. At best we could change the viewpoint by simply moving our head, but in many cases we would need to move our body to a very different position.

6.3.3 Occlusion Hides Information

The most powerful depth cue is **occlusion**, where some objects cannot be seen because they are hidden behind others. The visible objects are interpreted as being closer than the occluded ones. The occlusion relationships between objects change as we move around; this **motion parallax** allows us to build up an understanding of the relative distances between objects in the world.

When people look at realistic scenes made from familiar objects, the use of motion parallax typically does not impose cognitive load or require conscious attention. In synthetic scenes, navigation controls that allow the user to change the 3D viewpoint interactively invoke the same perceptual mechanisms to provide motion parallax. In sufficiently complex scenes where a single fixed viewpoint does not provide enough information about scene structure, interactive navigation capability is critical for understanding 3D structure. In this case, the cost is time: interactive navigation takes longer than inspecting a single image.

The overarching problem with occlusion in the context of visual encoding is that presumably important information is hidden, and discovering it via navigation has a time cost. In realistic environments, there is rarely a need to inspect all hidden surfaces. However, in a vis context, the occluded detail might be critical. It is especially likely to be important when using spatial position as a visual channel for abstract, nonspatial data.

Moreover, if the objects have unpredictable and unfamiliar shapes, understanding the three-dimensional structure of the scene can be very challenging. In this case there can be appreciable cognitive load because people must use internal memory to remember the shape from previous viewpoints, and internally synthesize an understanding of the structure. This case is common when using the spatial position channels for visual encoding. Figure 6.3 illustrates the challenges of understanding the topological structure of a node–link graph laid out in 3D, as an example of the unfamiliar structure that arises from visually encoding an abstract dataset. Synthesizing an understanding of the structure of the linkages hidden from the starting viewpoint shown here is likely to take a considerable amount of time. While sophisticated interaction idioms have been proposed to help users do this synthesis more quickly

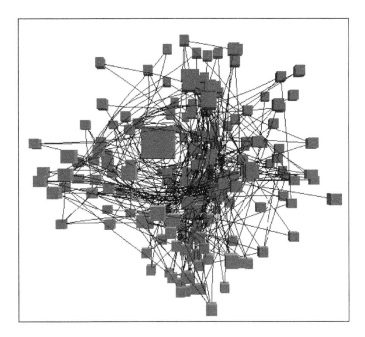

Figure 6.3. Resolving the 3D structure of the occluded parts of the scene is possible with interactive navigation, but that takes time and imposes cognitive load, even when sophisticated interaction idioms are used, as in this example of a node–link graph laid out in 3D space. From [Carpendale et al. 96, Figure 21].

than with simple realistic navigation, thus lowering the time cost, vis designers should always consider whether the benefits of 3D are worth the costs.

6.3.4 Perspective Distortion Dangers

The phenomenon of **perspective distortion** is that distant objects appear smaller and change their planar position on the image plane. Imagine a photograph looking along railroad tracks: although they are of course parallel, they appear to draw together as they recede into the distance. Although the tracks have the same width in reality, measuring with a ruler on the photograph itself would show that in the picture the width of the nearby track is much greater than that of the distant track.*

One of the major breakthroughs of Western art was the Renaissance understanding of the mathematics of perspective to create very realistic images, so many people think of perspective as a good

> ▶ The disparity in our perception of depth from our perception of planar spatial position is discussed in Section 6.3.2.

> ★ The phenomenon of *perspective distortion* is also known as **foreshortening**.

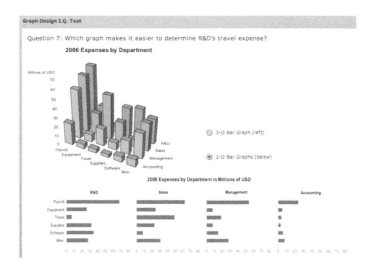

Figure 6.4. 3D bar charts are more difficult than 2D bar charts because of both perspective distortion and occlusion. From [Few 07, Question 7].

thing. However, in the context of visually encoding abstract data, perspective is a very bad thing! Perspective distortion is one of the main dangers of depth because the power of the plane is lost; it completely interferes with visual encodings that use the planar spatial position channels and the size channel. For example, it is more difficult to judge bar heights in a 3D bar chart than in multiple horizontally aligned 2D bar charts, as shown in Figure 6.4. Foreshortening makes direct comparison of bar heights difficult.

Figure 6.5 shows another example where size coding in multiple dimensions is used for bars that recede into the distance in 3D on a ground plane. The result of the perspective distortion is that the bar sizes cannot be directly compared as a simple perceptual operation.

Figure 6.5. With perspective distortion, the power of the planar spatial position channel is lost, as is the size channel. From [Mukherjea et al. 96, Figure 1].

6.3.5   Other Depth Cues

In realistic scenes, one of the depth cues is the size of familiar objects. We roughly know the size of a car, so when we see one at a distance we can estimate the size of a nearby unfamiliar object. If all objects in the scene are visually encoded representations of abstract information, we do not have access to this strong depth cue.

The depth cues of shadows and surface shading also communicate depth and three-dimensional structure information. Cast shadows are useful for resolving depth ambiguity because they allow us to infer the height of an object with respect to a ground plane. Shading and self-shadowing show the three-dimensional shape of an object. One problem with using these lighting-based cues when visualizing abstract data is that they create visual clutter that distracts the viewer's attention from the meaningful parts of the scene that represent information. Another problem is that cast shadows, regions of self-shadowing, or highlights could be mistaken by the viewer for true marks that are the substrate for the visual channels showing attribute information. Cast shadows could also cause problems by occluding true marks. The final problem is that surface shading effects interfere with the color channels: highlights can change the hue or saturation, and shadows change the luminance.

Stereoscopic depth is a cue that comes from the disparities between two images made from two camera viewpoints slightly separated in space, just like our two eyes are. In contrast, all of the previous discussion pertained to pictoral cues from a single camera. Although many people assume that stereo vision is the strongest depth cue, it is in fact a relatively weak one compared with the others listed above and contributes little for distant objects. Stereo depth cues are most useful for nearby objects that are at roughly the same depth, providing guidance for manipulating things within arm's reach.

Stereo displays, which deliver a slightly different image for each of our two eyes, do help people better resolve depth. Conveniently, they do not directly interfere with any of the main visual channels. Stereo displays do indeed improve the accuracy of depth perception compared with single-view displays—but even still depth cannot be perceived with the accuracy of planar position. Of course, stereo cannot solve any of the problems associated with perspective distortion.

The relatively subtle depth cue of atmospheric perspective, where the color of distant objects is shifted toward blue, would conflict with color encoding.

6.3.6   Tilted Text Isn't Legibile

Another problem with the use of 3D is dramatically impaired text legibility with most standard graphics packages that use current display technology [Grossman et al. 07]. Text fonts have been very carefully designed for maximum legibility when rendered on the grid of pixels that makes up a 2D display, so that characters as little as nine pixels high are easily readable. Although hardware graphics acceleration is now nearly pervasive, so that text positioned at arbitrary orientations in 3D space can be rendered *quickly*, this text is usually not rendered *well*. As soon as a text label is tilted in any way off of the image plane, it typically becomes blocky and jaggy. The combination of more careful rendering and very high-resolution displays of many hundred of dots per inch may solve this problem in the future, but legibility is a major problem today.

6.3.7   Benefits of 3D: Shape Perception

The great benefit of using 3D comes when the viewer's task fundamentally requires understanding the three-dimensional geometric structure of objects or scenes. In almost all of these cases, a 3D view with interactive navigation controls to set the 3D viewpoint will allow users to construct a useful mental model of dataset structure more quickly than simply using several 2D axis-aligned views. For these tasks, all of the costs of using 3D discussed above are outweighed by the benefit of helping the viewer build a mental model of the 3D geometry.

For example, although people can be trained to comprehend blueprints with a top view and two side views, synthesizing the information contained within these views to understand what a complex object looks like from some arbitrary 3D viewpoint is a difficult problem that incurs significant cognitive and memory load. The 2D blueprint views are better for the task of accurately discriminating the sizes of building elements, which is why they are still heavily used in construction. However, there is considerable experimental evidence that 3D outperforms 2D for shape understanding tasks [St. John et al. 01].

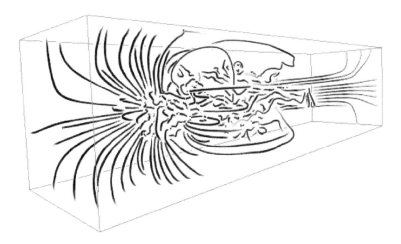

Figure 6.6. The use of 3D is well justified when the central task is shape understanding, as in this example of 3D streamline showing the patterns of fluid flow through a volume. From [Li and Shen 07, Figure 9].

Most tasks that have inherently 3D spatial data after the abstraction stage fall into this category. Some classical examples are fluid flow over an airplane wing, a medical imaging tomography dataset of the human body, or molecular interaction within a living cell. Figure 6.6 shows an example of streamlines in 3D fluid flow [Li and Shen 07], where geometric navigation based on 3D rotation is a good strategy to help users understand the complex shapes quickly.

▶ Streamlines are discussed further in Section 8.5, and geometric navigation in Section 11.5.

6.3.8 Justification and Alternatives

The question of whether to use two or three channels for spatial position has now been extensively studied. When computer-based vis began in the late 1980s, there was a lot of enthusiasm for 3D representations. As the field matured, researchers began to better appreciate the costs of 3D approaches when used for abstract datasets [Ware 01]. By now, the use of 3D for abstract data requires careful justification. In many cases, a different choice at the abstraction or visual encoding levels would be more appropriate.

Example: Cluster–Calendar Time-Series Vis

A good example is a system from van Wijk and van Selow designed to browse time-series data [van Wijk and van Selow 99]. The dataset has two

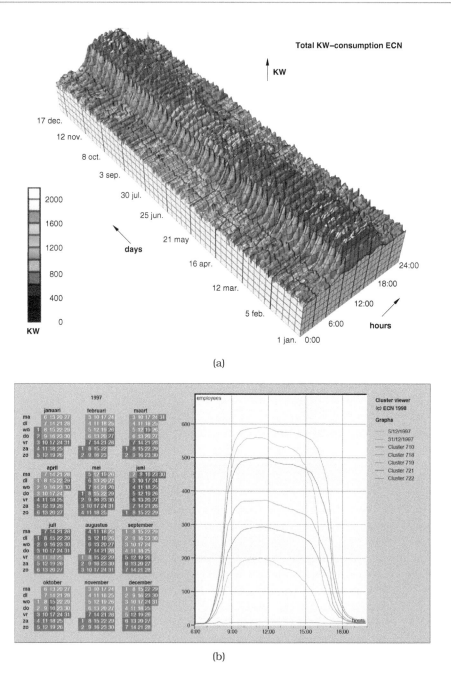

(a)

(b)

Figure 6.7. 3D versus 2D. (a) A 3D representation of this time-series dataset introduces the problems of occlusion and perspective distortion. (b) The linked 2D views of derived aggregate curves and the calendar allow direct comparison and show more fine-grained patterns. From [van Wijk and van Selow 99, Figures 1 and 4].

related sets of measurements: the number of people inside and amount of power used in an office building, with measurements over the course of each day for one full year. The authors compare a straightforward 3D representation with a carefully designed approach using linked 2D views, which avoids the problems of occlusion and perspective distortion. Figure 6.7(a) shows the straightforward 3D representation created directly from the original time-series data, where each cross-section is a 2D time series curve showing power consumption for one day, with one curve for each day of the year along the extruded third axis. Only very large-scale patterns such as the higher consumption during working hours and the seasonal variation between winter and summer are visible.

The final vis designed by the authors uses multiple linked 2D views and a different data abstraction. They created the derived data of a hierarchical clustering of the time-series curves through an iterative process where the most similar curves are merged together into a cluster that can be represented by the average of the curves within it.

▶ Linked views are discussed in Chapter 12.

Figure 6.7(b) shows a single aggregate curve for each of the highest-level groups in the clustering in the window on the right of the display. There are few enough of these aggregate curves that they can all be superimposed in the same 2D image without excessive visual clutter. Direct comparison between the curve heights at all times of the day is easy because there is no perspective distortion or occlusion. (The cluster–calendar vis shows the number of people in the building, rather than the power consumption of the 3D extruded vis.)

On the left side of Figure 6.7(b) is a calendar view. Calendars are a very traditional and successful way to show temporal patterns. The views are linked with shared color coding. The same large-scale patterns of seasonal variation between summer and winter that can be seen in 3D are still very visible, but smaller-scale patterns that are difficult or impossible to spot in the 3D view are also revealed. In this Dutch calendar, weeks are vertical strips with the weekend at the bottom. We can identify weekends and holidays as the nearly flat teal curve where nobody is in the building, and normal weekdays as the topmost tan curve with a full house. Summer and Fridays during the winter are the brown curve with one hundred fewer people, and Fridays in the summer are the green curve with nearly half of the employees gone. The blue and magenta curves show days between holiday times where most people also take vacation. The red curve shows the unique Dutch holiday of Santa Claus day, where everybody gets to leave work an hour early.

While unbridled enthusiasm for 3D is no longer common, there are indeed situations where its use is justifiable even for abstract data.

Figure 6.8 shows an example that is similar on the surface to the previous one, but in this case 3D is used with care and the design is well justified [Lopez-Hernandez et al. 10]. In this system for visualizing oscilloscope time-series data, the user starts by viewing the data using the traditional eye diagram where the signal is wrapped around in time and shown as many overlapping traces. Users can spread the traces apart using the metaphor of opening a drawer, as shown in Figure 6.8(a). This drawer interface does use 3D, but with many constraints. Layers are orthographically projected and always face the viewer. Navigation complexity is controlled by automatically zooming and framing as the user adjusts the drawer's orientation, as shown in Figure 6.8(b).

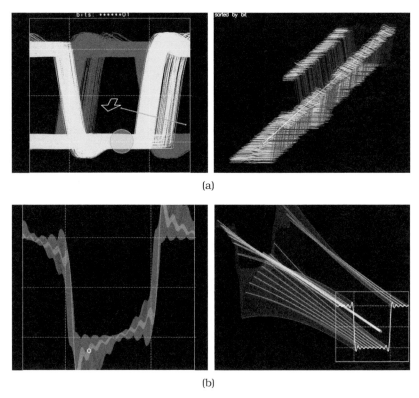

(a)

(b)

Figure 6.8. Careful use of 3D. (a) The user can evolve the view from the traditional overlapping eye diagram with the metaphor of opening a drawer. (b) The interaction is carefully designed to avoid the difficulties of unconstrained 3D navigation. From [Lopez-Hernandez et al. 10, Figures 3 and 7].

6.3.9 Empirical Evidence

Empirical experiments are critical in understanding user performance, especially because of the well-documented dissociation between stated preference for 3D and actual task performance [Andre and Wickens 95]. Experimental evidence suggests that 3D interfaces are better for shape understanding, whereas 2D are best for relative position tasks: those that require judging the precise distances and angles between objects [St. John et al. 01]. Most tasks involving abstract data do not benefit from 3D; for example, an experiment comparing 3D cone trees to an equivalent 2D tree browser found that the 3D interaction had a significant time cost [Cockburn and McKenzie 00].

Designing controlled experiments that untangle the efficacy of specific interfaces that use 3D can be tricky. Sometimes the goal of the experimenter is simply to compare two alternative interfaces that differ in many ways; in such cases it is dangerous to conclude that if an interface that happens to be 3D outperforms another that happens to be 2D, it is the use of 3D that made the difference. In several cases, earlier study results that were interpreted as showing benefits for 3D were superseded by more careful experimental design that eliminated uncontrolled factors. For example, the 3D Data Mountain interface for organizing web page thumbnail images was designed to exploit human spatial cognition and was shown to outperform the standard 2D Favorites display in Internet Explorer [Robertson et al. 98]. However, this study left open the question of whether the benefit was from the use of 3D or the use of the data mountain visual encoding, namely, a spatial layout allowing immediate access to every item in each pile of information. A later study compared two versions of Data Mountain, one with 3D perspective and one in 2D, and no performance benefit for 3D was found [Cockburn and McKenzie 01].

Another empirical study found no benefits for 3D landscapes created to reflect the density of a 2D point cloud, compared with simply showing the point cloud in 2D [Tory et al. 07]. In the 3D **information landscape** idiom, the density of the points on the plane is computed as a derived attribute and used to construct a surface whose height varies according to this attribute in order to show its value in a form similar to geographic terrain.* A third alternative to landscapes or points is a **contour plot**, where colored bands show the outlines of specific heights. A contour plot can be used alone as a 2D landscape or can be combined with 3D for a colored landscape. Proponents of this idiom have argued that landscapes

★ Other names for a 3D *landscape* are **height field** and **terrain**.

▶ Contour plots are discussed in Section 8.4.1.

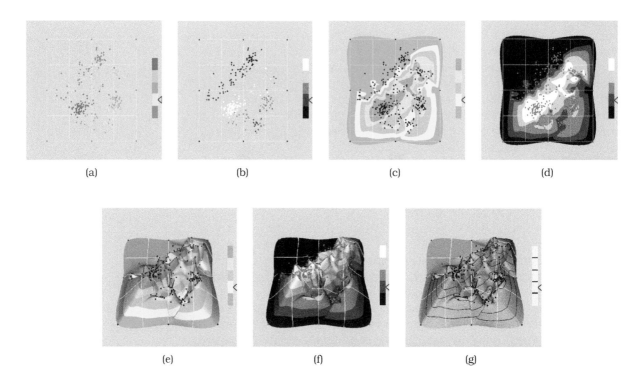

Figure 6.9. Point-based displays were found to outperform information landscapes in an empirical study of visual encodings for dimensionally reduced data. (a) Colored points. (b) Grayscale points. (c) Colored 2D landscape. (d) Grayscale 2D landscape. (e) Colored 3D landscape. (f) Grayscale 3D landscape. (g) Height only. From [Tory et al. 07, Figure 1].

▶ Dimensionality reduction is discussed in Section 13.4.3.

are familiar and engaging, and they have been used in several systems for displaying high-dimensional data after dimensionality reduction was used to reduce to two synthetic dimensions [Davidson et al. 01, Wise et al. 95].

Figure 6.9 shows the seven possibilities tested in the empirical study comparing points to colored and uncolored landscapes. The findings were that points were far superior to landscapes for search and point estimation tasks and in the landscape case 2D landscapes were superior to 3D landscapes [Tory et al. 07]. A follow-up study for a visual memory task yielded similar results [Tory et al. 09].

6.4   No Unjustified 2D

Laying out data in 2D space should also be explicitly justified, compared with the alternative of simply showing the data with a 1D list.

Lists have several strengths. First, they can show the maximal amount of information, such as text labels, in minimal space. In contrast, 2D layouts such as node–link representations of network data require considerably more space to show the same number of labels, so they have notably lower information density.

Second, lists are excellent for lookup tasks when they are ordered appropriately, for example in alphabetical order when the goal is to find a known label. In contrast, finding a specific label in a 2D node–link representation might require the user to hunt around the entire layout, unless a specific search capability is built into the vis tool.

When the task truly requires understanding the topological structure of the network, then the benefits of showing those relationships explicitly outweigh the cost of the space required. However, some tasks are handled well by linear lists, even if the original data has network structure.

6.5   Eyes Beat Memory

Using our eyes to switch between different views that are visible simultaneously has much lower cognitive load than consulting our memory to compare a current view with what was seen before. Many interaction idioms implicitly rely on the internal use of memory and thus impose cognitive load on the viewer. Consider navigation within a single view, where the display changes to show the scene from a different viewpoint. Maintaining a sense of orientation implicitly relies on using internal resources, either by keeping track of past navigation choices (for example, *I zoomed into the nucleus*) or by remembering past views (for example, *earlier all the stock options in the tech sector were in the top corner of the view*). In contrast, having a small overview window with a rectangle within it showing the position and size of the current camera viewport for the main view is a way to show that information through an external representation easily consulted by looking at that region of the screen, so that it can be read off by the perceptual system instead of remembered.

6.5.1 Memory and Attention

Broadly speaking, people have two different categories of memory: long-term memory that can last a lifetime, versus short-term memory that lasts several seconds, also known as **working memory**. While the capacity of long-term memory doesn't have a strict upper limit, human working memory is a very limited resource. When these limits are reached, people experience **cognitive load** and will fail to absorb all of the information that is presented.

Human attention also has severe limits. Conscious search for items is an operation that grows more difficult with the number of items there are to be checked. Vigilance is also a highly limited resource: our ability to perform visual search tasks degrades quickly, with far worse results after several hours than in the first few minutes.

6.5.2 Animation versus Side-by-Side Views

Some animation-based idioms also impose significant cognitive load on the viewer because of implicit memory demands. Animation is an overloaded word that can mean many different things considered through the lens of vis encoding and interaction. I distinguish between these three definitions:

- narrative storytelling, as in popular movies;

- transitions from just one state to another;

- video-style playback of a multiframe sequence: play, pause, stop, rewind, and step forward/back.

Some people have the intuition that because animation is a powerful storytelling medium for popular movies, it should also be suitable in a vis context. However, the situation is quite different. Successful storytelling requires careful and deliberate choreography to ensure that action is only occurring in one place at a time and the viewer's eyes have been guided to ensure that they are looking in the right place. In contrast, a dataset animation might have simultaneous changes in many parts of the view.

Animation is extremely powerful when used for transitions between two dataset configurations because it helps the user maintain context. There is considerable evidence that animated transitions can be more effective than jump cuts, because they help people track changes in object positions or camera viewpoints. These transitions are most useful when only a few things change; if the number of objects that change between frames is large, people will have a hard time tracking everything that occurs. We are blind to changes in regions of the image that are not the focus of our attention.

▶ Change blindness is covered in Section 6.5.3.

Although jump cuts are hard to follow when only seen once, giving the user control of jumping back and forth between just two frames can be effective for detecting whether there is a localized change between two scenes. This *blink comparator* idiom was used by the astronomer who found Pluto.

Finally, I consider animations as sequences of many frames, where the viewer can control the playback using video-style controls of play, pause, stop, rewind, and sometimes single-step forward or backward frame by frame. I distinguish animation from true interactive control, for example, navigation by flying through a scene. With animation the user does not directly control what occurs, only the speed at which the animation is played.

The difficulty of multiframe animations is that making comparisons between frames that do not adjoin relies on internal memory of what previous frames looked like. If changes only occur in one place at a time, the demands on attention and internal memory are small. However, when many things change all over the frame and there are many frames, we have a very difficult time in tracking what happens. Giving people the ability to pause and replay the animation is much better than only seeing it a single time straight through, but that control does not fully solve the problem.

For tasks requiring detailed comparison across many frames, seeing all the frames at once side by side can be more effective than animation. The number of frames must be small enough that the details within each can be discerned, so this approach is typically suitable for dozens but not hundreds of frames with current display resolutions. The action also should be segmented into meaningful chunks, rather than keyframes that are randomly chosen. Many vis idioms that use multiple views exploit this observation, especially small multiples.

▶ Small multiples are covered in Section 12.3.2.

6.5.3 Change Blindness

The human visual system works by querying the world around us using our eyes. Our visual system works so well that most people have the intuition that we have detailed internal memory of the visual field that surrounds us. However, we do not. Our eyes dart around, gathering information just in time for our need to use it, so quickly that we do not typically notice this motion at a conscious level.

The phenomenon of **change blindness** is that we fail to notice even quite drastic changes if our attention is directed elsewhere. For example, experimenters set up a real-world interaction where somebody was engaged by a stranger who asked directions, only to be interrupted by people carrying a door who barged in between them. The experimenters orchestrated a switch during this visual interruption, replacing the questioner with another person. Remarkably, most people did not notice, even when the new questioner was dressed completely differently—or was a different gender than the old one!

Although we are very sensitive to changes at the focus of our attention, we are surprisingly blind to changes when our attention is not engaged. The difficulty of tracking complex and widespread changes across multiframe animations is one of the implications of change blindness for vis.

6.6   Resolution over Immersion

Pixels are precious: if you are faced with a trade-off between resolution and immersion, resolution usually is far more important.

Immersive environments emphasize simulating realistic interaction and perception as closely as possible through technology such as stereo imagery delivered separately to each eye to enhance depth perception, and full six-degree-of-freedom head and position tracking so that the displays respond immediately to the user's physical motion of walking and moving the head around. The most common display technology is head-mounted displays, or small rooms with rear-projection displays on walls, floor, and ceilings. Immersion is most useful when a sense of presence is an important aspect of the intended task. With current display hardware, there is a trade-off between **resolution**, the number of available pixels divided by the display area, and **immersion**, the feeling of presence in virtual reality. The price of immersion is resolution; these displays cannot show as many pixels as state-of-the-art desktop displays of the equivalent area. The number of pixels available on a computer display is a limited resource that is usually the most critical constraint in vis design. Thus, it is extremely rare that immersion is worth the cost in resolution.

Another price of immersion is the integration of vis with the rest of a user's typical computer-based workflow. Immersive dis-

▶ Display resolution constraints are discussed in Section 1.13.

play environments are almost always special-purpose settings that are a different physical location than the user's workspace, requiring them to leave their usual office and go to some other location, whether down the hall or in another building. In most cases users stand rather than sit, so working for extended periods of time is physically taxing compared with sitting at a desk. The most critical problem is that they do not have access to their standard working environment of their own computer system. Without access to the usual input devices of mouse and keyboard, standard applications such as web browsing, email reading, text and spreadsheet editing, and other data analysis packages are completely unusable in most cases, and very awkward at best. In contrast, a vis system that fits into a standard desktop environment allows integration with the usual workflow and fast task switching between vis and other applications.

A compelling example of immersion is the use of virtual reality for phobia desensitization; somebody with a fear of heights would need a sense of presence in the synthetic environment in order to make progress. However, this example is not an application of vis, since the goal is to simulate reality rather than to visually encode information. The most likely case where immersion would be helpful for vis is when the chosen abstraction includes 3D spatial data. Even in this case, the designer should consider whether a sense of presence is worth the penalties of lower resolution and no workflow integration. It is very rare that immersion would be necessary for nonspatial, abstract data. Using 3D for visual encoding of abstract data is the uncommon case that needs careful justification. The use of an immersive display in this case would require even more careful justification.

▶ The need for justifying 3D for abstract data is covered in Section 6.3.

6.7 Overview First, Zoom and Filter, Details on Demand

Ben Shneiderman's influential mantra of **Overview First, Zoom and Filter, Details on Demand** [Shneiderman 96] is a heavily cited design guideline that emphasizes the interplay between the need for overview and the need to see details, and the role of data reduction in general and navigation in particular in supporting both.

A vis idiom that provides an **overview** is intended to give the user a broad awareness of the entire information space. Using the language of the what–why–how analysis framework, it's an idiom with the goal of *summarize*. A common goal in overview design is to show all items in the dataset simultaneously, without any need for navigation to pan or scroll. Overviews help the user find regions where further investigation in more detail might be productive. Overviews are often shown at the beginning of the exploration process, to guide users in choosing where to drill down to inspect in more detail. However, overview usage is not limited to initial reconnaissance; it's very common for users to interleave the use of overviews and detail views by switching back and forth between them many times.

When the dataset is sufficiently large, some form of *reduce* action must be used in order to show everything at once. Overview creation can be understood in terms of both filtering and aggregation. A simple way to create overviews is by zooming out geometrically, so that the entire dataset is visible within the frame. Each object is drawn smaller, with less room to show detail. In this sense, overviews are created by removing all filtering: an overview is created by changing from a zoomed-in view where some items are filtered out, to a zoomed-out view where all items are shown. When the number of items in a dataset is large enough, showing an overview of the entire dataset in a single screen using one mark per item is impossible, even if the mark size is decreased to a single pixel. When the number of items to draw outstrips the number of available pixels, the number of marks to show must be reduced with aggregation. Moreover, even for datasets of medium size, explicitly designing an overview display using a more sophisticated approach than simple geometric zooming can be fruitful. These custom overviews are similar in spirit to semantic zooming, in that the representation of the items is qualitatively different rather than simply being drawn smaller than the full-detail versions. These kinds of overviews often use dynamic aggregation that is implicitly driven by navigation, rather than being explicitly chosen by the user.

There is no crisp line dividing an "overview" from an "ordinary" vis idiom, because many idioms provide some form of overview or summary. However, it's often useful to make a relative distinction between a less detailed view that summarizes a lot of data and a more detailed view that shows a smaller number of data items with more information about each one. The former one is clearly the *overview*, the latter one is the *detail view*. It's particularly obvious how to distinguish between these when the idiom design choice of multiple views is being used; the mantra is particularly applicable when the detail view pops up in response to a *select* action by the

▶ Aggregation is discussed in Section 13.4.

▶ Geometric and semantic zooming are discussed in Section 11.5.

user, but it's also common for the detail view to be permanently visible side by side with the overview. There two other major families of idioms that support overviewing. One is to use a single view that dynamically changes over time by providing support for *reduce* actions such as zooming and filtering; then that single view sometimes acts as an overview and sometimes as a detail view. The third choice is to embed both detailed focus and overview context information together within a single view.

▶ Chapter 12 covers multiple views.

▶ Chapter 13 covers approaches to data reduction.

▶ Chapter 14 covers focus+context idioms.

This mantra is most helpful when dealing with datasets of moderate size. When dealing with enormous datasets, creating a useful overview for top-down exploration may not be feasible. In slogan form, an alternative approach is **Search, Show Context, Expand on Demand** [van Ham and Perer 09], where search results provide the starting point for browsing of local neighborhoods.

6.8   Responsiveness Is Required

The **latency** of interaction, namely, how much time it takes for the system to respond to the user action, matters immensely for interaction design. Our reaction to latency does not simply occur on a continuum, where our irritation level gradually rises as things take longer and longer. Human reaction to phenomena is best modeled in terms of a series of discrete categories, with a different time constant associated with each one. A system will feel responsive if these latency classes are taken into account by providing feedback to the user within the relevant time scale. The three categories most relevant for vis designers are shown in Table 6.1.

The perceptual processing time constant of one-tenth of a second is relevant for operations such as screen updates. The immediate response time constant of one second is relevant for operations such as visual feedback showing what item that user has selected with a mouse click, or the length of time for an animated transition from one layout to another. The brief task time constant of ten

Time Constant	Value (in seconds)
perceptual processing	0.1
immediate response	1
brief tasks	10

Table 6.1. Human response to interaction latency changes dramatically at these time thresholds. After [Card et al. 91, Table 3].

seconds is relevant for breaking down complex tasks into simpler pieces; a good granularity for the smallest pieces is this brief task time.

6.8.1   Visual Feedback

From the user's point of view, the latency of an interaction is the time between their action and some feedback from the system indicating that the operation has completed. In a vis system, that feedback would most naturally be some visual indication of state change within the system itself, rather than cumbersome approaches such as printing out status indications at the console or a popup dialog box confirmation that would interfere with the flow of exploration.

The most obvious principle is that the user should indeed have some sort of confirmation that the action has completed, rather than being left dangling wondering whether the action is still in progress, or whether the action never started in the first place (for example, because they missed the target and clicked on the background rather than the intended object). Thus, feedback such as highlighting a selected item is a good way to confirm that the desired operation has completed successfully. In navigation, feedback would naturally come when the user sees the new frame is drawn from the changed viewpoint. Visual feedback should typically take place within the immediate response latency class: around one second.

Another principle is that if an action could take significantly longer than a user would naturally expect, some kind of progress indicator should be shown to the user. A good rule of thumb for significantly longer is crossing from one latency class into another, as shown in Table 6.1.

6.8.2   Latency and Interaction Design

Successful interaction design for a vis system depends on having a good match between the latencies of the low-level interaction mechanism, the visual feedback mechanism, the system update time, and the cognitive load of operation itself.

For example, consider the operation of seeing more details for an item and the latency difference between three different low-level interaction mechanisms for doing so. Clicking on the item is slowest, because the user must move the mouse toward the target location, stop the motion in the right place, and press down on the mouse. Mouseover hover, where the cursor is placed over the object for some short period of dwell time but no click is required, may or may not be faster depending on the dwell time. Mouseover actions with no dwell time requirement, where the action is triggered by the cursor simply crossing the object, are of course the fastest because the second step is also eliminated and only the first step needs to take place.

For visual feedback, consider three different mechanisms for showing the information. One is showing the information on a fixed detail pane at the side of the screen. In order to see the information, the user's eyes need to move from the current cursor location to the side of the screen, so this operation has relatively high latency for making use of the visual feedback. On the other hand, from a visual encoding point of view, an advantage is that a lot of detail information can be shown without occluding anything else in the main display. A second feedback mechanism is a popup window at the current cursor location, which is faster to use since there is no need to move the eyes away from tracking the cursor. Since placing information directly in the view might occlude other objects, there is a visual encoding cost to this choice. A third mechanism is a visual highlight change directly in the view, for instance by highlighting all neighbors within the graph that are one hop from the graph node under the cursor through a color change.

System update time is another latency to consider. With tiny datasets stored completely locally, update time will be negligible for any of these options. With larger datasets, the time to redraw the entire view could be considerable unless the rendering* framework has been designed to deliver frames at a guaranteed rate. Similarly, scalable rendering frameworks can support fast update for changing a few items or a small part of the display without redrawing the entire screen, but most graphics systems do not offer this functionality by default. Thus, designing systems to guarantee immediate response to user actions can require significant algorithmic attention. With distributed datasets, obtaining details may require a round trip from the client to the server, possibly taking several seconds on a congested network.

★ The term **rendering** is used in computer graphics for drawing an image.

When systems are designed so that all of these latencies are well matched, the user interacts fluidly and can stay focused on high-level goals such as building an internal mental model of the dataset. When there is a mismatch, the user is jarred out of a state of flow [Csikszentmihalyi 91] by being forced to wait for the system.

6.8.3 Interactivity Costs

Interactivity has both power and cost. The benefit of interaction is that people can explore a larger information space than can be understood in a single static image. However, a cost to interaction is that it requires human time and attention. If the user must exhaustively check every possibility, use of the vis system may degenerate into human-powered search. Automatically detecting features of interest to explicitly bring to the user's attention via the visual encoding is a useful goal for the vis designer. However, if the task at hand could be completely solved by automatic means, there would be no need for a vis in the first place. Thus, there is always a trade-off between finding automatable aspects and relying on the human in the loop to detect patterns.

6.9 Get It Right in Black and White

▶ The principles of using color to visually encode data are discussed in Section 10.2. Figure 12.13 shows an example of explicitly checking luminance contrast between elements on different layers.

Maureen Stone has advocated the slogan **Get It Right in Black and White** as a design guideline for effective use of color [Stone 10]. That is, ensure that the most crucial aspects of visual representation are legible even if the image is transformed from full color to black and white. Do so by literally checking your work in black and white, either with image processing or by simply printing out a screenshot on a black and white printer. This slogan suggests encoding the most important attribute with the luminance channel to ensure adequate luminance contrast and considering the hue and saturation channels as secondary sources of information.

6.10 Function First, Form Next

The best vis designs should shine in terms of both form and function; that is, they should be both beautiful and effective. Nevertheless, in this book, I focus on function.

My rationale is that given an effective but ugly design, it's possible to refine the form to make it more beautiful while maintaining the base of effectiveness. Even if the original designer of the vis has no training in graphic design, collaboration is possible with people who do have that background.

In contrast, given a beautiful and ineffective design, you will probably need to toss it out and start from scratch. Thus, I don't advocate a "form first" approach, because progressive refinement is usually not possible. My argument mirrors the claims I made in the first chapter about the size of the vis design space and the fact that most designs are ineffective.

Equally important is the point that I don't advocate "form never": visual beauty does indeed matter, given that vis makes use of human visual perception. Given the choice of two equally effective systems, where one is beautiful and one is ugly, people will prefer the better form. Moreover, good visual form enhances the effectiveness of visual representations.

I don't focus on teaching the principles and practice of graphic design in this book because they are covered well by many other sources. I focus on the principles of vis effectiveness because of the lack of other resources.

6.11   Further Reading

No Unjustified 3D The differences between planar and depth spatial perception and the characteristics of 3D depth cues are discussed at length in both of Ware's books [Ware 08, Ware 13]. An in-depth discussion of the issues of 2D versus 3D [St. John et al. 01] includes references to many previous studies in the human factors and air traffic control literature including the extensive work of Wickens. Several careful experiments overturned previous claims of 3D benefits over 2D [Cockburn and McKenzie 00, Cockburn and McKenzie 01, Cockburn and McKenzie 04].

Memory Ware's textbook is an excellent resource for memory and attention as they relate to vis [Ware 13], with much more detail than I provide here. A recent monograph contains an interesting and thorough discussion of supporting and exploiting spatial memory in user interfaces [Scarr et al. 13].

Animation An influential paper on incorporating the principles of hand-drawn animation into computer graphics discusses the importance of choreography to guide the viewer's eyes during narrative storytelling [Lasseter 87]. A meta-review of animation argues that many seemingly promising study results are confounded by attempts to compare incommensurate situations; the authors find that small multiples are better than animation if equivalent information is shown [Tversky et al. 02] and the segmentation is carefully chosen [Zacks and Tversky 03]. An empirical study found that while trend animation was fast and enjoyable when used for presentation it did lead to errors, and it was significantly slower than both small multiples and trace lines for exploratory analysis [Robertson et al. 08].

Change Blindness A survey paper is a good starting point for the change blindness literature [Simons 00].

Overview, Zoom and Filter, Details on Demand This early and influential mantra about overviews is presented in a very readable paper [Shneiderman 96]. More recently, a synthesis review analyzes the many ways that overviews are used in infovis [Hornbæk and Hertzum 11].

Responsiveness Is Required Card pioneered the discussion of latency classes for vis and human–computer interaction [Card et al. 91]; an excellent book chapter covering these ideas appears in a very accessible book on interface design [Johnson 10, Chapter 12]. The costs of interaction are discussed in a synthesis review [Lam 08] and a proposed framework for interaction [Yi et al. 07].

Get It Right in Black and White A blog post on Get It Right in Black and White is a clear and concise starting point for the topic [Stone 10].

Function First, Form Next A very accessible place to start for basic graphic design guidelines is *The Non-Designer's Design Book* [Williams 08].

Arrange Tables

⊕ Express Values

⊕ Separate, Order, Align Regions

→ Separate   → Order   → Align

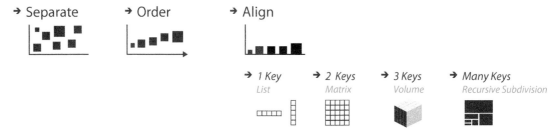

→ *1 Key*   → *2 Keys*   → *3 Keys*   → *Many Keys*
   List   *Matrix*   *Volume*   *Recursive Subdivision*

⊕ Axis Orientation

→ Rectilinear   → Parallel   → Radial

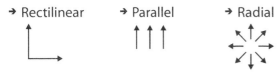

⊕ Layout Density

→ Dense   → Space-Filling

Figure 7.1. Design choices for arranging tables.

Chapter 7

Arrange Tables

7.1   The Big Picture

Figure 7.1 shows the four visual encoding design choices for how to arrange tabular data spatially. One is to express values. The other three are to separate, order, and align regions. The spatial orientation of axes can be rectilinear, parallel, or radial. Spatial layouts may be dense, and they may be space-filling.

> ▶ A fifth arrangement choice, to use a given spatial layout, is not an option for nonspatial information; it is covered in Chapter 8.

7.2   Why Arrange?

The **arrange** design choice covers all aspects of the use of spatial channels for visual encoding. It is the most crucial visual encoding choice because the use of space dominates the user's mental model of the dataset. The three highest ranked effectiveness channels for quantitative and ordered attributes are all related to spatial position: planar position against a common scale, planar position along an unaligned scale, and length. The highest ranked effectiveness channel for categorical attributes, grouping items within the same region, is also about the use of space. Moreover, there are no nonspatial channels that are highly effective for all attribute types: the others are split into being suitable for either ordered or categorical attributes, but not both, because of the principle of expressiveness.

> ▶ The primacy of the spatial position channels is discussed at length in Chapter 5, as are the principles of effectiveness and expressiveness.

7.3   Arrange by Keys and Values

The distinction between key and value attributes is very relevant to visually encoding table data. A **key** is an independent attribute that can be used as a unique index to look up items in a table, while a **value** is a dependent attribute: the value of a cell in a table. Key attributes can be categorical or ordinal, whereas values can be all

> ▶ See Section 2.6.1 for more on keys and values.

three of the types: categorical, ordinal, or quantitative. The unique values for a categorical or ordered attribute are called **levels**, to avoid the confusion of overloading the term *value*.

The core design choices for visually encoding tables directly relate to the semantics of the table's attributes: how many keys and how many values does it have? An idiom could only show values, with no keys; scatterplots are the canonical example of showing two value attributes. An idiom could show one key and one value attribute; bar charts are the best-known example. An idiom could show two keys and one value; for example, heatmaps. Idioms that show many keys and many values often recursively subdivide space into many regions, as with scatterplot matrices.

While datasets do only have attributes with value semantics, it would be rare to visually encode a dataset that has only key attributes. Keys are typically used to define a region of space for each item in which one or more value attributes are shown.

7.4   Express: Quantitative Values

Using space to express quantitative attributes is a straightforward use of the spatial position channel to visually encode data. The attribute is mapped to spatial position along an axis.

In the simple case of encoding a single value attribute, each item is encoded with a mark at some position along the axis. Additional attributes might also be encoded on the same mark with other nonspatial channels such as color and size. In the more complex case, a composite **glyph** object is drawn, with internal structure that arises from multiple marks. Each mark lies within a subregion in the glyph that is visually encoded differently, so the glyph can show multiple attributes at once.

▶ Glyphs and views are discussed further in Section 12.4.

Example: Scatterplots

The idiom of **scatterplots** encodes two quantitative value variables using both the vertical and horizontal spatial position channels, and the mark type is necessarily a point.

Scatterplots are effective for the abstract tasks of providing overviews and characterizing distributions, and specifically for finding outliers and extreme values. Scatterplots are also highly effective for the abstract task of judging the correlation between two attributes. With this visual encoding, that task corresponds the easy perceptual judgement of noticing

Figure 7.2. Scatterplot. Each point mark represents a country, with horizontal and vertical spatial position encoding the primary quantitative attributes of life expectancy and infant mortality. The color channel is used for the categorical country attribute and the size channel for quantitative population attribute. From [Robertson et al. 08, Figure 1c].

whether the points form a line along the diagonal. The stronger the correlation, the closer the points fall along a perfect diagonal line; positive correlation is an upward slope, and negative is downward. Figure 7.2 shows a highly negatively correlated dataset.

Additional transformations can also be used to shed more light on the data. Figure 7.3(a) shows the relationship between diamond price and weight. Figure 7.3(b) shows a scatterplot of derived attributes created by logarithmically scaling the originals; the transformed attributes are strongly positively correlated.

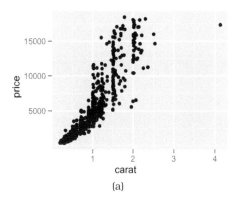 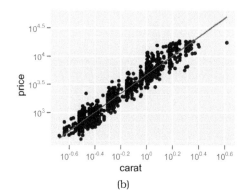

(a)   (b)

Figure 7.3. Scatterplots. (a) Original diamond price/carat data. (b) Derived log-scale attributes are highly positively correlated. From [Wickham 10, Figure 10].

When judging correlation is the primary intended task, the derived data of a calculated regression line is often superimposed on the raw scatterplot of points, as in Figures 7.3(b) and 1.3.

Scatterplots are often augmented with color coding to show an additional attribute. Size coding can also portray yet another attribute; size-coded scatterplots are sometimes called **bubble plots**. Figure 7.2 shows an example of demographic data, plotting infant mortality on the vertical axis against life expectancy on the horizontal axis.

The scalability of a scatterplot is limited by the need to distinguish points from each other, so it is well suited for dozens or hundreds of items.

The table below summarizes this discussion in terms of a what–why–how analysis instance. All of the subsequent examples will end with a similar summary table.

Idiom	Scatterplots
What: Data	Table: two quantitative value attributes.
How: Encode	Express values with horizontal and vertical spatial position and point marks.
Why: Task	Find trends, outliers, distribution, correlation; locate clusters.
Scale	Items: hundreds.

7.5   Separate, Order, and Align: Categorical Regions

The use of space to encode categorical attributes is more complex than the simple case of quantitative attributes where the value can be expressed with spatial position. Spatial position is an ordered magnitude visual channel, but categorical attributes have unordered identity semantics. The principle of expressiveness would be violated if they are encoded with spatial position.

The semantics of categorical attributes does match up well with the idea of a spatial **region**: regions are contiguous bounded areas that are distinct from each other. Drawing all of the items with the same values for a categorical attribute within the same region uses spatial proximity to encode the information about their similarity, in a way that adheres nicely to the expressiveness principle. The choice to separate into regions still leaves enormous flexibility in how to encode the data within each region: that's a different design choice. However, these regions themselves must be given spatial positions on the plane in order to draw any specific picture.

The problem becomes easier to understand by breaking down the distribution of regions into three operations: separating into regions, aligning the regions, and ordering the regions. The separation and the ordering always need to happen, but the alignment is optional. The separation should be done according to an attribute that is categorical, whereas alignment and ordering should be done by some other attribute that is ordered. The attribute used to order the regions must have ordered semantics, and thus it cannot be the categorical one that was used to do the separation. If alignment is done, the ordered attribute used to control the alignment *between* regions is sometimes the same one that is used to encode the spatial position of items *within* the region. It's also possible to use a different one.

7.5.1   List Alignment: One Key

With a single key, separating into regions using that key yields one region per item. The regions are frequently arranged in a one-dimensional **list alignment**, either horizontal or vertical. The view itself covers a two-dimensional area: the aligned list of items stretches across one of the spatial dimensions, and the region in which the values are shown stretches across the other.

Example: Bar Charts

The well-known bar chart idiom is a simple initial example. Figure 7.4 shows a bar chart of approximate weights on the vertical axis for each of three animal species on the horizontal axis. Analyzing the visual encoding, **bar charts** use a line mark and encode a quantitative value attribute with one spatial position channel. The other attribute shown in the chart, animal species, is a categorical key attribute. Each line mark is indeed in a separate region of space, and there is one for each level of the categorical attribute. These line marks are all aligned within a common frame, so that the highest-accuracy aligned position channel is used rather than the lower-accuracy unaligned channel. In Figure 7.4(a) the regions are ordered alphabetically by species name. Formally, the alphabetical ordering of the names should be considered a derived attribute. This frequent default choice does have the benefit of making lookup by name easy, but it often hides what could be meaningful patterns in the dataset. Figure 7.4(b) shows this dataset with the regions ordered by the values of the same value attribute that is encoded by the bar heights, animal weight. This kind of data-driven ordering makes it easier to see dataset trends. Bar charts are also well suited for the abstract task of looking up individual values.

The scalability issues with bar charts are that there must be enough room on the screen to have white space interleaved between the bar line marks so that they are distinguishable. A bar corresponds to a level of the categorical key attribute, and it's common to show between several and dozens of bars. In the limit, a full-screen chart with 1000 pixels could handle up to hundreds of bars, but not thousands.

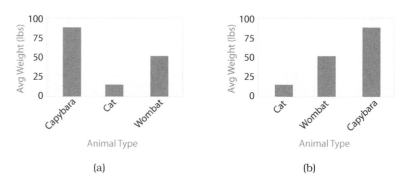

(a)   (b)

Figure 7.4. Bar chart. The key attribute, *species*, separates the marks along the horizontal spatial axis. The value attribute, *weight*, expresses the value with aligned vertical spatial position and line marks. (a) Marks ordered alphabetically according to species name. (b) Marks ordered by the weight attribute used for bar heights.

Idiom	Bar Charts
What: Data	Table: one quantitative value attribute, one categorical key attribute.
How: Encode	Line marks, express value attribute with aligned vertical position, separate key attribute with horizontal position.
Why: Task	Lookup and compare values.
Scale	Key attribute: dozens to hundreds of levels.

Example: Stacked Bar Charts

A **stacked bar chart** uses a more complex glyph for each bar, where multiple sub-bars are stacked vertically. The length of the composite glyph still encodes a value, as in a standard bar chart, but each subcomponent also encodes a length-encoded value. Stacked bar charts show information about multidimensional tables, specifically a two-dimensional table with two keys. The composite glyphs are arranged as a list according to a primary key. The other secondary key is used in constructing the vertical structure of the glyph itself. Stacked bar charts are an example of a list alignment used with more than one key attribute. They support the task of lookup according to either of the two keys.

Stacked bar charts typically use color as well as length coding. Each subcomponent is colored according to the same key that is used to determine the vertical ordering; since the subcomponents are all abutted end to end without a break and are the same width, they would not be distiguishable without different coloring. While it would be possible to use only black outlines with white fill as the rectangles within a bar, comparing subcomponents across different bars would be considerably more difficult.

Figure 7.5 shows an example of a stacked bar chart used to inspect information from a computer memory profiler. The key used to distribute composite bars along the axis is the combination of a processor and a procedure. The key used to stack and color the glyph subcomponents is the type of cache miss; the height of each full bar encodes all cache misses for each processor–procedure combination.

Each component of the bar is separately stacked, so that the full bar height shows the value for the combination of all items in the stack. The heights of the lowest bar component and the full combined bar are both easy to compare against other bars because they can be read off against the flat baseline; that is, the judgement is position against a common scale. The other components in the stack are more difficult to compare

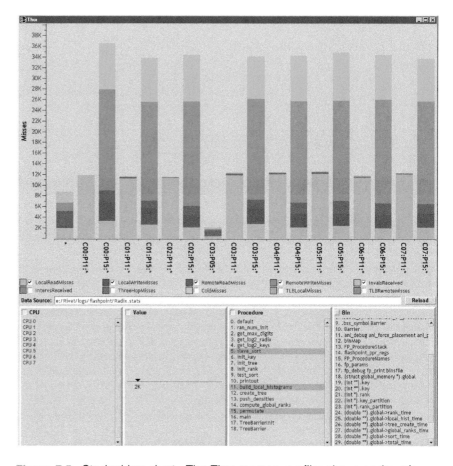

Figure 7.5. Stacked bar chart. The Thor memory profiler shows cache misses stacked and colored by miss type. From [Bosch 01, Figure 4.1].

▶ Stacked bars are typically used for absolute data; relative proportions of parts to a whole can be shown with a normalized stacked bar chart, where each bar shows the same information as in an entire pie chart, as discussed in Section 7.6.3.

across bars because their starting points are not aligned to a common scale. Thus, the order of stacking is significant for the kinds of patterns that are most easily visible, in addition to the ordering of bars across the main axis, as with standard bar charts.

The scalability of stacked bar charts is similar to standard bar charts in terms of the number of categories in the key attribute distributed across the main axis, but it is more limited for the key used to stack the subcomponents within the glyph. This idiom works well with several categories, with an upper limit of around one dozen.

Idiom	Stacked Bar Charts
What: Data	Multidimensional table: one quantitative value attribute, two categorical key attributes.
How: Encode	Bar glyph with length-coded subcomponents of value attribute for each category of secondary key attribute. Separate bars by category of primary key attribute.
Why: Task	Part-to-whole relationship, lookup values, find trends.
Scale	Key attribute (main axis): dozens to hundreds of levels. Key attribute (stacked glyph axis): several to one dozen

Example: Streamgraphs

Figure 7.6 shows a more complex generalized stacked graph display idiom with a dataset of music listening history, with one time series per artist counting the number of times their music was listened to each week [Byron and Wattenberg 08]. The streamgraph idiom shows derived geometry that emphasizes the continuity of the horizontal layers that represent the artists, rather than showing individual vertical glyphs that would emphasize listening behavior at a specific point in time.[1] The derived geometry is the result of a global computation, whereas individual glyphs can be constructed using only calculations about their own local region. The streamgraph idiom emphasizes the legibility of the individual streams with a deliberately organic silhouette, rather than using the horizontal axis as

Figure 7.6. Streamgraph of music listening history. From [Byron and Wattenberg 08, Figure 0].

---

[1]In this case, the main axis showing the quantitative time attribute is horizontal; both streamgraphs and stacked bar charts can be oriented either vertically or horizontally.

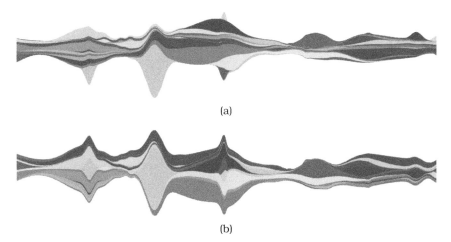

(a)

(b)

Figure 7.7. Streamgraphs with layers ordered by different derived attributes. (a) Volatility of artist's popularity. (b) Onset time when artist's music of first gained attention. From [Byron and Wattenberg 08, Figure 15].

the baseline. The shape of the layout is optimized as a trade-off between multiple factors, including the external silhouette of the entire shape, the deviation of each layer from the baseline, and the amount of wiggle in the baseline. The order of the layers is computed with an algorithm that emphasizes a derived value; Figure 7.7 shows the difference between sorting by the volatility of the artist's popularity, as shown in Figure 7.7(a), and the onset time when they begin to gain attention, as shown in Figure 7.7(b).

Streamgraphs scale to a larger number of categories than stacked bar charts, because most layers do not extend across the entire length of the timeline.

Idiom	Streamgraphs
What: Data	Multidimensional table: one quantitative value attribute (counts), one ordered key attribute (time), one categorical key attribute (artist).
What: Derived	One quantitative attribute (for layer ordering).
How: Encode	Use derived geometry showing artist layers across time, layer height encodes counts.
Scale	Key attributes (time, main axis): hundreds of time points. Key attributes (artists, short axis): dozens to hundreds

Example: Dot and Line Charts

The **dot chart** idiom is a visual encoding of one quantitative attribute using spatial position against one categorical attribute using point marks, rather than the line marks of a bar chart.[*] Figure 7.8(a) shows a dot chart of cat weight over time with the ordered variable of year on the horizontal axis and the quantitative weight of a specific cat on the vertical axis.

One way to think about a dot chart is like a scatterplot where one of the axes shows a categorical attribute, rather than both axes showing quantitative attributes. Another way to think about a dot chart is like a bar chart where the quantitative attribute is encoded with point marks rather than line marks; this way matches more closely with its standard use.

The idiom of **line charts** augments dot charts with line connection marks running between the points. Figure 7.8(b) shows a line chart for the same dataset side by side with the dot chart, plotting the weight of a cat over several years. The trend of constantly increasing weight, followed by loss after a veterinarian-imposed diet regime in 2010, is emphasized by the connecting lines.

★ The terms *dot chart* and *dot plot* are sometimes used as synonyms and have been overloaded. I use **dot chart** here for the idiom popularized by Cleveland [Becker et al. 96, Cleveland and McGill 84a], whereas Wilkinson [Wilkinson 99] uses **dot plot** for an idiom that shows distributions in a way similar to the histograms discussed in Section 13.4.1.

Idiom	Dot Charts
What: Data	Table: one quantitative value attribute, one ordered key attribute.
How: Encode	Express value attribute with aligned vertical position and point marks. Separate/order into horizontal regions by key attribute.

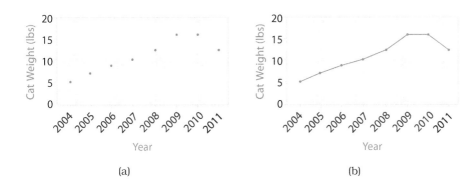

(a)   (b)

Figure 7.8. Line charts versus dot charts. (a) Dot charts use a point mark to show the value for each item. (b) Line charts use point marks connected by lines between them.

Idiom	Line Charts
What: Data	Table: one quantitative value attribute, one ordered key attribute.
How: Encode	Dot chart with connection marks between dots.
Why	Show trend.
Scale	Key attribute: hundreds of levels.

Line charts, dot charts, and bar charts all show one value attribute and one key attribute with a rectilinear spatial layout. All of these chart types are often augmented to show a second categorical attribute using color or shape channels. They use one spatial position channel to express a quantitative attribute, and use the other direction for a second key attribute. The difference is that line charts also use connection marks to emphasize the ordering of the items along the key axis by explicitly showing the relationship between one item and the next. Thus, they have a stronger implication of trend relationships, making them more suitable for the abstract task of spotting trends.

Line charts should be used for ordered keys but not categorical keys. A line chart used for categorical data violates the expressiveness principle, since it visually implies a trend where one cannot exist. This implication is so strong that it can override common knowledge. Zacks and Tversky studied how people answered questions about the categorical data type of gender versus the quantitative data type of age, as shown in Figure 7.9 [Zacks and Tversky 99]. Line charts for quantitative data elicited appropriate trend-related answers, such as "Height increases with age". Bar charts for quantitative data elicited equally appropriate discrete-comparison answers such as "Twelve year olds are taller than ten year olds". However, line charts for categorical data elicited inappropriate trend answers such as "The more male a person is, the taller he/she is".

When designing a line chart, an important question to consider is its **aspect ratio**: the ratio of width to height of the entire plot. While many standard charting packages simply use a square or some other fixed size, in many cases this default choice hides dataset structure. The relevant perceptual principle is that our ability to judge angles is more accurate at exact diagonals than at arbitrary directions. We can easily tell that an angle like 43° is off from the exact 45° diagonal, whereas we cannot tell 20° from 22°. The

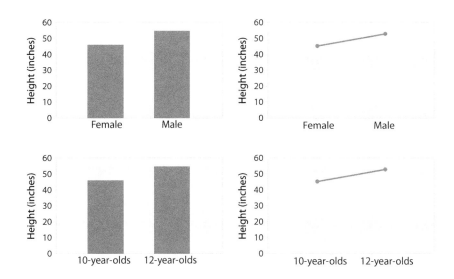

Figure 7.9. Bar charts and line charts both encode a single attribute. Bar charts encourage discrete comparisons, while line graphs encourage trend assessments. Line charts should not be used for categorical data, as in the upper right, because their implications are misleading. After [Zacks and Tversky 99, Figure 2].

idiom of **banking to 45°** computes the best aspect ratio for a chart in order to maximize the number of line segments that fall close to the diagonal. Multiscale banking to 45° automatically finds a set of informative aspect ratios using techniques from signal processing to analyze the line graph in the frequency domain, with the derived variable of the power spectrum. Figure 7.10 shows the classic sunspot example dataset. The aspect ratio close to 4 in Figure 7.10(a) shows the classic low-frequency oscillations in the maximum values of each sunspot cycle. The aspect ratio close to 22 in Figure 7.10(b) shows that many cycles have a steep onset followed by a more gradual decay. The blue line graphs the data itself, while the red line is the derived locally weighted regression line showing the trend.

7.5.2   Matrix Alignment: Two Keys

Datasets with two keys are often arranged in a two-dimensional **matrix alignment** where one key is distributed along the rows and

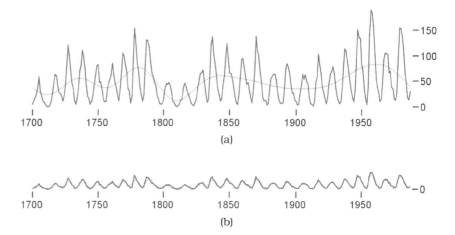

Figure 7.10. Sunspot cycles. The multiscale banking to 45° idiom exploits our orientation resolution accuracy at the diagonal. (a) An aspect ratio close to 4 emphasizes low-frequency structure. (b) An aspect ratio close to 22 shows higher-frequency structure: cycle onset is mostly steeper than the decay. From [Heer and Agrawala 06, Figure 5].

the other along the columns, so a rectangular cell in the matrix is the region for showing the item values.

Example: Cluster Heatmaps

The idiom of **heatmaps** is one of the simplest uses of the matrix alignment: each cell is fully occupied by an area mark encoding a single quantitative value attribute with color. Heatmaps are often used with bioinformatics datasets. Figure 7.11 shows an example where the keys are genes and experimental conditions, and the quantitative value attribute is the activity level of a particular gene in a particular experimental condition as measured by a microarray. This heatmap uses a diverging red–green colormap, as is common in the genomics domain. (In this domain there is a strong convention for the meaning of red and green that arose from raw images created by the optical microarray sensors that record fluorescence at specific wavelengths. Unfortunately, this choice causes problems for colorblind users.) The genes are a categorical attribute; experimental conditions might be categorical or might be ordered, for example if the experiments were done at successive times.

▶ See Section 10.3 for more on colormap design and Section 10.3.4 for the particular problem of colorblind-safe design.

The benefit of heatmaps is that visually encoding quantitative data with color using small area marks is very compact, so they are good for

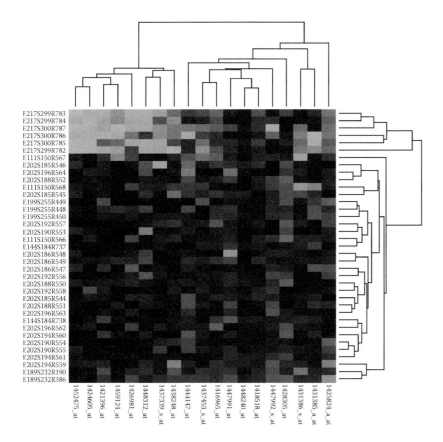

Figure 7.11. Cluster heatmap. A heatmap provides a compact summary of a quantitative value attribute with 2D matrix alignment by two key attributes and small area marks colored with a diverging colormap. The cluster heatmap includes trees drawn on the periphery showing how the matrix is ordered according to the derived data of hierarchical clusterings on its rows and columns.

providing overviews with high information density. The area marks in a heatmap are often several pixels on a side for easy distinguishability, so a matrix of 200 × 200 with 40,000 items is easily handled. The limit is area marks of a single pixel, for a dense heatmap showing one million items. Thus, the scalability limits are hundreds of levels for each of the two categorical key attributes. In contrast, only a small number of different levels of the quantitative attribute can be distinguishable, because of the limits on color perception in small noncontiguous regions: between 3 and 11 bins.[2]

---

[2]Again, all of the scalability analyses in this book related to screen-space limits assume a standard display size of 1000 × 1000, for a total of one million available pixels.

★ There are many synonyms for *matrix reordering*, including **matrix permutation**, **seriation**, **ordination**, **biclustering**, **coclustering**, and **two-mode clustering**. Matrix reordering has been studied in many different literatures beyond vis including cartography, statistics, operations research, data mining, bioinformatics, ecology, psychology, sociology, and manufacturing.

▶ Hierarchical clustering is further discussed in Section 13.4.1.

The *cluster heatmap* idiom combines the basic heatmap with **matrix reordering**, where two attributes are reordered in combination.* The goal of matrix reordering is to group similar cells in order to check for large-scale patterns between both attributes, just as the goal of reordering a single attribute is to see trends across a single one.

A **cluster heatmap** is the juxtaposed combination of a heatmap and two dendrograms showing the derived data of the cluster hierarchies used in the reodering. A **cluster hierarchy** encapsulates the complete history of how a clustering algorithm operates iteratively. Each leaf represents a cluster of a single item; the interior nodes record the order in which clusters are merged together based on similarity, with the root representing the single cluster of all items. A **dendrogram** is a visual encoding of tree data with the leaves aligned so that the interior branch heights are easy to compare. The final order used for the rows and the columns of the matrix view is determined by traversing the leaves in the trees.

Idiom	Heatmaps
What: Data	Table: two categorical key attributes (genes, conditions), one quantitative value attribute (activity level for gene in condition).
How: Encode	2D matrix alignment of area marks, diverging colormap.
Why: Task	Find clusters, outliers; summarize.
Scale	Items: one million. Categorical attribute levels: hundreds. Quantitative attribute levels: 3–11.

Idiom	Cluster Heatmaps
What: Derived	Two cluster hierarchies for table rows and columns.
How: Encode	Heatmap: 2D matrix alignment, ordered by both cluster hierarchies. Dendrogram: connection line marks for parent–child relationships in tree.

Example: Scatterplot Matrix

▶ SPLOMS are an example of small-multiple views, as discussed in Section 12.3.2.

A **scatterplot matrix (SPLOM)** is a matrix where each cell contains an entire scatterplot chart. A SPLOM shows all possible pairwise combinations of attributes, with the original attributes as the rows and columns. Figure 15.2 shows an example. In contrast to the simple heatmap matrix where each cell shows one attribute value, a SPLOM is an example of a more complex matrix where each cell shows a complete chart.

The key is a simple derived attribute that is the same for both the rows and the columns: an index listing all the attributes in the original dataset. The matrix could be reordered according to any ordered attribute. Usually only the lower or upper triangle of the matrix is shown, rather than the redundant full square. The diagonal cells are also typically omitted, since they would show the degenerate case of an attribute plotted against itself, so often labels for the axes are shown in those cells.

> ► Many extensions to SPLOMs have been proposed, including the scagnostics idiom using derived attributes described in Section 15.3 and the compact heatmap-style overview described in Section 15.5.

SPLOMs are heavily used for the abstract tasks of finding correlations, trends, and outliers, in keeping with the usage of their constituent scatterplot components.

Each scatterplot cell in the matrix requires enough room to plot a dot for each item discernably, so around 100×100 pixels is a rough lower bound. The scalability of a scatterplot matrix is thus limited to around one dozen attributes and hundreds of items.

Idiom	Scatterplot Matrix (SPLOM)
What: Data	Table.
What: Derived	Ordered key attribute: list of original attributes.
How: Encode	Scatterplots in 2D matrix alignment.
Why: Task	Find correlation, trends, outliers.
Scale	Attributes: one dozen. Items: dozens to hundreds.

7.5.3 Volumetric Grid: Three Keys

Just as data can be aligned in a 1D list or a 2D matrix, it is possible to align data in three dimensions, in a 3D volumetric grid. However, this design choice is typically not recommended for nonspatial data because it introduces many perceptual problems, including occlusion and perspective distortion. An alternative choice for spatial layout for multidimensional tables with three keys is recursive subdivision, as discussed below.

> ► The rationale for avoiding the unjustified use of 3D for nonspatial data is discussed in Section 6.3.

7.5.4 Recursive Subdivision: Multiple Keys

With multiple keys, it's possible to extend the above approaches by recursively subdividing the cell within a list or matrix. That is, ordering and alignment is still used in the same way, and containment is added to the mix.

There are many possibilities of how to partition data into separate regions when dealing with multiple keys. These design choices are discussed in depth in Section 12.4.

7.6   Spatial Axis Orientation

An additional design choice with the use of space is how to orient the spatial axes: whether to use rectilinear, parallel, or radial layout.

7.6.1   Rectilinear Layouts

In a **rectilinear** layout, regions or items are distributed along two perpendicular axes, horizontal and vertical spatial position, that range from minimum value on one side of the axis to a maximum value on the other side. Rectilinear layouts are heavily used in vis design and occur in many common statistical charts. All of the examples above use rectilinear layouts.

7.6.2   Parallel Layouts

> ▶ The potential drawbacks of using three spatial dimensions for abstract data are discussed in Section 6.3.

> ▶ The issue of separable versus integral channels is covered in Section 5.5.3.

The rectilinear approach of a scatterplot, where items are plotted as dots with respect to perpendicular axes, is only usable for two data attributes when high-precision planar spatial position is used. Even if the low-precision visual channel of a third spatial dimension is used, then only three data attributes can be shown using spatial position channels. Although additional nonspatial channels can be used for visual encoding, the problem of channel inseparability limits the number of channels that can be combined effectively in a single view. Of course, many tables contain far more than three quantitative attributes.

Example: Parallel Coordinates

> ★ In graphics terminology, the jagged line is a **polyline**: a connected set of straight line segments.

The idiom of **parallel coordinates** is an approach for visualizing many quantitative attributes at once using spatial position. As the name suggests, the axes are placed parallel to each other, rather than perpendicularly at right angles. While an item is shown with a dot in a scatterplot, with parallel coordinates a single item is represented by a jagged line that zigzags through the parallel axes, crossing each axis exactly once at the location of the item's value for the associated attribute.[*] Figure 7.12 shows an example of the same small data table shown both as a SPLOM and with parallel coordinates.

One original motivation by the designers of parallel coordinates was that they can be used for the abstract task of checking for correlation between attributes. In scatterplots, the visual pattern showing correlation is the tightness of the diagonal pattern formed by the item dots, tilting

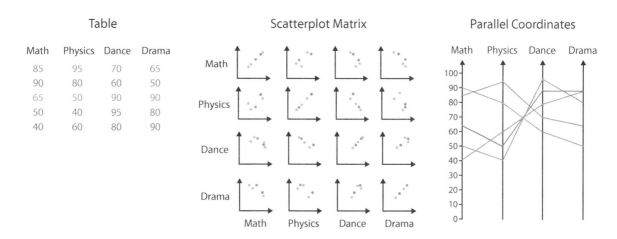

Figure 7.12. Comparison of scatterplot matrix and parallel coordinate idioms for a small data table. After [McGuffin 14].

upward for positive correlation and downward for negative correlation. If the attributes are not correlated, the points fall throughout the two-dimensional region rather than tightly along the diagonal. With parallel coordinates, correlation is also visible, but through different kinds of visual patterns, as illustrated in Figure 7.13. If two neighboring axes have high positive correlation, the line segments are mostly parallel. If two axes have high negative correlation, the line segments mostly cross over each other at a single spot between the axes. The pattern in between uncorrelated axes is a mix of crossing angles.

However, in practice, SPLOMs are typically easier to use for the task of finding correlation. Parallel coordinates are more often used for other tasks, including overview over all attributes, finding the range of individual attributes, selecting a range of items, and outlier detection. For example, in Figure 7.14(a), the third axis, labeled *manu_wrkrs*, has a broad range nearly to the normalized limits of *628.50* and *441.50*, whereas the range of values on the sixth axis, labeled *cleared*, is more narrow; the top item on the fourth axis, labeled *handgun_lc*, appears to be an outlier with respect to that attribute.

Parallel coordinates visually encode data using two dimensions of spatial position. Of course, any individual axis requires only one spatial dimension, but the second dimension is used to lay out multiple axes. The scalability is high in terms of the number of quantitative attribute values that can be discriminated, since the high-precision channel of planar spatial position is used. The exact number is roughly proportional to the screen space extent of the axes, in pixels. The scalability is moderate in

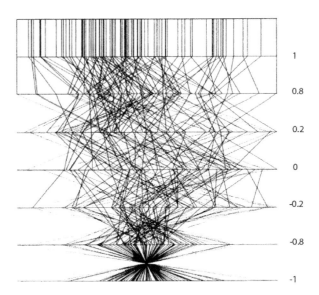

Figure 7.13. Parallel coordinates were designed to show correlation between neighboring axes. At the top, parallel lines show perfect positive correlation. At the bottom, all of the lines cross over each other at a single spot in between the two axes, showing perfect negative correlation. In the middle, the mix of crossings shows uncorrelated data. From [Wegman 90, Figure 3].

terms of number of attributes that can be displayed: dozens is common. As the number of attributes shown increases, so does the width required to display them, so a parallel coordinates display showing many attributes is typically a wide and flat rectangle. Assuming that the axes are vertical, then the amount of vertical screen space required to distinguish position along them does not change, but the amount of horizontal screen space increases as more axes are added. One limit is that there must be enough room between the axes to discern the patterns of intersection or parallelism of the line segments that pass between them.

The basic parallel coordinates idiom scales to showing hundreds of items, but not thousands. If too many lines are overplotted, the resulting occlusion yields very little information. Figure 7.14 contrasts the idiom used successfully with 13 items and 7 attributes, as in Figure 7.14(a), versus ineffectively with over 16,000 items and 5 attributes, as in Figure 7.14(b). In the latter case, only the minimum and maximum values along each axis can be read; it is nearly impossible to see trends, anomalies, or correlations.

▶ Section 13.4.1 covers scaling to larger datasets with hierarchical parallel coordinates.

The patterns made easily visible by parallel coordinates have to do with the pairwise relationships between neighboring axes. Thus, the cru-

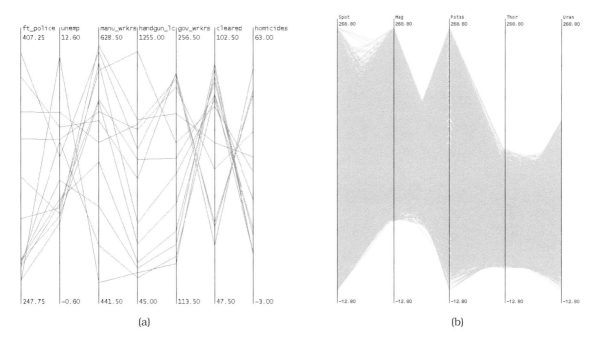

Figure 7.14. Parallel coordinates scale to dozens of attributes and hundreds of items, but not to thousands of items. (a) Effective use with 13 items and 7 attributes. (b) Ineffective use with over 16,000 items and 5 attributes. From [Fua et al. 99, Figures 1 and 2].

cial limitation of parallel coordinates is how to determine the order of the axes. Most implementations allow the user to interactively reorder the axes. However, exploring all possible configurations of axes through systematic manual interaction would be prohibitively time consuming as the number of axes grows, because of the exploding number of possible combinations.

Another limitation of parallel coordinates is training time; first-time users do not have intuitions about the meaning of the patterns they see, which must thus be taught explicitly. Parallel coordinates are often used in one of several multiple views showing different visual encodings of the same dataset, rather than as the only encoding. The combination of more familiar views such as scatterplots with a parallel coordinates view accelerates learning, particularly since linked highlighting reinforces the mapping between the dots in the scatterplots and the jagged lines in the parallel coordinates view.

▶ Multiple view design choices are discussed in Sections 12.3 and 12.4.

Idiom	Parallel Coordinates
What: Data	Table: many value attributes.
How: Encode	Parallel layout: horizontal spatial position used to separate axes, vertical spatial position used to express value along each aligned axis with connection line marks as segments between them.
Why: Tasks	Find trends, outliers, extremes, correlation.
Scale	Attributes: dozens along secondary axis. Items: hundreds.

7.6.3 Radial Layouts

In a **radial** spatial layout, items are distributed around a circle using the angle channel in addition to one or more linear spatial channels, in contrast to the rectilinear layouts that use only two spatial channels.

The natural coordinate system in radial layouts is **polar coordinates**, where one dimension is measured as an angle from a starting line and the other is measured as a distance from a center point. Figure 7.15 compares polar coordinates, as shown in Figure 7.15(a), with standard rectilinear coordinates, as shown in Figure 7.15(b). From a strictly mathematical point of view, rectilinear and radial layouts are equivalent under a particular kind of transformation: a box bounded by two sets of parallel lines is transformed into a disc where one line is collapsed to a point at the center and the other line wraps around to meet up with itself, as in Figure 7.15(c).

However, from a perceptual point of view, rectilinear and radial layouts are not equivalent at all. The change of visual channel has two major consequences from visual encoding principles alone. First, the angle channel is less accurately perceived than a rectilinear spatial position channel. Second, the angle channel is inherently cyclic, because the start and end point are the same, as opposed to the inherently linear nature of a position channel.* The expressiveness and effectiveness principles suggest some guidelines on the use of radial layouts. Radial layouts may be more effective than rectilinear ones in showing the periodicity of patterns, but encoding nonperiodic data with the periodic channel of angle

★ In mathematical language, the angle channel is **nonmonotonic**.

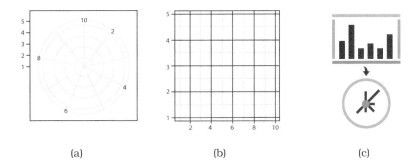

(a)   (b)   (c)

Figure 7.15. Layout coordinate systems. (a) Radial layouts use polar coordinates, with one spatial position and one angle channel. (b) Rectilinear layouts use two perpendicular spatial position channels. After [Wickham 10, Figure 8]. (c) Transforming rectilinear to radial layouts maps two parallel bounding lines to a point at the center and a circle at the perimeter.

may be misleading. Radial layouts imply an asymmetry of importance between the two attributes and would be inappropriate when the two attributes have equal importance.

Example: Radial Bar Charts

The same five-attribute dataset is encoded with a rectilinear bar chart in Figure 7.16(a) and with a radial alternative in Figure 7.16(b). In both cases, line marks are used to encode a quantitative attribute with the length channel, and the only difference is the radial versus the rectilinear orientation of the axes.

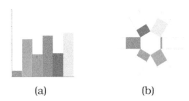

(a)   (b)

Figure 7.16. Radial versus rectilinear layouts. (a) Rectilinear bar chart. (b) Radial bar chart. After [Booshehrian et al. 11, Figure 4].

Idiom	Radial Bar Charts
What: Data	Table: one quantitative attribute, one categorical attribute.
How: Encode	Length coding of line marks; radial layout.

Example: Pie Charts

The most commonly used radial statistical graphic is the pie chart, shown in Figure 7.17(a). Pie charts encode a single attribute with area marks and the angle channel. Despite their popularity, pie charts are clearly problematic when considered according to the visual channel properties discussed in Section 5.5. Angle judgements on area marks are less accurate than length judgements on line marks. The wedges vary in width along the radial axis, from narrow near the center to wide near the outside, making the area judgement particularly difficult. Figure 7.17(b) shows a bar chart with the same data, where the perceptual judgement required to read the data is the high-accuracy position along a common scale channel. Figure 7.17(c) shows a third radial chart that is a more direct equivalent of a bar chart transformed into polar coordinates. The **polar area chart** also encodes a single quantitative attribute but varies the length of the wedge just as a bar chart varies the length of the bar, rather than varying the angle as in a pie chart.* The data in Figure 7.17 shows the clarity distribution of diamonds, where *I1* is worst and *IF* is best. These instances redundantly encode each mark with color for easier legibility, but these idioms could be used without color coding.

★ Synonyms for *polar area chart* are **rose plot** and **coxcomb plot**; these were first popularized by Florence Nightingale in the 19th century in her analysis of Crimean war medical data.

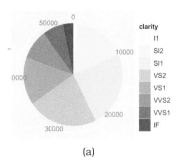
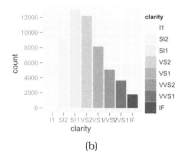
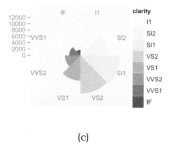

(a)   (b)   (c)

Figure 7.17. Pie chart versus bar chart accuracy. (a) Pie charts require angle and area judgements. (b) Bar charts require only high-accuracy length judgements for individual items. (c) Polar area charts are a more direct equivalent of bar charts, where the length of each wedge varies like the length of each bar. From [Wickham 10, Figures 15 and 16].

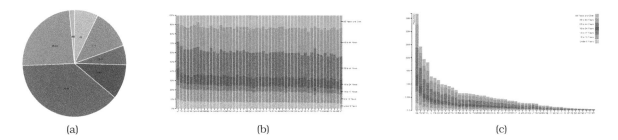

(a)   (b)   (c)

Figure 7.18. Relative contributions of parts to a whole. (a) A single pie chart shows the relative contributions of parts to a whole, such as percentages, using area judgements. (b) Each bar in a normalized stacked bar chart also shows the relative contributions of parts to a whole, with a higher-accuracy length encoding. (c) A stacked bar chart shows the absolute counts in each bar, in contrast to the percentages when each bar is normalized to the same vertical length. From http://bl.ocks.org/mbostock/3887235, http://bl.ocks.org/mbostock/3886208, http://bl.ocks.org/mbostock/3886394.

The most useful property of pie charts is that they show the relative contribution of parts to a whole. The sum of the wedge angles must add up to the 360° of a full circle, matching normalized data such as percentages where the parts must add up to 100%. However, this property is not unique to pie charts; a single bar in a normalized stacked bar chart can also be used to show this property with the more accurate channel of length judgements. A **stacked bar chart** uses a composite glyph made of stacking multiple sub-bars of different colors on top of each other; a **normalized stacked bar chart** stretches each of these bars to the maximum possible length, showing percentages rather than absolute counts. Only the lowest sub-bar in a stacked bar chart is aligned with the others in its category, allowing the very highest accuracy channel of position with respect to a common frame to be used. The other sub-bars use unaligned position, a channel that is less accurate than aligned position, but still more accurate than angle comparisons.

▶ Stacked glyphs are discussed further in Section 7.5.1.

Figure 7.18 compares a single pie chart showing aggregate population data for the entire United States to a normalized stacked bar chart and a stacked bar chart for all 50 states. An entire pie chart corresponds to a single bar in these charts; an equivalent display would be a list or matrix of pies.

Pie charts require somewhat more screen area than normalized stacked bar charts because the angle channel is lower precision than the length channel. The aspect ratio also differs, where a pie chart requires a square, whereas a bar chart requires a long and narrow rectangle. Both pie charts and normalized stacked bar charts are limited to showing a small number of categories, with a maximum of around a dozen categories.

Idiom	Pie Charts
What: Data	Table: one quantitative attribute, one categorical attribute.
Why: Task	Part–whole relationship.
How: Encode	Area marks (wedges) with angle channel; radial layout.
Scale	One dozen categories.

Idiom	Polar Area Charts
What: Data	Table: one quantitative attribute, one categorical attribute.
Why: Task	Part–whole relationship.
How: Encode	Area marks (wedges) with length channel; radial layout.
Scale	One dozen categories.

Idiom	Normalized Stacked Bar Charts
What: Data	Multidimensional table: one quantitative value attribute, two categorical key attributes.
What: Derived	One quantitative value attribute (normalized version of original attribute).
Why: Task	Part–whole relationship.
How: Encode	Line marks with length channel; rectilinear layout.
Scale	One dozen categories for stacked attribute. Several dozen categories for axis attribute.

Figure 7.19 compares rectilinear and radial layouts for 12 iconic time-series datasets: linear increasing, decreasing, shifted, single peak, single dip, combined linear and nonlinear, seasonal trends with different scales, and a combined linear and seasonal trend [Wickham et al. 12]. The rectilinear layouts in Figure 7.19(a) are more effective at showing the differences between the linear and nonlinear trends, whereas the radial plots Figure 7.19(b) are more effective at showing cyclic patterns.

A first empirical study on radial versus rectilinear grid layouts by Diehl et al. focused on the abstract task of memorizing positions of objects for a few seconds [Diehl et al. 10]. They compared performance in terms of accuracy and speed for rectilinear grids of rows and columns versus radial grids of sectors and rows. (The study did not investigate the effect of periodicity.) In general, rectilinear

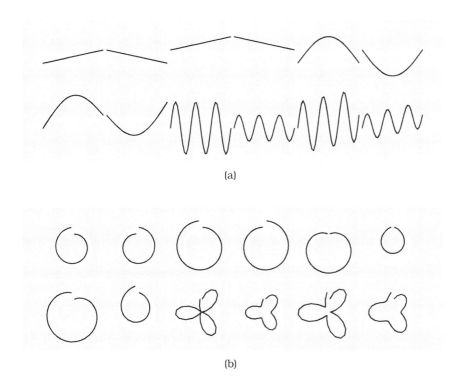

(a)

(b)

Figure 7.19. Glyphmaps. (a) Rectilinear layouts are more effective at showing the differences between linear and nonlinear trends. (b) Radial layouts are more effective at showing cyclic patterns. From [Wickham et al. 12, Figure 3].

layouts outperformed radial layouts: perception speed was faster, and accuracy tended to be better. However, their results also suggest the use of radial layouts can be justified when one attribute is more important than the other. In this case, the more important attribute should be encoded in the sectors and the less important attribute in the rings.

7.7 Spatial Layout Density

Another design choice with spatial visual encoding idioms is whether a layout is dense or sparse. A related, but not identical, choice is whether a layout is space-filling.

Dense

A **dense** layout uses small and densely packed marks to provide an overview of as many items as possible with very high information density.* A maximally dense layout has point marks that are only a single pixel in size and line marks that are only a single pixel in width. The small size of the marks implies that only the planar position and color channels can be used in visual encoding; size and shape are not available, nor are others like tilt, curvature, or shape that require more room than is available.

Section 15.4 presents a detailed case study of VisDB, a dense display for multidimensional tables using point marks.

★ A synonym for *dense* is **pixel-oriented**.

Example: Dense Software Overviews

Figure 7.20 shows the Tarantula system, a software engineering tool for visualizing test coverage [Jones et al. 02]. Dense displays using line marks have become popular for showing overviews of software source code. In these displays, the arrangement of the marks is dictated by the order and length of the lines of code, and the coloring of the lines encodes an attribute of interest.

Most of the screen is devoted to a large and dense overview of source code using one-pixel tall lines, color coded to show whether it passed, failed, or had mixed results when executing a suite of test cases. Although of course the code is illegible in the low-resolution overview, this view does convey some information about the code structure. Indentation and line length are preserved, creating visible landmarks that help orient the reader. The layout wraps around to create multiple horizontal columns out of a single long linear list. The small source code view in the lower left corner is a detail view showing a few lines of source code at a legible size; that is, a high-resolution view with the same color coding and same spatial position. The dense display scales to around ten thousand lines of code, handling around one thousand vertical pixels and ten columns.

The dataset used by Tarantula is an interesting complex combination of the software source code, the test results, and derived data. The original dataset is the software source code itself. Software code is highly structured text that is divided into numbered lines and has multiscale hierarchical structure with divisions into units such as packages, files, and methods. Most complex tasks in the software engineering domain require reading snippets of code line by line in the order that they were written by the programmer as a subtask, so changing or ignoring the order of lines within a method would not be an appropriate transformation. However, it's common with software engineering tasks that only a small number of the many units in a software project need to be read at any given time.

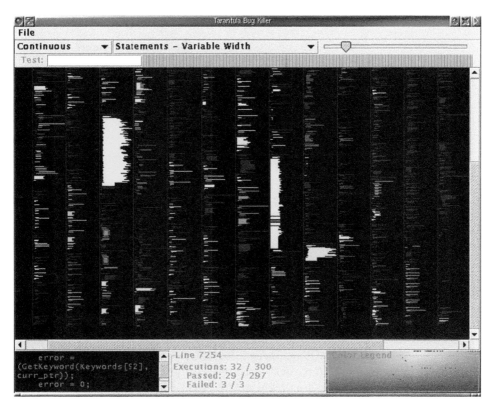

Figure 7.20. Tarantula shows a dense overview of source code with lines color coded by execution status of a software test suite. From [Jones et al. 02, Figure 4].

The design choice of a dense overview to provide orientation and a detail view where a small amount of text is shown legibly is thus reasonable.

    The original dataset also includes the tests, where each test has the categorical attribute of test or fail and is associated with a set of specific lines of the source code. Tarantula computes two derived quantitative attributes that are encoded with hue and brightness. The brightness encodes the percentage of coverage by the test cases, where dark lines represent low coverage and bright ones are high coverage. The hue encodes the relative percentage of passed versus failed tests.

    This example shows a full system that uses multiple idioms, rather than just a single idiom. For completeness, the what–why–how analysis instance includes material covered in later chapters, about the design choices of how to facet into multiple windows and how to reduce the amount of data shown.

> ▶ The overview and detail choice for multiple views is covered in Section 12.3.

Idiom	Dense Software Overviews
What: Data	Text with numbered lines (source code, test results log).
What: Derived	Two quantitative attributes (test execution results).
How: Encode	Dense layout. Spatial position and line length from text ordering. Color channels of hue and brightness.
Why: Task	Locate faults, summarize results and coverage.
Scale	Lines of text: ten thousand.
(How: Facet)	Same encoding, same dataset, global overview with detail showing subset of data, different resolutions, linking with color.
(How: Reduce)	Detail: filter to local neighborhood of selection

7.7.2 Space-Filling

A **space-filling** layout has the property that it fills all available space in the view, as the name implies. Any of the three geometric possibilties discussed above can be space-filling. Space-filling layouts typically use area marks for items or containment marks for relationships, rather than line or connection marks, or point marks. Examples of space-filling layouts using containment marks are the treemaps in Figures 9.8 and 9.9(f) and the nested circle tree in Figure 9.9(e). Examples of space-filling layouts using area marks and the spatial position channels are the concentric circle tree in Figure 9.9(d) and the icicle tree of Figure 9.9(b).

One advantage of space-filling approaches is that they maximize the amount of room available for color coding, increasing the chance that the colored region will be large enough to be perceptually salient to the viewer. A related advantage is that the available space representing an item is often large enough to show a label embedded within it, rather than needing more room off to the side.

In contrast, one disadvantage of space-filling views is that the designer cannot make use of **white space** in the layout; that is, empty space where there are no explicit visual elements. Many graphic design guidelines pertain to the careful use of white space for many reasons, including readability, emphasis, relative importance, and visual balance.

Space-filling layouts typically strive to achieve high information density. However, the property that a layout fills space is by no means a guarantee that is using space efficiently. More technically, the definition of space-filling is that the total area used by the layout is equal to the total area available in the view. There are many other possible metrics for analyzing the space efficiency of a layout. For instance, for trees, proposed metrics include the size of the smallest nodes and the area of labels on the nodes [McGuffin and Robert 10].

7.8 Further Reading

The Big Picture Many previous authors have proposed ways to categorize vis idioms. My framework was influenced by many of them, including an early taxonomy of the infovis design space [Card and Mackinlay 99] and tutorial on visual idioms [Keim 97], a book on the grammar of graphics [Wilkinson 05], a taxonomy of multidimensional multivariate vis [McGuffin 14], papers on generalized pair plots [Emerson et al. 12] and product plots [Wickham and Hofmann 11], and a recent taxonomy [Heer and Shneiderman 12]. Bertin's very early book *Semiology of Graphics* has been a mother lode of inspiration for the entire field and remains thought provoking to this day [Bertin 67].

History The rich history of visual representations of data, with particular attention to statistical graphics such as time-series line chart, the bar chart, the pie chart, and the circle chart, is documented at the extensive web site http://www.datavis.ca/milestones [Friendly 08].

Statistical Graphics A book by statistician Bill Cleveland has an excellent and extensive discussion of the use of many traditional statistical charts, including bar charts, line charts, dot charts, and scatterplots [Cleveland 93b].

Stacked Charts The complex stacked charts idiom of streamgraphs was popularized with the ThemeRiver system [Havre et al. 00]; later work analyzes their geometry and asthetics in detail [Byron and Wattenberg 08].

Bar Charts versus Line Charts A paper from the cognitive psychology literature provides guidelines for when to use bar charts versus line charts [Zacks and Tversky 99].

Banking to 45 Degrees **Early work proposed aspect ratio control by banking to 45° [Cleveland et al. 88, Cleveland 93b]; later work extended this idea to an automatic multiscale framework [Heer and Agrawala 06].**

Heatmaps and Matrix Reordering **One historical review covers the rich history of heatmaps, cluster heatmaps, and matrix reordering [Wilkinson and Friendly 09]; another covers matrix reordering and seriation [Liiv 10].**

Parallel Coordinates **Parallel coordinates were independently proposed at the same time by a geometer [Inselberg and Dimsdale 90, Inselberg 09] and a statistician [Wegman 90].**

Radial Layouts **Radial layouts were characterized through empirical user studies [Diehl et al. 10] and have also been surveyed [Draper et al. 09].**

Dense Layouts **Dense layouts have been explored extensively for many datatypes [Keim 00]. The SeeSoft system was an early dense layout for text and source code [Eick et al. 92]; Tarantula is a later system using that design choice [Jones et al. 02].**

Arrange Spatial Data

➔ **Use Given**

    ➔ Geometry

        ➔ *Geographic*

        ➔ *Other Derived*

    ➔ Spatial Fields

        ➔ *Scalar Fields (one value per cell)*

            ➔ *Isocontours*

            ➔ *Direct Volume Rendering*

        ➔ *Vector and Tensor Fields (many values per cell)*

            ➔ *Flow Glyphs (local)*

            ➔ *Geometric (sparse seeds)*

            ➔ *Textures (dense seeds)*

            ➔ *Features (globally derived)*

Figure 8.1. Design choices for using given spatial data: geometry or spatial fields.

Chapter 8

Arrange Spatial Data

8.1 The Big Picture

For datasets with spatial semantics, the usual choice for *arrange* is to *use* the given spatial information to guide the layout. In this case, the choices of *express*, *separate*, *order*, and *align* do not apply because the position channel is not available for directly encoding attributes. The two main spatial data types are geometry, where shape information is directly conveyed by spatial elements that do not necessarily have associated attributes, and spatial fields, where attributes are associated with each cell in the field. Figure 8.1 summarizes the major approaches for arranging these two data types. In a visualization context, geometry data typically either is geographic or has explicitly been derived from some other data type due to a design choice. For scalar fields with one attribute at each field cell, the two main visual encoding idiom families are isocontours and direct volume rendering. For both vector and tensor fields, with multiple attributes at each cell, there are four families of encoding idioms: flow glyphs that show local information, geometric approaches that compute derived geometry from a sparse set of seed points, texture approaches that use a dense set of seeds, and feature approaches where data is derived with global computations using information from the entire spatial field.

8.2 Why Use Given?

The common case with spatial data is that the given spatial position is the attribute of primary importance because the central tasks revolve around understanding spatial relationships. In these cases, the right visual encoding choice is to use the provided spatial position as the substrate for the visual layout, rather than to visually encode other attributes with marks using the spatial position channel. This choice may seem obvious from common sense alone. It also follows from the effectiveness principle, since the most effective channel of spatial position is used to show the most important aspect of the data, namely, the spatial relationships between elements in the dataset.

▶ The expressiveness principle is covered in Section 5.4.1.

Of course, it is possible that datasets with spatial attribute semantics might not have the task involving understanding of spatial relationships as the primary concern. In these cases, the question of which other attributes to encode with spatial position is once again on the table.

8.3 Geometry

Geometric data does not necessarily have attributes associated with it: it conveys shape information directly through the spatial position of its elements. The field of computer graphics addresses the problem of simply drawing geometric data. What makes geometry interesting in a vis context is when it is derived from raw source data as the result of a design decision at the abstraction level. A common source of derived geometry data is **geographic** information about the Earth. Geometry is also frequently derived from computations on spatial fields.

8.3.1 Geographic Data

Cartographers have grappled with design choices for the visual representation of geographic spatial data for many hundreds of years. The term **cartographic generalization** is closely related to the term *abstraction* as used in this book: it refers to the set of choices about how to derive an appropriate geometry dataset from raw data so that it is suitable for the intended task of the map users. This concept includes considerations discussed in this book such as filtering, aggregation, and level of detail. For example, a city might be indicated with a point mark in a map drawn at the scale of an entire country, or as an area mark with detailed geometric information showing the shape of its boundaries in a map at the scale of a city and its surrounding suburbs. Cartographic data includes what this book classifies as nonspatial information: for example, population data in the form of a table could be used to size code the point marks representing cities by their population.*

▶ Filtering, aggregation, and level of detail are discussed in Chapter 13.

★ The integration of nonspatial data with base spatial data is referred to as **thematic cartography** in the cartography literature.

Example: Choropleth Maps

A **choropleth** map shows a quantitative attribute encoded as color over regions delimited as area marks, where the shape of each region is determined by using given geometry. The region shapes might either be provided directly as the base dataset or derived from base data based on cartographic generalization choices. The major design choices for choropleths are how to construct the colormap, and what region boundaries to use.

Figure 8.2 shows an example of US unemployment rates from 2008 with a segmented sequential colormap. The white-to-blue colormap has a sequence of nine levels with monotonically decreasing luminance. The region granularity is counties within states.

▶ Sequential colormaps are covered in Section 10.3.2.

▶ The problem of spatial aggregation and its relationship to region boundaries is covered in Section 13.4.2.

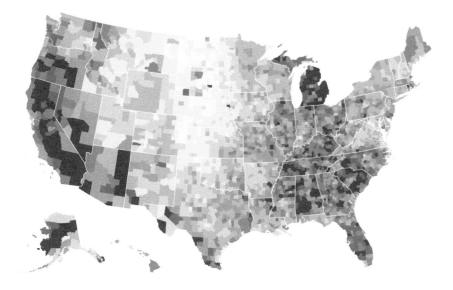

Figure 8.2. Choropleth map showing regions as area marks using given geometry, where a quantitative attribute is encoded with color. From http://bl.ocks.org/mbostock/4060606.

Idiom	Choropleth Map
What: Data	Geographic geometry data. Table with one quantitative attribute per region.
How: Encode	Space: use given geometry for area mark boundaries. Color: sequential segmented colormap.

8.3.2 Other Derived Geometry

Geometry data used in vis can also arise from spatial data that is not geographic. It is frequently derived through computations on spatial fields, as discussed below.

8.4 Scalar Fields: One Value

A scalar spatial field has a single value associated with each spatially defined cell. Scalar fields are often collected through medical imaging, where the measured value is radio-opacity in the case of computed tomography (CT) scans and proton density in the case of magnetic resonance imaging (MRI) scans.

There are three major families of idioms for visually encoding scalar fields: slicing, as shown in Figure 8.3(a); isocontours, as in shown Figure 8.3(b); and direct volume rendering, as shown in Figure 8.3(c). With the **isocontours** idiom, the derived data of lower-dimensional surface geometry is computed and then is shown using standard computer graphics techniques: typically 2D isosurfaces for a 3D field, or 1D isolines for a 2D field. With the **di-**

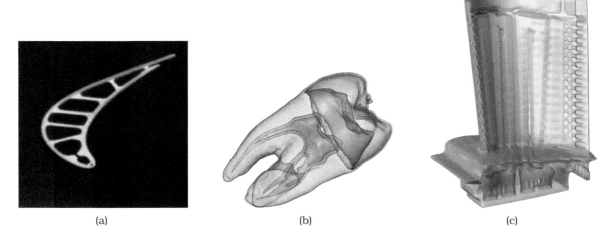

    (a)   (b)   (c)

Figure 8.3. Spatial scalar fields shown with three different idioms. (a) A single 2D slice of a turbine blade dataset. (b) Multiple semitransparent isosurfaces of a 3D tooth dataset. (c) Direct volume rendering of the entire 3D turbine dataset. From [Kniss 02, Figures 1.2 and 2.1b].

rect volume rendering idiom, the computation to generate an image from a particular 3D viewpoint makes use of all of the information in the full 3D spatial field. With the **slicing** idiom, information about only two dimensions at once is shown as an image; the slice might be aligned with the original axes of the spatial field or could have an arbitrary orientation in 3D space. In all of these cases, geometric navigation is the usual approach to interaction. The idioms can be combined, for example, by providing an interactively controllable widget for selecting the position and orientation of a slice embedded within direct volume rendering view.

> ▶ Slicing is also covered in Section 11.6.1, in the context of other idioms for attribute reduction.

> ▶ Section 11.5 covers geometric navigation.

8.4.1   Isocontours

A set of **isolines**, namely, lines that represent the contours of a particular level of the scalar value, can be derived from a scalar spatial field.* The isolines will occur far apart in regions of slow change and close together in regions of fast change but will never overlap; thus, contours for many different values can be shown simultaneously without excessive visual clutter. Color coding the regions between the contours with a sequential colormap yields a **contour plot**, as shown in Figure 6.9(c).

> ★ Synonyms for *isolines* are **contour lines** and **isopleths**.

Example: Topographic Terrain Maps

Topographic terrain maps are a familiar example of isolines in widespread use by the general public. They show the contours of equal elevation above sea level layered on top of the spatial substrate of a geographic map. Figure 8.4 shows contours every 10 meters, with nearly 80 levels in total. Small closed contours indicate mountain peaks, and the flat regions near sea level have no lines at all.

Idiom	Topographic Terrain Map
What: Data	2D spatial field; geographic data.
What: Derived	Geometry: set of isolines computed from field.
How: Encode	Use given geographic data geometry of points, lines, and region marks. Use derived geometry as line marks (blue).
Why: Tasks	Query shape.
Scale	Dozens of contour levels.

Figure 8.4. Topographic terrain map, with isolines in blue. From https://data.linz.govt.nz/layer/768-nz-mainland
-contours-topo-150k.

▶ Spatial navigation is
discussed further in Sec-
tion 11.5.

The idiom of **isosurfaces** transforms a 3D scalar spatial field
into one or more derived 2D surfaces that represent the contours
of a particular level of the scalar value. The resulting surface is
usually shown with interactive 3D navigation controls for changing
the viewpoint using rotation, zooming, and translation.

In the 3D case, simply showing all of the contour surfaces for
dozens of values at once is not feasible, because the outer contour
surfaces would occlude all of the inner ones. Thus, one crucial
question is how to determine which level will produce the most
useful result. Exploration is frequently supported by providing dynamic controls for changing the chosen level on the fly, for example, with a slider that allows the user to quickly change the contour
value from the minimum to the maximum value within the dataset.

With careful use of colors and transparency, several isosurfaces
can be shown at once. Figure 8.3(c) shows a 3D spatial field of a
human tooth with five distinguishable isosurfaces.

Example: Flexible Isosurfaces

The flexible isosurfaces idiom uses one more level of derived data, the *simplified contour tree*, to help users find structure that would be hidden with the standard single-level approach. There may be multiple disconnected isosurfaces for a given value: as the value changes, individual components could appear, join or split, or disappear. The **contour tree** tracks this evolution explicitly, showing how the connected isosurface components change their nesting structure. The full tree is very complex, as shown in Figure 8.5; there are over 1.5 million edges for the head dataset. Careful simplification of the tree yields a manageable result of under 100 edges, as shown in Figure 8.6. Using this structure for filtering and coloring via multiple coordinated views supports interactive exploration. Figure 8.6 shows several meaningful structures within the head that have been identified through this kind of exploration; seeing them all within the same 3D view allows users to understand both their shape and their relative position to each other.

▶ Filtering is discussed in Section 13.3.2 and coordinating multiple views is discussed in Section 12.3.

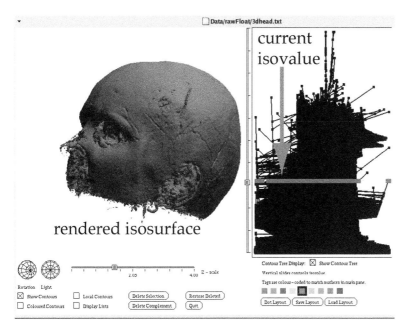

Figure 8.5. A full contour tree with over 1.5 million edges does not help the user explore isosurfaces. From [Carr et al. 04, Figure 1].

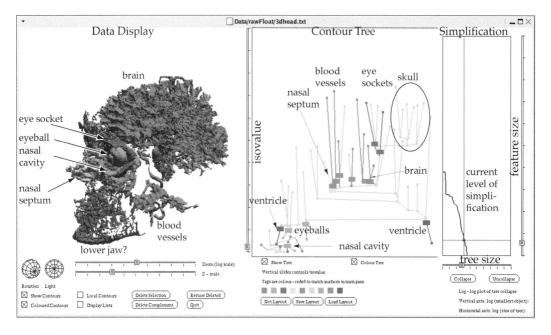

Figure 8.6. The flexible isosurfaces idiom uses the simplified contour tree of under 100 edges to help users identify meaningful structure. From [Carr et al. 04, Figure 1].

Idiom	**Flexible Isosurfaces**
What: Data	Spatial field.
What: Derived	Geometry: surfaces. Tree: simplified contour tree.
How: Encode	Surfaces: use given. Tree: line marks, vertical spatial position encodes isovalue.
Why: Tasks	Query shape.
Scale	One dozen contour levels.

8.4.2 Direct Volume Rendering

The **direct volume rendering** idiom creates an image directly from the information contained within the scalar spatial field, without deriving an intermediate geometric representation of a surface. The algorithmic issues involved in the computation are complex; a great deal of work has been devoted to the question of how to carry it out efficiently and correctly.

A crucial visual encoding design choice with direct volume rendering is picking the **transfer function** that maps changes in the scalar value to opacity and color. Finding the right transfer function manually often requires considerable trial and error because features of interest in the spatial field can be difficult to isolate: uninteresting regions in space may contain the same range of data values as interesting ones.

Example: Multidimensional Transfer Functions

The Simian system [Kniss 02, Kniss et al. 05] uses a derived space and a set of interactive widgets for specifying regions within it to help the user construct multidimensional transfer functions. The horizontal axis of this space corresponds to the data value of the scalar function. The vertical axis corresponds to the magnitude of the gradient,[1] the direction of fastest change, so that regions of high change can be distinguished from homogeneous regions. Figure 8.7(a) shows the information that can be considered part of a standard 1D transfer function: the histogram of the data values. The histogram shows both the linear scale values in black, and the log scale values in gray. In this view, only the basic three materials can be distinguished from each other: (A) air, (B) soft tissue, and (C) bone. Figure 8.7(b) shows that more information can be seen in the 2D joint histogram of the full derived space, where the vertial axis shows the gradient magnitude. This view is like a heatmap with very small area marks of one pixel each, where each cell shows a count of how many values occur within it using a grayscale colormap. In this view, boundaries between the basic surfaces also form distinguishable structures. Figure 8.7(c) presents a volume rendering of a head dataset using the resulting 2D transfer function, showing examples of the base materials and these three boundaries: (D) air–tissue, (E) tissue–bone, and (F) air–bone. A cutting plane has been positioned to show the internal structure of the head.

► The histogram visual encoding idiom is covered in Section 13.4.1.

► Cutting planes are covered in Section 11.6.2.

Idiom	Multidimensional Transfer Functions
What: Data	3D spatial field.
What: Derived	3D spatial field: gradient of original field.
What: Derived	Table: two key attributes, values binned from min to max for both data and derived data. One derived quantitative value attribute (item count per bin).
How: Encode	3D view: use given spatial field data, color and opacity from multidimensional transfer function. Joint histogram view: area marks in 2D matrix alignment, grayscale sequential colormap.

[1]Mathematically, the gradient is the first derivative.

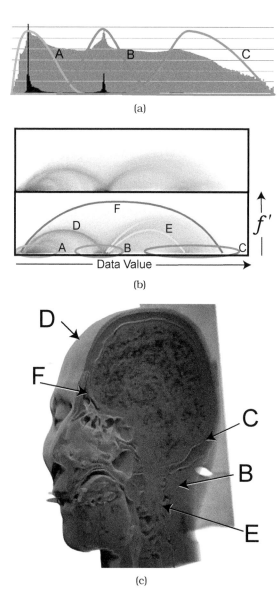

(a)

(b)

(c)

Figure 8.6. Simian allows users to construct multidimensional transfer functions for direct volume rendering using a derived space. (a) The standard 1D histogram can show the three basic materials: (A) air, (B) soft tissue, and (C) bone. (b) The full 2D derived space allows material boundaries to be distinguished as well. (c) Volume rendering of head dataset using the resulting 2D transfer function, showing material boundaries of (D) air–tissue, (E) tissue–bone, and (F) air–bone. From [Kniss et al. 05, Figure 9.1].

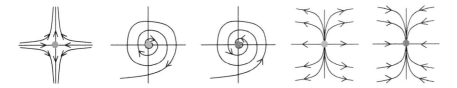

Figure 8.7. The main types of critical points in a flow field: saddle, circulating sinks, circulating sources, noncirculating sinks, and noncirculating sources. From [Tricoche et al. 02, Figure 1].

8.5 Vector Fields: Multiple Values

Vector field datasets are often associated with the application domain of computational fluid dynamics (CFD), as the outcome of flow simulations or measurements. Flow vis in particular deals with a specific kind of vector field, a velocity field, that contains information about both direction and magnitude at each cell. The three common cases are purely 2D spatial fields, purely 3D spatial fields, and the intermediate case of flow on a 2D surface embedded within 3D space. Time-varying flow datasets are called **unsteady**, as opposed to **steady** flows where the behavior does not change over time.

One of the features of interest in flows are the **critical points**, the points in a flow field where the velocity vanishes. They are classified by the behavior of the flow in their neighborhoods: the three main types are attracting **sources**, repelling **sinks**, and **saddle points** that attract from one direction and repel from another.[2] Also, sources and sinks may or may not have circulation around them.* Figure 8.7 shows these five types of critical points.

There are four major families of vector field spatial visual encoding idioms. The *flow glyph* idioms show local information at each cell. There are two major methods based on the derived data of tracing particle trajectories, either the *geometric flow* approach using a sparse set of seed points or the *texture flow* approach with a dense set of seeds. The *feature flow* approach uses global computation across the entire field to explicitly detect features, and these derived features are usually visually encoded with glyphs or geometry. Finally, a vector field can be reduced to a scalar field,

★ In flow vis, a source or sink with no circulation around it is called a **node**, and one with circulation is called a **focus**. I avoid these overloaded terms; in this book, I reserve *node* and *link* for network data and *focus+context* for the family of idioms that embed such information together in a single view.

---

[2]A fourth possible type is a *center* where the flow is perfectly circular, but this type is less important in practice.

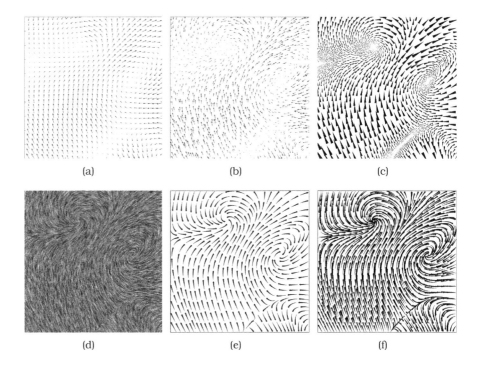

Figure 8.8. An empirical study compared human response to six different 2D flow vis idioms. (a) arrow glyphs on a regular grid. (b) arrow glyphs on a jittered grid. (c) triangular wedge glyphs inspired by oil painting strokes. (d) dense texture-based Line Integral Convolution (LIC). (e) curved arrow glyphs with image-guided streamline seeding. (f) curved arrow glyphs with regular grid streamline seeding. From [Laidlaw et al. 05, Figure 1].

allowing any of the scalar field idioms covered in the previous section to be used, such as direct volume rendering or isocontouring.

Laidlaw et al. conducted an empirical study comparing six visual encoding idioms for 2D vector fields [Laidlaw et al. 05]. Figures 8.8(a), 8.8(b), and 8.8(c) show local glyph idioms, Figure 8.8(d) shows a dense texture idiom, and Figures 8.8(e) and 8.8(f) show geometric idioms. The three tasks considered were finding all of the critical points and identifying their types; identifying what type of critical point is at a specific location; and predicting where a particle starting at a specified point will end up being transported.[*] While none of the idioms outperformed all of the others for all tasks, the two local glyph idioms using arrows fared worst.

★ The technical term for the transport of a particle within a fluid is **advection**.

8.5.1   Flow Glyphs

The **flow glyph** idioms show local information about a cell in the field using an object with internal substructure; one of the most basic choices is an arrow, as shown in Figure 8.8(a). An arrow glyph encodes magnitude with the length of the stem, direction with arrow orientation, and disambiguates directionality with the arrowhead on one side of the stem. In addition to the visual encoding of the glyphs themselves, another key design choice with this idiom is how many glyphs to show: a glyph for each cell in the field, or only a small subset. A limitation of glyph-based approaches is the problem of occlusion in 3D fields.

8.5.2   Geometric Flow

The **geometric flow** idioms compute derived geometric data from the original field using trajectories computed from a sparse set of seed points and then directly show the derived geometry. One major algorithmic issue is how to compute the trajectories.* A crucial design choice is the seeding strategy: poor choices result in visual clutter and occlusion problems, but a well-chosen strategy supports inspection of both 2D and 3D fields. In the 3D case, geometric navigation is a useful interaction idiom that helps with the shape and structure understanding tasks.

> ★ The geometric approaches typically approximate using numerical integration, and so this idiom is sometimes called **integration-based flow**.

The geometric flow idioms are based on intuitions from physical experiments that can be conducted in real-world settings such as wind tunnels, and the simpler cases all have direct physical analogs. The trajectory that a specific particle will follow is called a **streamline** for a steady field and a **pathline** for an unsteady (time-varying) field. The physical analogy is the path that a single ball would follow as time passes. In contrast, a **streakline** traces all the particles that pass through a specific point in space; the analogy is a trail of smoke particles released at different times from the same spot. A **timeline** is formed by connecting a front of pathlines over time: the analogy is placing several balls at the same time at different locations along a curve, and tracing the path between them at a later time step. All of these geometric structures have counterparts one dimension higher, formed by seeding from a curve rather than from a single point: **stream surfaces**, **path surfaces**, **streak surfaces**. Similarly, **time surfaces** are a generalization that is formed by connecting particles released from a surface rather than a curve.

Example: Similarity-Clustered Streamlines

Figure 8.9 shows a seeding strategy for streamlines and pathlines based on a derived similarity measure, proposed by McLoughlin et al. [McLoughlin et al. 13]. First, the derived geometry data of streamlines or pathlines is computed from the original 3D vector field. A set of derived attributes is computed for each streamline or pathline: curvature, namely, the curve's deviation from a straight line; torsion, namely, how much the curve bends

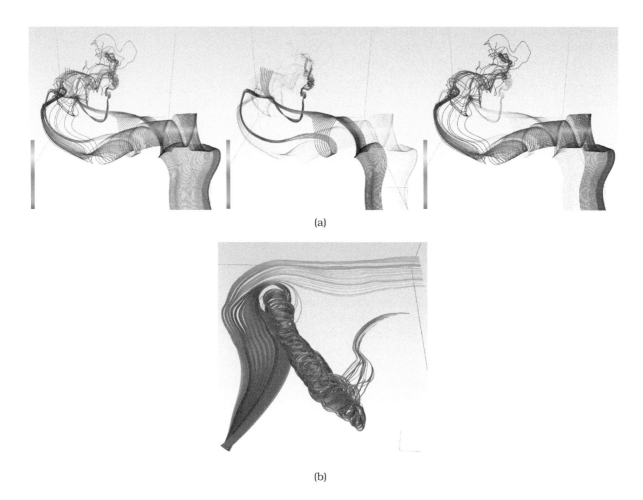

(a)

(b)

Figure 8.9. Geometric flow vis idioms showing a sparse set of particle trajectories, with seeding and coloring according to similarity. (a) Streamlines: all clusters equally opaque; purple cluster emphasized; red cluster emphasized. (b) Pathlines, colored by three clusters. From [McLoughlin et al. 13, Figures 7 and 11c].

out of its plane; and tortuosity, namely, how twisted the curve is. These three attributes are combined with a complex algorithm to form a fourth derived attribute, the line's *signature*. These signatures are used to construct a similarity matrix, and that is in turn used to create a cluster hierarchy. The user can interactively filter which lines are seeded according to cluster membership so that as much detail as possible is preserved. The streamline or pathline spatial geometry is drawn in 3D. Each line is colored according to its cluster membership, and the user has interactive control of how many clusters to show. The user can also select a cluster to emphasize as a foreground layer with high opacity, where the others are drawn in low opacity to form a translucent background layer. Figure 8.9(a) shows three views: all of the streamlines at full opacity, the purple cluster emphasized, and the red cluster emphasized. Figure 8.9(b) shows an unsteady field, with three clusters of pathlines. The interaction idiom of geometric 3D navigation allows the user to rotate to any desired viewpoint.

> ▶ Filtering is covered in Section 13.3.

> ▶ Layering is covered in Section 12.5.

Idiom	Similarity-Clustered Streamlines
What: Data	Spatial field: 3D vector field.
What: Derived	Geometry: streamlines or pathlines.
What: Derived	One attribute per streamline/pathline (signature).
What: Derived	Cluster hierarchy of streamlines/pathlines.
How: Encode	Use derived geometry of lines, color, and opacity according to cluster.
Why: Tasks	Find features, query shape.
Scale	Field: millions of samples. Geometry: hundreds of streamlines.

8.5.3   Texture Flow

The **texture flow** idioms also rely on particle tracing, but with dense coverage across the entire field rather than from a carefully selected set of seed points.* They are most commonly used for 2D fields or fields on 2D surfaces. Figure 8.8(d) shows an example of the Line Integral Convolution (LIC) idiom, where white noise is smeared according to particle flow [Cabral and Leedom 93].

> ★ The name of **texture** arises from a set of data structures and algorithms in computer graphics that efficiently manipulate high-resolution images without intermediate geometric representations; these operations are supported in hardware on modern machines.

8.5.4   Feature Flow

The **feature flow** vis idioms rely on global computations across the entire vector field to explicitly locate all instances of specific structures of interest, such as critical points, vortices, and shock

★ An alternative name for *feature-based flow* is **topological flow** vis.

waves.* The goal is to partition the field into subregions where the qualitative behavior is similar. The resulting derived data is then directly visually encoded with one of the previously described flow idioms, for a geometric representation or a glyph showing each feature. In contrast, the previous idioms are intended to help the user to infer the existence of these structures, but they are not necessarily shown directly. A major challenge of feature-based flow vis is the algorithmic problem of computationally locating these structures efficiently and correctly.

8.6 Tensor Fields: Many Values

Flow vis is concerned with both vector and tensor data. Tensor fields typically contain a matrix at each cell in the field, capturing more complex structure than what can be expressed in a vector field.[3] Tensor fields can measure properties such as stress, conductivity, curvature, and diffusivity. One example of a tensor field is diffusion tensor data, where the extent to which the rate of water diffusion varies as a function of direction is measured with magnetic resonance imaging. This kind of medical imaging is often used to study the architecture of the human brain and find abnormalities.

All of the idiom families used for vector fields are also used for tensor fields: local *glyphs*, sparse *geometry*, dense *textures*, and explicitly derived *features*.

One major family of idioms for visually encoding tensor fields is **tensor glyphs**, where local information at cells in the field is shown by controlling the shape, orientation, and appearance of a base geometric shape. Just as with vector glyphs, another design choice is whether to show a glyph in all cells or only a carefully chosen subset. While the glyph idiom is the same fundamental design choice for both tensor and vector glyphs, tensor glyphs necessarily have a more complex geometric structure because they must encode more information.

Example: Ellipsoid Tensor Glyphs

Tensor quantities can be naturally decomposed into orientation and shape information; these quantities can be visually encoded with a 3D glyph.[4] A

---

[3] Mathematically, in the 3D case second-order tensors are 3×3 matrices that may be symmetric or nonsymmetric.

[4] Mathematically, the shape information can be computed from the eigenvalues and the orientation from the eigenvectors.

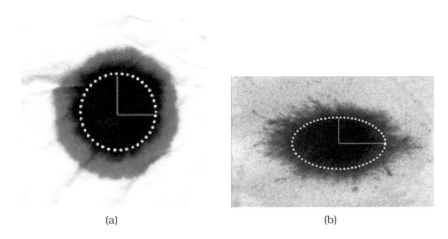

(a)   (b)

Figure 8.10. 2D diffusion illustrated with ink and paper. (a) Isotropic Kleenex. (b) Anisotropic newspaper.

shape may be **isotropic**, where each direction is the same, or **anisotropic**, where there is a directional asymmetry. For diffusion in biological tissue, anisotropy occurs when the water moves through tissue faster in some directions than in others; Figure 8.10 shows a physical example of the 2D case where two different kinds of paper are stained with ink. There is isotropic diffusion through Kleenex, where the ink spreads at the same rate in all directions as shown in Figure 8.10(a), whereas the newspaper has a preferred direction where the ink moves faster with anisotropic diffusion as shown in Figure 8.10(b).

Figure 8.11 shows the three basic shapes that are possible in 3D. The fully isotropic case is a perfect sphere, as in Figure 8.11(a); the partially anisotropic planar case is a sphere flattened in only one direction, as in

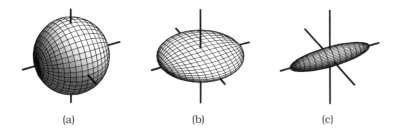

(a)   (b)   (c)

Figure 8.11. Ellipsoid glyphs can show three basic shapes. (a) Isotropic: sphere. (b) Partially anisotropic: planar. (c) Fully anisotropic: linear. From [Kindlmann 04, Figure 1].

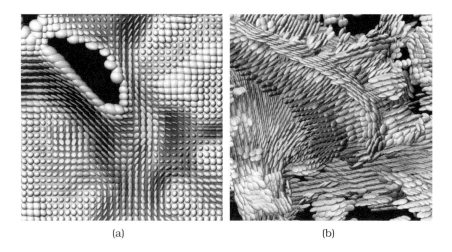

(a)   (b)

Figure 8.12. Ellipsoid glyphs show shape and orientation of tensors at each cell in a field. (a) 2D slice. (b) 3D field, with isotropic glyphs filtered out. From [Kindlmann 04, Figures 10a and 11a].

Figure 8.11(b); and the completely anisotropic linear case is flattened differently each of two directions to become a cigar-shaped ellipsoid, as in Figure 8.11(c). One way to encode this shape information in a 3D glyph is with an ellipsoid, where the direction that it points is an intuitive way to encode the orientation. Figure 8.12(a) shows using ellipsoid glyphs to inspect a 2D slice of a tensor field with the orientation attributes also used for coloring. In the 3D case shown in Figure 8.12(b), the isotropic glyphs are filtered out so that the anisotropic regions are visible.

Ellipsoid tensor glyphs have the weakness that different glyphs cannot be disambiguated from a single viewpoint; superquadric tensor glyphs are a more sophisticated approach that resolve this ambiguity [Kindlmann 04].

Idiom	Ellipsoid Tensor Glyphs
What: Data	Spatial field: 3D tensor field.
What: Derived	Three quantitative attributes: tensor shape. Three vectors: tensor orientation.
How: Encode	Glyph showing six derived attributes, color and opacity according to cluster.

The **geometric tensor flow** visual encoding idioms are based on similar intuitions as in the vector case, by computing sparse derived geometry such as hyperstreamlines or tensorlines; the same situation holds for the **texture tensor flow** idioms. Similarly, **feature tensor flow** idioms explicitly detect features in tensor fields, where simpler cases that occur in vector fields are generalized to the more complex possibilities of tensor fields.

8.7   Further Reading

History   Thematic cartography, where statistical data is overlaid on geographic maps, blossomed in the 19th century. Choropleth maps, where shading is used to show a variable of interest, were introduced, as were dot maps and proportional symbol maps. The history of thematic cartography, including choropleth maps, is documented at the extensive web site http://www.datavis.ca/milestones [Friendly 08].

Cartography   A more scholarly but still accessible historical review of thematic cartography is structured around the ideas of marks and channels [MacEachren 79]; MacEachren's full-length book contains a deep analysis of cartographic representation, visualization, and design with respect to both cognition and semiotics [MacEachren 95]. Slocum's textbook on cartography is a good general reference for the vis audience [Slocum et al. 08].

Spatial Fields   One overview chapter covers a broad set of spatial field visual encoding and interaction idioms [Schroeder and Martin 05]; another covers isosurfaces and direct volume rendering in particular [Kaufman and Mueller 05].

Isosurfaces   Edmond Halley presented isolines in 1686 and contour plots in 1701. The standard algorithm for creating isosurfaces is Marching Cubes, proposed in 1987 [Lorensen and Cline 87]; a survey covers some of the immense amount of followup work that has occurred since then [Newman and Yi 06]. Flexible isosurfaces are discussed in a paper [Carr et al. 04].

Direct Volume Rendering   The *Real-Time Volume Graphics* book is an excellent springboard for further investigation of direct volume rendering [Engel et al. 06]. The foundational algorithm papers both appeared in 1988 from two independent sources: Pixar [Drebin et al. 88], and UNC Chapel Hill [Levoy 88]. The Simian system supports multidimensional transfer function construction [Kniss 02, Kniss et al. 05].

Vector Fields An overview chapter provides a good introduction to flow vis [Weiskopf and Erlebacher 05]. A series of state-of-the-art reports provide more detailed discussion of three flow vis idioms families: geometric [McLouglin et al. 10], texture based [Laramee et al. 04], and feature based [Post et al. 03]. The foundational algorithm for texture-based flow vis is Line Integral Convolution (LIC) [Cabral and Leedom 93].

Tensor Fields The edited collection *Visualization and Processing of Tensor Fields* contains 25 chapters on different aspects of tensor field vis, providing a thorough overview [Weickert and Hagen 06]. One of these chapters is a good introduction to diffusion tensor imaging in particular [Vilanova et al. 06], including a comparison between ellipsoid tensor glyphs and superquadric tensor glyphs [Kindlmann 04].

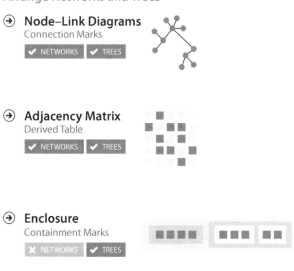

Figure 9.1. Design choices for arranging networks.

Chapter 9

Arrange Networks and Trees

The Big Picture

This chapter covers design choices for arranging network data in space, summarized in Figure 9.1. The node–link diagram family of visual encoding idioms uses the connection channel, where marks represent links rather than nodes. The second major family of network encoding idioms are matrix views that directly show adjacency relationships. Tree structure can be shown with the containment channel, where enclosing link marks show hierarchical relationships through nesting.

9.2   Connection: Link Marks

The most common visual encoding idiom for tree and network data is with **node–link diagrams**, where nodes are drawn as point marks and the links connecting them are drawn as line marks. This idiom uses connection marks to indicate the relationships between items. Figure 9.2 shows two examples of trees laid out as node–link diagrams. Figure 9.2(a) shows a tiny tree of 24 nodes laid out with a triangular vertical node–link layout, with the root on the top and the leaves on the bottom. In addition to the connection marks, it uses vertical spatial position channel to show the depth in the tree. The horizontal spatial position of a node does not directly encode any attributes. It is an artifact of the layout algorithm's calculations to ensure maximum possible information density while guaranteeing that there are no edge crossings or node overlaps [Buchheim et al. 02].

Figure 9.2(b) shows a small tree of a few hundred nodes laid out with a spline radial layout. This layout uses essentially the same algorithm for density without overlap, but the visual encoding is radial rather than rectilinear: the depth of the tree is encoded as distance away from the center of the circle. Also, the links of

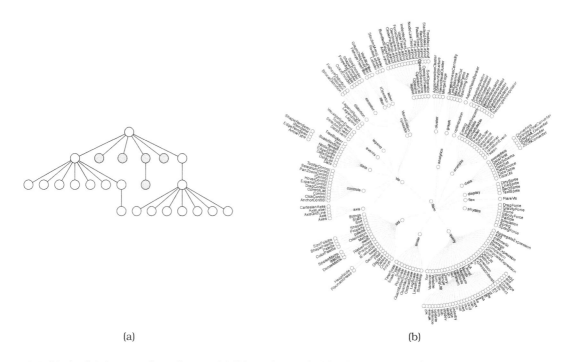

(a)   (b)

Figure 9.2. Node–link layouts of small trees. (a) Triangular vertical for tiny tree. From [Buchheim et al. 02, Figure 2d]. (b) Spline radial layout for small tree. From http://mbostock.github.com/d3/ex/tree.html.

the graph are drawn as smoothly curving **splines** rather than as straight lines.

Figure 9.3(a) shows a larger tree of 5161 nodes laid out as a rectangular horizontal node–link diagram, with the root on the left and the leaves stretching out to the right. The edges are colored with a purple to orange continuous colormap according to the Strahler centrality metric discussed in Section 3.7.2. The spatial layout is fundamentally the same as the triangular one, but from this zoomed-out position the edges within a subtree form a single perceptual block where the spacing in between them cannot be seen. Figure 9.3(b) shows the same tree laid out with the BubbleTree algorithm [Grivet et al. 06]. BubbleTree is a radial rather than rectilinear approach where subtrees are laid out in full circles rather than partial circular arcs. Spatial position does encode information about tree depth, but as relative distances to the center of the parent rather than as absolute distances in screen space.

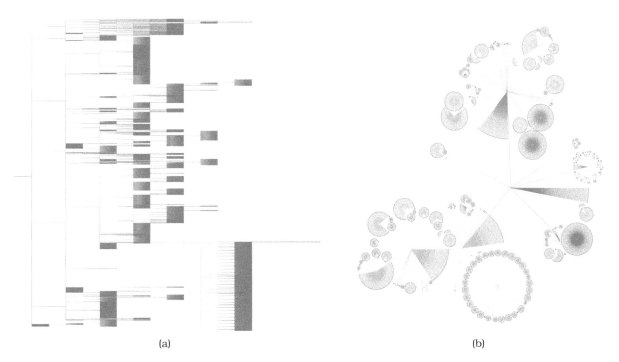

Figure 9.3. Two layouts of a 5161-node tree. (a) Rectangular horizontal node–link layout. (b) BubbleTree node–link layout.

Networks are also very commonly represented as node–link diagrams, using connection. Nodes that are directly connected by a single link are perceived as having the tightest grouping, while nodes with a long path of multiple hops between them are less closely grouped. The number of **hops** within a path—the number of individual links that must be traversed to get from one node to another—is a network-oriented way to measure distances. Whereas distance in the 2D plane is a continuous quantity, the network-oriented distance measure of hops is a discrete quantity. The connection marks support path tracing via these discrete hops.

Node–link diagrams in general are well suited for tasks that involve understanding the network **topology**: the direct and indirect connections between nodes in terms of the number of hops between them through the set of links. Examples of topology tasks include finding all possible paths from one node to another, finding the shortest path between two nodes, finding all the adjacent nodes one hop away from a target node, and finding nodes that act as a bridge between two components of the network that would otherwise be disconnected.

Node–link diagrams are most often laid out within a two-dimensional planar region. While it is algorithmically straightforward to design 3D layout algorithms, it is rarely an effective choice because of the many perceptual problems discussed in Section 6.3, and thus should be carefully justified.

Example: Force-Directed Placement

One of the most widely used idioms for node–link network layout using connection marks is **force-directed placement**. There are many variants in the force-directed placement idiom family; in one variant, the network elements are positioned according to a simulation of physical forces where nodes push away from each other while links act like springs that draw their endpoint nodes closer to each other.* Many force-directed placement algorithms start by placing nodes randomly within a spatial region and then iteratively refine their location according to the pushing and pulling of these simulated forces to gradually improve the layout. One strength of this approach is that a simple version is very easy to implement. Another strength is that it is relatively easy to understand and explain at a conceptual level, using the analogy of physical springs.

★ *Force-directed placement* is also known as **spring embedding**, **energy minimization**, or **nonlinear optimization**.

Force-directed network layout idioms typically do not directly use spatial position to encode attribute values. The algorithms are designed to minimize the number of distracting artifacts such as edge crossings and node overlaps, so the spatial location of the elements is a side effect of the computation rather than directly encoding attributes. Figure 9.4(a) shows a node–link layout of a graph, using the idiom of force-directed placement. Size and color coding for nodes and edges is also common. Figure 9.4(a) shows size coding of edge attributes with different line widths, and Figure 9.4(b) shows size coding for node attributes through different point sizes.

Analyzing the visual encoding created by force-directed placement is somewhat subtle. Spatial position does not directly encode any attributes of either nodes or links; the placement algorithm uses it indirectly. A tightly interconnected group of nodes with many links between them will often tend to form a visual clump, so spatial proximity does indicate grouping through a strong perceptual cue. However, some visual clumps may simply be artifacts: nodes that have been pushed near each other because they were repelled from elsewhere, not because they are closely connected in the network. Thus, proximity is sometimes meaningful but sometimes arbitrary; this ambiguity can mislead the user. This situation is a specific instance of the general problem that occurs in all idioms where spatial position is implicitly chosen rather than deliberately used to encode information.

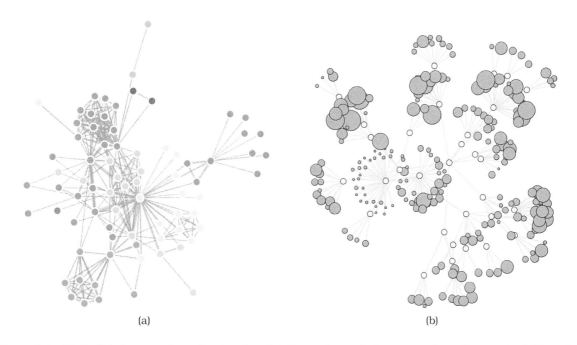

             (a)   (b)

Figure 9.4. Node–link layouts of small networks. (a) Force-directed placement of small network of 75 nodes, with size coding for link attributes. (b) Larger network, with size coding for node attributes. From http://bl.ocks.org/mbostock/4062045 and http://bl.ocks.org/1062288.

One weakness of force-directed placement is that the layouts are often **nondeterministic**, meaning that they will look different each time the algorithm is run, rather than **deterministic** approaches such as a scatterplot or a bar chart that yield an identical layout each time for a specific dataset. Most idioms that use randomness share this weakness.[1] The problem with nondeterministic visual encodings is that spatial memory cannot be exploited across different runs of the algorithm. Region-based identifications such as "the stuff in the upper left corner" are not useful because the items placed in that region might change between runs. Moreover, the randomness can lead to different proximity relationships each time, where the distances between the nodes reflect the randomly chosen initial positions rather than the intrinsic structure of the network in terms of how the links connect the nodes. Randomness is particularly tricky with dynamic layout, where the network is a dynamic stream with nodes and links that are added, removed, or changed rather than a static file that is fully available when the layout begins. The visual encoding goal of disrupting the spatial stability of the layout as little as possible, just enough

---
[1]There are simple algorithmic solutions for supporting repeatability with most random layouts by using the same *seed* for the pseudorandom number generator.

to adequately reflect the changing structure, requires sophisticated algorithmic strategies.

A major weakness of force-directed placement is scalability, both in terms of the visual complexity of the layout and the time required to compute it. Force-directed approaches yield readable layouts quickly for tiny graphs with dozens of nodes, as shown in Figure 9.4. However, the layout quickly degenerates into a **hairball** of visual clutter with even a few hundred nodes, where the tasks of path following or understanding overall structural relationships become very difficult, essentially impossible, with thousands of nodes or more. Straightforward force-directed placement is unlikely to yield good results when the number of nodes is more than roughly four times the number of links. Moreover, many force-directed placement algorithms are notoriously brittle: they have many parameters that can be tweaked to improve the layout for a particular dataset, but different settings are required to do well for another. As with many kinds of computational optimization, many force-directed placement algorithms search in a way that can get stuck in **local minimum** energy configuration that is not the globally best answer.

In the simplest force-directed algorithms, the nodes never settle down to a final location; they continue to bounce around if the user does not explicitly intervene to halt the layout process. While seeing the force-directed algorithm iteratively refine the layout can be interesting while the layout is actively improving, continual bouncing can be distracting and should be avoided if a force-directed layout is being used in a multiple-view context where the user may want to attend to other views without having motion-sensitive peripheral vision invoked. More sophisticated algorithms automatically stop by determining that the layout has reached a good balance between the forces.

Idiom	Force-Directed Placement
What: Data	Network.
How: Encode	Point marks for nodes, connection marks for links.
Why: Tasks	Explore topology, locate paths.
Scale	Nodes: dozens/hundreds. Links: hundreds. Node/link density: $L < 4N$

▶ Compound networks are discussed further in Section 9.5.

▶ Cluster hierarchies are discussed in more detail in Section 13.4.1.

Many recent approaches to scalable network drawing are **multi-level network** idioms, where the original network is augmented with a derived cluster hierarchy to form a compound network. The cluster hierarchy is computed by **coarsening** the original network into successively simpler networks that nevertheless attempt to capture the most essential aspects of the original's structure. By laying out the simplest version of the networks first, and then improving the layout with the more and more complex versions, both the speed and quality of the layout can be improved. These approaches do better at avoiding the local minimum problem.

Example: sfdp

Figure 9.5(a) shows a network of 7220 nodes and 13,800 edges using the multilevel scalable force-directed placement (sfdp) algorithm [Hu 05], where the edges are colored by length. Significant cluster structure is indeed visible in the layout, where the dense clusters with short orange and yellow edges can be distinguished from the long blue and green edges between them. However, even these sophisticated idioms hit their limits with sufficiently large networks and fall prey to the hairball problem. Figure 9.5(b) shows a network of 26,028 nodes and 100,290 edges, where the sfdp layout does not show much visible structure. The enormous number of overlapping lines leads to overwhelming visual clutter caused by occlusion.

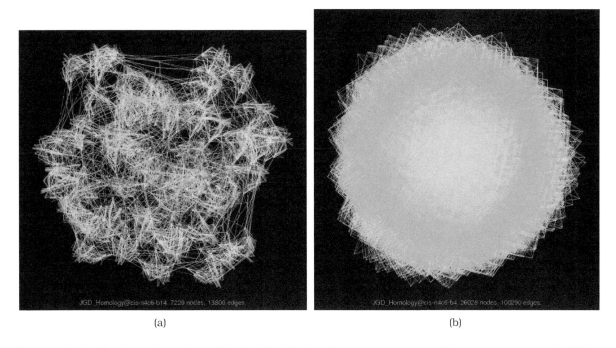

(a)   (b)

Figure 9.5. Multilevel graph drawing with sfdp [Hu 05]. (a) Cluster structure is visible for a large network of 7220 nodes and 13,800 edges. (b) A huge graph of 26,028 nodes and 100,290 edges is a "hairball" without much visible structure. From [Hu 14].

Idiom	Multilevel Force-Directed Placement (sfdp)
What: Data	Network.
What: Derived	Cluster hierarchy atop original network.
What: Encode	Point marks for nodes, connection marks for links.
Why: Tasks	Explore topology, locate paths and clusters.
Scale	Nodes: 1000–10,000. Links: 1000–10,000. Node/link density: L < 4N.

9.3 Matrix Views

Network data can also be encoded with a matrix view by deriving a table from the original network data.

Example: Adjacency Matrix View

A network can be visually encoded as an **adjacency matrix** view, where all of the nodes in the network are laid out along the vertical and horizontal edges of a square region and links between two nodes are indicated by coloring an area mark in the cell in the matrix that is the intersection between their row and column. That is, the network is transformed into the derived dataset of a table with two key attributes that are separate full lists of every node in the network, and one value attribute for each cell records whether a link exists between the nodes that index the cell. Figure 9.6(a) shows corresponding node–link and adjacency matrix views of a small network. Figures 9.6(b) and 9.6(c) show the same comparison for a larger network.

▶ Adjacency matrix views use 2D alignment, just like the tabular matrix views covered in Section 7.5.2.

Additional information about another attribute is often encoded by coloring matrix cells, a possibility left open by this spatially based design choice. The possibility of size coding matrix cells is limited by the number of available pixels per cell; typically only a few levels would be distinguishable between the largest and the smallest cell size. Network matrix views can also show weighted networks, where each link has an associated quantitative value attribute, by encoding with an ordered channel such as luminance or size.

For undirected networks where links are symmetric, only half of the matrix needs to be shown, above or below the diagonal, because a link from node A to node B necessarily implies a link from B to A. For directed networks, the full square matrix has meaning, because links can be asymmetric.

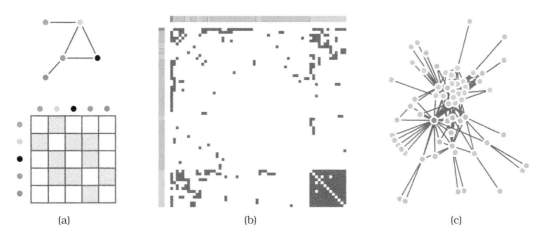

Figure 9.6. Comparing node–link matrix and matrix views of a network. (a) Node–link and matrix views of small network. (b) Matrix view of larger network. (c) Node–link view of larger network. From [Gehlenborg and Wong 12, Figures 1 and 2].

Matrix views of networks can achieve very high information density, up to a limit of one thousand nodes and one million edges, just like cluster heatmaps and all other matrix views that use small area marks.

Idiom	Adjacency Matrix View
What: Data	Network.
What: Derived	Table: network nodes as keys, link status between two nodes as values.
How: Encode	Area marks in 2D matrix alignment.
Scale	Nodes: 1000. Links: one milllion.

9.4 Costs and Benefits: Connection versus Matrix

The idiom of visually encoding networks as node–link diagrams, with connection marks representing the links between nodes, is by far the most popular way to visualize networks and trees. In addition to all of the examples in Section 9.2, many of the other examples in other parts of this book use this idiom. Node–link network examples inclue the genealogical graphs of Figure 4.6, the telecommunications network using linewidth to encode bandwidth of Figure 5.9, the gene interaction network shown with Cerebral in Figure 12.5, and the graph interaction examples of Figure 14.10. Node–link tree views include the DOITree of Figure 14.2, the Cone Trees of Figure 14.4, a file system shown with H3 in Figure 14.6, and the phylogenetic trees shown with TreeJuxtaposer in Figure 14.7.

The great strength of node–link layouts is that for sufficiently small networks they are extremely intuitive for supporting many of the abstract tasks that pertain to network data. They particularly shine for tasks that rely on understanding the topological structure of the network, such as path tracing and searching local topological neighborhoods a small number of hops from a target node, and can also be very effective for tasks such as general overview or finding similar substructures. The effectiveness of the general idiom varies considerably depending on the specific visual encoding idiom used; there has been a great deal of algorithmic work in this area.

Their weakness is that past a certain limit of network size and link density, they become impossible to read because of occlusion from edges crossing each other and crossing underneath nodes. The **link density** of a network is the number of links compared with the number of nodes. Trees have a link density of one, with one edge for each node. The upper limit for node–link diagram effectiveness is a link density of around three or four [Melançon 06].

Even for networks with a link density below four, as the network size increases the resulting visual clutter from edges and nodes occluding each other eventually causes the layout to degenerates into an unreadable *hairball*. A great deal of algorithmic work in graph drawing has been devoted to increasing the size of networks that can be laid out effectively, and multilevel idioms have led to significant advances in layout capabilities. The legibility limit depends on the algorithm, with simpler algorithms supporting hundreds of nodes while more state-of-the-art ones handle thousands well but degrade in performance for tens of thousands. Limits do and will remain; interactive navigation and exploration idioms can address the problem partially but not fully. Filtering, aggregation, and navigation are design choices that can ameliorate the clutter problem, but they do impose cognitive load on the user who must then remember the structure of the parts that are not visible.

The other major approach to network drawing is a matrix view. A major strength of matrix views is perceptual scalability for both large and dense networks. Matrix views completely eliminate the occlusion of node–link views, as described above, and thus are effective even at very high information densities. Whereas node–link views break down once the density of edges is more than about three or four times the number of nodes, matrix views can handle dense graphs up to the mathematical limit where the edge count is the number of nodes squared. As discussed in the scalability analyses of Sections 7.5.2 and 13.4.1, a single-level matrix view can handle up to one million edges and an aggregated multilevel matrix view might handle up to ten billion edges.

Another strength of matrix views is their predictability, stability, and support for reordering. Matrix views can be laid out within a predictable amount of screen space, whereas node–link views may require a variable amount of space depending on dataset characteristics, so the amount of screen real estate needed for a legible layout is not known in advance. Moreover, matrix views are stable; adding a new item will only cause a small visual change. In contrast, adding a new item in a force-directed view might cause a major change. This stability allows multilevel matrix views to easily support geometric or semantic zooming. Matrix views can also be used in conjunction with the interaction design choice of reordering, where the linear ordering of the elements along the axes is changed on demand.

▶ Reordering is discussed further in Section 7.5.

Matrix views also shine for quickly estimating the number of nodes in a graph and directly supporting search through fast node lookup. Finding an item label in an ordered list is easy, whereas finding a node given its label in node–link layout is time consuming because it could be placed anywhere through the two-dimensional area. Node–link layouts can of course be augmented with interactive support for search by highlighting the matching nodes as the labels are typed.

One major weakness of matrix views is unfamiliarity: most users are able to easily interpret node–link views of small networks without the need for training, but they typically need training to interpret matrix views. However, with sufficient training, many aspects of matrix views can become salient. These include the tasks of finding specific types of nodes or node groups that are supported by both matrix views and node–link views, through different but roughly equally salient visual patterns in each view. Figure 9.7 shows three such patterns [McGuffin 12]. The completely interconnected lines showing a clique in the node–link graph is instead a square block of filled-in cells along the diagonal in the matrix view. After training, it's perhaps even easier to tell the differences between a proper clique and a cluster of highly but not completely interconnected nodes in the matrix view. Similarly, the biclique

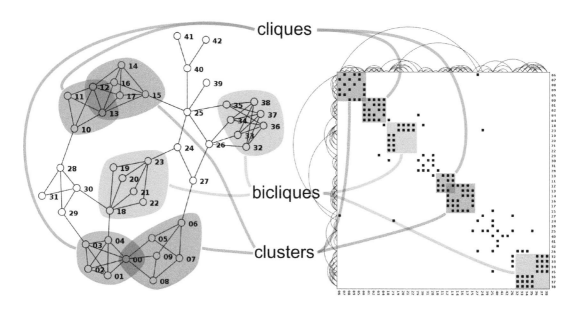

Figure 9.7. Characteristic patterns in matrix views and node–link views: both can show cliques and clusters clearly. From [McGuffin 12, Figure 6].

structure of node subsets where edges connect each node in one subset with one in another is salient, but different, in both views. The degree of a node, namely, the number of edges that connect to it, can be found by counting the number of filled-in cells in a row or column.

The most crucial weakness of matrix views is their lack of support for investigating topological structure because they show links in a more indirect way than the direct connections of node–link diagrams. This weakness is a direct trade-off for their strength in avoiding clutter. One reason that node–link views are so popular, despite the many other strengths of matrix views listed above, might be that most complex domain tasks involving network exploration end up requiring topological structure inspection as a subtask. Hybrid multiple-view systems that use both node–link and matrix representations are a nice way to combine their complementary strengths, such as the MatrixExplorer system shown in Figure 4.8.

An empirical investigation [Ghoniem et al. 05] compared node–link and matrix views for many low-level abstract network tasks. It found that for most tasks studied, node–link views are best for small networks and matrix views are best for large networks. In specific, several tasks became more difficult for node–link views as size increased, whereas the difficulty was independent of size for matrix views: approximate estimation of the number of nodes and of edges, finding the most connected node, finding a node given its label, finding a direct link between two nodes, and finding a common neighbor between two nodes. However, the task of finding a multiple-link path between two nodes was always more difficult in matrix views, even with large network sizes. This study thus meshes with the analysis above, that topological structure tasks such as path tracing are best supported by node–link views.

9.5   Containment: Hierarchy Marks

Containment marks are very effective at showing complete information about hierarchical structure, in contrast to connection marks that only show pairwise relationships between two items at once.

Example: Treemaps

The idiom of **treemaps** is an alternative to node–link tree drawings, where the hierarchical relationships are shown with containment rather than connection. All of the children of a tree node are enclosed within the area allocated that node, creating a nested layout. The size of the nodes is mapped to some attribute of the node. Figure 9.8 is a treemap view of the

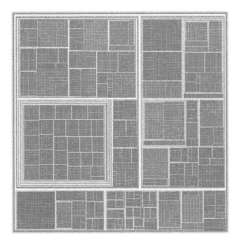

Figure 9.8. Treemap layout showing hierarchical structure with containment rather than connection, in contrast to the node–link diagrams of the same 5161-node tree in Figure 9.3.

same dataset as Figure 9.3, a 5161-node computer file system. Here, node size encodes file size. Containment marks are not as effective as the pairwise connection marks for tasks focused on topological structure, such as tracing paths through the tree, but they shine for tasks that pertain to understanding attribute values at the leaves of the tree. They are often used when hierarchies are shallow rather than deep. Treemaps are very effective for spotting the outliers of very large attribute values, in this case large files.

Idiom	Treemaps
What: Data	Tree.
How: Encode	Area marks and containment, with rectilinear layout.
Why: Tasks	Query attributes at leaf nodes.
Scale	Leaf nodes: one million. Links: one million.

Figure 9.9 shows seven different visual encoding idioms for tree data. Two of the visual encoding idioms in Figure 9.9 use containment: the treemap in Figure 9.9(f) consisting of nested rectangles, and the nested circles of Figure 9.9(e). Two use connection: the vertical node–link layout in Figure 9.9(a) and the radial node–link layout in Figure 9.9(c).

Although connection and containment marks that depict the link structure of the network explicitly are very common ways to encode networks, they are not the only way. In most of the trees in Figure 9.9, the spatial position channel is explicitly used to show

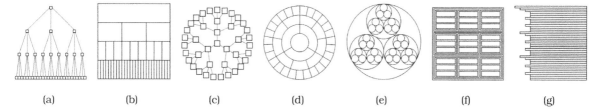

(a)   (b)   (c)   (d)   (e)   (f)   (g)

Figure 9.9. Seven visual encoding idioms showing the same tree dataset, using different combinations of visual channels. (a) Rectilinear vertical node–link, using connection to show link relationships, with vertical spatial position showing tree depth and horizontal spatial position showing sibling order. (b) Icicle, with vertical spatial position and size showing tree depth, and horizontal spatial position showing link relationships and sibling order. (c) Radial node–link, using connection to show link relationships, with radial depth spatial position showing tree depth and radial angular position showing sibling order. (d) Concentric circles, with radial depth spatial position and size showing tree depth and radial angular spatial position showing link relationships and sibling order. (e) Nested circles, using radial containment, with nesting level and size showing tree depth. (f) Treemap, using rectilinear containment, with nesting level and size showing tree depth. (g) Indented outline, with horizontal spatial position showing tree depth and link relationships and vertical spatial position showing sibling order. From [McGuffin and Robert 10, Figure 1].

the tree depth of a node. However, three layouts show parent–child relationships without any connection marks at all. The rectilinear icicle tree of Figure 9.9(b) and the radial concentric circle tree of Figure 9.9(d) show tree depth with one spatial dimension and parent–child relationships with the other. Similarly, the indented outline tree of Figure 9.9(g) shows parent–child relationships with relative vertical position, in addition to tree depth with horizontal position.

Example: GrouseFlocks

The containment design choice is usually only used if there is a hierarchical structure; that is, a tree. The obvious case is when the network is simply a tree, as above. The other case is with a **compound network**, which is the combination of a network and tree; that is, in addition to a base network with links that are pairwise relations between the network nodes, there is also a *cluster hierarchy* that groups the nodes hierarchically.* In other words, a compound network is a combination of a network and a tree on top of it, where the nodes in the network are the leaves of the tree. Thus, the interior nodes of the tree encompass multiple network nodes.

⋆ The term **multilevel network** is sometimes used as a synonym for *compound network*.

▶ Cluster hierarchies are discussed further in Section 7.5.2.

Containment is often used for exploring such compound networks. In the sfdp example above, there was a specific approach to coarsening the network that created a single derived hierarchy. That hierarchy was used only to accelerate force-directed layout and was not shown directly to the user. In the GrouseFlocks system, users can investigate multiple possible hierarchies and they are shown explicitly. Figure 9.10(a) shows a network and Figure 9.10(b) shows a cluster hierarchy built on top of it.

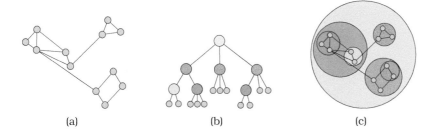

| (a) | (b) | (c) |

Figure 9.10. GrouseFlocks uses containment to show graph hierarchy structure. (a) Original graph. (b) Cluster hierarchy built atop the graph, shown with a node–link layout. (c) Network encoded using connection, with hierarchy encoded using containment. From [Archambault et al. 08, Figure 3].

Figure 9.10(c) shows a combined view using of containment marks for the associated hierarchy and connection marks for the original network links.

System	**GrouseFlocks**
What: Data	Network.
What: Derived	Cluster hierarchy atop original network.
What: Encode	Connection marks for original network, containment marks for cluster hierarchy.

9.6 Further Reading

Network Layout An early survey of network vis [Herman et al. 00] was followed by one covering more recent developments [von Landesberger et al. 11]. A good starting point for network layout algorithms is a tutorial that covers node–link, matrix, and hybrid approaches, including techniques for ordering the nodes [McGuffin 12]. An analysis of edge densities in node–link graph layouts identifies the limit of readability as edge counts beyond roughly four times the node count [Melançon 06].

Force-Directed Placement Force-directed placement has been heavily studied; a good algorithmically oriented overview appears in a book chapter [Brandes 01]. The Graph Embedder (GEM) algorithm is a good example of a sophisticated placement algorithm with built-in termination condition [Frick et al. 95].

Multilevel Network Layout Many multilevel layouts have been proposed, including sfdp [Hu 05], FM^3 [Hachul and Jünger 04], and TopoLayout [Archambault et al. 07b].

Matrix versus Node–Link Views The design space of matrix layouts, node–link layouts, and hybrid combinations were considered for the domain of social network analysis [Henry and Fekete 06, Henry et al. 07]. The results of an empirical study were used to characterize the uses of matrix versus node–link views for a broad set of abstract tasks [Ghoniem et al. 05].

Design Space of Tree Drawings A hand-curated visual bibliography of hundreds of different approaches to tree drawing is available at http://treevis.net [Schulz 11]. Design guidelines for a wide variety of 2D graphical representations of trees are the result of analyzing their space efficiency [McGuffin and Robert 10]. Another analysis covers the design space of approaches to tree drawing beyond node–link layouts [Schulz et al. 11].

Treemaps Treemaps were first proposed at the University of Maryland [Johnson and Shneiderman 91]. An empirical study led to perceptual guidelines for creating treemaps by identifying the data densities at which length-encoded bar charts become less effective than area-encoded treemaps [Kong et al. 10].

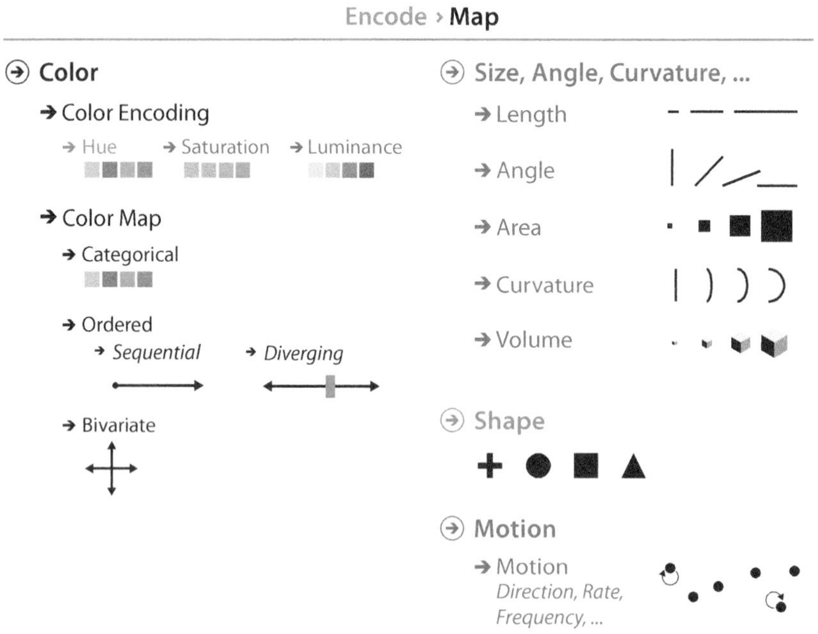

⊕ Color

→ Color Encoding

→ Hue → Saturation → Luminance

→ Color Map

→ Categorical

→ Ordered
  → *Sequential*   → *Diverging*

→ Bivariate

⊕ Size, Angle, Curvature, ...

→ Length

→ Angle

→ Area

→ Curvature

→ Volume

⊕ Shape

⊕ Motion

→ Motion
  Direction, Rate,
  Frequency, ...

Figure 10.1. Design choices for mapping color and other visual encoding channels.

Chapter 10

Map Color and Other Channels

10.1   The Big Picture

This chapter covers the mapping of color and other nonspatial channels in visual encoding design choices, summarized in Figure 10.1. The colloquial term *color* is best understood in terms of three separate channels: luminance, hue, and saturation. The major design choice for colormap construction is whether the intent is to distinguish between categorical attributes or to encode ordered attributes. Sequential ordered colormaps show a progression of an attribute from a minimum to a maximum value, while diverging ordered colormaps have a visual indication of a zero point in the center where the attribute values diverge to negative on one side and positive on the other. Bivariate colormaps are designed to show two attributes simultaneously using carefully designed combinations of luminance, hue, and saturation.

The characteristics of several more channels are also covered: the magnitude channels of size, angle, and curvature and the identity channels of shape and motion.

10.2   Color Theory

Color is a rich and complex topic, and here I only touch on the most crucial aspects that apply to vis.

10.2.1   Color Vision

The retina of the eye has two different kinds of receptors. The **rods** actively contribute to vision only in low-light settings and provide low-resolution black and white information. I will thus not discuss them further in this book. The main sensors in normal lighting conditions are the **cones**. There are three types of cones, each with peak sensitivities at a different wavelength within the spectrum of visible light. The visual system immediately processes these signals into three **opponent color channels**: one from red to green, one from blue to yellow, and one from black and white encoding luminance information. The luminance channel conveys high-resolution edge information, while the red–green and blue–yellow channels are lower resolution. This split between luminance and **chromaticity**—what most people informally call would normally call *color*—is a central issue in visual encoding design.

The theory of opponent color channels explains what is colloquially called **color blindness**, which affects around 8% of men in its most common form. A more accurate term is **color deficiency**, since a "colorblind" person's ability to differentiate color along the red–green channel is reduced or absent but their blue–yellow channel is still in full working order.[*]

★ There is a type of color deficiency where the blue–yellow channel is impaired, **tritanopia**, but it is extremely rare and not sex linked. The two common forms of red–green color blindness are **deuteranopia** and **protanopia**; both are sex linked.

10.2.2   Color Spaces

The **color space** of what colors the human visual system can detect is three dimensional; that is, it can be adequately described using three separate axes. There are many ways to mathematically describe color as a space and to transform colors from one such space into another. Some of these are extremely convenient for computer manipulation, while others are a better match with the characteristics of human vision.

The most common color space in computer graphics is the system where colors are specified as triples of red, green, and blue values, which is called the **RGB** system. Although this system is computationally convenient, it is a very poor match for the mechanics of how we see. The red, green, and blue axes of the RGB color space are not useful as separable channels; they give rise to the integral perception of a color. I do not discuss them further as channels in my analysis of visual encoding.

Another color space, the hue–saturation–lightness or **HSL** system, is more intuitive and is heavily used by artists and designers. The **hue** axis captures what we normally think of as pure colors that are not mixed with white or black: red, blue, green, yellow, purple, and so on. The **saturation** axis is the amount of white mixed with that pure color. For instance, pink is a partially desaturated red. The **lightness** axis is the amount of black mixed with a color. A common design for color pickers is a disk with white at the center and the hue axis wrapped around the outside, with separate linear control for the amount of darkness versus lightness, as shown in Figure 10.2. The HSV space is very similar, where V stands for grayscale value and is linearly related to L.

Figure 10.2. A common HSL/HSV colorpicker design, as in this example from Mac OS X, is to show a color wheel with fully saturated color around the outside and white at the center of the circle, and a separate control for the darkness.

Despite the popularity of the HSL space, it is only pseudoperceptual: it does not truly reflect how we perceive color. In particular, the lightness L is wildly different from how we perceive luminance. Figure 10.3 shows six different hues, arranged in order of their luminance. The corresponding computed L values are all identical. The true luminance is a somewhat better match with our perceptual experience: there is some variation between the boxes. However, our perception of luminance does not match what

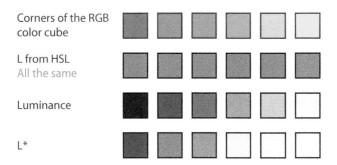

Figure 10.3. Comparing HSL lightness, true luminance, and perceptually linear luminance L^* for six colors. The computed HSL lightness L is the same for all of these colors, showing the limitations of that color system. The true luminance values of these same six colors, as could be measured with an instrument. The computed perceptually linear luminance L^* of these colors is the best match with what we see. After [Stone 06].

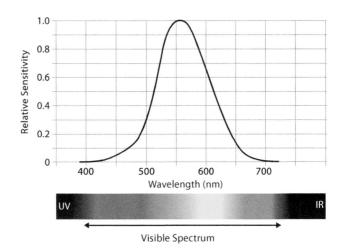

Figure 10.4. The spectral sensitivity of our eyes to luminance depends on the wavelength of the incoming light. After [Kaiser 96], http://www.yorku.ca/eye/photopik.htm.

an instrument would measure: the amount of luminance that humans perceive depends on the wavelength. Figure 10.4 shows the roughly bell-shaped **spectral sensitivity** curve for daylight vision. We are much more sensitive to middle wavelengths of green and yellow than to the outer wavelengths of red and blue.

There are several color spaces that attempt to provide a perceptually uniform space, including one known as $L^*a^*b^*$. This space has a single black and white luminance channel L^*, and the two color axes a^* and b^*. Figure 10.3 also shows the L^* values for the same six boxes, which is even a better match with what we see than true luminance. The L^* axis is a nonlinear transformation of the luminance perceived by the human eye. Our perception of luminance is compressed, as shown by the exponent of $n = 0.5$ for the brightness power law curve in Figure 5.7. The L^* axis is designed to be perceptually linear, so that equally sized steps appear equal to our visual systems, based on extensive measurement and calibration over a very large set of observers. The color axes have also been designed to be as perceptually linear as possible. The $L^*a^*b^*$ space is thus well suited for many computations, including interpolation and finding differences between colors, that should not be executed in the perceptually nonlinear RGB or HSL spaces.

▶ Accuracy of perception is discussed in Section 5.5.1.

In this book, I use the term *luminance* as an evocative way to describe the black and white visual channel.* I use *saturation* and *hue* for the other two chromaticity channels.*

10.2.3 Luminance, Saturation, and Hue

Color can be confusing in vis analysis because it is sometimes used as a magnitude channel and sometimes as a identity channel. When I use the precise terms *luminance*, *hue*, and *saturation*, I mean the three separable visual channels that pertain to color in the analysis of visual encoding. Luminance and saturation are magnitude channels, while hue is a identity channel. When I use the generic term color, I mean the integral perception across all three of these channels at once, and I am analyzing it as an identity channel.

The magnitude channel of luminance is suitable for ordered data types. However, one consideration with luminance is our low accuracy in perceiving whether noncontiguous regions have the same luminance because of contrast effects. Thus, the number of discriminable steps is small, typically less then five when the background is not uniform: Ware suggests avoiding grayscale if more than two to four bins are required [Ware 13].

Moreover, a fundamental problem with using it for encoding a specific data attribute is that luminance is then "used up" and cannot be used for other purposes. A crucial consideration when visual encoding with color is that luminance contrast is the only way we can resolve fine detail and see crisp edges; hue contrast or saturation contrast does not provide detectable edges. In particular, text is not readable without luminance contrast. The standard guidelines are that 10:1 is a good luminance contrast ratio for text, with 3:1 as a minimum [Ware 13]. If it's important that fine-grained features are legible, ensure that you provide sufficient luminance contrast.

The magnitude channel of saturation is also suitable for ordered data. Saturation shares the problem of low accuracy for noncontiguous regions. The number of discriminable steps for saturation is low: around three bins [Ware 13].

Moreover, saturation interacts strongly with the size channel: it is more difficult to perceive in small regions than in large ones. Point and line marks typically occupy small regions, so using just two different saturation levels is safer in these cases. Finally,

★ I avoid the term *perceptually linear luminance* as inaccurate for visualization analysis because very few visual encoding idioms carry out this computation. Similarly, I avoid the term brightness, the technical term for the human perceptual experience of luminance, because it is affected by many factors such as illumination levels and surrounding context; again, visual encoding idioms typically manipulate luminance rather than attempting to deliver true brightness.

★ This hybrid usage of luminance, saturation, and hue does not correspond exactly to any of the standard color spaces used in computer graphics.

Luminance

Saturation

Hue

Figure 10.5. The luminance and saturation channels are automatically interpreted as ordered by our perceptual system, but the hue channel is not.

saturation and hue are not separable channels within small regions for the purpose of categorical color coding.

For small regions, designers should use bright, highly saturated colors to ensure that the color coding is distinguishable. When colored regions are large, as in backgrounds, the design guideline is the opposite: use low-saturation colors; that is, pastels.

The identity channel of **hue** is extremely effective for categorical data and showing groupings. It is the highest ranked channel for categorical data after spatial position.

However, hue shares the same challenges as saturation in terms of interaction with the size channel: hue is harder to distinguish in small regions than large regions. It also shared the same challenges as saturation and luminance for separated regions: we can make fine distinctions in hue for contiguous regions, but we have very limited discriminability between separated regions. The number of discriminable steps for hue in small separated regions is moderate, around six or seven bins.

Unlike luminance and saturation, hue does not have an implicit perceptual ordering, as shown in Figure 10.5. People can reliably order by luminance, always placing gray in between black and white. With saturation, people reliably place the less saturated pink between fully saturated red and zero-saturation white. However, when they are asked to create an ordering of red, blue, green, and yellow, people do not all give the same answer. People can and do learn conventions, such as green–yellow–red for traffic lights, or the order of colors in the rainbow, but these constructions are at a higher level than pure perception.

10.2.4 Transparency

A fourth channel strongly related to the other three color channels is **transparency**: information can be encoded by decreasing the opacity of a mark from fully opaque to completely see-through. Transparency cannot be used independently of the other color channels because of its strong interaction effects with them: fully transparent marks cannot convey any information at all with the other three channels. In particular, transparency coding interacts strongly with luminance and saturation coding and should not be used in conjunction with them at all. It can be used in conjunction with hue encoding with a very small number of discriminable steps, most frequently just two. Transparency is used most often with superimposed layers, to create a foreground layer that is distinguishable from the background layer. It is frequently used redundantly, where the same information is encoded with another channel as well.

▶ Superimposing layers is covered in Section 12.5.

10.3 Colormaps

A **colormap** specifies a mapping between colors and data values; that is, a visual encoding with color.* Using color to encode data is a powerful and flexible design choice, but colormap design has many pitfalls for the unwary.

★ *Colormapping* is also called **pseudocoloring**, especially in earlier literature. Another synonym for *colormap* is **color ramp**.

Figure 10.6 shows the taxonomy of colormaps; it is no coincidence that it mirrors the taxonomy of data types. Colormaps can be **categorical** or **ordered**, and ordered colormaps can be either **sequential** or **diverging**. Of course, it is important to match colormap to data type characteristics, following the expressiveness principle. Colormaps for ordered data should use the magnitude channels of luminance and saturation, since the identity channel of hue does not have an implicit ordering.

▶ The principle of expressivness is covered in Section 5.4.1.

Colormaps can either be a **continuous** range of values, or **segmented** into discrete bins of color.* Continuous colormaps are heavily used for showing quantitative attributes, especially those associated with inherently spatial fields. Segmented colormaps are suitable for categorical data. For ordinal data, segmented colormaps would emphasize its discrete nature, while continuous would emphasize its ordered nature. Bivariate colormaps encode two attributes simultaneously. While bivariate colormaps are straightforward to understand when the second attribute is binary, with only two levels, they are more difficult for people to interpret when both attributes have multiple levels.

★ There are many synonyms for *segmented colormap*: **quantized colormap**, **stepped colormap**, **binned colormap**, **discretized colormap**, and **discrete colormap**.

▶ Continuous versus discrete data semantics is discussed in Section 2.4.3.

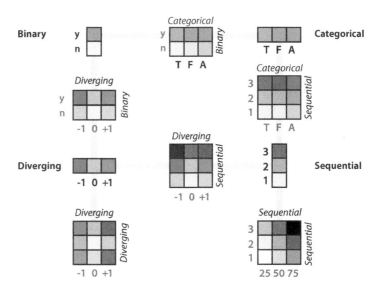

Figure 10.6. The colormap categorization partially mirrors the data types: categorical versus ordered, and sequential and diverging within ordered. Bivariate encodings of two separate attributes at once is safe if one has only two levels, but they can be difficult to interpret when both attributes have multiple levels. After [Brewer 99].

10.3.1 Categorical Colormaps

A **categorical** colormap uses color to encode categories and groupings. Categorical colormaps are normally segmented.* They are very effective when used appropriately; for categorical data, they are the next best channel after spatial position.

> ★ *Categorical colormaps* are also known as **qualitative** colormaps.

Categorical colormaps are typically designed by using color as an integral identity channel to encode a single attribute, rather than to encode three completely separate attributes with the three channels of hue, saturation, and luminance.

The number of discriminable colors for coding small separated regions is limited to between six and twelve bins. You should remember to include background color and any default object colors in your total count: some or all of the most basic choices of black, white, and gray are often devoted to those uses. Easily nameable colors are desirable, both for memorability and ability to discuss them using words. A good set of initial choices are the fully saturated and easily nameable colors, which are also the opponent

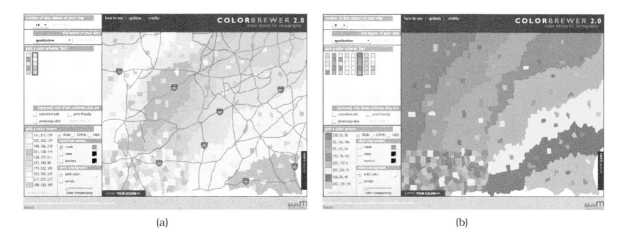

(a)   (b)

Figure 10.7. Saturation and area. (a) The ten-element low-saturation map works well with large areas. (b) The eight-element high-saturation map would be better suited for small regions and works poorly for these large areas. Made with ColorBrewer, http://www.colorbrewer2.org.

color axes: red, blue, green, and yellow. Other possibilities when more colors are needed are orange, brown, pink, magenta, purple, and cyan. However, colormap design is a tricky problem: careful attention must be paid to luminance and saturation. Luminance constrast is a major issue: for some uses, the colors should be close in luminance to avoid major differences in salience and to ensure that all can be seen against the same background. For example, fully saturated yellow and green will have much less luminance contrast against a white background than red and blue. For other uses, colors should be sufficiently different in luminance that they can be distinguished even in black and white. Moreover, colormaps for small regions such as lines should be highly saturated, but large regions such as areas should have low saturation. Thus, the appropriate colormap may depend on the mark type.

A good resource for creating colormaps is ColorBrewer at http://www.colorbrewer2.org, a system that incorporates many perceptual guidelines into its design in order to provide safe suggestions. It was used to create both the ten-element low-saturation map in Figure 10.7(a) and the eight-element high-saturation map in Figure 10.7(b). The low-saturation pastel map is well suited for large regions, leaving fully saturated colors for small road marks. In contrast, the eight-element map that uses highly saturated colors is much too bright for the large areas shown here, but would be a good fit for small line or point marks.

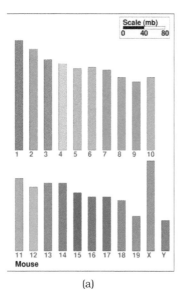

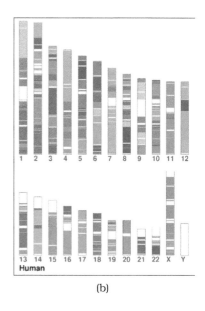

(a)   (b)

Figure 10.8. Ineffective categorical colormap use. (a) The 21 colors used as an index for each mouse chromosome can indeed be distinguished in large regions next to each other. (b) In noncontiguous small regions only about 12 bins of color can be distinguished from each other, so a lot of information about how regions in the mouse genome map to the human genome is lost. From [Sinha and Meller 07, Figure 2].

Figure 10.8 illustrates an attempt to use categorical color that is ineffective because of a mismatch between the number of color bins that we can distinguish in noncontiguous small regions and the number of levels in the categorical attribute being encoded. Figure 10.8(a) shows that one color has been assigned to each of the 21 chromosomes in the mouse. All 21 of these colors can indeed be distinguished from each other in this view that acts as a legend and an index, because regions are large and the most subtle differences are between regions that are right next to each other.

In Figure 10.8(b), the regions of the human chromosomes that correspond to those in the mouse chromosomes have been colored to illustrate how genomic regions have moved around as the species evolved independently from each other after diverging from a common ancestor. In this case, the colored regions are much smaller and not contiguous. The 21 colors are definitely not distinguishable from each other in this view: for example, only about three bins of green can be distinguished in the human view, rather than the full set of seven in the mouse view. Similarly, the full set of five pinks and purples in the mouse view has collapsed into about three distinguishable bins in the human view. In total, only around 12 bins of color can be distinguished in the human view.

When you are faced with the problem of discriminability mismatch, there are two good design choices. One choice is to reduce the number of bins explicitly through a deliberate data transformation that takes into account the nature of the data and task, so that each bin can be encoded with a distinguishable color. This choice to derive a new and smaller set of attributes is better than the inadvertent segmentation into bins that arises from the user's perceptual system, which is unlikely to match meaningful divisions in the underlying data. For example, the attribute may have hierarchical structure that can be exploited to derive meaningful aggregate groups, so that one color can be used per group. Another possibility is to filter the attributes to only encode a small set of the most important ones with color, and aggregate all of the rest into a new category of *other*; the Constellation system analyzed in Section 15.8 takes this approach to color coding links, where a few dozen categories were narrowed down to fit within eight bins.

▶ Aggregation and filtering idioms are covered in Chapter 13.

The other choice is to use a different visual encoding idiom that uses other visual channels instead of, or in addition to, the color channel alone. Figure 10.9 shows an example of systematically considering a large space of visual encoding possibilities for visualizing biological experiment workflows. The dataset has 27 categorical levels in total that are gathered into seven categories with between three and seven levels each. Seven designs were considered, using multiple channels in addition to color: shape, size, and more complex glyphs that evoke metaphoric associations. Figure 10.10 shows the final choice made, where the color channel was only used to encode the four levels in category S7, and other channels were used for the other categories.

10.3.2   Ordered Colormaps

An **ordered** colormap is appropriate for encoding ordinal or quantitative attributes. The two major variants of continuous colormaps for ordered data have expressiveness charactistics that should match up with the attribute type. A **sequential** colormap ranges from a minimum value to a maximum value. If only the luminance channel is used, the result is a grayscale ramp. When incorporating hue, one end of the ramp is a specific hue at full saturation and brightness. If saturation is the variable, the other end is pale

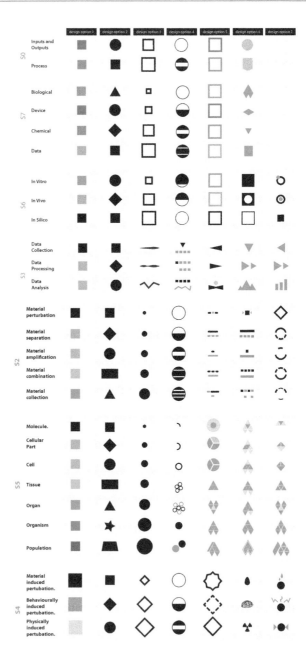

Figure 10.9. Effective categorical colormap use: A large space of visual encoding possibilities for 27 categories was considered systematically in addition to the color channel, including size and shape channels and more complex glyphs. From [Maguire et al. 12, Figure 5].

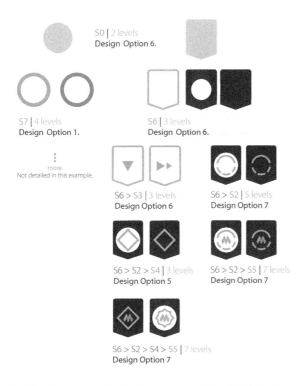

Figure 10.10. Effective categorical colormap use: The final design uses the color channel for only four of the categories. From [Maguire et al. 12, Figure 6].

or white; when luminance is the varying quantity, the other end is dark or black. A **diverging** colormap has two hues at the endpoints and a neutral color as a midpoint, such as white, gray, or black, or a high-luminance color such as yellow.

The question of how many unique hues to use in continuous colormaps depends on what level of structure should be emphasized: the high-level structure, the middle range of local neighborhoods, or fine-grained detail at the lowest level. Figure 10.11 shows the same fluid flow data with two different colormaps. Figure 10.11(a) emphasizes mid-level neighborhood structure with many hues. Figure 10.11(b) emphasizes large-scale structure by ranging between two fully saturated hues, with saturation smoothly varying to a middle point: in this sequential case, the ends are purple and yellow, and the midpoint is gray.

One advantage of the rainbow colormap shown in Figure 10.11(a) is that people can easily discuss specific subranges because the

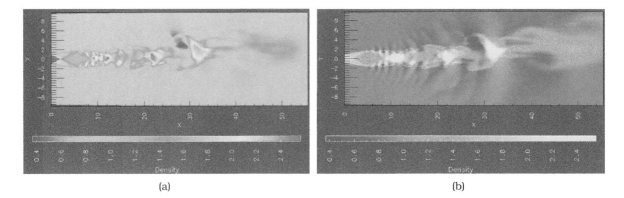

Figure 10.11. Rainbow versus two-hue continuous colormap. (a) Using many hues, as in this rainbow colormap, emphasizes mid-scale structure. (b) Using only two hues, the blue–yellow colormap emphasizes large-scale structure. From [Bergman et al. 95, Figures 1 and 2].

differences are easily nameable: "the red part versus the blue part versus the green part". In colormaps that use just saturation or luminance changes, there are only two hue-based semantic categories: "the purple side versus the yellow side". It is not easy to verbally distinguish between smaller neighborhoods—we cannot easily demarcate the "sort-of-bright purple" from the "not-quite-so-bright purple" parts.

However, rainbow colormaps suffer from three serious problems at the perceptual level; it is rather unfortunate that they are a default choice in many software packages. Figure 10.12 illustrates all three problems. First, hue is used to indicate order, despite being an identity channel without an implicit perceptual ordering. Second, the scale is not perceptually linear: steps of the same size at different points in the colormap range are not perceived equally by our eyes. A range of 1000 units in Figure 10.12(a) has different characteristics depending on where within the colormap it falls. While the range from –2000 to –1000 has three distinct colors, cyan and green and yellow, a range of the same size from –1000 to 0 simply looks yellow throughout. Third, fine detail cannot be perceived with the hue channel; the luminance channel would be a much better choice, because luminance contrast is required for edge detection in the human eye.

One way to address all three problems is to design **monotonically increasing luminance** colormaps: that is, where the multiple hues are ordered according to their luminance from lowest to high-

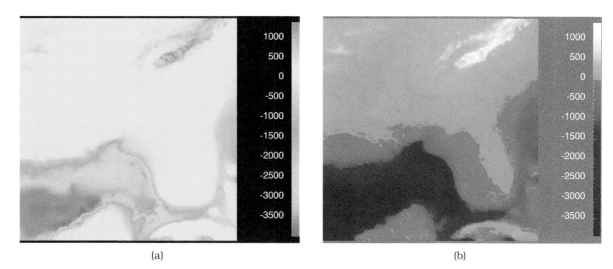

(a)   (b)

Figure 10.12.   Rainbow versus multiple-hue continuous colormap with monotonically increasing luminance.
(a) Three major problems with the common continuous rainbow colormap are perceptual nonlinearity, the expressivity mismatch of using hue for ordering, and the accuracy mismatch of using hue for fine-grained detail. (b) A colormap that combines monotonically increasing luminance with multiple hues for semantic categories, with a clear segmentation at the zero point, succeeds in showing high-level, mid-level, and low-level structure. From [Rogowitz and Treinish 98, Figure 1].

est. The varying hues allow easy segmentation into categorical regions, for both seeing and describing mid-level neighborhoods. Luminance is a magnitude channel, providing perceptual ordering. It supports both high-level distinctions between one end ("the dark parts") and the other ("the light parts") and low-level structure perception because subtle changes in luminance are more accurately perceived than subtle changes in hue. Figure 10.12(b) illuminates the true structure of the dataset with a more appropriate colormap, where the luminance increases monotonically. Hue is used to create a semantically meaningful categorization: the viewer can discuss structure in the dataset, such as the dark blue sea, the cyan continental shelf, the green lowlands, and the white mountains. The zero point matches with sea level, a semantically meaningful point for this dataset.

It is possible to create a perceptually linear rainbow colormap, but at the cost of losing part of the dynamic range because the fully saturated colors are not available for use. Figure 10.13 shows an example created with a system for calibrating perceptually based colormaps [Kindlmann 02]. The perceptually nonlinear rainbow

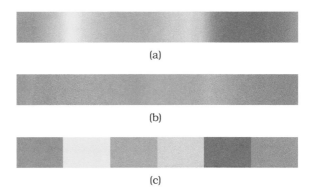

Figure 10.13. Appropriate use of rainbows. (a) The standard rainbow colormap is perceptually nonlinear. (b) Perceptually linear rainbows are possible [Kindlmann 02], but they are less bright with a decreased dynamic range. (c) Segmented rainbows work well for categorical data when the number of categories is small.

in Figure 10.13(a) can be converted to the perceptually linear one shown in Figure 10.13(b); however, it is so much less bright than the standard one that it seems almost dingy, so this solution is not commonly used.

Rainbows are not always bad; a segmented rainbow colormap is a fine choice for categorical data with a small number of categories. Figure 10.13(c) shows an example. Segmented rainbows could also be used for ordered data; while not ideal, at least the perceptual nonlinearity problem is solved because the colormap range is explicitly discretized into bins. Using a segmented colormap on quantitative data is equivalent to transforming the datatype from quantitative to ordered. This choice is most legitimate when task-driven semantics can be used to guide the segmentation into bins. The intuition behind the technique is that it is better to deliberately bin the data explicitly, rather than relying on the eye to create bins that are of unequal size and often do not match meaningful divisions in the underlying data.

10.3.3   Bivariate Colormaps

The safest use of the color channel is to visually encode a single attribute; these colormaps are known as **univariate**. Figure 10.6 includes several colormaps that encode two separate attributes, called **bivariate**. When one of the two attributes is **binary**, meaning it has only two levels, then it is straightforward to create a comprehensible bivariate colormap with two families of colors by fixing a base set of hues and varying their saturation, as in the bivariate categorical–binary and diverging–binary examples in Figure 10.6. This approach can also be useful for a single categorical attribute that has a hierarchical structure.

When both attributes are categorical with multiple levels, results will be poor [Wainer and Francolini 80], and thus there are no bivariate categorical–categorical maps in Figure 10.6. The case of encoding combinations of two sequential or diverging attributes with multiple levels is a middle ground. Figure 10.6 shows several examples with three levels for each attribute: sequential–sequential, diverging–diverging, diverging–sequential, and categorical–sequential. While these colormaps do appear frequently in vis systems, you should be aware that some people do have difficulty in interpreting their meaning.

10.3.4 Colorblind-Safe Colormap Design

Designers using color should take the common problem of red–green color blindness into account. It is a sex-linked inherited trait that affects 8% of males and a much smaller proportion of females, 0.5%. In the common forms of color blindness the ability to sense along the red–green opponent color axis is limited or absent. The problem is not limited to simply telling red apart from green; many pairs that are discriminable to people with normal color vision are confused, including red from black, blue from purple, light green from white, and brown from green.

▶ Opponent color is discussed in Section 10.2.

On the theoretical side, the safest strategy is to avoid using only the hue channel to encode information: design categorical colormaps that vary in luminance or saturation, in addition to hue. Clearly, avoiding colormaps that emphasize red–green, especially divergent red–green ramps, would be wise. In some domains there are strong conventions with the use of red and green, so those user expectations can be accommodated by ensuring luminance differences between reds and greens.

▶ For example, the historical and technical reasons behind red–green usage in bioinformatics domain are discussed in Section 7.5.2.

On the practical side, an excellent way to ensure that a design uses colors that are distinguishable for most users is to check it with a color blindness simulator. This capability is built into many desktop software tools including Adobe Illustrator and Photoshop, and also available through web sites such as http://www.rehue.net, http://www.color-blindness.com, and http://www.etre.com/tools/colourblindsimulator.

10.4   Other Channels

While the previously discussed channels pertaining to position and color are highly salient, other visual channels are also an important part of the visual encoding design space. Other magnitude visual channels include the size channels of length, area, and volume; the angle/orientation/tilt channel; and curvature. Other identity channels are shape and motion. Textures and stippling use combinations of multiple channels.

10.4.1   Size Channels

Size is a magnitude channel suitable for ordered data. It interacts with most other channels: when marks are too small, encodings in another channel such as shape or orientation simply cannot be seen. Size interacts particularly strongly with color hue and color saturation.

Length is one-dimensional (1D) size; more specifically, height is vertical size and width is horizontal size. Area is two-dimensional (2D) size, and volume is three-dimensional (3D) size. The accuracy of our perceptual judgements across these three channels varies considerably.

Our judgements of length are extremely accurate. Length judgements are very similar to unaligned planar position judgements: the only channel that is more accurate is aligned planar position.

In contrast, our judgement of area is significantly less accurate. Stevens assigns a power law exponent of 0.7 for area, as shown in Figure 5.7. The area channel is in the midde of the rankings, below angle but above 3D depth.

The volume channel is quite inaccurate. The volume channel is at the bottom of the rankings, in an equivalence class with curvature. Encoding with volume is rarely the right choice.

A larger-dimensional size coding clearly subsumes a smaller-dimensional one: length and area cannot be simultaneously used to encode different dimensions. Similarly, the combination of smaller-dimensional sizes is usually integral rather than separable, as illustrated in Figure 5.10 where the combination of small width, large width, small height, and large height yielded three groups rather than four: small areas, large areas, and flattened areas. It is possible that people asked to make area judgements might take the shortcut of simply making length judgements.

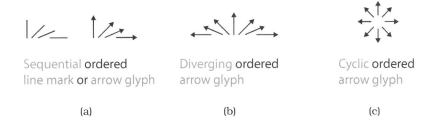

Sequential **ordered**   Diverging **ordered**   Cyclic **ordered**
line mark **or** arrow glyph   arrow glyph   arrow glyph

(a)   (b)   (c)

Figure 10.14. Tiltmaps using the angle channel to show three different types of ordered data. (a) A sequential attribute can be shown with either a line mark or an arrow glyph in one quadrant. (b) A diverging attribute can be shown with two quadrants and an arrow glyph. (c) A cyclic attribute can be shown with all four quadrants and arrow glyphs.

10.4.2   Angle Channel

The *angle* channel encodes magnitude information based on the **orientation** of a mark: the direction that it points. There are two slightly different ways to consider orientation that are essentially the same channel. With **angle**, the orientation of one line is judged with respect to another line. With **tilt**, an orientation is judged against the global frame of the display.* While this channel is somewhat less accurate than length and position, it is more accurate than area, the next channel down on the effectiveness ranking.

★ The terms *angle*, *tilt*, and **orientation** are often used as synonyms.

Angles can act as a sequential channel within a single $90°$ quadrant, as shown in Figure 10.14(a). However, as shown in Figure 10.14(c), an angle also has cyclic properties: a mark returns to its starting position after it swings all the way around. A simple line mark cycles four times when swinging around a full circle of $360°$. A more complex shape like an arrow, where the top can be distinguished from the bottom, cycles once for each full circle turn. Tilting an arrow glyph through a half-circle range of $180°$ yields a diverging **tiltmap**, as shown in Figure 10.14(b), where the central vertical position acts like the central neutral color that is the zero point in a diverging colormap, lying between orientations to the left or right.

The accuracy of our perception of angle is not uniform. We have very accurate perceptions of angles near the exact horizontal, vertical, or diagonal positions, but accuracy drops off in between them. We can tell $89°$ from $90°$, $44°$ from $45°$, and $1°$ from $0°$; however, we cannot tell $37°$ from $38°$.

10.4.3 Curvature Channel

The **curvature** channel is not very accurate, and it can only be used with line marks. It cannot be used with point marks that have no length, or area marks because their shape is fully constrained. The number of distinguishable bins for this channel is low, probably around two or three; it is in an equivalence class with volume (3D size) at the bottom of the magnitude channel ranking.

10.4.4 Shape Channel

The term **shape** is a catch-all word for a complex perceptual phenomenon. Vision scientists have identified many lower-level features that we can preattentively identify, including closure, curvature, termination, intersection, and others. For the purposes of analyzing visual encoding with marks and channels, I simplify by considering shape as a identity channel that can be used with point and line marks. Applying shape to point marks is the common case, and is easy to understand. Applying the shape channel to line marks results in stipple patterns such as dotted and dashed lines, as discussed below. The shape channel cannot be applied to area marks because their shape is constrained by definition.

If the point size is sufficiently large, the number of discriminable bins for the shape channel is dozens or even hundreds. However, there is a strong interaction between shape and size. When the region in which the shape must be drawn is small, then far fewer discriminable bins exist. For example, given a limit of 10×10 pixels, with careful design it might be possible to create roughly a dozen distinguishable shapes.

Shape can interfere with other channels in the same way that size coding does, and it can interfere with size coding itself. For example, filled-in shapes like disks are a good substrate for also encoding with color hue. Sparse line-oriented marks like crosses have fewer pixels available for color coding, so that channel will be impaired.

10.4.5 Motion Channels

Several kinds of **motion** are also visual channels, including **direction** of motion, **velocity** of motion, and flicker **frequency**. In order to use motion for visual encoding given a fixed spatial layout, the typical motion is a cyclic pattern where items somehow oscillate around their current location, so that they do not move outside the viewpoint, as would occur if they just continued to move in a single direction.

Motion is less studied than the other visual channels, but some results are known already. Motion is extremely salient, and moreover motion is very separable from all other static channels. In particular, it is strongly separable from the highly ranked channels typically used for showing groups and categories, such as color and spatial position.

The strength and weakness of motion is that it strongly draws attention; it is nearly impossible to ignore. The idea behind using separable channels for visual encoding is that the viewer can selectively attend to any of the channels; however, directing attention selectively to the nonmoving channels may be difficult when motion is used. Flicker and blinking are so difficult to ignore that they can be very annoying and should only be used with great care.

It is not clear whether different motion channels are separable from each other, or how many discriminable bins exist in each. A safe strategy with motion is to create a single combined motion channel and use it for a binary category of just two levels: items that move versus items that don't move. Thus, although an individual motion subchannel such as velocity could in theory act as a magnitude channel, I simplify the complex situation by classifying motion as a identity channel, much like shape.

The motion channels are most appropriate for highlighting, where drawing the user's attention away from the rest of the scene is exactly the goal, particularly when the highlighting is transitory rather than ongoing. Temporary highlighting is often used with lightweight actions such as mouseover or clicking, as opposed to more heavyweight actions such as using search, where a text string is typed into a control panel. Many uses of highlighting are indeed binary, where the selected items just need to be distinguished from the nonselected ones. Even blinking could be appropriate in cases where very strong emphasis is desired, for example with dynamic layouts where new items at multiple locations have just been added to the view in a single timestep.

▶ Section 11.4.2 covers highlighting.

10.4.6   Texture and Stippling

The term **texture** refers to very small-scale patterns. Texture is also a complex perceptual phenomenon that can be simplified by considering it as the combination of three perceptual dimensions: orientation, scale, and contrast. The first two pertain to the individual texture elements and have obvious mappings to the angle and size channels, respectively. Contrast refers to luminance contrast, which is related to the *density* of the texture elements; it maps to the luminance channel.

Texture can be used to show categorical attributes, in which case the goal is to create patterns that are distinguishable from each other using the combination of all three channels. In this case, with sufficient care it is possible to create at least one or two dozen distingishable bins.

Texture can also be used to show ordered attributes, for example, by mapping separate attributes to each of the three channels. In this case, no more than three or four bins can be distinguished for each. Another possibility is to use all three channels in combination to encode more bins of a single attribute; with careful design, around a dozen bins can be distinguishable.

The term **stippling** means to fill in regions of drawing with short strokes. It is a special case of texture. Stippling is still in regular use for lines; a familiar example is the use of dotted or dashed lines. Stippling was heavily used for area marks with older printing technology because it allows shades of gray to be approximated using only black ink; now that color and grayscale printing are cheap and pervasive, area stippling is less popular than in the past.*

★ The terms **hatching** and **cross-hatching** are synonyms for *stippling* in two-dimensional areas.

10.5 Further Reading

The Big Picture Ware's textbook is an excellent resource for further detail on all of the channels covered in this chapter [Ware 13].

Color Theory Stone's brief article [Stone 10] and longer book [Stone 03] are an excellent introduction to color.

Colormap Design The design of segmented colormaps has been extensively discussed in the cartographic literature: Brewer offers very readable color use guidelines [Brewer 99] derived from that community, in conjunction with the very useful ColorBrewer tool at http://www.colorbrewer2.org. Early guidelines on quantitative colormap creation and the reasons to avoid rainbow colormaps are in series of papers [Bergman et al. 95, Rogowitz and Treinish 96, Rogowitz and Treinish 98], with more recent work continuing the struggle against rainbows as a default [Borland and Taylor 07]. An empirical study of bivariate colormaps showed their serious limitations for encoding two categorical attributes [Wainer and Francolini 80].

Motion An empirical study investigated different kinds of motion highlighting and confirmed its effectiveness in contexts where color coding was already being used to convey other information [Ware and Bobrow 04].

Texture Ware proposes breaking down texture into orientation, scale, and constrast subchannels, as part of a thorough discussion of the use of texture for visual encoding in his textbook [Ware 13, Chapter 6].

Manipulate

→ **Change over Time**

→ **Select**

→ **Navigate**

→ Item Reduction

→ *Zoom*
Geometric or *Semantic*

→ *Pan/Translate*

→ *Constrained*

→ Attribute Reduction

→ *Slice*

→ *Cut*

→ *Project*

Figure 11.1. Design choices for idioms that change a view.

Chapter 11

Manipulate View

11.1   The Big Picture

Figure 11.1 shows the design choices for how to manipulate a view: to change anything about it, to select items or attributes within it, and to navigate to a different viewpoint.

The ways to change a view cover the full set of all other design choices for idioms. A change could be made from one choice to another to change idioms, and any of the parameters for a particular idiom can be changed. Any aspect of visual encoding can be changed, including the ordering, any other choice pertaining to the spatial arrangement, and the use of other visual channels such as color. Changes could be made concerning what elements are filtered, the level of detail of aggregation, and how the data is partitioned into multiple views.

A change often requires a set of items or attributes within the vis as input. There are several choices about how a user can select elements: what kind of elements can be targets, how many selection types are supported, how many elements can be in the selected set, and how to highlight the elements.

Navigation is a change of viewpoint; that is, changing what is shown in a view based on the metaphor of a camera looking at the scene from a moveable point of view. It's a rich enough source of design choices that it's addressed separately in the framework as a special case. Zooming in to see fewer items in more detail can be done geometrically, matching the semantics of real-world motion. With semantic zooming, the way to draw items adapts on the fly based on the number of available pixels, so appearance can change dramatically rather than simply shrinking or enlarging. The camera metaphor also motivates the idea that attributes are assigned to spatial dimensions, leading to the slice idiom of extracting a single slice from the view volume and the cut idiom of separating the volume into two parts with a plane and eliminating everything on one side of it. The project idiom reduces the number of dimensions using one of many possible transformations.

11.2   Why Change?

> ▶ One is deriving new data as discussed in Chapter 3. The other three options are covered in subsequent chapters: faceting the data by partitioning it into multiple juxtaposed views or superimposed layers in Chapter 12, reducing the amount of data to show within a view in Chapter 13, and embedding focus and context information together within a single view in Chapter 14.

Datasets are often sufficiently large and complex that showing everything at once in a single static view would lead to overwhelming visual clutter. There are five major options for handling complexity; a view that changes over time is one of them. These five choices are not mutually exclusive and can be combined together.

Changing the view over time is the most obvious, most popular, and most flexible choice in vis design. The most fundamental breakthrough of vis on a computer display compared with printed on paper is the possibility of interactivity: a view that changes over time can dynamically respond to user input, rather than being limited to a static visual encoding. Obviously, all interactive idioms involve a view that changes over time.

11.3   Change View over Time

The possibilities for how the view changes can be based on any of the other design choices of *how* to construct an idiom: change the encoding, change the arrangement, change the order, change the viewpoint, change which attributes are filtered, change the aggregation level, and so on.

For example, the visual encoding could be changed to a completely different idiom. Some vis tools allow the user to manually change between several different idioms, such as switching from a node–link layout to a matrix layout of a network. Giving the user control of the encoding is particularly common in general-purpose systems designed to flexibly accommodate a large range of possible datasets, rather than special-purpose systems fine tuned for a very particular task. Figure 11.2 shows a sequence of different visual encodings of the same product sales dataset created with the Tableau system, which supports fluidly moving between encodings via drag and drop interactions to specify which attributes to encode with which channels. Figure 11.2(a) shows the data encoded with simple bars, changed to stacked bars in Figure 11.2(b). Figure 11.2(c) shows a recommendation of alternate encodings that are good choices taking into account the types and semantics of

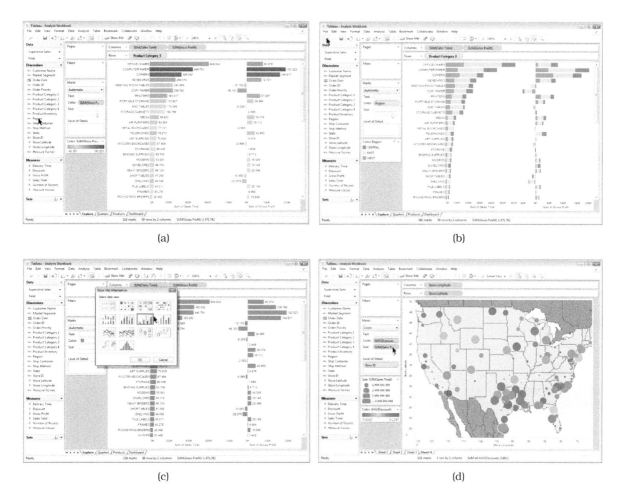

Figure 11.2. Tableau supports fluid changes between visual encoding idioms with drag and drop interaction. (a) Data encoded with bars. (b) Data encoded with stacked bars. (c) The user selects a completely different visual encoding. (d) Data encoded using geographic positions.

the attributes. Figure 11.2(d) shows the use of given spatial geometry as a substrate, with circular area marks size coded for the sum of sales and color coded with a diverging red–green colormap showing the average discount.

Another kind of view change is to alter some parameter of the existing encoding, such as the range of possible mark sizes.

Many kinds of change involve rearrangement of some or all of the items in the view. Reordering, often called **sorting**, is a powerful choice for finding patterns in a dataset by interactively changing the attribute that is used to order the data. For example, a common interaction with tables is to sort the rows according to the values in a chosen column. The same principle holds for more exotic visual encodings as well. The power of reordering lies in the privileged status of spatial position as the highest ranked visual channel. Reordering data spatially allows us to invoke the pattern-finding parts of our visual system to quickly check whether the new configuration conveys new information. It can be used with any categorical attribute. In contrast, reordering does not make sense for ordered attributes, which have a given order already.

▶ Visual channels are discussed in detail in Chapter 5.

▶ Ordering regions containing categorical data is covered in Section 7.5.

Example: LineUp

The LineUp system is designed to support exploration of tables with many attributes through interactive reordering and realigning. In addition to sorting by any individual attribute, the user can sort by complex weighted combinations of multiple attributes. LineUp is explicitly designed to support the comparison of multiple rankings.

Figure 11.3 compares several different rankings of top universities. On the left is a customized combination of attributes and weights for the 2012 data, and in the middle is the official ranking for 2012, with colored

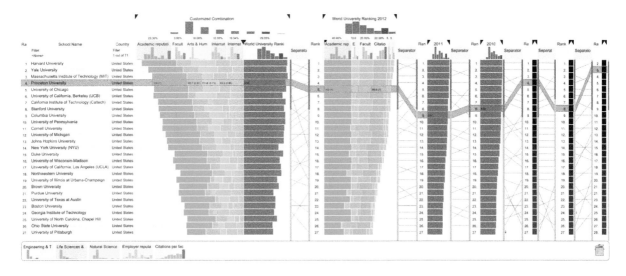

Figure 11.3. The LineUp system for comparing multiattribute rankings with reordering and realignment. From [Gratzl et al. 13, Figure 1].

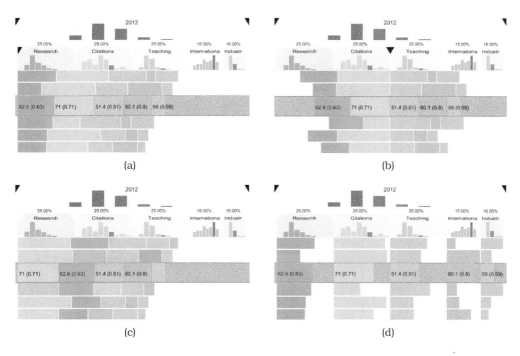

Figure 11.4. Changing the alignment in Lineup. (a) Classical stacked bars. (b) Diverging stacked bars. (c) Ordered stacked bars. (d) Separately aligned bars: small multiple bar charts. From [Gratzl et al. 13, Figure 4].

stacked bar charts showing the contribution of the component attributes for both. The next two columns show a compressed view with a single summary bar for two more rankings, using the data for years 2011 and 2010, and the last three columns have a collapsed heatmap view with the value encoded in grayscale rather than with bar length. The uncollapsed columns are scented widgets, with histograms showing the distributions within them at the top. Between the bar chart columns are **slope graphs**, where connecting line marks link the same items together.* Items that do not change their ranking between neighboring columns are connected by straight lines, while highly sloped lines that cross many others show items whose ranking changed significantly.

Figure 11.4 shows the results of changing the alignment to each of the four different possibilities. In addition to classical stacked bars as in Figure 11.4(a), any of the attributes can be set as the baseline from which the alignment diverges, as in Figure 11.4(b). Figure 11.4(c) shows the bars sorted by decreasing size separately in each row, for the purpose of emphasizing which attributes contribute most to that item's score. Figure 11.4(d) shows each attribute aligned to its own baseline, which yields a small-multiple view with one horizontal bar chart in each column. When

▶ Scented widgets are covered in Section 13.3.1.

★ *Slope graphs* are also known as **bump charts**.

▶ Partitioning data into small-multiple views is covered in Section 12.4.

▶ Animated transitions are discussed in the next example.

the alignment is changed, an animated transition between the two states occurs.

In contrast to many of the previous examples of using derived data, where the vis designer is the one who makes choices about deriving data, with LineUp the user decides what data to derive on the fly during an analysis session.

System	LineUp
What: Data	Table.
What: Derived	Ordered attribute: weighted combination of selected attributes.
How: Encode	Stacked bar charts, slope graphs.
How: Manipulate	Reorder, realign, animated transitions.
Why: Task	Compare rankings, distributions.

▶ Design choices for reducing and increasing the data shown are discussed in Chapter 13.

▶ The Eyes Beat Memory rule of thumb in Section 6.5 discusses some of the strengths and weaknesses of animation.

Many kinds of change involve reducing or increasing the amount of data that is shown: changes to aggregation and filtering are at the heart of interactive data reduction idioms.

Many kinds of changes to a view over time fall into the general category of **animation**, including changes to the spatial layout. While animation has intuitive appeal to many beginning designers, it is valuable to think carefully about cognitive load and other trade-offs.

Example: Animated Transitions

★ The term *jump cut* comes from cinematography.

▶ Navigation is covered in Section 11.5.

One of the best-justified uses of animation is the idiom of **animated transition**, where a series of frames is generated to smoothly transition from one state to another. Animated transitions are thus an alternative to a **jump cut**, where the display simply changes abruptly from one state to the next.* This idiom is often used for navigation, in which case the two states are different camera viewpoints. More generally, they can be constructed to bridge between the start and end state of any kind of change, including reordering items, filtering by adding or removing items from the view, changing the visual encoding, or updating item values as they change over time.

The benefit of animated transitions is that they help users maintain a sense of context between the two states by explicitly showing how an item in the first state moves to its new position in the second state, rather than forcing users to do item tracking on their own using internal cognitive and memory resources. These transitions are most useful when the amount of change is limited, because people cannot track everything that occurs

Figure 11.5. Frames from an animated transition showing zoom between levels in a compound network arranged as an adjacency matrix. From [van Ham 03, Figure 4].

if many items change in different ways all over the frame. They work well when either a small number of objects change while the rest stay the same, or when groups of objects move together in similar ways. Transitions can also be broken down into a small number of stages. An empirical study showed that carefully designed animated transitions do indeed support better graphical perception of change [Heer and Robertson 07].

Figure 11.5 shows an example of five frames from an animated transition of a network shown as an adjacency matrix. The data type shown is a compound network, where there is a cluster hierarchy associated with the base network. The transition shows a change from one level of hierarchical aggregation to the next, providing more detail. Accordingly, the scope of what is shown narrows down to show only a subset of what is visible in the first frame. The middle block gradually stretches out to fill all of the available space, and additional structure appears within it; the other blocks gradually squish down to nothing, with their structure gradually becoming more aggregated as the amount of available screen space decreases.

▶ Visually encoding a network as an adjacency matrix is covered in Section 9.3.

▶ Compound networks are discussed in Section 9.5.

▶ Hierarchical aggregation is covered in Section 13.4.1.

Idiom	Animated Transitions
What: Data	Compound network.
How: Manipulate	Change with animated transition. Navigate between aggregation levels.

11.4   Select Elements

Allowing users to **select** one or more elements of interest in a vis is a fundamental action that supports nearly every interactive idiom. The output of a selection operation is often the input to a subsequent operation. In particular, the *change* choice is usually dependent on a previous *select* result.

11.4.1 Selection Design Choices

A fundamental design choice with selection is what kinds of elements can be selection targets. The most common element is data items, and another element is links in the case of network data. In some vis tools, data attributes are also selectable. It's also common to be able to select by **levels** within an attribute; that is, all items that share a unique value for that attribute. When the data is faceted across multiple views, then a view itself can also be a selection target.

▶ Multiple views are covered further in Chapter 12.

The number of independent selection types is also a design choice. In the simplest case, there is only one kind of selection: elements are either selected or not selected. It's also common to support two kinds of selection, for example in some cases a mouse click produces one kind of selection and a mouse **hover**, where the cursor simply passes over the object, produces another. It's also common to have multiple kinds of clicks. The low-level details of interface hardware often come into play with this design choice. With a mouse, clicks and hovers are easy to get, and if the mouse has several buttons there are several kinds of clicks. If there is also a keyboard, then key presses can be added to the mix, either in addition to or instead of a multi-button mouse. Some kinds of touch screens provide hover information, but others don't. It's much more rare for hardware to support multiple levels of proximity, such as *nearby* as an intermediate state between *hover* and *distant*.

Another design choice is how many elements can be in the selection set. Should there be exactly one? Can there be many? Is a set of zero elements acceptable? Is there a primary versus secondary selection? If many elements can be selected, do you support only the selection of a spatially contiguous group of items, or allow the user to add and remove items from the selection set in multiple passes?

For some tasks there should only be one item selected at a time, which means that choosing a new item replaces the old one. While occasionally task semantics require that there must always be a selected item, often it makes sense that the selection set could be empty. In this case, selection is often implemented as a toggle, where a single action such as clicking switches between select and deselect. For example, a vis tool might be designed so that there is a specific view of fixed size where detailed information about a single selected item is shown. That choice implies the detail selection set should have a maximum of one item at a time, and a set size of zero can be easily accommodated by leaving the pane blank.

In other tasks, it is meaningful to have many items selected at once, so there must be actions for adding items, removing items, and clearing the selection set. For example, a vis tool might allow the user to interactively assign items into any of seven main groups, change the name of a group, and change the color of items in the group. In this situation, it's a good design choice to move beyond simply using different selection types into a design that explicitly tracks group membership using attributes. For example, if an element can only belong to one group, then a single categorical attribute can be used to store group membership. If items can belong to many, then the information can be stored with multiple attributes, one for each group, with an indication for each item whether it's in that group or not. In this case, straightforward selection can be used to pick a group as the current target and then to add and remove items to that group. For most users, it would be more natural to think about groups than about attribute levels, but it's sometimes useful to think about the underlying attribute structure as a designer.

In the previous example the selection set could contain multiple items, but all items within the set were interchangeable. Some abstract tasks require a distinction between a primary and secondary selection, for example, path traversal in a directed graph from a source to a target node. Once again, some tasks require that these sets contain only one item apiece, while other tasks may require multi-item sets for one, the other, or both.

11.4.2 Highlighting

The action of selection is very closely tied to **highlighting**, where the elements that were chosen are indicated by changing their visual appearance in some way. Selection should trigger highlighting in order to provide users with immediate visual feedback, to confirm that the results of their operations match up with their intentions. The requirement to highlight the selection is so well understood that these two actions are sometimes treated as synonyms and used interchangeably. However, you should consider two different design choices that can be independently varied: the interaction idiom of how the user selects elements and the visual encoding idiom of how the selected elements are highlighted.

For data items, nearly any change of visual encoding strategy can be used for highlighting. For example, it's a very common

▶ The timing requirements for this kind of visual feedback are discussed in Section 6.8.

design choice to highlight selected items by changing their color. Another important caveat is that the highlight color should be sufficiently different from the other colors that a visual popout effect is achieved with sufficient hue, luminance, or saturation contrast.

▶ Popout is discussed in Section 5.5.4.

A fundamental limitation of highlighting by color change is that the existing color coding is temporarily hidden. For some abstract tasks, that limitation constitutes a major problem. An alternative design choice that preserves color coding is to highlight with an outline. You could either add an outline mark around the selected object or change the color of an existing outline mark to the highlight color. It's safest to highlight the items individually rather than to assume the selection set is a spatially contiguous group, unless you've built that selection constraint into the vis tool.

This choice may not provide enough visual salience when marks are small, but it can be very effective for large ones. Another design choice is to use the size channel, for example by increasing an item's size or the linewidth of a link. For links, it's also common to highlight with the shape channel, by changing a solid line to a dashed one. These choices can be combined for increased salience, for example, by highlighting lines with increased width and a color change.

Another possible design choice is to use motion coding, such as moving all selected points in small circular orbits oscillating around their usual location, or by moving all selected items slightly back and forth relative to their original position, or by having a dash pattern crawl along selected links. Although this choice is still unusual, Ware and Bobrow ran experiments finding that motion coding often outperformed more traditional highlighting approaches of coloring, outlining, and size changes [Ware and Bobrow 04].

If attributes are directly encoded with marks within a view, then they can be highlighted with the same set of design choices as data items. For example, a selected parallel coordinates axis could be highlighted with a color change or by adding an outline. In other cases, the attribute selection might be done through a control panel rather than in a full vis view, in which case the visual feedback could be accomplished through standard 2D user interface (UI) widgets such as radio buttons and lists. Similarly, the highlighting for a selected view is often simply a matter of using the existing UI widget support for windows in the user's operating system.

Another different design choice for highlighting is to add connection marks between the objects in the selection set. This choice

to explicitly draw links is a contrast to the more implicit alternative
choices discussed above, where existing marks are changed.

Example: Context-Preserving Visual Links

Figure 11.6 shows the idiom of context-preserving visual links, where links
are drawn as curves that are carefully routed between existing elements
in a vis [Steinberger et al. 11]. The route takes into account trade-offs
between four criteria: minimizing link lengths, minimizing the occlusion
of salient regions, maximizing the difference between the link's color and
the colors of the existing elements that it crosses, and maximizing the
bundling of links together.

▶ Edge bundling is dis-
cussed further in Sec-
tion 12.5.2.

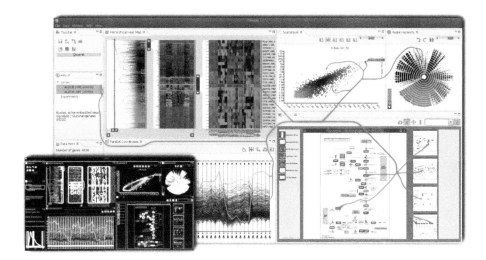

Figure 11.6. The context-preserving visual links idiom is an example of the design choice to coordinate betweeen views by explicitly drawing links as connection marks between items and regions of interest. From [Steinberger et al. 11, Figure 1].

Idiom	Context-Preserving Visual Links
What: Data	Any data.
How: Encode	Any encoding. Highlight with link marks connecting items across views.
How: Manipulate	Select any element.
(How: Coordinate)	Juxtaposed multiple views.

11.4.3   Selection Outcomes

Sometimes the outcome of selection is additional actions, beyond simply highlighting. Selection is often a first step in a multistage sequence, allowing the user to indicate specific elements that should be the target of the next action. That is, the output of a select action is often the input to the next action. Nearly all of the other major design choices of how idioms are constructed can accommodate a selected set of elements as input. For example, selected items might be filtered or aggregated, or their visual encoding could be changed. A selected set of regions or items might be reordered within a view. A navigation trajectory could be constructed so that a selected item is centered within the view at the end of an animated transition.

> ▶ Chained sequences of tasks are discussed in Section 1.14 and 3.7.

11.5   Navigate: Changing Viewpoint

Large and complex datasets often cannot be understood from only a single point of view. Many interactive vis systems support a metaphor of navigation, analogous to navigation through the physical world. In these, the spatial layout is fixed and navigation acts as a change of the viewpoint.

The term **navigation** refers to changing the point of view from which things are drawn. The underlying metaphor is a virtual camera located in a particular spot and aimed in a particular direction. When that camera **viewpoint** is changed, the set of items visible in the camera **frame** also changes.

Navigation can be broken down into three components. The action of **zooming** moves the camera closer to or farther from the plane. Zooming the camera in close will show fewer items, which appear to be larger. Zooming out so that the camera is far away will show more items, and they will appear smaller. The action of **panning** the camera moves it parallel to the plane of the image, either up and down or from side to side.* In 3D navigation, the general term **translating** is more commonly used for any motion that changes camera position.* The action of **rotating** spins the camera around its own axis. Rotation is rare in two-dimensional navigation, but it is much more important with 3D motion.

Since changing the viewpoint changes the visible set of items, the outcome of navigation could be some combination of filtering and aggregation. Zooming in or panning with a zoomed-in camera

> ★ In 2D navigation, the term **scrolling** is a synonym for *panning*.

> ★ In this book, *pan* and *zoom* are used to mean translating the camera parallel to and perpendicular to the image plane; this loose sense matches the usage in the infovis literature. In cinematography, these motions are called *trucking* and *dollying*. The action of **trucking**, where the camera is translated parallel to the image plane, is distinguished from **panning**, where the camera stays in the same location and turns to point in a different direction. The action of **dollying**, where the camera is translated closer to the scene, is distinguished from **zooming** by changing the focal length of the camera lens.

filters based on the spatial layout; zooming out can act as aggregation that creates an overview.

Navigation by panning or translating is straightfoward; zooming is the more complex case that requires further discussion.

> ▶ Filtering and aggregation
> are covered in Chapter 13.

11.5.1 Geometric Zooming

An intuitive form of navigation is **geometric zooming** because it corresponds almost exactly with our real-world experience of walking closer to objects, or grasping objects with our hands and moving them closer to our eyes. In the 2D case, the metaphor is moving a piece of paper closer to or farther from our eyes, while keeping it parallel to our face.

11.5.2 Semantic Zooming

With geometric zooming, the fundamental appearance of objects is fixed, and moving the viewpoint simply changes the size at which they are drawn in image space. An alternative, nongeometric approach to motion does not correspond to simply moving a virtual camera. With **semantic zooming**, the representation of the object adapts to the number of pixels available in the image-space region occupied by the object. The visual appearance of an object can change subtly or dramatically at different scales.

For instance, an abstract visual representation of a text file might always be a rectangular box, but its contents would change considerably. When the box was small, it would contain only a short text label, with the name of the file. A medium-sized box could contain the full document title. A large box could accommodate a multiline summary of the file contents. If the representation did not change, the multiple lines of text would simply be illegible when the box was small.

Figure 11.7 shows an example from the LiveRAC system for analyzing large collections of time-series data, in this case resource usage for large-scale system administration [McLachlan et al. 08]. Line charts in a very large grid use semantic zooming, automatically adapting to the amount of space available as rows and columns are stretched and squished. When the available box is tiny, then only a single categorical variable is shown with color coding. Slightly larger boxes also use **sparklines**, very concise line charts with dots marking the minimum and maximum values for that time period. As the box size passes thresholds, axes are

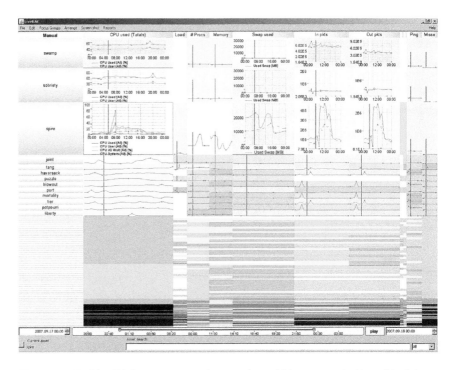

Figure 11.7. LiveRAC uses semantic zooming within a stretchable grid of time-series line charts. From [McLachlan et al. 08, Figure 2b].

▶ Focus+context approaches are discussed further in Chapter 14.

drawn and multiple line charts are superimposed. The stretch-and-squish navigation idiom is an example of a focus+context approach.

11.5.3 Constrained Navigation

With **unconstrained navigation**, the camera can move anywhere at all. It is very easy to implement for programmers who have learned the framework of standard computer graphics. It does have the conceptual appeal of allowing users access to a clearly defined mathematical category of transformations. However, users often have difficulty figuring out how to achieve a desired viewpoint with completely free navigation, especially in three dimensions. Navigating with the six degrees of freedom available in 3D space is not a skill that most people have acquired; pilots of airplanes and helicopters are the exception rather than the rule. To make matters worse, when interacting with virtual objects drawn with computer graphics, it is easy to inadvertently move the viewpoint inside objects that are intended to be solid. The physics of reality prevent interpenetration between our heads and objects like walls, floors, or basketballs. With computer graphics, collision detection is a computationally intensive process that is separate from drawing and does not come for free. Another problem is ending up with the camera pointed at nothing at all, so that the entire frame is empty and it is not obvious where to go in order to see something interesting. This problem is especially common in 3D settings, but it can still be a problem in 2D settings with unconstrained panning and zooming. A button to reset the view is of course a good idea, but it is far from a complete solution.

In contrast, **constrained navigation** idioms have some kind of limit on the possible motion of the camera. One of the simplest approaches in a 2D setting is to limit the zoom range, so that the camera cannot zoom out much farther than the distance where the entire drawn scene is visible or zoom in much farther than the size of the smallest object.

Many approaches allow the user to easily select some item of interest, to which the system can then automatically calculate a smooth camera trajectory for an **animated transition** from the current viewpoint to a viewpoint better suited to viewing the selected item, thus maintaining context. Figure 15.20 shows an example where the final viewpoint is zoomed in enough that labels are clearly visible, zoomed out far enough that the full extent of the object fits in the frame, and panned so that the object is within the frame. In this case, a click anywhere within the green box enclosing a set of words is interpreted as a request to frame the entire complex object in the view, not a request to simply zoom in to that exact point in space. In 3D, a useful additional constraint is that final orientation looks straight down at the object along a vector perpendicular to it, with the up vector of the camera consistent with the vertical axis of the object.

Constrained navigation is particularly powerful when combined with linked navigation between multiple views. For example, a tabular or list view could be sorted by many possible attributes, including simple alphabetical ordering. These views support search well, where the name of a unique item is known in advance. Clicking on that object in the list view could trigger navigation to ensure that the object of interest is framed within another, more elaborate, view designed for browsing local neighborhoods where the items are laid out with a very different encoding for spatial position.

Many vis tools support both types of navigation. For example, constrained navigation may be designed to provide shortcuts for common use, with unconstrained navigation as a backup for the uncommon cases where the user needs completely general controls.

11.6 Navigate: Reducing Attributes

The geometric intuitions that underlie the metaphor of navigation with a virtual camera also lead to a set of design choices for reducing the number of attributes: slice, cut, and project. In this section I often use the term *dimensions* instead of the synonym *attributes* to emphasize this intuition of moving a camera through space. Although these idioms are inspired by ways to manipulate a virtual camera in a 3D scene, they also generalize to higher-dimensional spaces. These idioms are very commonly used for spatial field datasets, but they can sometimes be usefully applied to abstract data.

11.6.1 Slice

With the **slice** design choice, a single value is chosen from the dimension to eliminate, and only the items matching that value for the dimension are extracted to include in the lower-dimensional slice. Slicing is a particularly intuitive metaphor when reducing spatial data from 3D to 2D.

Figure 11.8(a) shows a classic example of inspecting a 3D scan of a human head by interactively changing the slice location to different heights along the skull. That is, the value chosen is a specific height in the third dimension, and the information extracted is the 2D position and color for each point matching that height. Here the slicing plane is aligned to one of the major axes of the human body, which are also the original dimensions used to gather the data. One benefit of axis-aligned slices is that they may correspond to views that are familiar to the viewer: for example, medical students learn anatomy in terms of cross sections along the standard coronal, sagittal, and horizontal planes.

It is also possible to slice along a plane at an arbitrary orientation that does not match the original axes, exploiting the same intuition. Mathematically, the operation is more complex, because finding the values to extract may require a significant computation rather than a simple look-up.*

★ Using the vocabulary of signal processing, care must taken to minimize **sampling** and **interpolation** artifacts. These questions are also discussed in Section 8.4.

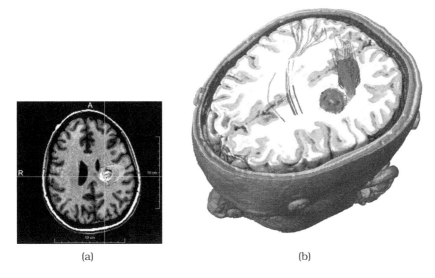

(a)   (b)

Figure 11.8. The *slice* choice eliminates a dimension/attribute by extracting only the items with a chosen value in that dimension. The *cut* choice eliminates all data on one side of a spatial cutting plane. (a) Axis-aligned slice. (b) Axis-aligned cut. From [Rieder et al. 08, Figures 7c and 0].

Slicing is not restricted to a change from 3D to 2D. The same idea holds in the more general case, where the slicing plane could be a **hyperplane**; that is, the higher-dimensional version of a plane. In the case of reducing to just one dimension, the hyperplane would simply be a line. Slicing can be used to eliminate multiple dimensions at once, for example by reducing from six dimensions to one.

Example: HyperSlice

The HyperSlice system uses the design choice of slicing for attribute reduction to display abstract data with many attributes: scalar functions with many variables [van Wijk and van Liere 93]. The visual encoding is a set of views showing all possible orthogonal two-dimensional slices aligned in a matrix. Figure 11.9(a) shows the intuition behind the system for a simple 3D example of three planes that intersect at right angles to each other. The views are coordinated with linked navigation of the high-dimensional space, where each view is both a display and a control: dragging with a view changes the slice value based on its pair of dimen-

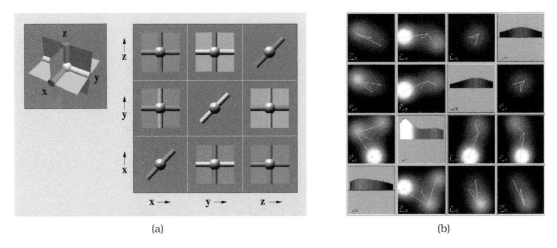

(a)   (b)

Figure 11.9. The HyperSlice system uses extracting only the items with a chosen value in that dimension. (a) Three 3D planes that intersect at right angles. (b) Four-dimensional dataset where function value is encoded with luminance. From [van Wijk and van Liere 93, Figures 1 and 4].

sions. Figure 11.9(b) shows a more complex four-dimensional dataset, where the function value is coded with luminance.

11.6.2   Cut

The interaction idiom of **cut** allows the user to position a plane that divides the viewing volume in two, and everything on the side of the plane nearest to the camera viewpoint is not shown. This **cutting plane** can either be axis aligned or arbitrarily oriented, just as with the slices.* Cutting is often used to see features in the interior of a 3D volume. Figure 11.8(b) shows an example, again with medical image data of a human brain. The cutting plane is set to the same level as the slice in Figure 11.8(a). The *cut* design choice shows more information than just the 2D slice alone, since the surrounding 3D context behind the cutting plane is also visible. Figure 8.6(c) also shows a cutting plane in use on a human head dataset, but with the visual encoding idiom of direct volume rendering.

★ In computer graphics, this plane is often called a **clipping plane**.

11.6.3   Project

With the **project** design choice, all items are shown, but without the information for specific dimensions chosen to exclude. For instance, the shadow of an object on a wall or floor is a projection from 3D to 2D. There are many types of projection; some retain partial information about the removed dimensions, while others eliminate that completely.

A very simple form of projection is **orthographic projection**: for each item the values for excluded dimensions are simply dropped, and no information about the eliminated dimensions is retained. In the case of orthographic projection from 3D to 2D, all information about depth is lost.* Projections are often used via multiple views, where there can be a view for each possible combination of dimensions. For instance, standard architectural blueprints show the three possible views for axis-aligned 2D views of a 3D XYZ scene: a floor plan for the XY dimensions, a side view for YZ, and a front view for XZ.

> ★ The term **dimensional filtering**, common when working with abstract data, is essentially a synonym for **orthographic projection**, more commonly used when working with spatial data.

A more complex yet more familiar form of projection is the standard **perspective projection**, which also projects from 3D to 2D. This transformation happens automatically in our eyes and is mathematically modeled in the perspective transformation used in the computer graphics virtual camera. While a great deal of information about depth is lost, some is retained through the **perspective distortion** foreshortening effect, where distant objects are closer together on the image plane than nearby objects would be.

Many **map projections** from the surface of the Earth to 2D maps have been proposed by cartographers, including the well-known Mercator projection. These projections transform from a curved to a flat space, and most of the design choices when creating them concern whether distorting angles or areas is less problematic for the intended abstract task.[1]

11.7   Further Reading

Change An early paper argues for adding interaction support to previously static visual encoding idioms as a good starting point for thinking about views that change [Dix and Ellis 98].

---

[1]Mathematically, cartographic projections are a transformation from a 2D curved space that is embedded in three dimensions, namely, the surface of the Earth, to a 2D flat space, so they do not cleanly fit the intuition of projection as a way to reduce dimensionality.

Animated Transitions A taxonomy of animated transition types includes design guidelines for constructing transitions, and an empirical study showing strong evidence that properly designed transitions can improve graphical perception of changes [Heer and Robertson 07].

Select The entertainingly named *Selection: 524,288 Ways to Say "This Is Interesting"* contains nicely reasoned arguments for narrowing selection operations across linked views to a small set of combinations [Wills 96].

Semantic Zooming The Pad++ system was an early exploration into semantic zooming [Bederson and Hollan 94]; LiveRAC is a more recent system using that idiom [McLachlan et al. 08].

Constrained Navigation Early work evangelized the idea of constrained navigation in 3D [Mackinlay et al. 90]; later work provides a framework for calculating smooth and efficient 2D panning and zooming trajectories [van Wijk and Nuij 03].

Facet

⊕ Juxtapose and Coordinate Multiple Side-by-Side Views

→ Share Encoding: Same/Different

→ *Linked Highlighting*

→ Share Data: All/Subset/None

→ Share Navigation

		Data		
		All	Subset	None
Encoding	Same	Redundant	Overview/Detail	Small Multiples
	Different	Multiform	Multiform, Overview/Detail	No Linkage

⊕ Partition into Side-by-Side Views

⊕ Superimpose Layers

Figure 12.1. Design choices of how to facet information between multiple views.

Chapter 12

Facet into Multiple Views

12.1   The Big Picture

This chapter covers choices about how to facet data across multiple views, as shown in Figure 12.1. One option for showing views is juxtapose them side by side, leading to many choices of how to coordinate these views with each other. The other option is to superimpose the views as layers on top of each other. When the views show different data, a set of choices covers how to partition data across multiple views.

The main design choices for juxtaposed views cover how to coordinate them: which visual encoding channels are shared between them, how much of the data is shared between them, and whether the navigation is synchronized. Other juxtaposition choices are when to show each view and how to arrange them. The design choices for partitioning are how many regions to use, how to divide the data up into regions, the order in which attributes are used to split, and when to stop. The design choices for how to superimpose include how elements are partitioned between layers, how many layers to use, how to distinguish them from each other, and whether the layers are static or dynamically constructed.

12.2   Why Facet?

The verb **facet** means to split; this chapter covers the design choices that pertain to splitting up the display, into either multiple views or layers. One of the five major approaches to handling visual complexity involves faceting information: juxtaposing coordinated views side by side and superimposing layers within a single view. In both of these cases, the data needs to be partitioned into the views or layers.

Multiple views juxtaposed side by side are spread out in space, an alternative to a changing view where the information presented

▶ The other four approaches are covered in other chapters: Chapter 3 covers deriving new data to include in a view, Chapter 11 covers changing a single view over time, Chapter 13 covers reducing the amount of data to show in a view, and Chapter 14 covers embedding focus and context information within the same view.

▶ For more on the ideas behind the slogan *Eyes Beat Memory*, see Section 6.5.

to the user is spread out over time. Comparing two views that are simultaneously visible is relatively easy, because we can move our eyes back and forth between them to compare their states. In contrast, for a changing view, comparing its current state to its previous state requires users to consult their working memory, a scarce internal resource.

The *multiform* design choice for coordinating juxtaposed views is to use a different encoding in each one to show the same data. The rationale is that no single visual encoding is optimal for all possible tasks; a multiform vis tool can thus support more tasks, or faster switching between tasks, than a tool that only shows a single view. Cooordinating multiform views with linked highlighting allows users to see whether a spatial neighborhood in one view also falls into contiguous regions in the other views or whether it is distributed differently.

The *small multiples* coordination choice involves partitioning the data between views. Partitioning is a powerful and general idea, especially when used hierarchically with a succession of attributes to slice and dice the dataset up into pieces of possible interest. The choice of which attributes to partition versus which to directly encode with, as well as the order of partitioning, has a profound effect on what aspects of the dataset are visually salient.

The obvious and significant cost to juxtaposed views is the display area required to show these multiple windows side by side. When two views are shown side by side, they each get only half the area that a single view could provide. Display area is a scarce external resource. The trade-off between the scarcity of display area and working memory is a major issue in choosing between juxtaposing additional views and changing an existing view.

In contrast, superimposing layers does not require more screen space. Visual layering is a way to control visual clutter in complex visual encodings, leading to a less cluttered view than a single view without any layers. Superimposing layers and changing the view over time are not mutually exclusive: these two design choices are often used together. In particular, the choice to dynamically construct layers necessarily implies an interactive view that changes. One limitation of superimposing is that creating visually distinguishable layers imposes serious constraints on visual encoding choices. A major difference between layering and juxtaposing is the strong limits on the number of layers that can be superimposed on each other before the visual clutter becomes overwhelming: two is very feasible and three is possible with care, but more would be difficult. In contrast, the juxtaposing choice can accommodate a much larger number of views, where several is straightforward and up to a few dozen is viable with care.

12.3   Juxtapose and Coordinate Views

Using multiple juxtaposed views involves many choices about how to coordinate between them to create **linked views**.* There are four major design choices for how to establish some sort of linkage between the views. Do the views share the same visual encoding or use different encodings? In particular, is highlighting linked between the views? Do the views show the same data, does one show a subset of what's in the other, or do the views show a disjoint partitioning where each shows a different set? Is navigation synchronized between the views?

> ★ *Linked views*, multiple views, coordinated views, coordinated multiple views, and **coupled views** are all synonyms for the same fundamental idea.

12.3.1   Share Encoding: Same/Different

The most common method for linking views together is to have some form of shared visual encoding where a visual channel is used in the same way across the multiple views. The design choice of **shared encoding views** means that all channels are handled the same way for an identical visual encoding. The design choice of **multiform views** means that some, but not necessarily all, aspects of the visual encoding differ between the two views.* For example, in a multiform system two views might have different spatial layouts but the same color coding, so there is a shared encoding through the color channel. Another option is that two views could be aligned in one spatial direction but not in the other. These forms of linking don't necessarily require interactivity and can be done with completely static views.

> ★ The generic term **multiple views** is often used as a synonym for *multiform views*.

Interactivity unleashes the full power of linked views. One of the most common forms of linking is **linked highlighting**, where items that are interactively selected in one view are immediately highlighted in all other views using in the same highlight color.* Linked highlighting is a special case of a shared visual encoding in the color channel. The central benefit of the linked highlighting idiom is in seeing how a region that is contiguous in one view is distributed within another.

> ★ *Linked highlighting* is also called **brushing** or **cross-filtering**.

The rationale behind multiform encoding across views is that a single monolithic view has strong limits on the number of attributes that can be shown simultaneously without introducing too much visual clutter. Although simple abstract tasks can often be fully supported by a single view of a specific dataset, more complex ones often cannot. With multiple views as opposed to a single view, each view does not have to show all of the attributes; they can each show only a subset of the attributes, avoiding the visual clutter of trying to superimpose too many attributes in a single view. Even if two views show exactly the same set of attributes, the visual channels used to encode can differ. The most important channel change is what spatial position encodes; this most salient channel dominates our use of the view and strongly affects what tasks it best supports. Multiform views can thus exploit the strengths of multiple visual encodings.

Example: Exploratory Data Visualizer (EDV)

The EDV system features the idiom of linked highlighting between views [Wills 95]. Figure 12.2 shows a baseball statistics dataset with linked bar charts, scatterplots, and a histogram [Wills 95]. In Figure 12.2(a), the viewer has selected players with high salaries in the smoothed histogram view on the upper right. The distribution of these players is very different in the other plots. In the *Years* played view bar chart on the upper left, there are no rookie players. The *Assists-PutOuts* scatterplot does not show much correlation with salary. Comparing the *CHits/Years* plot showing batting ability in terms of career home runs with average career hits shows that the hits per year is more correlated with salary than the home runs

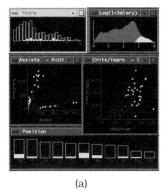 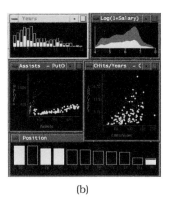

(a)   (b)

Figure 12.2. Linked highlighting between views shows how regions that are contiguous in one view are distributed within another. (a) Selecting the high salaries in the upper right window shows different distributions in the other views. (b) Selecting the bottom group in the *Assists-PutOuts* window shows that the clump corresponds to specific positions played. From [Wills 95, Figures 4 and 5].

per year. The bottom *Position* window shows a loose relationship between salary and the player's position in the field. The *Assists-PutOuts* window shows a clustering into two major groups. Figure 12.2(b) shows the result of selecting the bottom clump. The bottom *Position* window shows that this clump corresponds to specific positions played, whereas these players are fairly evenly distributed in the other windows.

System	Exploratory Data Visualizer (EDV)
What: Data	Tables.
How: Encode	Bar charts, scatterplots, and histograms.
How: Facet	Partition: multiform views. Coordinate: linked highlighting.

12.3.2   Share Data: All, Subset, None

A second design choice is how much data is shared between the two views. There are three alternatives: with **shared data**, both views could each show all of the data; with **overview–detail**, one view could show a subset of what is in the other, or with **small multiples**, the views could show different partitions of the dataset into disjoint pieces.

The *shared data* choice to show all of the data in each view is common with multiform systems, where the encoding differs between the views. It's not usual to combine shared data with shared encoding, since then the two views would be identical and thus redundant.

With the *overview–detail* choice, one of the views shows information about the entire dataset to provide an overview of everything. One or more additional views show more detailed information about a subset of the data that is selected by the viewer from the larger set depicted in the broader view.

A popular overview–detail idiom is to combine shared encoding and shared data with navigation support so that each view shows a different viewpoint of the same dataset. When two of these views are shown they often have different sizes, a large one with many pixels versus a small one with few. For some tasks, it's best to have the large window be the main view for exploring the details and the small window be the zoomed-out overview; for others, the large view would be devoted to the overview, with a smaller window for details. While it's theoretically possible to set both views to the same zoom level, so that they show identical information, the

▶ For more on changing the viewpoint with navigation, see Section 11.5.

normal case is that one view shows only a subset of the other. Also, zooming is only one form of navigation: even two viewpoints at the same zoom level can still show different subsets of the data due to different rotation or translation settings.

There are several standard approaches in choosing how many views to use in total. A common choice is to have only two views, one for overview and one for detail. When the dataset has multilevel structure at discrete scales, multiple detail views may be appropriate to show structure at these different levels. The user can zoom down in to successively smaller subsets of the data with a series of selections, and the other views act as a concise visual history of what region they selected that can be accessed at a glance. In contrast, with the change design choice, users are more likely to lose track of their location because they have no scaffolding to augment their own internal memory.

Example: Bird's-Eye Maps

Interactive online geographic maps are a widely used idiom that combines the shared encoding and overview–detail choices for geographic data, with a large map exploration view augmented by a small "bird's-eye" view providing an orienting overview, as shown in Figure 12.3. A small rectangle

Figure 12.3. Overview–detail example with geographic maps, where the views have the same encoding and dataset; they differ in viewpoint and size. Made with Google Maps, http://maps.google.com.

within the overview shows the region viewable within the detail view. The minimum navigational linkage is unidirectional, where position and size of the rectangle in the overview updates as the user pans and zooms within the large detail view. With bidirectionally linked views, the rectangle can also be moved within the small view to update the region shown in the large one.

Idiom	Bird's-Eye Maps
What: Data	Geographic.
How: Encode	Use given.
How: Facet	Partition into two views with same encoding, overview–detail.
(How: Reduce)	Navigate.

Another common approach is to combine the choices of overview–detail for data sharing with multiform views, where the detail view has a different visual encoding than the overview. A detail view that shows additional information about one or more items selected in a central main view is sometimes called a **detail-on-demand** view. This view might be a popup window near the cursor or a fixed window in another part of the display.

Example: Multiform Overview–Detail Microarrays

Figure 12.4 shows an example of a multiform overview–detail vis tool designed to support the visual exploration of microarray time-series data by biologists [Craig and Kennedy 03]. It features coordination between the scatterplot view in the center and the graph view in the upper left. The designers carefully analyzed the domain situation to generate an appropriate data and task abstraction and concluded that no single view would suffice.

Microarrays measure gene expression, which is the activity level of a gene. They are used to compare gene activity across many different situations; examples include different times, different tissue types such as brain versus bone, exposure to different drugs, samples from different individuals, or samples from known groups such as cancerous or noncancerous.

The designers identified the five tasks of finding genes that were on or off across the whole time period, finding genes whose values rose or fell over a specified time window, finding genes with similar time-series patterns, relating all these sets to known functional groups of genes, and exporting the results for use within other tools.

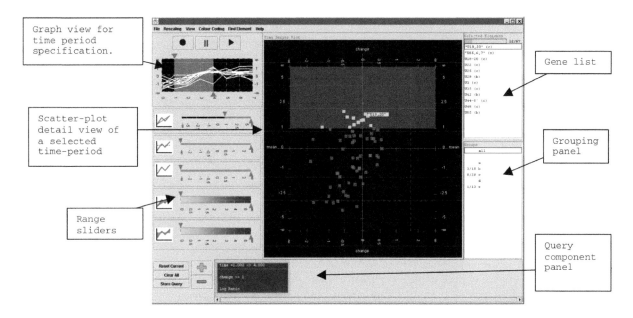

Graph view for time period specification.

Scatter-plot detail view of a selected time-period

Range sliders

Gene list

Grouping panel

Query component panel

Figure 12.4. Multiform overview–detail vis tool for microarray exploration features a central scatterplot linked with the graph view in the upper left. From [Craig and Kennedy 03, Figure 3].

In the *why* analysis framework, the first four tasks are examples of the *consume* goal, while the last is *produce*. All of the *consume* tasks involve the *discover* goal at the high level and the *locate* goal for the mid-level search. At the query level, the first three tasks focus on the *identify* case, and the last on the *compare* case. In the *what* analysis framework, the targets are distributions and trends for a single attribute and similarity between multiple attributes.

The data abstraction identified five key parameters: the original quantitative attribute of microarray value indexed by the keys of gene and time and three derived quantitative attributes of value change, percentage of max value, and fold change (a log-scale change measure frequently used in microarray data analysis).

The graph view shows time-series data plotted with globally superimposed line charts. Each line mark represents a gene, with the horizontal axis showing time and the vertical axis showing value. The user interacts with this overview to select a time period of interest to show in the scatterplot detail view by changing the position or width of the time slider. The time-series graph view does not support visual queries about value change or fold change, which are derived values computed within the time window chosen. In the scatterplot view, the horizontal axis can be set to either of

▶ For more on superimposed line charts, see Section 12.5.2.

these derived variables. In the scatterplot, each gene is represented by a point mark. This view also encodes the functional groups with color coding and dynamically shows the label for the gene under the cursor.

The list view on the right shows the gene names for all genes within the active time window, ordered alphabetically. Although a text list might appear to be a trivial vis when considered as a stand-alone view, these kinds of simpler views often play useful roles in a multiple-view system. This particular list view provides a textual overview and also supports both browsing and lookup. While interaction via hovering over an item is useful for discovering the identify of a mark in a specific place, it would be a very frustrating way to get an overview of all labels because the user would have to click in many places and try to remember all of the previous labels. Glancing at the list view provides a simple overview of the names and allows the user to quickly select an item with a known name.

System	Multiform Overview–Detail Microarrays
What: Data	Multidimensional table: one categorical key attribute (gene), one ordered key attribute (time), one quantitative value attribute (microarray measurement of gene activity at time).
What: Derived	Three quantitative value attributes: (value change, percentage of max value, fold change).
Why: Tasks	Locate, identify, and compare; distribution, trend, and similarity. Produce.
How: Encode	Line charts, scatterplots, lists.
How: Facet	Partition into multiform views. Coordinate with linked highlighting. Overview+detail filtering of time range. Superimpose line charts.

The third alternative for data sharing between views is to show a *different partition* of the dataset in each. Multiple views with the same encoding and different partitions of the data between them are often called **small multiples**. The shared visual encoding means that the views have a common reference frame so that comparison of spatial position between them is directly meaningful. Small multiples are often aligned into a list or matrix to support comparison with the highest precision. The choice of small-multiple views is in some sense the inverse of multiform views, since the encoding is identical but the data differs.

▶ The design choice of how to partition data between views is covered in Section 12.4.

▶ For more on aligning regions, see Section 7.5.

The weakness of small multiples, as with all juxtaposed view combinations, is the screen real estate required to show all of these views simultaneously. The operational limit with current displays of around one million pixels is a few dozen views with several hundred elements in each view.

The strength of the small-multiple views is in making different partitions of the dataset simultaneously visible side by side, allowing the user to glance quickly between them with minimal interaction cost and memory load. Small multiples are often used as an alternative to animations, where all frames are visible simultaneously rather than shown one by one. Animation imposes a massive memory load when the amount of change between each frame is complex and distributed spatially between many points in the scene.

▶ The relationship between animation and memory is discussed in Section 6.5.

Example: Cerebral

Figure 12.5 shows an example of small-multiple views in the Cerebral system [Barsky et al. 08]. The dataset is also from the bioinformatics domain, a multidimensional table with the two keys of genes and experimental condition and the value attribute of microarray measurements of gene activity for the condition. The large view on the upper right is a node–link network diagram where nodes are genes and links are the known interactions between genes, shown with connection marks. The layout also encodes an ordered attribute for each node, the location within the cell where the interaction occurs, with vertical spatial position. Containment marks show the groups of coregulated genes. The small-multiple views to the left of the large window show a partitioning of the dataset by condition. The views are aligned to a matrix and are reorderable within it.

In each small-multiple network view the nodes are colored with a diverging red–green colormap showing the quantitative attribute of gene activity for that view's condition. This colormap follows bioinformatics domain conventions; other colormaps that better serve colorblind users are also available. In the large network view, the color coding for the nodes is a diverging orange–blue colormap based on the derived attribute of difference in values between the two selected small multiples, whose titlebars are highlighted in blue.

▶ The convention of red–green colormaps in bioinformatics is discussed in Section 7.5.2.

Cerebral is also multiform; the view at the bottom uses parallel coordinates for the visual encoding, along with a control panel for data clustering. The navigation between the views is linked, as discussed next.

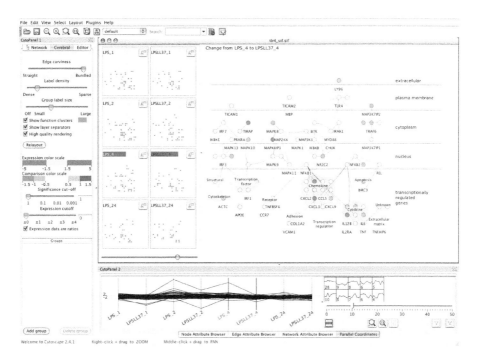

Figure 12.5. Cerebral uses small-multiple views to show the same base graph of gene interactions colored according to microarray measurements made at different times. The coloring in the main view uses the derived attribute of the difference in values between the two chosen views. From [Barsky et al. 08, Figure 2].

System	Cerebral
What: Data	Multidimensional table: one categorical key attribute (gene), one categorical key attribute (condition), one quantitative value attribute (gene activity at condition). Network: nodes (genes), links (known interaction between genes), one ordered attribute on nodes: location within cell of interaction.
What: Derived	One quantitative value attribute (difference between measurements for two partitions).
How: Encode	Node–link network using connection marks, vertical spatial position expressing interaction location, containment marks for coregulated gene groups, diverging colormap. Small-multiple network views aligned in matrix. Parallel coordinates.
How: Facet	Partition: small multiple views partitioned on condition, and multiform views. Coordinate: linked highlighting and navigation.

Figure 12.6. Design choices for how to coordinate between views relating to sharing encoding and data.

12.3.3 Share Navigation: Synchronize

Another way to coordinate between views is to share navigation. With **linked navigation**, moving the viewpoint in one view is synchronized to movement in the others. For example, linked navigation is common with map views that have a smaller bird's-eye overview window in addition to a larger detail view, where interaction in the small window changes the viewpoint in the large one.

▶ Navigation is covered further in Section 11.5.

12.3.4 Combinations

Figure 12.6 summarizes the design choices for coordinating views in terms of whether the encoding and data are shared or different and how these choices interact with each other. The encoding could be the same or different; the data could be the same, a subset, or a partition. Two of the six possibilities are not useful. When everything is shared, with both the data and encoding identical, the two views would be redundant. When nothing is shared, with different data in each view and no shared channels in the visual encoding, there is no linkage between the views. Otherwise, the choices of sharing for encoding and data are independent. For example, the overview–detail choice of creating subsets of the data can be used with either *multiform* or *shared* encoding.

Complex systems will use these methods in combination, so in this book these terms are used to mean that at least one pair of views differs along that particular axis. For example, *multiform* means that at least one pair of views differs, not necessarily that every single view has a different encoding from every other one.

Example: Improvise

Figure 12.7 shows a vis of census data that uses many views. In addition to geographic information, the demographic information for each county includes population, density, genders, median age, percentage change since 1990, and proportions of major ethnic groups. The system is multiform with geographic, scatterplot, parallel coordinate, tabular, and matrix views. These multiform views all share the same bivariate sequential–sequential color encoding, documented with a legend in the bottom middle. A set of small-multiple views appears in the lower left in the form of a scatterplot matrix, where each scatterplot shows a different pair of attributes. All of the views are linked by highlighting: the blue selected items are close together in some views and spread out in others. A set of small-multiple reorderable list views result from partitioning the data by

> ▶ Bivariate colormaps are covered in Section 10.3.3.

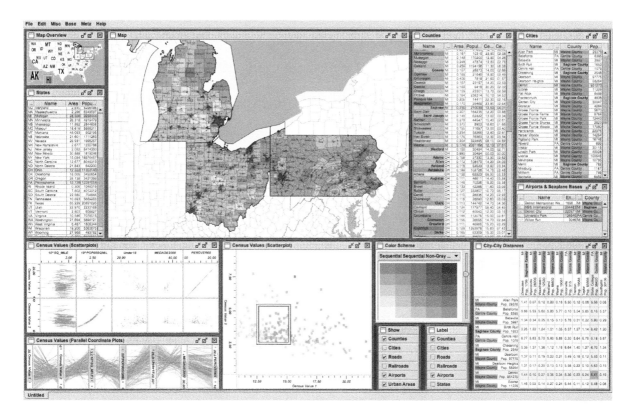

Figure 12.7. The Improvise toolkit [Weaver 04] was used to create this census vis that has many forms of coordination between views. It has many multiform views, some of which use small multiples, and some of which provide additional detail information. From http://www.cs.ou.edu/~weaver/improvise/examples/census.

attribute. The list views allow direct sorting by and selection within an attribute of interest. The map in the upper left view is a small overview, with linked navigation to the large geographic detail view in the top middle.

System	Improvise
What: Data	Geographic and multidimensional table (census data): one key attribute (county), many quantitative attributes (demographic information).
How: Encode	Scatterplot matrix, parallel coordinates, choropleth map with size-coded city points, bird's-eye map overview, scatterplot, reorderable text lists, text matrix. Bivariate sequential–sequential colormap.
How: Facet	Partition: small-multiple, multiform, overview–detail views; linked highlighting.

12.3.5 Juxtapose Views

Two additional design choices that pertain to view juxtaposition do not directly involve view coordination: when to show each view and how to arrange them.

The usual choice with juxtaposition is that all of the views are permanently visible so that users can glance between them, as suggested by the synonym *side-by-side*. However, another option is to have a view that temporarily pops up in response to a user action.

Sometimes the arrangement of the views is not under the direct control of the vis designer and is left to the built-in functionality of the window system running on the user's computer. If the number of views is large, then manually arranging them could be a burdensome load to the user. A more sophisticated choice is to arrange the views themselves automatically, just like regions and items can be arranged. For example, views can be aligned and ordered linearly in a list, or two-dimensionally in a matrix, to support higher-precision comparison than unaligned views. This case is common when data is partitioned between the views, as discussed in the next section.

12.4   Partition into Views

The design choice of how to **partition** a multiattribute dataset into meaningful groups has major implications for what kind of patterns are visible to the user.* This choice encodes association between items using spatial proximity, a highly ranked channel.

The primary design choice within partitioning is how to divide the data up between the views, given a hierarchy of attributes.*

One design choice is how many splits to carry out: splitting could continue through as many attributes as are available until the simplest case of one region per item has been reached and it can be encoded with a single mark, or the partitioning could stop at a higher level where there is more complex structure to show within each region. Another design choice within partitioning is the order in which attributes are used to split things up. A final design choice is how many views to use; while this decision is often data driven, it could be determined in advance.

A partitioning attribute is typically a categorical variable that has only a limited number of unique values; that is, **levels**. It can also be a derived attribute, for example created by a transformation from a quantitative attribute by dividing it up into a limited number of bins. Partitioning can be carried out with either key or value attributes. An attribute can be categorical without being a key; that attribute can still be used to separate into regions and partition the dataset according to the levels for that attribute. When dealing with key attributes, it is possible to partition the data down to the item level, since each item is uniquely indexed by the combination of all keys. With a value attribute, multiple items can all share the same value, so the final division might be a group of items rather than just a single one.

> ★ *Partitioning* and *grouping* are inverse terms; the term **partitioning** is natural when considering starting from the top and gradually refining; the term **grouping** is more natural when considering a bottom-up process of gradually consolidating. The term **conditioning** is a synonym for *partitioning* that is used heavily in the statistics literature.

> ★ Synonyms for *partitioning* are **hierarchical partitioning** and **dimensional stacking**.

12.4.1   Regions, Glyphs, and Views

Partitioning is an action on a dataset that separates data into groups. To connect partioning to visual encoding choices, the crucial idea is that a partitioned group can be placed within a **region** of space, so partitioning is an action that addresses the separate choice when arranging data in space. These regions then need to be ordered, and often aligned, to resolve the other spatial arrangement choices. For example, after space is subdivided into regions, they can be aligned and ordered within a 1D list, or 2D matrix. Recursive subdivision allows these regions to nest inside each other;

> ▶ Section 7.5 covers separation, ordering, and alignment.

these nested regions may be arranged using the same choices as their enclosing regions or different choices.

When a dataset has only one key attribute, then it is straightforward to use that key to separate into one region per item. When a dataset has multiple keys, there are several possibilities for separation. Given two keys, X and Y, you could first separate by X and then by Y, or you could first separate by Y and then by X. A third option is that you might separate into regions by only one of the keys and then draw something more complex within the region. The complexity of what is encoded in a region falls along a continuum. It could be just a single **mark**, a single geometric primitive. It could be a more complex **glyph**: an object with internal structure that arises from multiple marks. It could be a full *view*, showing a complete visual encoding of marks and attributes.

There is no strict dividing line between a *region*, a *view*, and a *glyph*.* A **view** is a contiguous region in which visually encoded data is shown on the display.* Sometimes a view is a full-blown window controlled by the computer's operating system, sometimes it is a subcomponent such as a panel or a pane, and sometimes it simply means a region of the display that is visually distinguishable from other regions through some kind of visible boundary. A spatial region showing data visually encoded by a specific idiom might be called either a *glyph* or a *view* depending on its screen size, the amount of additional information beyond the visual encoding alone that is shown, and whether it is nested within another region. Large, stand-alone, highly detailed regions are likely to be called *views*, and small, nested, schematic regions are likely to be called *glyphs*. For example, a single bar chart that is 800 pixels wide and 400 pixels high, with axes that have labels and tick marks, confidence intervals shown for each bar, and both a legend and a title would usually be called a view. If there is a set of bar charts that are each 50 by 25 pixels, each with a few schematic bars and two thin unlabeled lines to depict the axes, where each appears within a geographic region on a map, each chart might be called a glyph.

The term *glyph* has been used for structures at a range of sizes. Glyphs like the schematic bar chart example just mentioned would fall into the category of **macroglyphs**. Another example is a glyph with a complex 3D shape that represents several aspects of local fluid flow all simultaneously. Designing these glyphs is a microcosm of vis design more generally!

In the middle of the size spectrum are simpler structures such as a single multipart bar in a stacked bar chart. At the extreme end

★ The word *glyph* is used very ambiguously in the vis literature. My definitions unify many ideas within a common framework but are not standard. In particular, my distinction between a *mark* and a *glyph* made of multiple marks is not universal.

★ Other synonyms for *view* include **display**, **window**, **panel**, and **pane**.

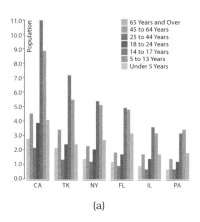 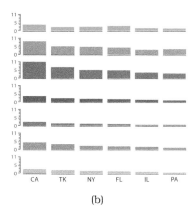

(a)   (b)

Figure 12.8. Partitioning and bar charts. (a) Single bar chart with grouped bars: separated by *state* key into regions, using seven-mark glyphs within each region. (b) Four aligned small-multiple bar chart views: separated by *group* key into vertically aligned list of regions, with a full bar chart in each region. From http://bl.ocks.org/mbostock/3887051, after http://bl.ocks.org/mbostock/4679202.

of the spectrum, **microglyphs** can be so small that their structure is not intended to be directly distinguishable: for example, five very short connected line segments, where the angle between each pair of segments encodes a quantitative attribute, and the entire glyph fits within an 15 by 4 pixel region. Microglyphs are typically used as a dense 2D array that forms a sea of visual texture, where the hope is that noticeable boundaries will emerge where attribute values change.

12.4.2 List Alignments

A concrete and simple example of how different partitioning decisions enable different tasks comes from comparing grouped bar charts to small-multiple aligned bar charts, as shown in Figure 12.8.

In a **grouped bar chart**, a multibar glyph is drawn within each region where a single mark would be drawn in a standard bar chart. In Figure 12.8(a), the regions are the states, and the bars within each glyph show demographic category. In contrast, the small-multiple design choice simply shows several standard bar charts, one in each view. In Figure 12.8(b), each view shows a demographic category, with the states spread along each standard bar chart axis. The grouped bar chart facilitates comparison between the attributes, whereas the small multiple bar charts facilitate comparison within a single attribute.

These two encodings can be interpreted in a unified way: either both as glyphs, or both in terms of partitions. From a glyph point of view, the grouped bars idiom uses a smaller multibar glyph, and the small-multiple bars idiom uses a larger bar-chart glyph. From a partitioning point of view, both idioms use two levels of partitioning: at the high level by a first key, and then at a lower level by a second key, and finally a single mark is drawn within each subregion. The difference is that with grouped bars the second-level regions are interleaved within the first-level regions, whereas with small multiple bars the second-level regions are contiguous within a single first-level region.

12.4.3 Matrix Alignments

Example: Trellis

> ► Dot charts are discussed in Section 7.5.1.

The Trellis [Becker et al. 96] system is a more complex example. This system features partitioning a multiattribute dataset into multiple views and ordering them within a 2D matrix alignment as the main avenue for exploration. Figure 12.9 shows a dataset of barley yields shown with dot charts. This dataset is a multidimensional table with three categorical attributes that act as keys. The *site* attribute has six unique levels, the locations where the barley was grown. The *variety* attribute for the type of barley grown has ten levels. The *year* attribute has only two levels, and although it technically is a number it is treated as categorical rather than ordered. The dataset also has a fourth quantitative attribute, the *yield*.

In this figure, the partitioning is by *year* for the matrix columns and by *site* for the rows. Within the individual dot chart views the vertical axis is separated by *variety*, with *yield* as the quantitative value expressed with horizontal spatial position. The ordering idiom used is **main-effects ordering**, where the derived attribute of the median value is computed for each group created by the partitioning and used to order them. In Trellis, main-effects ordering can be done at every partitioning scale. In Figure 12.9(a) the matrix rows are ordered by the medians for the site, and the rows within each dot chart are ordered by the medians for the varieties.

The value of main-effects ordering is that outliers countervailing to the general trends are visible. The Morris plots in the third row do not match up with the others, suggesting that perhaps the years had been switched. Figure 12.9(b) shows a trellis where the vertical ordering between and within the plots is alphabetical. This display does not provide any useful

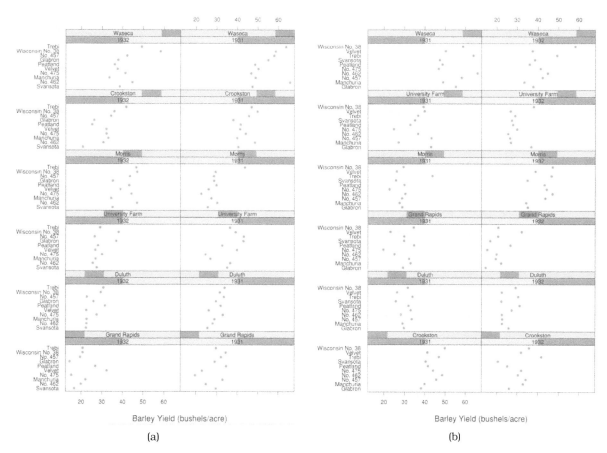

Figure 12.9. Trellis facets the data into a matrix of dot chart views, allowing the user control of partitioning and orderering. (a) With main-effects ordering, the plots are ordered by median values within the plots for the sites, and the shared vertical axis within each plot is ordered by median values within the varieties. The Morris site in the third row is a visible outlier that does not fit the general trends. (b) With a simple alphabetical ordering of plots and axes, no trends are visible, so no outliers can be detected. From [Becker et al. 96, Figures 1 and 3].

hints of outliers versus the trends, since no particular general trend is visible at all. Main-effects ordering is useful because it is a data-driven way to spatially order information so that both general trends and outliers can be spotted.

Figure 12.10 shows another plot with a different structure to further investigate the anomaly. The plots are still partitioned vertically by *site*, but no further. Both years are thus included within the same view and distinguished from each other by color. The switch in color patterns in the third row shows convincing evidence for the theory that the Morris data is incorrect.

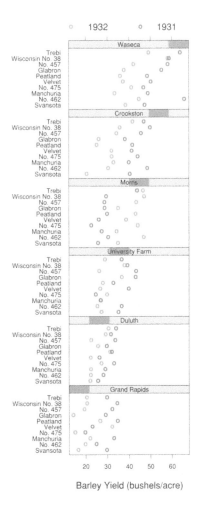

Figure 12.10. A second Trellis plot combines the years into a single plot with year encoded by color, showing strong evidence of an anomaly in the data. From [Becker et al. 96, Figure 2].

System	Trellis
What: Data	Multidimensional table: three categorical key attributes, one quantitative value attribute.
What: Derived	Medians for each partition.
How: Encode	Dot charts aligned in 2D matrix.
How: Facet	Partitioned by any combination of keys into regions.

12.4.4   Recursive Subdivision

Partitioning can be used in an exploratory way, where the user can reconfigure the display to see different choices of partioning and encoding variables. The Hierarchical Visual Expression (HiVE) system supports this kind of exploration, shown in the examples that follow on a dataset of over one million property transactions in the London area. The categorical attribute of *residence type* has four levels: flats *Flat*, attached terrace houses *Ter*, semidetached houses *Semi*, and fully detached houses *Det*. The *price* attribute is quantitative. The *time of sale* attribute is provided as a year and a month, for an ordered attribute with hierarchical internal structure. The *neighborhood* attribute, with 33 levels, is an interesting case that can be considered either as categorical or as spatial.

Figure 12.11(a) shows a view where the top-level partition is a split into four regions based on the *type* attribute, arranged in a matrix. The next split uses the neighborhood attribute, with the same matrix alignment choice. The final split is by time, again in a matrix ordered with year from left to right and month from top to bottom. At the base level, each square is color coded by the derived attribute of price variation within the group.

This encoding emphasizes that the patterns within the top-level squares, which show the four different house types, are very different. In contrast, the coloring within each second-level square representing a neighborhood is more consistent; that is, houses within the same neighborhood tend to have similar prices.

One way to consider this arrangement is as a recursive subdivision using matrix alignment. Another way to interpret it is that containment is used to indicate the order of partitioning, where each of the higher-level regions contains everything at the next level within it. A third way is as four sets of 33 small multiples each, where each small multiple view shows a heatmap for the neighborhood. The consistent ordering and alignment within the matrices allows easy comparison of the same time cell across the different neighborhood heatmaps.

Figure 12.11(b) shows another configuration of the same dataset with the same basic spatial arrangement but a different order of partitioning. It is partitioned first by neighborhood and then by residence type, with the bottom levels by year and month as in the previous example. The color coding is by a slightly different derived attribute, the average price within the group. In this encoding it is easy to spot expensive neighborhoods, which are the views near the center. It is also easy to see that detached houses, in the lower right corner of each view, are more expensive than the other types.

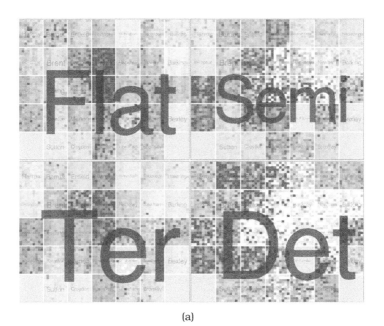

(a)

(b)

Figure 12.11. The HiVE system supports exploration through different partitioning choices. (a) Recursive matrix alignment where the first split is by the house type attribute, and the second by neighborhood. The lowest levels show time with years as rows and months as columns. (b) Switching the order of the first and second splits shows radically different patterns. From [Slingsby et al. 09, Figures 7b and 2c].

(a)

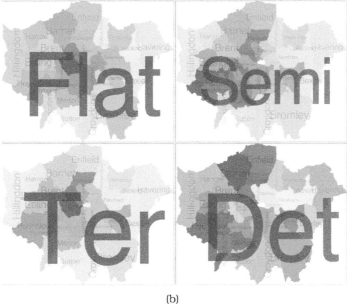

(b)

Figure 12.12. HiVE with different arrangements. (a) Sizing regions according to sale counts yields a treemap. (b) Arranging the second-level regions as choropleth maps. From [Slingsby et al. 09, Figures 7a and 7c].

Figure 12.12(a) shows a third configuration with the same order of partitioning as Figure 12.11(a) but an important difference in the spatial arrangement: the regions created by the recursive subdivision are sized according to the number of sales, yielding variably sized rectangles rather than equally sized squares. This encoding can be interpreted as a treemap, where the tree structure being shown is implicitly derived by the order of partitioning decisions rather than being explicitly provided.

▶ Treemaps are discussed in detail in Section 9.5.

Figure 12.12(b) shows a fourth configuration with a more dramatic change of arrangement: the top level still has rectangular regions, but the next level shows the information geographically using choropleth maps. The structural similarities between heatmaps, treemaps, and choropleth maps are particularly obvious from this progression. All three have color-coded area marks, where the shape results from visual encoding choices for the first two cases and using given spatial geometry in the latter case.

▶ Choropleth maps are covered in Section 8.3.1.

The rough correspondence between the ordering in the rectangular layouts and the geographic view is no coincidence: it arises from using a variant of the treemap idiom that is spatially aware [Wood and Dykes 08], for a hybrid layout that combines aspects of using given spatial data and the design choices for arranging table data.

12.5 Superimpose Layers

The **superimpose** family of design choices pertains to combining multiple layers together by stacking them directly on top of each other in a single composite view. Multiple simple drawings are combined on top of each other into a single shared frame. All of the drawings have the same horizontal and vertical extent and are blended together as if the single drawings are completely transparent where no marks exist.*

★ In graphics terminology, *superimpose* is an **image-space compositing** operation, where the drawings have an identical coordinate system.

A visual **layer** is simply a set of objects spread out over a region, where the set of objects in each layer is a visually distinguishable group that can be told apart from objects in other layers at a perceptual level. The extent of the region is typically the entire view, so layering multiple views on top of each other is a direct alternative to showing them as separate views juxtaposed side by side.

The design choices for how to superimpose views include: How many layers are used? How are the layers visually distinguished from each other? Is there a small static set of layers that do not change, or are the layers constructed dynamically in response to user selection?

A final design choice is how to partition items into layers. For static layers, it is common to approach this question in a similar spirit to partitioning items into views, with heavyweight divisions according to attribute types and semantics. For dynamically constructed layers, the division is often a very lightweight choice driven by the user's changing selection, rather than being directly tied to the structure of dataset attributes.

12.5.1 Visually Distinguishable Layers

One good way to make distinguishable layers is to ensure that each layer uses a different and nonoverlapping range of the visual channels active in the encoding. A common choice is to create two visual layers, a foreground versus a background. With careful design, a few layers can be created. The main limitation of layering is that the number of layers that can be visually distinguished is limited to very few if the layers contain a substantial number of area marks: two layers is definitely achievable, and three layers is possible with careful design. Layering many views is only feasible if each layer contains very little, such as a single line.

The term *layer* usually implies multiple objects spread through the region spatially intermixed with objects that are not part of that visual layer. However, a single highlighted object could be considered as constituting a very simple visual layer.

12.5.2 Static Layers

The design choice of **static layers** is that all of the layers are displayed simultaneously; the user can choose which to focus on with the selective direction of visual attention. Mapmakers usually design maps in exactly this way.

Example: Cartographic Layering

Figure 12.13 shows an example that lets the viewer easily shift attention between layers. In Figure 12.13(a), area marks form a background layer, with three different unsaturated colors distinguishing water, parks, and other land. Line marks form a foreground layer for the road network, with main roads encoded by wide lines in a fully saturated red color and small roads with thinner black lines. This layering works well because of the luminance contrast between the elements on different layers, as seen in Figure 12.13(b) [Stone 10].

> ► Checking luminance contrast explicitly is an example of the slogan *Get It Right in Black and White* discussed in Section 6.9.

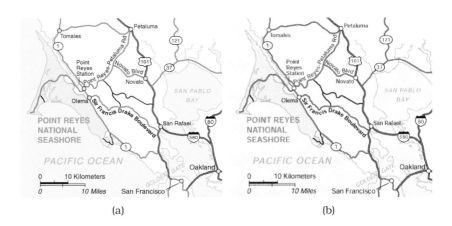

(a)   (b)

Figure 12.13. Static visual layering in maps. (a) The map layers are created by differences in the hue, saturation, luminance, and size channels on both area and line marks. (b) The grayscale view shows that each layer uses a different range in the luminance channel, providing luminance contrast. From [Stone 10].

Idiom	Cartographic Layering
What: Data	Geographic
How: Encode	Area marks for regions (water, parks, other land), line marks for roads, categorical colormap.
How: Facet	Superimpose: static layers distinguished with color saturation, color luminance, and size channels.

Example: Superimposed Line Charts

Figure 12.14 shows a common use of the superimpose design choice, where several lines representing different data items are superimposed to create combined charts. The alignment of the simple constituent drawings is straightforward: they are all superimposed directly on top of each other so that they share the same frame. This simple superimposition works well because the only mark is a thin line that is mostly disjoint with the other marks. Figure 12.14(a) shows that the amount of occlusion is very small with only three lines. This idiom is still usable with even nearly one dozen items superimposed, as shown in Figure 12.14(b). However, Figure 12.14(c) shows that this approach does not scale to many dozens or hundreds of items.

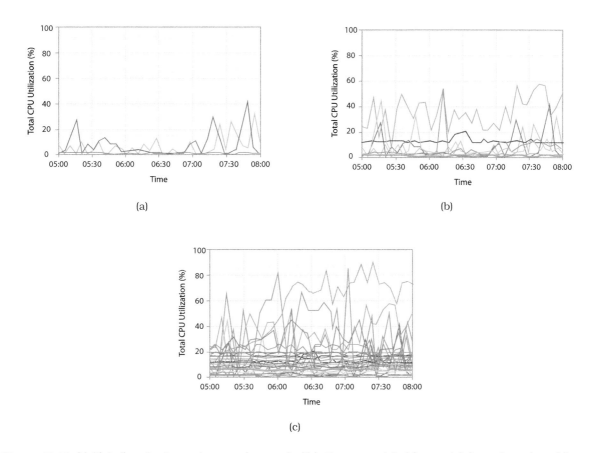

Figure 12.14. Multiple line charts can be superimposed within the same global frame. (a) A small number of items is easily readable. (b) Up to a few dozen lines can still be understood. (c) This technique does not scale to hundreds of items.

Idiom	Superimposed Line Charts
What: Data	Multidimensional table: one ordered key attribute (time), one categorical key attribute (machine), one quantitative value attribute (CPU utilization).
How: Encode	Line charts, colored by machine attribute.
How: Facet	Superimpose: static layers, distinguished with color.
Scale	Ordered key attribute: hundreds. Categorical key attribute: one dozen.

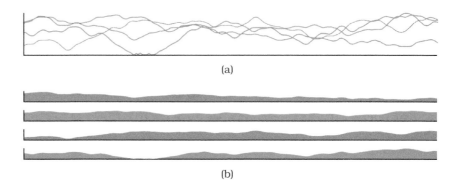

Figure 12.15. Empirical study comparing superimposed line charts to juxtaposed filled-area line charts. (a) Superimposed line charts performed best for tasks carried out within a local visual span. (b) Juxtaposed filled area charts were best for global tasks, especially as the number of time series increased. From [Javed et al. 10, Figures 1 and 2].

Figure 12.15 shows two interfaces from an empirical study: one where line charts are superimposed as layers, and another where juxtaposed small multiples show filled-area charts. The study explicitly considers the trade-offs between less vertical space available for the small multiples and less visual clutter by controlling the screen area to be commensurate: the complete set of small multiples fit within the same area as the single superimposed view. The studied tasks were the local *maximum* task of finding the time series with the highest value at a specific point in time, the global *slope* task of finding the time series with the highest increase during the entire time period, and the global *discrimination* task to check whether values were higher at different time points across the series. The number of time series displayed was either 2, 4, or 8 simultaneously. They proposed the guideline that superimposing layers, as in Figure 12.15(a), is the best choice for comparison within a local visual span, while juxtaposing multiple views, as in Figure 12.15(b), is a better choice for dispersed tasks that require large visual spans, especially as the number of series increases.

Example: Hierarchical Edge Bundles

▶ Compound networks are defined and discussed in Section 9.5.

A more complex example of static superimposition is the **hierarchical edge bundles** idiom [Holten 06]. It operates on a **compound network**, a combination of a base network and a cluster hierarchy that groups its nodes.

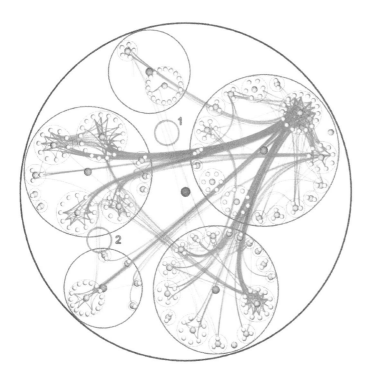

Figure 12.16. The hierarchical edge bundles idiom shows a compound network in three layers: the tree structure in back with containment circle marks, the red–green graph edges with connection marks in a middle layer, and the graph nodes in a front layer. From [Holten 06, Figure 13].

The software engineering example in Figure 12.16 shows the call graph network, namely, which functions call what other functions in a software system, in conjunction with the hierarchical structure of the source code in which these function calls are defined.

The idiom creates two easily distinguishable visual layers through the use of color: the source code hierarchy layer is gray, as opposed to the semitransparent red–green layer with the call graph network edges. The gray hierarchical structure is shown with circular containment marks, in contrast to the colored connection link marks for the network edges. The idiom's name comes from *bundling* the network edges together to reduce occlusion with the underlying tree structure, just like physical cables can be bundled together with cable ties to keep them tidy. Without bundling, most of the background layer structure would be very difficult to see. The use of layering is also an important aspect of the idiom; if all of the network edges were also gray and opaque, the resulting image would be much harder to interpret. The idiom does not rely on a specific spatial layout for the tree; it can be applied to many different tree layouts.

Idiom	Hierarchical Edge Bundles
What: Data	Compound graph: network, hierarchy whose leaves are nodes in network.
How: Encode	Back layer shows hierarchy with containment marks colored gray, middle layer shows network links colored red–green, front layer shows nodes colored gray.
How: Facet	Superimpose static layers, distinguished with color.

Layering is often carried out with modern graphics hardware to manage rendering with planes oriented in the screen plane that are blended together in the correct order from back to front, as if they were at slightly different 3D depths. This approach is one of the many ways to exploit modern graphics hardware to create complex drawings that have the spirit of 2D drawings, rather than true 3D scenes with full perspective.

12.5.3 Dynamic Layers

With **dynamic layers**, a layer with different salience than the rest of the view is constructed interactively, typically in response to user selection. The number of possible layers can be huge, since they are constructed on the fly rather than chosen from a very small set of possibilities that must be simultaneously visually distinguishable.

The Cerebral system, shown also in Figure 12.5, uses the design choice of dynamic layering. Figure 12.17 shows the dynamic creation of a foreground layer that updates constantly as the user moves the cursor. When the cursor is directly over a node, the foreground layer shows its one-hop neighborhood: all of the nodes in the network that are a single topological hop away from it, plus the links to them from the target node. The one-hop neighborhood is visually emphasized with a distinctive fully saturated red to create a foreground layer that is visually distinct from the background layer, which has only low-saturation colors. The marks in the foreground layer also have larger linewidth.

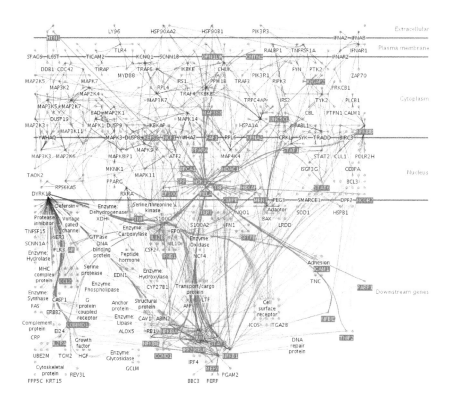

Figure 12.17. Cerebral dynamically creates a foreground visual layer of all nodes one topological hop away in the network from the node underneath the cursor. From [Barsky et al. 07, Figure 1].

12.6   Further Reading

The Big Picture An extensive survey discusses many idioms that use the design choices of partitioning into multiple views, superimposing layers, changing the viewpoint through navigation, and embedding focus into context, and includes an assessment of the empirical evidence on their strengths and weaknesses [Cockburn et al. 08]. A monograph also presents an extensive discussion of the trade-offs between these design choices and guidelines for when and how to use them [Lam and Munzner 10]. A more specific paper quantifies costs and benefits of multiple views versus navigation within a single view for visual comparisons at multiple scales [Plumlee and Ware 06].

A thoughtful discussion of the design space of "composite vis" proposes the categories of juxtapose views side by side, superimpose views on top of each other, overload views by embedding, nest one view inside another, and integrate views together with explicit link marks between them [Javed and Elmqvist 12]. Another great discussion of approaches to comparison identifies juxtapose, superimpose and encode with derived data [Gleicher et al. 11].

Coordinating Juxtaposed Views A concise set of guidelines on designing multiple-view systems appears in an early paper [Baldonado et al. 00], and many multiple-view idioms are discussed in a later surveys [Roberts 07]. The Improvise toolkit supports many forms of linking between views [Weaver 04], and follow-on work has explored in depth the implications of designing coordinated multiple view systems [Weaver 10].

Partitioning The HiVE system supports flexible subdivision of attribute hierarchies with the combination of interactive controls and a command language, allowing systematic exploration of the design space of partitioning [Slingsby et al. 09], with spatially ordered treemaps as one of the layout options [Wood and Dykes 08].

Glyphs A recent state of the art report on glyphs is an excellent place to start with further reading [Borgo et al. 13]; another good overview of glyph design in general appears in a somewhat earlier handbook chapter [Ward 08]. The complex and subtle issues in the design of both macroglyphs and microglyphs are discussed extensively Chapters 5 and 6 of Ware's vis textbook [Ware 13]. Glyph placement in particular is covered a journal article [Ward 02]. The space of possible glyph designs is discussed from a quite different point of view in a design study focused on biological experiment workflows [Maguire et al. 12]. Empirical experiments on visual channel use in glyph design are discussed in a paper on color enhanced star plot glyphs [Klippel et al. 09].

Linked Highlighting Linked highlighting was proposed at Bell Labs, where it was called *brushing* [Becker and Cleveland 87]; a chapter published 20 years later contains an in-depth discussion following up these ideas [Wills 08].

Superimposing Layers A concise and very readable blog post discusses layer design and luminance constrast [Stone 10]. An-

other very readable article discusses the benefits of superimposed dot charts compared to grouped bar charts [Rob-
bins 06].

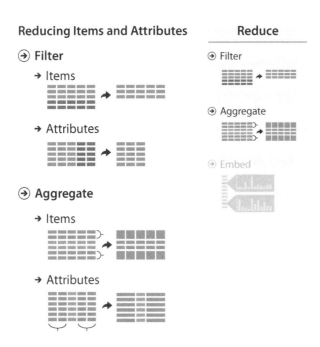

Figure 13.1. Design choices for reducing (or increasing) the amount of data items and attributes to show.

Chapter 13

Reduce Items and Attributes

13.1   The Big Picture

Figure 13.1 shows the set of design choices for reducing—or increasing—what is shown at once within a view. Filtering simply eliminates elements, whereas aggregation combines many together. Either choice can be applied to both items or attributes.

13.2   Why Reduce?

Reduction is one of five major strategies for managing complexity in visualizations; as pointed out before, these five choices are not mutually exclusive, and various combinations of them are common.

Typically, static data reduction idioms only reduce what is shown, as the name suggests. However, in the dynamic case, the outcome of changing a parameter or a choice may be an increase in the number of visible elements. Thus, many of the idioms covered in this chapter are bidirectional: they may serve to either reduce or increase the number of visible elements. Nevertheless, they are all named after the reduction action for brevity.

Reducing the amount of data shown in a view is an obvious way to reduce its visual complexity. Of course, the devil is in the details, where the challenge is to minimize the chances that information important to the task is hidden from the user. Reduction can be applied to both items and attributes; the word **element** will be used to refer to either items or attributes when design choices that apply to both are discussed. Filtering simply eliminates elements, whereas aggregation creates a single new element that stands in for multiple others that it replaces. It's useful to consider the trade-offs between these two alternatives explicitly when making design choices: filtering is very straightforward for users to understand, and typically also to compute. However, people tend to have an

> ► Deriving new data is covered in Chapter 3, changing a view over time is covered in Chapter 11, faceting data into multiple views is covered in Chapter 12, and embedding focus and contextual information together within one view is covered in Chapter 14.

"out of sight, out of mind" mentality about missing information: they tend to forget to take into account elements that have been filtered out, even when their absence is the result of quite recent actions. Aggregation can be somewhat safer from a cognitive point of view because the stand-in element is designed to convey information about the entire set of elements that it replaces. However, by definition, it cannot convey all omitted information; the challenge with aggregation is how and what to summarize in a way that matches well with the dataset and task.

13.3 Filter

The design choice of **filtering** is a straightforward way to reduce the number of elements shown: some elements are simply eliminated. Filtering can be applied to both items and attributes. A straightforward approach to filtering is to allow the user to select one or more ranges of interest in one or more of the elements. The range might mean what to show or what to leave out.

The idea of filtering is very obvious; the challenge comes in designing a vis system where filtering can be used to effectively explore a dataset. Consider the simple case of filtering the set of items according to their values for a single quantitative attribute. The goal is to select a range within it in terms of minimum and maximum numeric values and eliminate the items whose values for that attribute fall outside of the range. From the programmer's point of view, a very simple way to support this functionality would be to simply have the user enter two numbers, a minimum and maximum value. From the user's point of view, this approach is very difficult to use: how on earth do they know what numbers to type? After they type, how do they know whether that choice is correct? When your goal is to support exploration of potentially unknown datasets, you cannot assume that the users already know these kinds of answers.

In an interactive vis context, filtering is often accomplished through **dynamic queries**, where there is a tightly coupled loop between visual encoding and interaction, so that the user can immediately see the results of the intervention. In this design choice, a display showing a visual encoding of the dataset is used in conjunction with controls that support direct interaction, so that the display updates immediately when the user changes a setting. Often these controls are standard graphical user interface widgets such as sliders, buttons, comboboxes, and text fields. Many extensions of off-the-shelf widgets have also been proposed to better support the needs of interactive vis.

13.3.1 Item Filtering

In **item filtering**, the goal is to eliminate items based on their values with respect to specific attributes. Fewer items are shown, but the number of attributes shown does not change.

Example: FilmFinder

Figure 13.2 shows the FilmFinder system [Ahlberg and Shneiderman 94] for exploring a movie database. The dataset is a table with nine value attributes: genre, year made, title, actors, actresses, directors, rating, popularity, and length. The visual encoding features an interactive scatterplot where the items are movies color coded by genre, with scatterplot axes of year made versus movie popularity; Figure 13.2(a) shows the full dataset. The interaction design features filtering, with immediate update of the visual display to filter out or add back items as sliders are moved and buttons are pressed. The visual encoding adapts to the number of items to display; the marks representing movies are automatically enlarged and labeled when enough of the dataset has been filtered away that there is enough room to do so, as in Figure 13.2(b). The system uses multiform overview–detail views, where clicking on any mark brings up a popup detail view with more information about that movie, as in Figure 13.2(c).

FilmFinder is a specific example of the general dynamic queries approach, where browsing using tightly coupled visual encoding and interaction is an alternative to searching by running queries, as for example with a database. All of the items in a database are shown at the start of a session to provide an overview, and direct manipulation of interface widgets replaces reformulating new queries. This approach is well suited to browsing, as opposed to a search where the user must formulate an explicit query that might return far too many items, or none at all.

Figure 13.2 shows the use of two augmented slider types, a **dual slider** for movie length that allows the user to select both a minimum and maximum value, and several **alpha sliders** that are tuned for selection with text strings rather than numbers.

System	FilmFinder
What: Data	Table: nine value attributes.
How: Encode	Scatterplot; detail view with text/images.
How: Facet	Multiform, overview–detail.
How: Reduce	Item filtering.

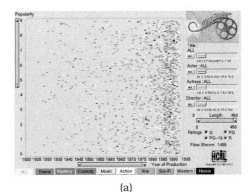

(a)

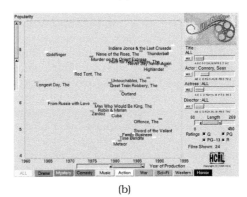

(b)

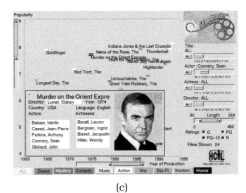

(c)

Figure 13.2. FilmFinder features tightly coupled interactive filtering, where the result of moving sliders and pressing buttons is immediately reflected in the visual encoding. (a) Exploration begins with an overview of all movies in the dataset. (b) Moving the actor slider to select Sean Connery filters out most of the other movies, leaving enough room to draw labels. (c) Clicking on the mark representing a movie brings up a detail view. From [Ahlberg and Shneiderman 94, Color Plates 1, 2, and 3].

Figure 13.3. The scented widget idiom adds visual encoding information directly to standard graphical widgets to make filtering possible with high information density displays. From [Willett et al. 07, Figure 2].

Standard widgets for filtering controls can be augmented by concisely visually encoding information about the dataset, but in the part of the screen normally thought of as the control panel rather than a separate display area. The idea is to do so while using no or minimal additional screen real estate, in order to create displays that have high information density. These augmented widgets are called **scented widgets** [Willett et al. 07], alluding to the idea of **information scent**: cues that help a searcher decide whether there is value in drilling down further into a particular information source, versus looking elsewhere [Pirolli 07]. Figure 13.3 shows several examples. One way to add information is by inserting a concise statistical graphic, such as a bar or line chart. Another choice is by inserting icons or text labels. A third choice is to treat some part of the existing widget as a mark and encode more information into that region using visual channels such as hue, saturation, and opacity.

The Improvise system shown in Figure 12.7 is another example of the use of filtering. The checkbox list view in the lower middle part of the screen is a simple filter controlling whether various geographic features are shown. The multiform microarray explorer in Figure 12.4 also supports several kinds of filtering, with simple range sliders and a more complex view that allows range selection on top of line charts of time-series data. The selected range in the line chart view acts as a filter for the scatterplot view.

13.3.2   Attribute Filtering

Attributes can also be filtered. With **attribute filtering**, the goal is to eliminate attributes rather than items; that is, to show the same number of items, but fewer attributes for each item.

Item filtering and attribute filtering can be combined, with the result of showing both fewer items and fewer attributes.

Example: DOSFA

Figure 13.4 shows an example of the Dimensional Ordering, Spacing, and Filtering Approach (DOSFA) idiom [Yang et al. 03a]. As the name suggests, the idiom features attribute filtering.* Figure 13.4 shows DOSFA on a dataset of 215 attributes representing word counts and 298 points representing documents in a collection of medical abstracts. DOSFA can be used with many visual encoding approaches; this figure shows it in use with star plots. In Figure 13.4(a) the plot axes are so densely packed that little structure can be seen. Figure 13.4(b) shows the plots after the dimensions are ordered by similarity and filtered by both similarity and importance thresholds. The filtered display does show clear visual patterns.

★ Many idioms for attribute filtering and aggregation use the alternative term **dimension** rather than *attribute* in their names.

▶ For more on star plots, see Section 7.6.3.

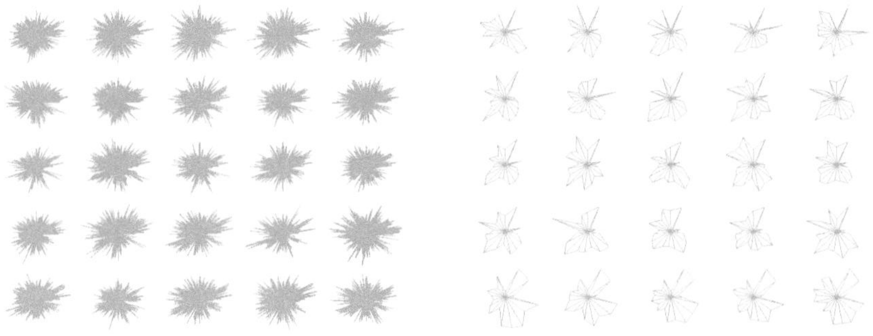

(a)   (b)

Figure 13.4. The DOSFA idiom shown on star glyphs with a medical records dataset of 215 dimensions and 298 points. (a) The full dataset is so dense that patterns cannot be seen. (b) After ordering on similarity and filtering on both similarity and importance, the star glyphs show structure. From [Yang et al. 03a, Figures 3a and 3d].

System	DOSFA
What: Data	Table: many value attributes.
How: Encode	Star plots.
How: Facet	Small multiples with matrix alignment.
How: Reduce	Attribute filtering.

Attribute filtering is often used in conjunction with **attribute ordering**.* If attributes can be ordered according to a derived attribute that measures the similarity between them, then all of the high-scoring ones or low-scoring ones can be easily filtered out interactively. A **similarity measure** for an attribute creates a quantitative or ordered value for each attribute based on all of the data item values for that attribute.* One approach is to calculate the **variance** of an attribute: to what extent the values within that attribute are similar to or different from each other. There are many ways to calculate a similarity measure between attributes; some focus on global similarity, and others search for partial matches [Ankerst et al. 98].

★ A synonym for *attribute ordering* is **dimensional ordering**.

★ A synonym for *similarity measure* is **similarity metric**. Although I am combining the ideas of measure and metric here for the purposes of this discussion, in many specialized contexts such as mathematics and business analysis they are carefully distinguished with different definitions.

▶ An example of a complex combination of both aggregation and filtering is cartographic generalization, discussed in Section 8.3.1.

13.4 Aggregate

The other major reduction design choice is **aggregation**, so that a group of elements is represented by a new derived element that stands in for the entire group. Elements are merged together with aggregation, as opposed to eliminated completely with filtering. Aggregation and filtering can be used in conjunction with each other. As with filtering, aggregation can be used for both items and attributes.

Aggregation typically involves the use of a derived attribute. A very simple example is computing an average; the four other basic aggregation operators are minimum, maximum, count, and sum. However, these simple operators alone are rarely an adequate solution. The challenge of aggregation is to avoid eliminating the interesting signals in the dataset in the process of summarization. The Anscombe's Quartet example shown in Figure 1.3 exactly illustrates the difficulty of adequately summarizing data, and thus the limits of static visual encoding idioms that use aggregation. Aggregation is nevertheless a powerful design choice, particularly when used within interactive idioms where the user can change the level of aggregation on the fly to inspect the dataset at different levels of detail.

13.4.1 Item Aggregation

The most straightforward use of item aggregation is within static visual encoding idioms; its full power and flexibility can be harnessed by interactive idioms where the view dynamically changes.

Example: Histograms

The idiom of **histograms** shows the distribution of items within an original attribute. Figure 13.5 shows a histogram of the distribution of weights for all of the cats in a neighborhood, binned into 5-pound blocks. The range of the original attribute is partitioned into bins, and the number of items that fall into each bin is computed and saved as a derived ordered attribute. The visual encoding of a histogram is very similar to bar charts, with a line mark that uses spatial position in one direction and the bins distributed along an axis in the other direction. One difference is that histograms are sometimes shown without space between the bars to visually imply continuity, whereas bar charts conversely have spaces between the bars to imply discretization. Despite their visual similarity, histograms are very different than bar charts. They do not show the original table directly; rather, they are an example of an aggregation idiom that shows a derived table that is more concise than the original dataset. The number of bins in the histogram can be chosen independently of the number of items in the dataset. The choice of bin size is crucial and tricky: a histogram can look quite different depending on the discretization chosen. One possible solution to the problem is to compute the number of bins based on dataset characteristics; another is to provide the user with controls to easily change the number of bins interactively, to see how the histogram changes.

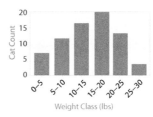

Figure 13.5. The histogram idiom aggregates an arbitrary number of items into a concise representation of their distribution.

Idiom	Histograms
What: Data	Table: one quantitative value attribute.
What: Derived	Derived table: one derived ordered key attribute (bin), one derived quantitative value attribute (item count per bin).
How: Encode	Rectilinear layout. Line mark with aligned position to express derived value attribute. Position: key attribute.

Example: Continuous Scatterplots

Another example of aggregation is continuous scatterplots, where the problem of occlusion on scatterplots is solved by plotting an aggregate value at each pixel rather than drawing every single item as an individual point. Occlusion can be a major readability problem with scatterplots, because many dots could be overplotted on the same location. Size coding exacerbates the problem, as does the use of text labels. Continuous scatterplots use color coding at each pixel to indicate the density of overplotting, often in conjunction with transparency. Conceptually, this approach uses a derived attribute, overplot density, which can be calculated after the layout is computed. Practically, many hardware acceleration techniques sidestep the need to do this calculation explicitly.

Figure 13.6 shows a continuous scatterplot of a tornado air-flow dataset, with the magnitude of the velocity on the horizontal and the z-direction velocity on the vertical. The density is shown with a log-scale sequential colormap with monotonically increasing luminance. It starts with dark blues at the low end, continues with reds in the middle, and has yellows and whites at the high end.

Scatterplots began as a idiom for discrete, categorical data. They have been generalized to a mathematical framework of density functions for continuous data, giving rise to continuous scatterplots in the 2D case

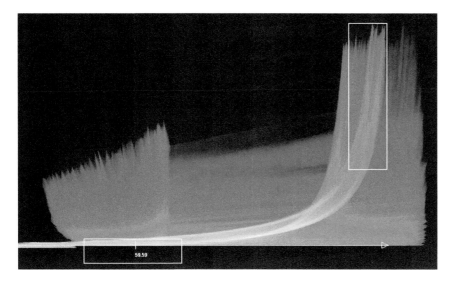

Figure 13.6. The continuous scatterplot idiom uses color to show the density at each location, solving the problem of occlusion from overplotting and allowing scalability to large datasets. From [Bachthaler and Weiskopf 08, Figure 9].

and continuous histograms in the 1D case [Bachthaler and Weiskopf 08]. Continuous scatterplots use a dense, space-filling 2D matrix alignment, where each pixel is given a different color. Although the idiom of continuous scatterplots has a similar name to the idiom of scatterplots, analysis via the framework of design choices shows that the approach is in fact very different.

Idiom	Continuous Scatterplots
What: Data	Table: two quantitative value attributes.
What: Derived	Derived table: two ordered key attributes (x, y pixel locations), one quantitative attribute (overplot density).
How: Encode	Dense space-filling 2D matrix alignment, sequential categorical hue + ordered luminance colormap.
How: Reduce	Item aggregation.

Example: Boxplot Charts

The visually concise idiom of **boxplots** shows an aggregate statistical summary of all the values that occur within the distribution of a single quantitative attribute. It uses five derived variables carefully chosen to provide information about the attribute's distribution: the median (50% point), the lower and upper quartiles (25% and 75% points), and the upper and lower fences (chosen values near the extremes, beyond which points should be counted as outliers). Figure 13.7(a) shows the visual encoding of these five numbers using a simple glyph that relies on vertical spatial position. The eponymous box stretches between the lower and upper quartiles and has a horizontal line at the median. The **whiskers** are vertical lines that extend from the core box to the fences marked with horizontal lines.* Outliers beyond the range of the chosen fence cutoff are shown explicitly as discrete dots, just as in scatterplots or dot charts.

★ *Boxplots* are also known as **box-and-whisker** diagrams.

A boxplot is similar in spirit to an individual bar in a bar chart in that only a single spatial axis is used to visually encode data, but boxplots show five numbers through the use of a glyph rather than the single number encoded by the linear mark in a bar chart. A boxplot chart features multiple boxplots within a single shared frame to contrast different attribute distributions, just as bar charts show multiple bars along the second axis. In Figure 13.7, the quantitative value attribute is mapped to the vertical axis and the categorical key attribute to the horizontal one.

The boxplot can be considered an item reduction idiom that provides an aggregate view of a distribution through the use of derived data. Box-

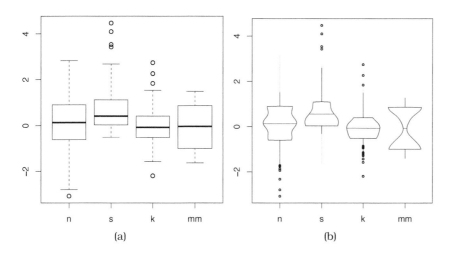

(a)   (b)

Figure 13.7. The boxplot is an idiom presenting summary statistics for the distribution of a quantitative attribute, using five derived values. These plots illustrate four kinds of distributions: normal (n), skewed (s), peaked (k), and multimodal (mm). (a) Standard box plots. (b) Vase plots, which use horizontal spatial position to show density directly. From [Wickham and Stryjewski 12, Figure 5].

plots are highly scalable in terms of aggregating the target quantitative attribute from what could be an arbitrarily large set of values down to five numbers; for example, it could easily handle from thousands to millions of values within that attribute. The spatial encoding of these five numbers along the central axis requires only a moderate amount of screen space, since we have high visual acuity with spatial position. Each boxplot requires only a very small amount of screen space along the secondary axis, leading to a high level of scalability in terms of the number of categorical values that can be accommodated in a boxplot chart; roughly hundreds.

Boxplots directly show the **spread**, namely, the degree of dispersion, with the extent of the box. They show the **skew** of the distribution compared with a normal distribution with the peak at the center by the asymmetry between the top and bottom sections of the box. Standard boxplots are designed to handle **unimodal** data, where there is only one value that occurs the most frequently. There are many variants of boxplots that augment the basic visual encoding with more information. Figure 13.7(b) shows a variable-width variant called the **vase plot** that uses an additional spatial dimension within the glyph by altering the width of the central box according to the density, allowing a visual check if the distribution is instead **multimodal**, with multiple peaks. The variable-width variants require more screen space along the secondary axis than the simpler version, in an example of the classic cost–benefit trade-off where conveying more information requires more room.

Idiom	Boxplot Charts
What: Data	Table: many quantitative value attributes.
What: Derived	Five quantitative attributes for each original attribute, representing its distribution.
Why: Tasks	Characterize distribution; find outliers, extremes, averages; identify skew.
How: Encode	One glyph per original attribute expressing derived attribute values using vertical spatial position, with 1D list alignment of glyphs into separated with horizontal spatial position.
How: Reduce	Item aggregation.
Scale	Items: unlimited. Attributes: dozens.

Many of the interesting uses of aggregation in vis involve dynamically changing sets: the mapping between individual items and the aggregated visual mark changes on the fly. The simple case is to allow the user to explicitly request aggregation and deaggregation of item sets. More sophisticated approaches do these operations automatically as a result of higher-level interaction and navigation, usually based on spatial proximity.

Example: SolarPlot

Figure 13.8 shows the example of SolarPlot, a radial histogram with an interactively controllable aggregation level [Chuah 98]. The user directly manipulates the size of the base circle that is the radial axis of the chart. This change of radius indirectly changes the number of available histogram bins, and thus the aggregation level. Like all histograms, the SolarPlot aggregation operator is *count*: the height of the bar represents the number of items in the set. The dataset shown is ticket sales over time, starting from the base of the circle and progressing counterclockwise to cover 30 years in total. The small circle in Figure 13.8(a) is heavily aggregated. It does show an increase in ticket sales over the years. The larger circle in Figure 13.8(b) is less aggregated, and seasonal patterns within each year can be distinguished.

Idiom	SolarPlot
What: Data	Table: one quantitative attribute.
What: Derived	Derived table: one derived ordered key attribute (bin), one derived quantitative value attribute (item

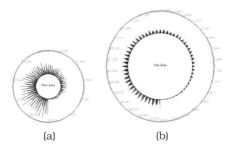

            (a)   (b)

Figure 13.8. The SolarPlot circular histogram idiom provides indirect control of aggregation level by changing the circle size. (a) The small circle shows the increase in ticket sales over time. (b) Enlarging the circle shows seasonal patterns in addition to the gradual increase. From [Chuah 98, Figures 1 and 2].

	count per bin). Number of bins interactively controlled.
How: Encode	Radial layout, line marks. Line length: express derived value attribute; angle: key attribute.
How: Reduce	Item aggregation.
Scale	Original items: unlimited. Derived bins: proportional to screen space allocated.

The general design choice of **hierarchical aggregation** is to construct the derived data of a hierarchical clustering of items in the original dataset and allow the user to interactively control the level of detail to show based on this hierarchy. There are many specific examples of idioms that use variants of this design choice. The cluster–calendar system in Figure 6.7 is one example of hierarchical aggregation. Another is hierarchical parallel coordinates.

Example: Hierarchical Parallel Coordinates

The idiom of **hierarchical parallel coordinates** [Fua et al. 99] uses interactively controlled aggregation as a design choice to increase the scalability of the basic parallel coordinates visual encoding to hundreds of thousands of items. The dataset is transformed by computing derived data: a hierarchical clustering of the items. Several statistics about each cluster are computed, including the number of points it contains; the mean, minimum, and maximum values; and the depth in the hierarchy. A cluster is represented by a band of varying width and opacity, where the mean is in the middle and width at each axis depends on the minimum and

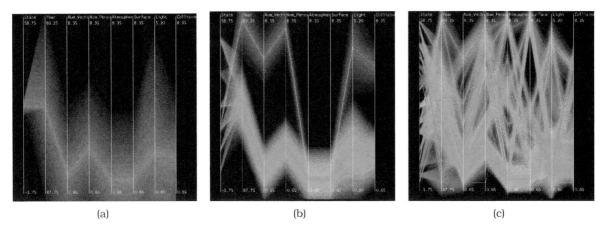

(a)   (b)   (c)

Figure 13.9. Hierarchical parallel coordinates provide multiple levels of detail. (a) The single top cluster has large extent. (b) When several clusters are shown, each has a smaller extent. (c) When many clusters are shown, the proximity-based coloring helps them remain distinguishable from each other. From [Fua et al. 99, Figure 4].

maximum item values for that attribute within the cluster. Thus, in the limit, a cluster of a single item is shown by a single line, just as with the original idiom. The cluster bands are colored according to their proximity in the cluster hierarchy, so that clusters far away from each other have very different colors.

The level of detail displayed at a global level for the entire dataset can be interactively controlled by the user using a single slider. The parameter controlled by that slider is again a derived variable that varies the aggregate level of detail shown in a smooth and continuous way. Figure 13.9 shows a dataset with eight attributes and 230,000 items at different levels of detail. Figure 13.9(a) is the highest-level overview showing the single top-level cluster, with very broad bands of green. Figure 13.9(b) is the mid-level view showing several clusters, where the extents of the tan cluster are clearly distinguishable from the now-smaller green one. Figure 13.9(c) is a more detailed view with dozens of clusters that have tighter bands; the proximity-based coloring mitigates the effect of occlusion.

Idiom	Hierarchical Parallel Coordinates
What: Data	Table.
What: Derived	Cluster hierarchy atop original table of items. Five per-cluster attributes: count, mean, min, max, depth.
How: Encode	Parallel coordinates. Color clusters by proximity in hierarchy.
How: Reduce	Interactive item aggregation to change level of detail.
Scale	Items: 10,000–100,000. Clusters: one dozen.

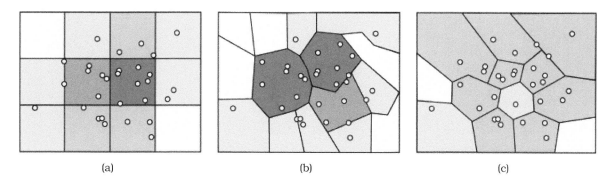

Figure 13.10. Modifiable Areal Unit Problem (MAUP) example, showing how different boundaries for aggregation regions lead to very different visual patterns on choropleth maps. (a) Central region is high density. (b) Central region is medium density. (c) Central region is low density. From http://www.e-education.psu.edu/geog486/l4_p7.html, Figure 4.cg.6.

13.4.2   Spatial Aggregation

The challenge of **spatial aggregation** is to take the spatial nature of data into account correctly when aggregating it. In the cartography literature, the **modifiable areal unit problem (MAUP)** is a major concern: changing the boundaries of the regions used to analyze data can yield dramatically different results. Even if the number of units and their size does not change, any change of spatial grouping can lead to a very significant change in analysis results. Figure 13.10 shows an example, where the same location near the middle of the map has a different density level depending on the region boundaries: high in Figure 13.10(a), medium in Figure 13.10(b), and low in Figure 13.10(c). Moreover, changing the scale of the units also leads to different results. The problem of **gerrymandering**, where the boundaries of voting districts are manipulated for political gain, is the instance of the MAUP best known to the general public.

Example: Geographically Weighted Boxplots

The **geowigs** family of idioms, namely, geographically weighted interactive graphics, provides sophisticated support for spatial aggregation using geographically weighted regression and geographically weighted summary statistics [Dykes and Brunsdon 07]. Figure 13.11 shows a multivariate geographic dataset used to explore social issues in 19th century France. The six quantitative attributes are population per crime against persons ($x1$), population per crime against property ($x2$), percentage who can read

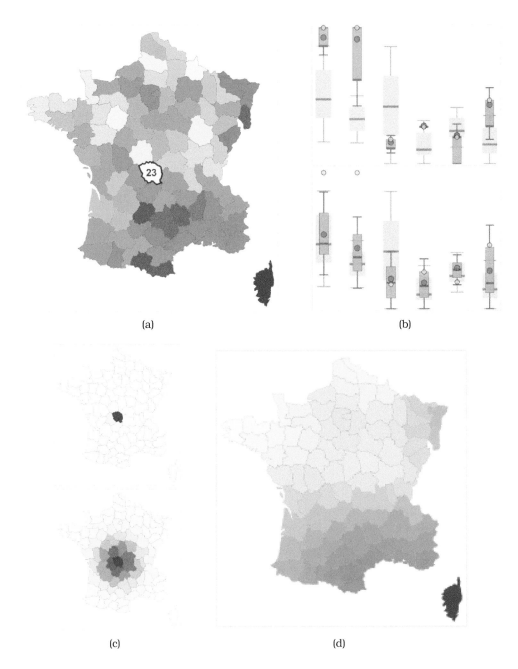

(a)   (b)

(c)   (d)

Figure 13.11. Geowigs are geographically weighted interactive graphics. (a) A choropleth map showing attribute *x1*. (b) The set of gw-boxplots for all six attributes at two scales. (c) Weighting maps showing the scales: local and larger. (d) A gw-mean map at the larger scale. From [Dykes and Brunsdon 07, Figures 7a and 2].

and write (*x3*), donations to the poor (*x4*), population per illegitimate birth (*x5*), and population per suicide (*x6*).

Figure 13.11(a) shows a standard choropleth map colored by personal crime attribute *x1*, with the interactively selected region *Creuse (23)* highlighted. Figure 13.11(b) shows gw-boxplots for all six attributes, at two scales. The **gw-boxplot**, a geographically weighted boxplot geowig, supports comparison between the global distribution and the currently chosen spatial scale using the design choice of superimposed layers. The global statistical distribution is encoded by the gray boxplot in the background, and the local statistics for the interactively chosen scale are encoded by a foreground boxplot in green. Figure 13.11(c) shows the weighting maps for the currently chosen scale of each gw-boxplot set: very local on top, and a larger scale on the bottom. Figure 13.11(d) shows a **gw-mean** map, a geographically weighted mean geowig, weighted according to the same larger scale.

> ▶ Choropleth maps are covered in Section 8.3.1.

> ▶ Boxplots are covered in Section 13.4.1.

At the local level, the first *x1* attribute is clearly an outlier in the gw-boxplot, matching that region's pale color in the choropleth map. When weighted according to a larger scale, that attribute's distribution is close to the global one in both the boxplot, matching the mid-range color in the gw-mean map geowig in Figure 13.11(d).

Idiom	Geographically Weighted Boxplots
What: Data	Geographic geometry with area boundaries. Table: Key attribute (area), several quantitative value attributes. Table: Five-number statistical summary distributions for each original attribute.
What: Derived	Multidimensional table: key attribute (area), key attribute (scale), quantitative value attributes (geographically weighted statistical summaries for each area at multiple scales).
How: Encode	Boxplot.
How: Facet	Superimposed layers: global boxplot as gray background, current-scale boxplot as green foreground.
How: Reduce	Spatial aggregation.

13.4.3 Attribute Aggregation: Dimensionality Reduction

Just as attributes can be filtered, attributes can also be aggregated, where a new attribute is synthesized to take the place of multiple original attributes. A very simple approach to aggregating attributes is to group them by some kind of similarity measure, and then synthesize the new attribute by calculate an average across that similar set. A more complex approach to aggregation is **dimensionality reduction (DR)**, where the goal is to preserve the meaningful structure of a dataset while using fewer attributes to represent the items.

13.4.3.1 Why and When to Use DR?

In the family of idioms typically called *dimensionality reduction*, the goal is to preserve the meaningful structure of a dataset while using fewer attributes to represent the items.* The rationale that a small set of new synthetic attributes might be able to faithfully represent most of the structure or variance in the dataset hinges on the assumption that there is hidden structure and significant redundancy in the original dataset because the underlying latent variables could not be measured directly.

Nonlinear methods for dimensionality reduction are used when the new dimensions cannot be expressed in terms of a straightforward combination of the original ones. The **multidimensional scaling (MDS)** family of approaches includes both linear and nonlinear variants, where the goal is to minimize the differences in distances between points in the high-dimensional space versus the new lower-dimensional space.

Example: Dimensionality Reduction for Document Collections

A situation where dimensionality reduction is frequently used is when users are faced with the need to analyze a large collection of text documents, ranging from thousands to millions or more. Although we typically read text when confronted with only a single document, document collection vis is typically used in situations where there are so many documents in the collection that simply reading each one is impractical. Document collections are not directly visualizeable, but they can be transformed into a dataset type that is: a derived high-dimensional table.

Text documents are usually transformed by ignoring the explicit linear ordering of the words within the document and treating it as a **bag of words**: the number of times that each word is used in the document is simply counted. The result is a large **feature vector**, where the elements in the vector are all of the words in the entire document collection. Very common words are typically eliminated, but these vectors can still contain tens of thousands of words. However, these vectors are very **sparse**, where the overwhelming number of values are simply zero: any individual document contains only a tiny fraction of the possible words.

★ The words **attribute aggregation**, **attribute synthesis**, and **dimensionality reduction (DR)** are all synonyms. The term *dimensionality reduction* is very common in the literature. I use *attribute aggregation* as a name to show where this design choice fits into the taxonomy of the book; it is not a typical usage by other authors. Although the term *dimensionality reduction* might logically seem to include attribute filtering, it is more typically used to mean attribute synthesis through aggregation.

▶ Deriving new data is discussed in Section 3.4.2.3.

The result of this transformation is a derived table with a huge number of quantitative attributes. The documents are the items in the table, and the attribute value for a particular word contains the number of times that word appears in the document. Looking directly at these tables is not very interesting.

This enormous table is then transformed into a much more compact one by deriving a much smaller set of new attributes that still represents much of the structure in the original table using dimensionality reduction. In this usage, there are two stages of constructing derived data: from a document collection to a table with a huge number of attributes, and then a second step to get down to a table with the same number of items but just a few attributes.

The bag-of-words DR approach is suitable when the goal is to analyze the differential distribution of words between the documents, or to find clusters of related documents based on common word use between them. The dimensionally reduced data is typically shown with a scatterplot, where the user's goal is cluster discovery: either to verify an existing conjecture about cluster structure or to find previously unknown cluster structure.

Images, videos, and other multimedia documents are usually transformed to create derived attributes in a similar spirit to the transformations done to text documents. One major question is how to derive new attributes that compactly represent an image as a set of **features**. The features in text documents are relatively easy to identify because they're based on the words; even in this case, natural language processing techniques are often used to combine synonyms and words with the same stem together. Image features typically require even more complex computations, such as detecting edges within the image or the set of colors it contains. Processing individual videos to create derived feature data can take into account temporal characteristics such as interframe coherence.

A typical analysis scenario is complex enough that it is useful to break it down into a chained sequence, rather than just analyzing it as a single instance. In the first step, a low-dimensional table is derived from the high-dimensional table using multidimensional scaling. In the second step, the low-dimensional data is encoded as a color-coded scatterplot, according to a conjectured clustering. The user's goal is a discovery task, to verify whether there are visible clusters and identify those that have semantic meaning given the documents that comprise them. Figure 13.12 shows a scatterplot view of a real-world document collection dataset, dimensionally reduced with the Glimmer multidimensional scaling (MDS) algorithm [Ingram et al. 09]. In this scenario, the user can interactively navigate within the scatterplot, and selecting a point shows document keywords in a popup display and the full text of the document in another view. In the third step, the user's goal is to produce annotations by adding text labels to the verified clusters. Figure 13.13 summarizes this what–why–how analyis.

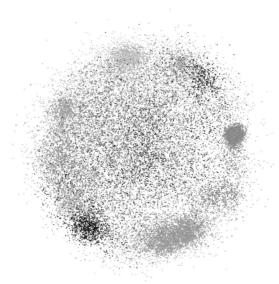

Figure 13.12. Dimensionality reduction of a large document collection using Glimmer for multidimensional scaling. The results are laid out in a single 2D scatterplot, allowing the user to verify that the conjectured clustering shown with color coding is partially supported by the spatial layout. From [Ingram et al. 09, Figure 8].

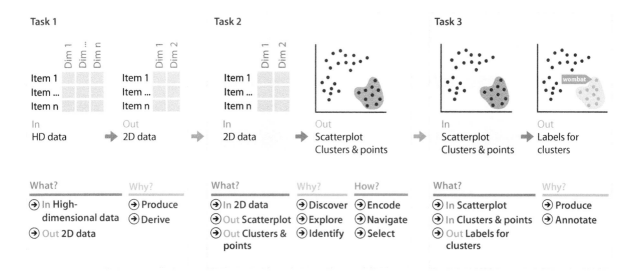

Figure 13.13. A chained sequence of what–why–how analysis instances for the scenario of dimensionality reduction of document collection data.

Idiom	Dimensionality Reduction for Document Collections
What: Data	Text document collection.
What: Derived	Table with 10,000 attributes.
What: Derived	Table with two attributes.
How: Encode	Scatterplot, colored by conjectured clustering.
How: Reduce	Attribute aggregation (dimensionality reduction) with MDS.
Scale	Original attributes: 10,000. Derived attributes: two. Items: 100,000.

13.4.3.2 How to Show DR Data?

With standard dimensionality reduction techniques, the user chooses the number of synthetic attributes to create. When the target number of new attributes is two, the dimensionally reduced data is most often shown as a scatterplot. When more than two synthetic attributes are created, a scatterplot matrix (SPLOM) may be a good choice. Although in general scatterplots are often used to check for correlation between two attributes, that is not the goal when inspecting scatterplots of dimensionally reduced data. The point of dimensionality reduction is to automatically collapse correlated dimensions together into new synthetic dimensions; the techniques are designed so that these new dimensions will not be correlated. The tasks with scatterplots of dimensionally reduced data are to verify or find whether the data items form meaningful clusters and to verify or check whether the new synthetic attributes are meaningful.

For both of these tasks, an important function is to be able to select a low-dimensional point in the scatterplot and inspect the high-dimensional data that it represents. Typically, the user investigates by clicking on points and seeing if the spatial layout implied by the low-dimensional positions of the points seems to properly reflect the high-dimensional space.

Sometimes the dataset has no additional information, and the scatterplot is simply encoding two-dimensional position. In many cases there is a conjectured categorization of the points, which are colored according to those categories. The task is then to check whether the patterns of colors match up well with the patterns of the spatial clusters of the reduced data, as shown in Figure 13.12.

When you are interpreting dimensionally reduced scatterplots it is important to remember that only relative distances matter. The absolute position of clusters is not meaningful; most techniques create layouts where the image would have the same meaning if it is rotated in an arbitrary direction, reflected with mirror symmetry across any line, or rescaled to a different size.*

> ★ In mathematical ter-
> minology, the layouts are
> **affine invariant**.

Another caution is that this inspection should be used only to find or verify large-scale cluster structure. The fine-grained structure in the lower-dimensional plots should not be considered strongly reliable because some information is lost in the reduction. That is, it is safe to assume that major differences in the distances between points are meaningful, but minor differences in distances may not be a reliable signal.

Empirical studies have shown that two-dimensional scatter-plots or SPLOMS are the safest idiom choices for inspecting dimensionally reduced data [Sedlmair et al. 13]. While the idiom of three-dimensional scatterplots has been proposed many times, they are susceptible to all of the problems with 3D representations. As discussed in Section 6.3, they are an example of the worst possible case for accurate depth perception, an abstract cloud of points floating in three-dimensional space. Although some systems use the idiom of 3D landscapes for dimensionally reduced data, this approach is similarly problematic, for reasons also covered in Section 6.3.

13.5   Further Reading

Filtering Early work in dynamic queries popularized filtering with tightly coupled views and extending standard widgets to better support these queries [Ahlberg and Shneiderman 94].

Scented Widgets Scented widgets [Willett et al. 07] allude to the idea of information scent proposed within the theory of information foraging from Xerox PARC [Pirolli 07].

Boxplots The boxplot was originally proposed by Tukey and popularized through his influential book on *Exploratory Data Analysis* [Tukey 77]. A recent survey paper discusses the many variants of boxplots that have been proposed in the past 40 years [Wickham and Stryjewski 12].

Hierarchical Aggregation A general conceptual framework for analyzing hierarchical aggregation is presented in a recent paper

[Elmqvist and Fekete 10]. Earlier work presented hierarchical parallel coordinates [Fua et al. 99].

Spatial Aggregation The Modifiable Areal Unit Problem is covered in a recent handbook chapter [Wong 09]; a seminal booklet lays out the problem in detail [Openshaw 84]. Geographically weighted interactive graphics, or geowigs for short, support exploratory analysis that explicitly takes scale into account [Dykes and Brunsdon 07].

Attribute Reduction DOSFA [Yang et al. 03a] is one of many approaches to attribute reduction from the same group [Peng et al. 04, Yang et al. 04, Yang et al. 03b]. The DimStiller system proposes a general framework for attribute reduction [Ingram et al. 10]. An extensive exploration of similarity metrics for dimensional aggregation was influential early work [Ankerst et al. 98].

Dimensionality Reduction The foundational ideas behind multidimensional scaling were first proposed in the 1930s [Young and Householder 38], then further developed in the 1950s [Torgerson 52]. An early proposal for multidimensional scaling (MDS) in the vis literature used a stochastic force simulation approach [Chalmers 96]. The Glimmer system exploits the parallelism of graphics hardware for MDS; that paper also discusses the history and variants of MDS in detail [Ingram et al. 09]. Design guidelines for visually encoding dimensionally reduced data suggest avoiding the use of 3D scatterplots [Sedlmair et al. 13].

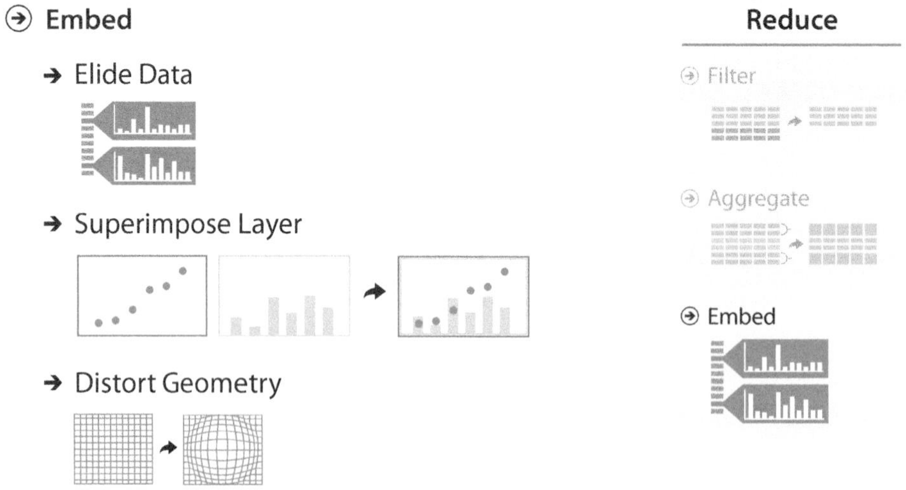

Embed

→ Elide Data

→ Superimpose Layer

→ Distort Geometry

Reduce

⊕ Filter

⊕ Aggregate

⊕ Embed

Figure 14.1. Design choices for embedding focus information within context.

Chapter 14

Embed: Focus+Context

14.1 The Big Picture

The family of idioms known as **focus+context** are based on the design choice to **embed** detailed information about a selected set—the **focus**—within a single view that also contains overview information about more of the data—the **context**. These idioms reduce the amount of data to show in the view through sophisticated combinations of filtering and aggregation. The design considerations are sufficiently complex that embedding is addressed separately in the analysis framework as a special case. A very large family of specific idioms that use some form of focus+context embedding has been proposed.*

One design choice for embedding is to elide items, where some items are filtered out completely while others are summarized using dynamic aggregation for context; only the focus items are shown in detail. Another choice is to superimpose layers, where a local region of focus information can be moved against the background layer of contextual information. A third choice is to distort the geometry, where context regions are compressed to make room for magnified focus regions. In all of these cases, there is a choice of single or multiple regions of focus. With geometric distortion, there are choices for region shape, region extent, and interaction metaphor. Figure 14.1 summarizes this set of design choices.

14.2 Why Embed?

The goal of embedding focus and context together is to mitigate the potential for disorientation that comes with standard navigation techniques such as geometric zooming. With realistic camera motion, only a small part of world space is visible in the image when the camera is zoomed in to see details for a small region. With

★ Many names are essentially synonyms for or special cases of *focus+context*: **bifocal displays**, **degree-of-interest models**, **detail in context**, **distortion-oriented presentations**, **distortion viewing**, **elastic presentation spaces**, **fisheye lens**, **generalized fisheye views**, **hyperbolic geometry**, **multifocal displays**, **nonlinear magnification fields**, **pliable surfaces**, **polyfocal projections**, **rubber sheet navigation**, and **stretch and squish navigation**.

▶ Zooming is discussed in Section 11.5.1.

geometric navigation and a single view that changes over time, the only way to maintain orientation is to internally remember one's own navigation history. Focus+context idioms attempt to support orientation by providing contextual information intended to act as recognizable landmarks, using external memory to reduce internal cognitive load.

Focus+context idioms are thus an example of nonliteral navigation, in the same spirit as semantic zooming. The shared idea with all of them is that a subset of the dataset items are interactively chosen by the user to be the focus and are drawn in detail. The visual encoding also includes information about some or all of the rest of the dataset shown for context, integrated into and embedded within the same view that shows the focus items. Some idioms achieve this selective presentation without the use of geometric distortion, but many use carefully chosen distortion to combine magnified focus regions and minimized context regions into a unified view.

Embedding idioms cannot be fully understood when considered purely from the visual encoding point of view *or* purely from the interaction point of view; they are fundamentally a synthesis of both. The key idea of focus+context is that the focus set changes dynamically as the user interacts with the system, and thus the visual representation also changes dynamically. Many of the idioms involve indirect control, where the focus set is inferred via the combination of the user's navigation choices and the inherent structure of the dataset.

14.3 Elide

One design choice for embedding is **elision**: some items are omitted from the view completely, in a form of dynamic filtering. Other items are summarized using dynamic aggregation for context, and only the focus items are shown in detail.

A general framework for reasoning about these three sets of items is a **degree of interest (DOI)** function: $DOI = I(x) - D(x, y)$. In this equation, I is an interest function; D is the distance, either semantic or spatial; x is the location of an item; y is the current focus point [Furnas 86]. There could be only one focus point, or multiple independent foci. The DOI function can be thought of as a continuous function that does not explicitly distinguish between focus items to show in detail, context items to aggregate, and com-

pletely elided items to filter out. Those interpretations are made by
algorithms that use the function, often based on threshold values.
These interest functions typically exploit knowledge about dataset
structure, especially hierarchical relationships. For example, if a
few subsections of a document were selected to be the foci, then a
good context would be their enclosing sections.

Example: DOITrees Revisited

The DOITrees Revisited system shown in Figure 14.2 uses multiple foci
to show an elided version of a 600,000 node tree. The shaded triangles
provide an aggregate representation showing the size of the elided subtrees. The context in which to show them is computed using tree traversal
from the many focus nodes up toward their common ancestors and the
tree root. In this case, distance is computed topologically based on hops
through the tree, rather than geometrically through Euclidean space. The
focus nodes can be chosen explicitly by clicking, or indirectly through
searching.

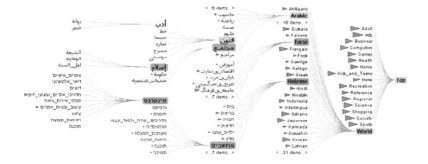

Figure 14.2. DOITrees Revisited uses elision to show multiple focus nodes within
context in a 600,000 node tree. From [Heer and Card 04, Figure 1].

System	DOITrees Revisited
What: Data	Tree.
How: Encode	Node–link layout.
How: Reduce	Embed: elide, multiple foci.
Scale	Nodes: hundreds of thousands.

14.4   Superimpose

▶ Superimposing layers globally is discussed in Section 12.5.

Another choice for integrating focus and context is the use of superimposed layers. In this case, the focus layer is limited to a local region, rather than being a global layer that stretches across the entire view to cover everything.

Example: Toolglass and Magic Lenses

The Toolglass and Magic Lenses system shown in Figure 14.3 uses a see-through lens to show color-coded Gaussian curvature in a foreground layer, atop the background layer consisting of the rest of the 3D scene. Within the lens, details are shown, and the unchanged remainder of the other view provides context. The lens layer occludes the region beneath it. The system handled many different kinds of data with different visual encodings of it; this example shows 3D spatial data. The curvature lens shows that the object in the scene that appears to be a perfect sphere when rendered with standard computer graphics techniques is in fact a faceted object made from multiple patches.

Figure 14.3. The Toolglass and Magic Lenses idiom provides focus and context through a superimposed local layer: the see-through lens color codes the patchwork sphere with Gaussian curvature information and provides a numeric value for the point at the center. From [Bier et al. 93, Figure 12].

System	Toolglass and Magic Lenses
What: Data	Spatial, quantitative curvature attribute across surface.
How: Encode	Use given, color by curvature.
How: Reduce	Embed: superimpose.

14.5   Distort

In contrast to using elision or layers, many focus+context idioms solve the problem of integrating focus and context into a single view using geometric distortion of the contextual regions to make room for the details in the focus regions.

There are several major design choices that underlie all geometric distortion idioms. As with the other two choices, there is the choice of the number of focus regions: is there only a single region of focus, or does the idiom allow multiple foci? Another choice is the shape of the focus: is it a radial, rectangular, or a completely arbitrary shape? A third choice is the extent of the focus: is it global across the entire image, or constrained to just a local region? A fourth choice is the interaction metaphor. One possibility is constrained geometric navigation. Another is moveable lenses, evocative of the real-world use of a magnifying glass lens. A third is stretching and squishing a rubber sheet. A fourth is working with vector fields.

These choices are now illustrated through five examples of distortion idioms: 3D perspective, fisheye lenses, hyperbolic geometry, stretch and squish navigation, and magnification fields.

Example: 3D Perspective

Several early idioms used 3D perspective to provide a global distortion region with a single focus point. The interaction metaphor was constrained geometric navigation. The perspective distortion arising from

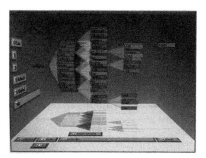

Figure 14.4. The Cone Tree system used 3D perspective for focus+context, providing a global distortion region with a single focus point, and using standard geometric navigation for interaction. From [Card and Mackinlay 99, Figure 10].

the standard 3D computer graphics transformations is a very intuitive and familiar effect. It was used with the explicit intention of providing a distortion-based focus+context user experience in many early vis systems, such as the influential Cone Tree system shown in Figure 14.4 [Robertson et al. 91].

Although many people found it compelling and expressed a strong preference for it on their first encounter, this approach lost popularity as the trade-offs between the costs and benefits of 3D spatial layout for abstract information became more understood.

> ▶ The costs and benefits of 3D are discussed in Section 6.3.

System	Cone Trees
What: Data	Tree.
How: Encode	3D node–link layout.
How: Reduce	Embed: distort with 3D perspective; single global focus region.
Scale	Nodes: thousands.

Example: Fisheye Lens

The **fisheye lens** distortion idiom uses a single focus with local extent and radial shape and the interaction metaphor of a draggable lens on top of the main view. The fisheye idiom provides the same radial distortion effect as the physical optical lenses used with cameras and for door peepholes. The lens interaction provides a foreground layer that completely replaces what is beneath it, like the magic lens idiom, rather than preserving what is beneath and superimposing additional information on top of it, like the superimposing layer design choice for faceting data between views. The lens can be moved with the standard navigation approach of 2D translation. The mathematics of fisheye distortion is straightforward; modern graphics hardware supports high performance fisheye lenses using vertex shaders [Lambert et al. 10].

Figure 14.5 shows two examples of a fisheye lens used with an online poker player dataset. The scatterplot in Figure 14.5(a) shows the percentage of time that a player goes to showdown (playing until people have to show all of their cards) versus the flop (playing until the point where three cards are placed face-up on the board). In the dense matrix view of Figure 14.5(b), blocks representing players are color coded according to their winning rate, and a space-filling curve is used to lay out these blocks in order of a specific derived attribute; in this case, a particular betting strategy. In the parts of the scene under the fisheye lens, the labels are large enough to read; that focus region remains embedded within

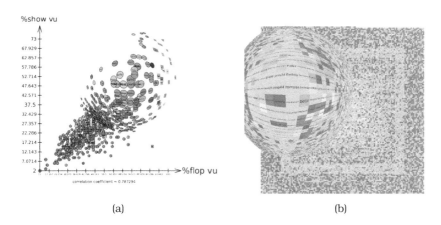

(a)   (b)

Figure 14.5. Focus+context with interactive fisheye lens, with poker player data-set. (a) Scatterplot showing correlation between two strategies. (b) Dense matrix view showing correlation between a specific complex strategy and the player's winning rate, encoded by color.

the surrounding context, showing the global pattern within the rest of the dataset.

Idiom	Fisheye Lens
What: Data	Any data.
How: Encode	Any layout.
How: Reduce	Embed: distort with fisheye; single focus, local radial region, moveable lens interaction metaphor.

Example: Hyperbolic Geometry

The distortion idiom of hyperbolic geometry uses a single radial global focus with the interaction metaphor of hyperbolic translation. This approach exploits the mathematics of non-Euclidean geometry to elegantly accommodate structures such as trees that grow by an exponential factor, in contrast to standard Euclidean geometry where there is only a polynomial amount of space available for placing items. An infinite non-Euclidean plane can be mapped to a finite Euclidean circle, and similarly an infinite non-Euclidean volume can be mapped to a finite sphere in Euclidean space. The interaction metaphor is hyperbolic translation, which corresponds to changing the focus point of the projection; the visual effect

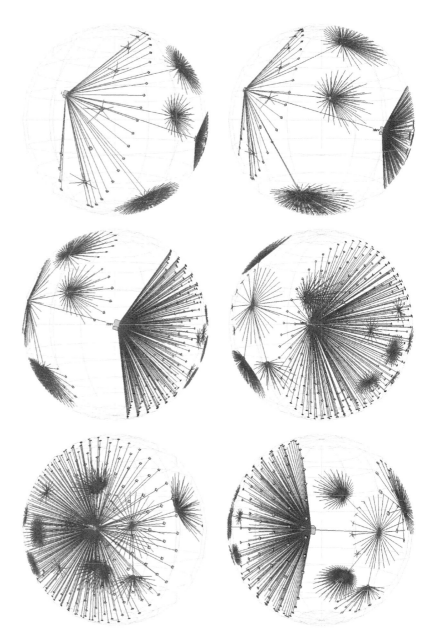

Figure 14.6. Animated transition showing navigation through 3D hyperbolic geometry for a file system tree laid out with the H3 idiom, where the first three frames show hyperbolic translation changing the focus point and the last three show standard 3D rotation spinning the structure around. From [Munzner 98, Figure 3].

is changing which items are magnified at the center, versus minimized at the periphery, for a global effect with similarities to using a fisheye lens that extends across the entire scene.

Figure 14.6 shows a 3D hyperbolic node–link tree representing the structure of a file system laid out with the H3 idiom [Munzner 98], through a sequence of frames from an animated transition as the view changes over time. The first three frames show hyperbolic translation to change what part of the tree is magnified, where the subtree on the right side gets larger as it moves toward the center of projection. The last three frames show standard rotation to clarify the 3D structure. The rationale for using 3D rather than 2D was to achieve greater information density, but at the cost that any single frame is partially occluded.

▶ The costs and benefits of using 3D for abstract data are covered in Section 6.3.

Idiom	Hyperbolic Geometry
What: Data	Tree or network.
How: Encode	Hyperbolic layout.
How: Reduce	Embed: distort by projecting from hyperbolic to Euclidean space; single global radial focus; hyperbolic translation interaction metaphor.

Example: Stretch and Squish Navigation

The **stretch and squish navigation** idiom uses multiple rectangular foci of global extent for distortion, and the interaction metaphor where enlarging some regions causes others to shrink. In this metaphor, the entire scene is considered to be drawn on a rubber sheet where stretching one region squishes the rest, as shown in Figures 11.7, 14.7, and 14.8. Figure 14.7 shows stretch and squish navigation with the TreeJuxtaposer system [Munzner et al. 03], where Figure 14.7(a) shows two small trees juxtaposed with linked highlighting and navigation, and Figure 14.7(b) shows the result of multiple successive stretches within a single large tree. The borders of the sheet stay fixed so that all items stay visible within the viewport, although they may be projected to arbitrarily small regions of the image. The user can choose to separately stretch the rectangular focal regions in the horizontal and vertical directions.

These figures also illustrate the visual encoding idiom of **guaranteed visibility** that ensures that important objects are always visible within the scene, even if they are very small. Guaranteed visibility is an example of aggregation that operates at the subpixel level and takes the importance attribute of each item into account. Standard graphics systems use assumptions that work well when drawing realistic scenes but are not necessarily true for abstract data. In reality, distant objects are not visually

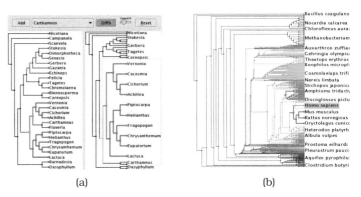

(a)   (b)

Figure 14.7. TreeJuxtaposer uses stretch and squish navigation with multiple rectangular foci for exploring phylogenetic trees. (a) Stretching a single region when comparing two small trees. (b) Stretching multiple regions within a large tree. From [Munzner et al. 03, Figures 5 and 1].

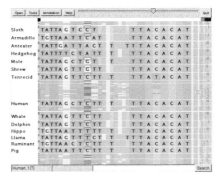

Figure 14.8. PRISequenceJuxtaposer supports comparing gene sequences using the stretch and squish navigation idiom with the guaranteed visibility of marks representing items with a high importance value, via a rendering algorithm with custom subpixel aggregation. From [Slack et al. 06, Figure 3].

salient, so it is a reasonable optimization to simply not draw items that are sufficiently far away. If the viewpoint is moved closer to these objects, they will become larger on the image plane and will be drawn. However, in abstract scenes the distance from the camera is a poor stand-in for the **importance** value for an object; often an original or derived attribute is used instead of or in combination with geometric distance. The example in Figure 14.8 is a collection of gene sequences that are over 16,000 nucleotides in width displayed in a frame of less than 700 pixels wide [Slack et al. 06]. The red marks that indicate differences between gene sequences stay visible at all times because they are given a high importance value, even in very squished regions where hundreds or thousands of items may fall within a single pixel. Figure 11.7 also illustrates this idiom: the value used for the box color coding also indicates importance, so the boxes representing alerts that are colored red are always visible.

Idiom	Stretch and Squish Navigation
What: Data	Any data.
How: Encode	Any layout.
How: Reduce	Embed: distort with stretch and squish; multiple foci, global rectangular regions, stretch and squish navigation interaction metaphor.

Example: Nonlinear Magnification Fields

The nonlinear magnification fields idiom relies on a general computational framework featuring multiple foci of arbitrary magnification levels and shapes, whose scope can be constrained to affect only local regions. The underlying mathematical framework supports calculations of the implicit

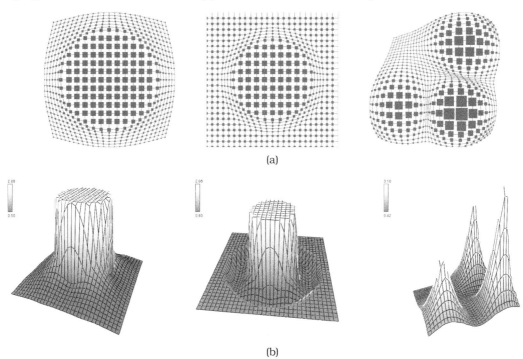

(a)

(b)

Figure 14.9. General frameworks calculate the magnification and minimization fields needed to achieve desired transformations in the image. (a) Desired transformations. (b) Calculated magnification fields. From [Keahey 98, Figure 3].

magnification field required to achieve a desired transformation effect, as shown in Figure 14.9(a). The framework supports many possible interaction metaphors including lenses and stretchable surfaces. It can also expose the magnification fields shown in Figure 14.9(b) directly to the user, for example, to support data-driven magnification trails of moving objects.

Idiom	Nonlinear Magnification Fields
What: Data	Any data.
How: Encode	Any layout.
How: Reduce	Embed: distort with magnification fields; multiple foci, local arbitrary regions, lens or stretch or data-driven interaction metaphors.

14.6   Costs and Benefits: Distortion

Embedding focus information within surrounding context in a single view is one of five major alternatives to showing complex information. The other four choices are deriving new data, manipulating a single changing view, faceting into multiple views, and reducing the amount of data to show. The trade-offs of cost and benefits between these five approaches are still not fully understood.

What has gradually become clear is that distortion-based focus+context in particular has measurable costs, in addition to whatever benefits it may provide. One cost is the problem that distance or length judgements are severely impaired, so distortion is a poor match with any tasks that require such comparisons. Thus, one of the most successful use cases for geometric distortion is with exploration of node–link layouts for networks and trees. The task of understanding the topological structure of the network is likely to be robust to distortion when that structure is shown using lines to connect between nodes, or containment to show nested parent–child node relationships, because precise angle and length judgements are not necessary.

One potential cost is that users may not be aware of the distortion, and thus misunderstand the underlying object structure. This risk is highest when the user is exploring an unfamiliar or sparse structure, and many idioms incorporate explicit indications of distortion to lessen this risk. Hyperbolic views typically show the enclosing circle or sphere, magnification fields often show a superimposed grid or shading to imply the height of the stretched surface.

Even when users do understand the nature of the distortion, another cost is the internal overhead of maintaining object constancy, which is the understanding that an item seen in two different frames represents the same object, just seen from a different viewpoint. Understanding the underlying shape of a complex structure could require mentally subtracting the effect of the transformation in order to recognize the relationship between the components of an image before and after the transformation. Although in most cases we do this calculation almost effortlessly for standard 3D perspective distortion, the cost of mentally tracking general distortions increases as the amount of distortion increases [Lam et al. 06]. Some empirical evidence shows that constrained and predictable distortion is better tolerated than more drastic distortion [Lam and Munzner 10].

The originator of the generalized fisheye view approach has expressed surprise about the enthusiasm with which others have embraced distortion and suggests that the question *what* is being shown in terms of selective filtering is more central than that of *how* it is shown with any specific distortion idiom [Furnas 06]. For example, the fisheye metaphor is not limited to a geometric lens used after spatial layout; it can be used directly on structured data, such as a hierarchical document where some sections are collapsed while others are left expanded.

Figure 14.10 illustrates four different approaches on the same node–link graph [Lambert et al. 10]: a fisheye lens in Figure 14.10(a), an ordinary magnifying lens in Figure 14.10(b), a neighborhood highlighting idiom using only superimposed layers in Figure 14.10(c), and a combination of that layering with the Bring and Go interaction idiom in Figure 14.10(d). Discussing these examples in detail will shed some light on the costs and benefits of distortion versus occlusion versus other interaction.

The local fisheye distortion has a small circle region of very high magnification at the center of the lens surrounded by a larger intermediate region that continuously varies from medium magnification to very high compression, returning to low compression in the outer periphery. Although fisheye lenses were developed with the goal of reducing the viewer's disorientation, unfortunately they can be quite disorienting. The continuous magnification change introduces some amount of cognitive load to untangle the underlying shape from the imposed distortion. Distortion is less problematic with familiar shapes, like geographic maps of known places, be-

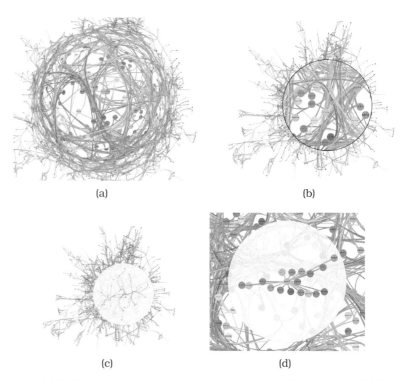

(a)   (b)

(c)   (d)

Figure 14.10. Four approaches to graph exploration. (a) Fisheye lens. (b) Magnifying lens. (c) Neighborhood highlighting with layering. (d) Neighborhood highlighting with both layering and Bring and Go interaction. From [Lambert et al. 10, Figures 2a, 2b, 3b, and 4b].

cause people can interpret the distortion as a change to a known baseline. With unfamiliar structures, it can be difficult to reconstruct the basic shape by mentally removing the distortion effects. While these idioms are designed to be used in an interactive setting, where the user quickly moves the lens around and compares the undistorted to the distorted states, there is still some cognitive load.

In contrast, the superimposed local magnifying lens has just two discrete levels: a highly magnified circle of medium size, and the low-compression periphery of medium size. There is a discontinuous jump between these two levels, where the lens occludes the immediately surrounding region. In this particular example, the fisheye lens may be more difficult to use than the magnifying lens; it is not clear that the benefit of avoiding occlusion is worth the cost of interpreting the continuous magnification change.

The last two approaches show a specific region of interest, in this case a local topological neighborhood of nodes reachable within one or two hops from a chosen target node. The neighborhood highlighting lens does not distort spatial position at all; it uses layering by reducing the opacity of items not in that neighborhood, automatically calculating a lens diameter to accommodate the entire neighborhood. While this approach would not help for tasks where magnification is critical, such as reading node labels, it does a good job of supporting path tracing.

A fisheye lens can be interpreted as a temporary warping that affects the location of all objects within the active region. The **Bring and Go** interaction idiom for network data [Moscovich et al. 09] is also temporary, but selectively changes the location of only specific objects of interest, by bringing the one-hop neighbors close to the target node. The layout is designed to simplify the configuration as much as possible while still preserving direction and relative distance information, in hopes of minimizing potential disorientation. This interaction idiom exploits topological structure information to reduce the cognitive load cost of tracking moving objects: only the one-hop neighbors move during animated transitions, in contrast to fisheye lenses that affect the positions of all items within their span.

14.7 Further Reading

The Big Picture Two extensive surveys discuss a broad set of idioms that use the choices of changing the viewpoint through navigation, partitioning into multiple views, and embedding focus into context, including an assessment of the empirical evidence on the strengths and weaknesses of these three approaches and guidelines for design [Cockburn et al. 08, Lam and Munzner 10].

Early Work Early proposals for focus+context interfaces were the Bifocal Display [Spence and Apperley 82] and polyfocal cartography [Kadmon and Shlomi 78]. An early taxonomy of distortion-based interfaces introduced the unifying vocabulary of magnification and transformation functions [Leung and Apperley 94].

Fisheye Views The fundamental idea of generalized fisheye views [Furnas 82, Furnas 86] was followed up 20 years later with a paper questioning the overwhelming emphasis on geometric distortion in the work of many others in the intervening decades [Furnas 06].

3D Perspective Influential 3D focus+context interfaces from Xerox PARC included the Perspective Wall [Mackinlay et al. 91] and Cone Trees [Robertson et al. 91].

Frameworks Two general frameworks for focus+context magnification and minimization are elastic presentation spaces [Carpendale et al. 95, Carpendale et al. 96] and nonlinear magnification fields [Keahey and Robertson 97].

Hyperbolic Geometry Hyperbolic 2D trees were proposed at Xerox PARC [Lamping et al. 95] and 3D hyperbolic networks were investigated at Stanford [Munzner 98].

Stretch and Squish Navigation The TreeJuxtaposer system proposed the guaranteed visibility idiom and presented algorithms for stretch and squish navigation of large trees [Munzner et al. 03], followed by the PRISAD framework that provided further scalability and handled several data types [Slack et al. 06].

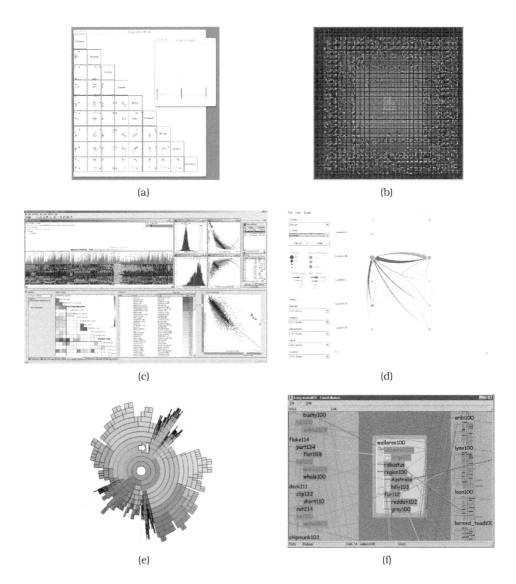

(a)

(b)

(c)

(d)

(e)

(f)

Figure 15.1. Six case studies of full vis systems. (a) Scagnostics, from [Wilkinson et al. 05, Figure 5]. (b) VisDB, from [Keim and Kriegel 94, Figure 6]. (c) Hierarchical Clustering Explorer, from [Seo and Shneiderman 05, Figure 1]. (d) PivotGraph, from [Wattenberg 06, Figure 5]. (e) InterRing, from [Yang et al. 02, Figure 4]. (f) Constellation, from [Munzner 00, Figure 5.5].

Chapter 15

Analysis Case Studies

15.1 The Big Picture

Figure 15.1 shows the six vis systems analyzed in this chapter as full case studies. The Scagnostics system provides a scalable summary of large scatterplot matrices through a derived SPLOM based on classifying the geometric shapes formed by the point distributions in the original scatterplots [Wilkinson et al. 05, Wilkinson et al. 06]. The VisDB system for database vis treats an entire database as a very large table of data, visually encoding it with dense and space-filling layouts with items colored according to their relevance for a specific query [Keim and Kriegel 94]. The Hierarchical Clustering Explorer (HCE) system supports systematic exploration of a multidimensional tables, such as those representing microarray measurements of gene expression in the genomics domain, with an associated hierarchical clustering [Seo and Shneiderman 02, Seo and Shneiderman 05]. The PivotGraph system summarizes networks using the succinct data abstraction of a derived network created by rolling up groups of nodes and links into aggregate nodes based on two categorical attributes [Wattenberg 06]. The InterRing system for tree exploration uses a space-filling, radial layout with interaction built around a multifocus focus+context distortion [Yang et al. 02]. The Constellation system supports browsing a complex multilevel linguistic network with a layout that encodes query relevance with spatial position and dynamic layering to avoid the perceptual impact of edge crossings [Munzner 00, Munzner et al. 99].

15.2 Why Analyze Case Studies?

The ability to concisely describe existing systems gives you a firm foundation for considering the full array of possibilities when you generate new systems. These case studies illustrate how to use the analysis framework presented in the book to decompose a vis approach, however complex, into pieces that you can systematically think about and compare with other approaches. These examples continue the analysis gradually introduced in the previous chapters. Now that all design choices have been introduced, each example has a complete analysis.

At the abstraction level, these analyses include the types and semantics of the data abstraction including any derived data and the targeted task abstraction. At the idiom level, the choices are decomposed into the design choices of how to encode data, facet data between multiple views, and reduce the data shown within a view. The analyses also include a discussion of scalability and continue with the practice of assuming available screen space of one million pixels in a standard format of 1000 by 1000 pixels.

A few of these systems have simple data abstractions and can be unambiguously classified as handling a particular simple dataset type: tables, or networks, or spatial data. Most of them have more complex data abstractions, which is the common case in real-world problems. Many of these systems carry out significant transformations of the original data to create derived data and handle combinations of multiple basic types. Often the system is designed to support exploration of interesting structure at multiple levels.

The following analyses are descriptive examinations of the final design of each system, not prescriptive statements that the particular choices made by these designers are the only good solution that fits the requirements. As you read through this chapter, it is a useful exercise to generate a set of alternatives for each choice made by these designers and to consider the pros and cons of each.

15.3   Graph-Theoretic Scagnostics

▶ Scatterplots are discussed in Section 7.4.

▶ SPLOMs are an example of the design choice of matrix alignments, discussed in Section 7.5.2, and small multiples, discussed in Section 12.3.2.

Graph-theoretic scagnostics is a scalable idiom for the exploration of scatterplot matrices, or SPLOMs [Wilkinson et al. 05, Wilkinson et al. 06]. A scagnostics SPLOM is a next step beyond a standard SPLOM, just as a SPLOM is a step beyond a single scatterplot. A single scatterplot supports direct comparison between two attributes by plotting their values along two spatial axes. A **scatterplot matrix** is the systematic way to compare all possible pairs of attributes, with the attributes ordered along both the rows and the columns and one scatterplot at each cell of the matrix. Figure 15.2 shows a SPLOM for a dataset of abalone measurements that has nine attributes.

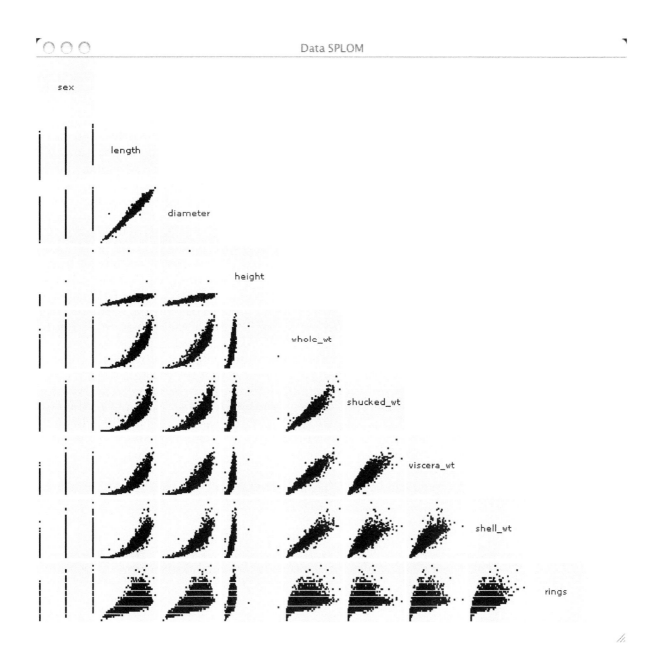

Figure 15.2. Scatterplot matrices (SPLOM) showing abalone data. From [Wilkinson et al. 05, Figure 1].

The scalability challenge of a SPLOM is that the size of the matrix grows quadratically. Each individual plot requires enough screen space to distinguish the points within it, so this idiom does not scale well past a few dozen attributes.

The idea of **scagnostics**, short for scatterplot computer-guided diagnostics, is to identify a small number of measurements that nicely categorize the shape of the point distributions within each scatterplot. The nine measures are *outlying* for outlier detection; *skewed*, *clumpy*, *sparse*, and *striated* for point distribution and density; *convex*, *skinny*, and *stringy* for shape, and *monotonic* for the association. Figure 15.3 shows examples of real-world datasets rated low, medium, and high with respect to each of these measures.

These measurements are then shown in a new scagnostics SPLOM that is a scatterplot of scatterplots. That is, each point in the scagnostics SPLOM represents an entire scatterplot in the original SPLOM, which is shown when the point is selected. Figure 15.4 shows the scagnostics matrix for the abalone dataset. As with standard SPLOMs, there is linked highlighting between views, and selecting a point also triggers a popup detail view showing the full scatterplot.

The idea is that the distribution of points in the scagnostics SPLOM should provide a fast overview of the most important characteristics of the original SPLOM, because the measures have been carefully chosen to reflect scatterplot shape. Looking at the outliers in this scagnostics SPLOM guides the user to the unusually shaped, and thus potentially interesting, scatterplots in the original SPLOM.

System	Scagnostics
What: Data	Table.
What: Derived	Nine quantitative attributes per scatterplot (pairwise combination of original attributes).
Why: Tasks	Identify, compare, and summarize; distributions and correlation.
How: Encode	Scatterplot, scatterplot matrix.
How: Manipulate	Select.
How: Facet	Juxtaposed small-multiple views coordinated with linked highlighting, popup detail view.
Scale	Original attributes: dozens.

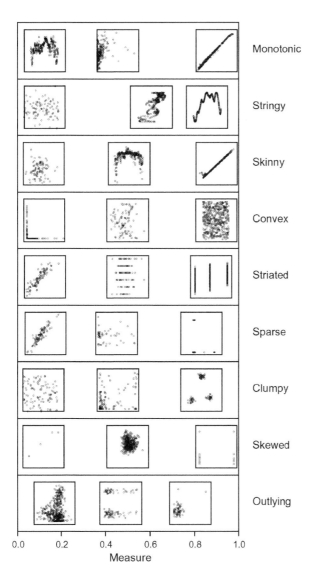

Figure 15.3. The nine scagnostics measures that describe scatterplot shape, with examples of real-world datasets rated low, medium, and high for each of the nine measures. From [Wilkinson and Wills 08, Figure 6].

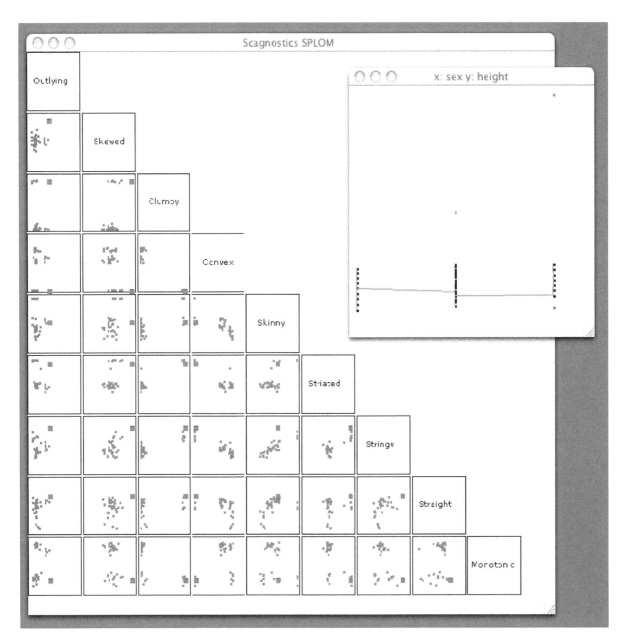

Figure 15.4. Scagnostics SPLOM for the abalone dataset, where each point represents an entire scatterplot in the original matrix. The selected point is highlighed in red in each view, and the scatterplot corresponding to it is shown in a popup detail view. From [Wilkinson et al. 05, Figure 5].

15.4 VisDB

The VisDB system for database vis [Keim and Kriegel 94] treats an entire database as a very large table of data. The system shows that table with respect to a specific query that matches some subset of the items in it. VisDB computes a set of derived attributes that measure the relevance of the query with respect to the original attributes and items, as shown in Figure 15.5(a). Each item is given a relevance score for the query for each original attribute. An overall relevance score is computed that combines these individual scores, adding an additional derived attribute column to the original table.

VisDB supports two different layout idioms that are dense, space-filling, and use square color-coded area marks. Figure 15.5 shows schematic views of the layouts, and Figure 15.6 shows the corresponding screenshots.

The spatial ordering of regions within VisDB views is not a standard aligned rectilinear or radial layout; it follows a spiral pattern emanating from the center, as shown in Figure 15.7(a). The sequential colormap, shown in Figure 15.7(b), uses multiple hues ordered with monotonically increasing luminance to support both categorical and ordered perception of the encoded data. At the bottom is dark red, the mid-range has purple and blue, it continues with cyan and then even brighter green, and there is a very bright yellow at the high end to emphasize the top of the range.

One of the two layouts partitions the dataset by attribute into small multiple views shown side by side, with one view for each attribute. Figure 15.5(a) illustrates the idiom schematically, and Figure 15.6(a) shows an example with a dataset of 1000 items. The items are placed in the same order across all views but colored according to relevance score for that view's attribute. They are ordered by the derived overall relevance attribute, which is also the coloring attribute in the upper left view; spatial position and color provide redundant information in this view. In the other views with coloring by each other attribute, there are different visual patterns of color. The user can inspect the patterns within the individual views to carry out the abstract task of characterizing distributions and finding groups of similar values within individual attributes and per-attribute outlier detection. Comparing between the patterns in different views corresponds to the abstract task of looking for correlations between attributes.

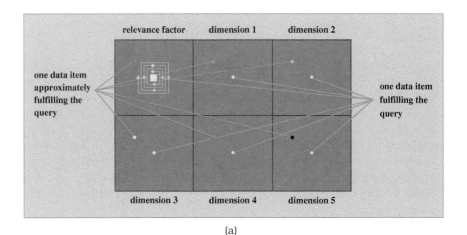

(a)

(b)

Figure 15.5. VisDB layouts schematically, for a dataset with five attributes. (a) Each attribute is shown in a separate small-multiple view. (b) In an alternate VisDB layout, each item is shown with a glyph with per-attribute sections in a single combined view. From [Keim and Kriegel 94, Figures 2 and 4].

The second layout uses a single view where the space has been partitioned into one region for each item, containing a glyph that shows all of the attributes for that item. Figure 15.5(b) shows the schematic diagram, and Figure 15.6(b) shows a screenshot. This item-based partition supports the abstract task of comparison across items and finding groups of similar items, rather than comparison across attributes.

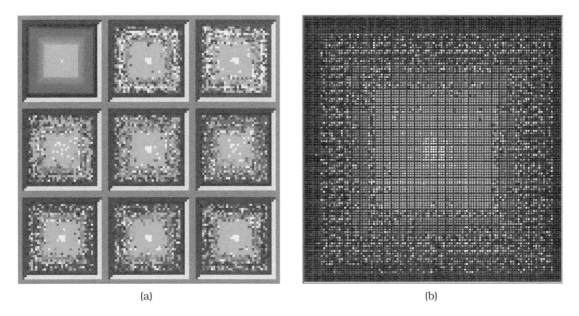

(a)   (b)

Figure 15.6. VisDB screenshots with a dataset of eight attributes and 1000 items. (a) Attribute-based grouping with one small-multiple view for each attribute. (b) Item-based grouping has a single combined view with multiattribute glyph. From [Keim and Kriegel 94, Figure 6].

Both of these layouts use filtering for data reduction. When the number of items is greater than the available room for the view, items are filtered according to the relevance values. The total table size handled by the system thus can be up to several million, even though only one million items can be shown at once in a single screen of one million pixels.

The small-multiples layout is effective for up to 10–12 attributes, where each per-attribute view shows around 100,000 items, and one million items are shown across all the views. In contrast, the layout idiom using a single large glyph-based view only can handle up to around 100,000 visible items, an order of magnitude fewer than the other idiom. The elements within the glyph need to be boxes larger than a single pixel in order to be salient, and glyphs need borders around them in order to be distinguished from neighboring ones.

VisDB is an early example of a very information-dense design that tests the upper limits of useful information density. It is also a very clear example of how different strategies for partitioning space can be used to support different tasks.

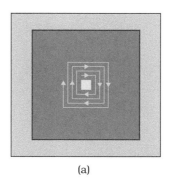

(a)   (b)

Figure 15.7. VisDB layout orientation and colors. (a) Layouts are are ordered internally in a spiral emanating from the center. (b) The VisDB sequential colormap uses multiple hues with monotonically increasing luminance. From [Keim and Kriegel 94, Figures 2 and 3].

System	VisDB
What: Data	Table (database) with k attributes; query returning table subset (database query).
What: Derived	$k + 1$ quantitative attributes per original item: query relevance for the k original attributes plus overall relevance.
Why: Tasks	Characterize distribution within attribute, find groups of similar values within attribute, find outliers within attribute, find correlation between attributes, find similar items.
How: Encode	Dense, space-filling; area marks in spiral layout; colormap: categorical hues and ordered luminance.
How: Facet	Layout 1: partition by attribute into per-attribute views, small multiples. Layout 2: partition by items into per-item glyphs.
How: Reduce	Filtering
Scale	Attributes: one dozen. Total items: several million. Visible items (using multiple views, in total): one million. Visible items (using glyphs): 100,000

15.5   Hierarchical Clustering Explorer

The Hierarchical Clustering Explorer (HCE) system supports systematic exploration of a multidimensional table with an associated hierarchical clustering [Seo and Shneiderman 02, Seo and Shneiderman 05]. It was originally designed for the genomics domain where the table reprents microarray measurements of gene expression. The original data is a multidimensional table with two key attributes, genes and experimental conditions, and a single quantitative value attribute, measurements of the activity of each gene under each experimental condition. The derived data is a cluster hierarchy of the items based on a similarity measure bewteen items.[1]

HCE is a good example of achieving scalability through carefully designed combination of visual encoding and interaction idioms in order to support datasets much larger than could be handled by a single static view. The scalability target of HCE is between 100 and 20,000 gene attributes and between 2 and 80 experimental condition attributes. This target is reached with the reduction design choices of interactively controlled aggregation, filtering, and navigation, and with the view coordination design choices of overview–detail, small multiple, and multiform side-by-side views with linked highlighting.

Figure 15.8 shows HCE on a genomics dataset. Two cluster heatmap views are coordinated with the overview–detail design choice, and scatterplot and histogram views provide different encodings.

▶ For more on cluster heatmaps, see Section 7.5.2.

The overview cluster heatmap at the top uses an aggregated representation where an entire dataset of 3614 genes is shown with fewer than 1500 pixels by replacing individual leaves with the average values of adjacent leaves. The density level of the overview can be interactively changed by the user, for a tradeoff between an aggregate view where some detail is lost but the entire display is visible at once, and a more zoomed-in view where only some of the columns are visible simultaneously and navigation by horizontal panning is required to see the rest. The horizontal line through the dendrogram labeled *Minimum Similarity* is an interactive filtering control. Dragging it down vertically dynamically filters out the columns in the heatmap that correspond to the parts of the den-

---

[1]The clustering is computed outside the tool itself and is expected as input to the system; for the purposes of this decompositional analysis, I consider it derived rather than original data.

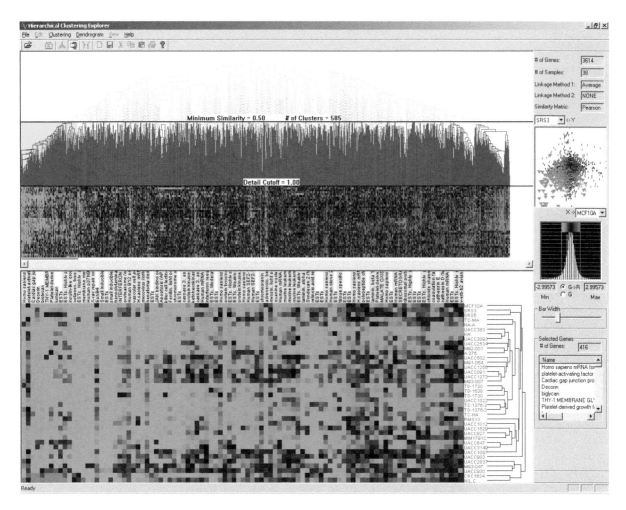

Figure 15.8. Hierachical Clustering Explorer uses interactive aggregation and filtering for the scalable display of a multidimensional table showing gene activity in different conditions using multiple overview+detail cluster heatmap views. From [Seo and Shneiderman 02, Figure 2].

drogram above the bar and partitions the heatmap into pieces that correspond to the number of clusters just below the bar.

The detail view at the bottom shows a heatmap of the cluster selected in the top overview. It also shows the second dendrogram for hierarchical clustering of the rows on the side; this dendrogram is not shown above in order to to maximize the number of columns that can fit within the overview. The background of the

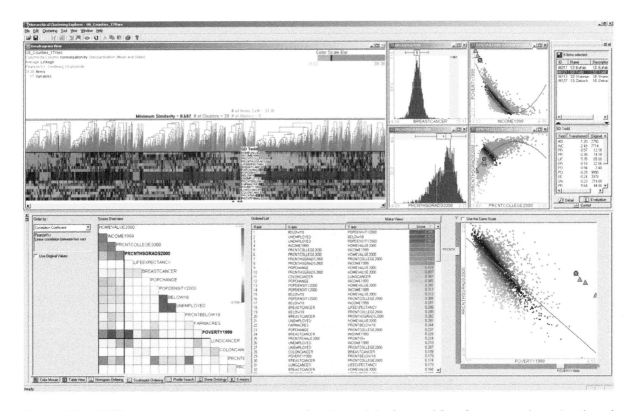

Figure 15.9. HCE on a demographics dataset showing the rank-by-feature idiom for systematic exploration of pairwise combinations of attributes using a matrix overview and scatterplot. From [Seo and Shneiderman 05, Figure 1].

selected cluster is highlighted in yellow in the overview, and the correspondence between the views is emphasized by coloring the column labels along the top of the detail view yellow as well, for linked highlighting.

HCE has also been used for exploring datasets from other domains, including census demographic information, as shown in Figure 15.9. This screenshot focuses on the **rank-by-feature** idiom that combines the design choice of changing the order and the reduction design choice of aggregation to guide exploration and achieve scalability. In this idiom, the data abstraction is augmented with many new derived attributes. Orderings for each original attribute and pairwise combination of attributes are computed for several choices of ordering criteria, and the user can select which of them to use.*

> ★ Mapping the name of this idiom into the vocabulary used in this book, *rank* is used as a synonym for *order*, and *feature* means either *attribute* or *attribute pair*.

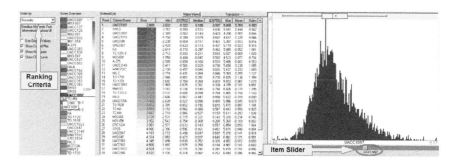

Figure 15.10. Detail of HCE rank-by-feature views for ranking individual attributes using a list overview and histogram/boxplot. From [Seo and Shneiderman 05, Figure 2].

The results appear in three views, as shown at the bottom of Figure 15.9 and in the detail screenshot in Figure 15.10. The lower left of Figure 15.9 shows an aggregate compact view with the same matrix alignment as a SPLOM, where each cell of the matrix has only a single area mark colored by the chosen criterion with a diverging blue–white–brown colormap. On the left of Figure 15.10 is a compact aggregate overview display with list alignment that matches the ordering used in the cluster heatmap, with the same area mark coloring. In the middle of Figure 15.10 is an intermediate level of detail view for all attributes that shows them in a list alignment that is both ordered and colored by the criterion. This list is less compact, showing a middle level of detail for each attribute, and thus it supports navigation through scrolling. On the right is a detail view to show the full details for the selected attribute with a histogram as shown in Figure 15.10, or the selected attribute pair with a scatterplot as shown in Figure 15.9. The user can select by clicking on a cell in the list or matrix views or by flipping through alternatives quickly using the single or double sliders in the respective detail views.*

★ Although the slider in the Figure 15.10 screenshot is labeled *Item Slider*, in my vocabulary it is being used to choose which *attribute* to display in the detail view.

System	Hierarchical Clustering Explorer (HCE)
What: Data	Multidimensional table: two categorical key attributes (genes, conditions); one quantitative value attribute (gene activity level in condition).

What: Derived	Hierarchical clustering of table rows and columns (for cluster heatmap); quantitative derived attributes for each attribute and pairwise attribute combination; quantitative derived attribute for each ranking criterion and original attribute combination.
Why: Tasks	Find correlation between attributes; find clusters, gaps, outliers, trends within items.
How: Encode	Cluster heatmap, scatterplots, histograms, boxplots. Rank-by-feature overviews: continuous diverging colormaps on area marks in reorderable 2D matrix or 1D list alignment.
How: Reduce	Dynamic filtering; dynamic aggregation.
How: Manipulate	Navigate with pan/scroll.
How: Facet	Multiform with linked highlighting and shared spatial position; overview–detail with selection in overview populating detail view.
Scale	Genes (key attribute): 20,000. Conditions (key attribute): 80. Gene activity in condition (quantitative value attribute): 20,000 × 80 = 1,600,000.

15.6   PivotGraph

Connection, containment, and matrix views of networks are different visual encodings of the same data abstraction; they both depict the link structure of a network. In contrast, the PivotGraph idiom [Wattenberg 06] visually encodes a different data abstraction: a new network derived from the original one by aggregating groups of nodes and links into a **roll-up** according to categorical attribute values on the nodes. The user can also select attributes of interest that filter the derived network. Roll-ups can be made for up to two attributes at once; for two dimensions nodes are laid out on a grid, and for one dimension they are laid out on a line. Node positions in the grid are computed to minimize link-crossing clutter, and the links between them are drawn as curves. The user interactively explores the graph through roll-up and selection to see visual encodings that directly summarize the high-level relationships between the attribute-based groups and can drill down to see more details for any node or link on demand. When the user chooses a different roll-up, an animated transition smoothly interpolates between the two layouts.

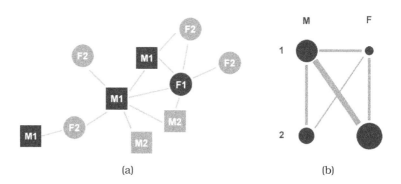

              (a)   (b)

Figure 15.11. The PivotGraph idiom. (a) Node–link view of small network with two attributes on nodes: gender (*M/F*) is encoded by node shape, and company division (*1/2*) is encoded by grayscale value. (b) The schematic PivotGraph roll-up of the same simple network where size of nodes and links of the derived graph shows the number of items in these aggregated groups. From [Wattenberg 06, Figure 4].

    Figure 15.11 shows an example of a simple node–link drawing in Figure 15.11(a) side by side with a PivotGraph roll-up in Figure 15.11(b). The network has two categorical attributes: gender, shown with *M* for male and *F* for female, and company division, shown with *1* or *2*. In the node–link view, node shape represents gender with squares for *M* and circles for *F*, and grayscale value represents company division with black for *1* and gray for *2*. The full original network is shown, emphasizing its topological structure. In the PivotGraph view, the derived network has four nodes that represent the four possible groups of the combination of these two attributes: males in division 1 in the upper left, females in division 1 in the upper right, males in division 2 on the lower left, and females in division 2 on the lower right. The size of each of these aggregate groups is encoded with node size. Similarly, a single link in this derived graph represents the entire group of edges in the original graph that linked items in these groups, and the size of that group is encoded with line width. In this example, all possible gender/division pairs are connected except for men and women in division 2.

    Figure 15.12 shows a more complex example rolled up by gender and office locations; the dataset is an anonymized version of a real corporate social network. Most of the cross-gender communication occurs in location B, and there are no women at location A. An additional quantitative attribute is encoded with a diverging

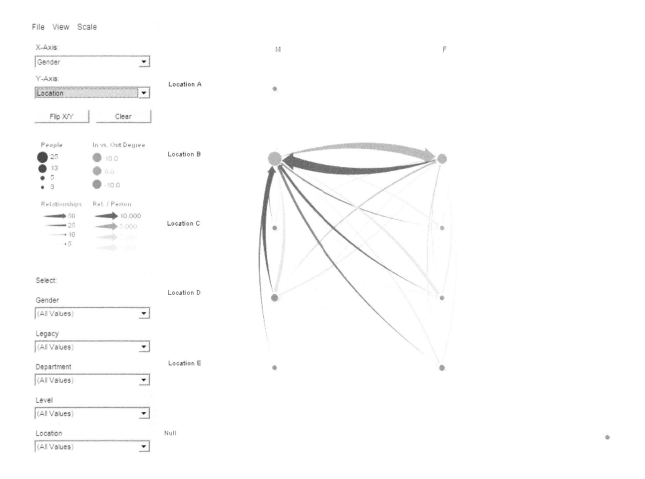

Figure 15.12. PivotGraph on graph rolled up by gender and location, showing most cross-gender communication occurs in location B. From [Wattenberg 06, Figure 5].

red–green colormap, the number of inward links versus outward links at each node.

The PivotGraph idiom is highly scalable because it summarizes an arbitrarily large number of nodes and links in the original network, easily handling from thousands to millions. The visual complexity of the derived network layout depends only on the number of attribute levels for the two attributes chosen for roll-up.

PivotGraph complements the standard approaches to network layout, node–link and matrix views, and thus could serve as one of several linked multiform views in addition to being used on its

▶ Section 9.4 compares the strengths and weaknesses of the standard approaches to network layout.

own as a single view. PivotGraph is very well suited for the task of comparisons across attributes at the aggregate level, a task that is difficult with previous approaches. Conversely, it is poorly suited for understanding topological features of networks, a task that is easy with node–link views when the network is not too large.

Idiom	PivotGraph
What: Data	Network.
What: Derived	Derived network of aggregate nodes and links by roll-up into two chosen attributes.
Why: Tasks	Cross-attribute comparison of node groups.
How: Encode	Nodes linked with connection marks, size.
How: Manipulate	Change: animated transitions.
How: Reduce	Aggregation, filtering.
Scale	Nodes/links in original network: unlimited. Roll-up attributes: 2. Levels per roll-up attribute: several, up to one dozen.

15.7 InterRing

The InterRing system [Yang et al. 02] for tree exploration uses a space-filling, radial layout for visually encoding the hierarchy. The interaction is built around a multifocus focus+context distortion approach to change the amount of room allocated to different parts of the hierarchy. Figure 15.13(a) shows the undisorted base layout. Figure 15.13(b) shows that the result of enlarging the blue subtree is shrinking the room allocated to its siblings. Figure 15.13(c) shows a subsequent use of interactive distortion, where the tan region is also enlarged for emphasis.

The proposed structure-based coloring redundantly emphasizes the hierarchical information encoded spatially. Structure-based coloring could be eliminated if InterRing is used as the only view, in order to show a different attribute with color coding. Structure-based coloring is particularly useful when shared color coding is used to coordinate between multiple views, so that items are colored by the tree hierarchy in other linked views with different spatial layouts.

The scalability of InterRing is moderate; it handles hundreds of nodes easily, where the leaf labels are large enough to read. The space-filling geometric configuration yields about three times

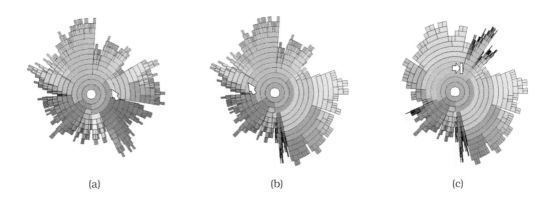

(a)   (b)   (c)

Figure 15.13. The InterRing hierarchy vis idiom uses a space-filling radial visual encoding and distortion-based focus+context interaction. (a) The hierarchy before distortion. (b) The blue selected subtree is enlarged. (c) A second tan region is enlarged. From [Yang et al. 02, Figure 4].

as many legible labels as with a classical node–link layout using labels of the same size. In the extreme case, where each leaf is encoded with a single pixel and the idiom uses the entire screen, InterRing could scale to several thousand nodes. The number of edges in a tree is the same as the number of nodes, so there is no need to separately analyze that aspect. Another useful factor to consider with trees is the maximum **tree depth** supported by the encoding; that is, the number of levels between the root and the farthest away leaves. InterRing can handle up to several dozen levels, whereas hundreds would be overwhelming.

In addition to being a viable single-view approach when tree exploration is the only task, InterRing is designed to work well with other views where a hierarchy view should support selection, navigation, and roll-up/drill-down operations. It also supports directly editing the hierarchy itself. In contrast, many tree browsing systems do not support modification of the hierarchy.

System	InterRing
What: Data	Tree.
Why: Tasks	Selection, rollup/drilldown, hierarchy editing.
How: Encode	Radial, space-filling layout. Color by tree structure.
How: Facet	Linked coloring and highlighting.
How: Reduce	Embed: distort; multiple foci.
Scale	Nodes: hundreds if labeled, thousands if dense. Levels in tree: dozens.

15.8 Constellation

The Constellation system [Munzner 00, Munzner et al. 99] supports browsing a complex multilevel linguistic network. Several of the visual encoding decisions diverge from the traditional node–link network layout. The perceptual impact of edge crossings is minimized by using dynamic highlighting of a foreground layer rather than by an algorithm to minimize crossings, allowing the use of spatial position to encode two ordered attributes. Nodes in the graph that have links to multiple subgraphs are duplicated within each to maximize readability at the subgraph level. The traditional approach of drawing a node in only one location would increase the cognitive load of understanding subgraph structure by requiring too much tracing back and forth along links; the duplication is signalled by dynamic highlighting on hover.

Constellation is an example of a highly specialized vis tool designed for a very small audience to use for a limited period of time. It was intended to support computational linguistics researchers who were developing algorithms for traversing a very large network created from an online dictionary. The tool was intended to "work itself out of a job" and be abandoned after their algorithms were fully tuned.

In this multilevel network, a low-level node represents a *word sense*: the narrow meaning of a word used in a particular way, where most words have multiple senses. For example, *bank* has the two distinct meanings of a financial institution and the side of a river. The metanodes at the next level of the graph each contain a subgraph of around 10–12 nodes representing a dictionary definition, with links between the *headword* node being defined, and all of the *leafword* nodes used in the defining sentence. The large-scale structure of the network arises from combining these subgraphs together, since the same word may be used in many different definitions: as a headword in one definition, and as leafwords in several others.

There is a categorical attribute for the relationship encoded by each link, such as *is-a* or *part-of*. While there are in total a few dozen possible values for this type, most are rarely used; we binned this attribute into eight bins, preserving the seven most frequently used types and combining all others into an eighth *other* category.

The linguistics researchers did not need to inspect the full network; rather, they wanted to see the results of their query algorithms that traversed the network, returning an ordered set of the

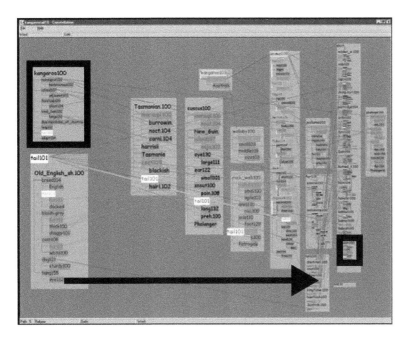

Figure 15.14. The Constellation high-level layout bases horizontal spatial position on the plausibility attribute, where more room is allocated to definitions on highly plausible and usually short paths on the left, and less room to those on less plausible and typically longer paths on the right. From [Munzner 00, Figure 5.4].

top 10 or 50 highest-ranking paths between two words, a source and a sink. The paths are ranked with the quantitative attribute of *plausibility*, as computed by their traversal algorithms. Each path consists of an ordered list of words, and attached to each of these words is the set of all the definitions that were used during the computation to place it within the path.

The primary task of the linguists was to hand-check the results to see how well the computed plausibility matched up to their human intuition: were all high-ranking paths believable, and conversely were all believable paths highly ranked? The secondary task was to check the data quality, to ensure that extremely common *stop words* had been appropriately excluded from the computation. The task abstraction is the *consume-discover* case, where the search requirements include both browsing the high-ranking paths and locating the low-belivability paths, and the querying requirements include both identification and comparison. All of these tasks require extensive reading of node labels.

The high-level Constellation spatial layout is based on a curvilinear grid, where each path flows along a vertical column with the words ordered from the source on top to the sink on the bottom, and the horizontal order of the paths is determined by the plausibility attribute with highly plausible ones on the left. The layout is designed so that definitions on the plausible left side have more room than those on the implausible right side, as shown in Figure 15.14. Paths have different lengths, and less plausible ones tend to be longer and have more definitions associated with each word. Paths on the implausible right are given less horizontal space. This variability leads to many empty cells in the base grid shown in Figure 15.15(a); full cells are expanded both horizontally as in Figure 15.15(b) and vertically as in Figure 15.15(c) to fill the available space and achieve high information density.

The choice to use spatial position to encode information precludes algorithmic approaches to minimizing edge crossings. Instead, Constellation uses the design choice of superimposed dynamic layers to minimize the perceptual impact of crossings. Figure 15.16(a) shows an example of the background version of a definition graph, while Figure 15.16(b) shows the foreground version. Four different kinds of structures can be highlighted to create different *constellations*, motivating the system's name: paths, definition graphs, all of the direct connections to a single word, and all links of a particular type. Figure 15.17 shows a constellation with all links of type *Part* highlighted. It also illustrates the "sideways T" layout characteristic of a query where the source and sink words are highly related, so all of the high-ranking paths are very short; in this case, *aspirin* and *headache*.

The mid-level spatial layout handles a path *segment*: one word in the path along with all of the definitions associated with it, using containment marks to show the hierarchical relationships. Figure 15.18(a) shows an example where the box allocated to the entire segment is tan, and the path word has its own definition that is also drawn in the tan section. Figure 15.18(b) shows an example where the path word itself is not defined, but each of the other definitions assigned to it is enclosed in a green box nested within the tan segment.

The low-level spatial layout of a definition is illustrated in Figure 15.19(a). A ladder-like rectilinear structure encodes with both spatial position and line marks. Each leafword is enclosed in its own blue label box. Vertical lines show the hierarchical microstructure inside the definition and are colored white, and horizontal edges are color coded to show the link type.

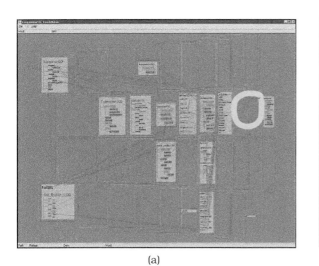

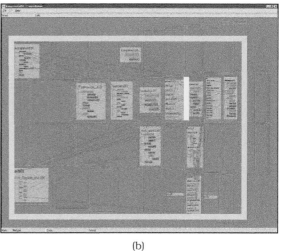

(a)   (b)

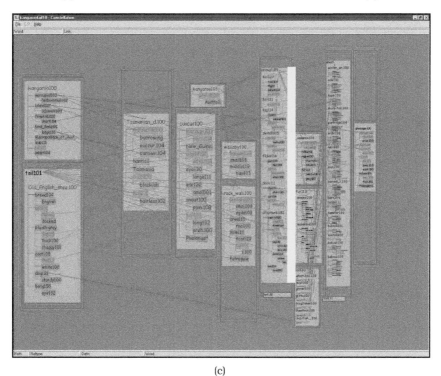

(c)

Figure 15.15. Resizing grid cells to increase information density. (a) Base curvilinear grid. (b) After eliminating the empty columns. (c) After eliminating empty cell rows in each column. From [Munzner 00, Figure 5.13].

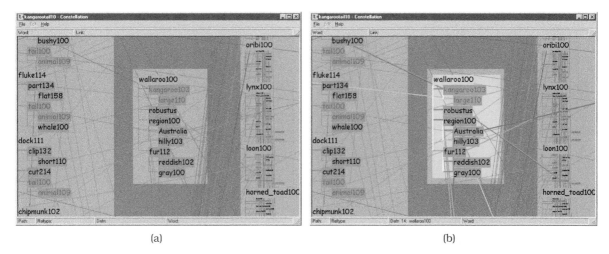

(a)   (b)

Figure 15.16. Constellation uses the design choice of dynamic superimposed layers. (a) Edges in the background layer are not obtrusive. (b) The newly selected foreground layer is distinguished from the background with changes of the size, luminance, and saturation channels. From [Munzner 00, Figure 5.5].

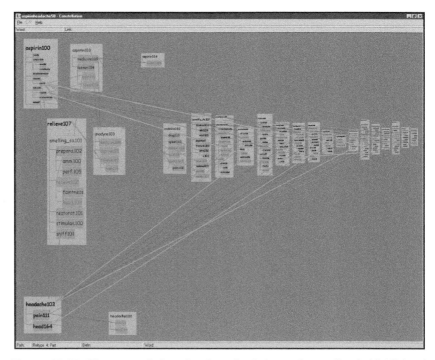

Figure 15.17. The constellation showing all relations of type *Part* is highlighted. From [Munzner 00, Figure 5.16a].

(a)   (b)

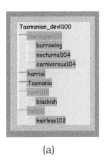

(a)   (b)

Figure 15.18. Mid-level Constellation path segment layout, using containment to show hierarchical relationship between path word in tan and its associated definitions in green. (a) One of the definitions is for the path word itself. (b) Path word that is not itself defined, but only appears within other definitions. From [Munzner 00, Figure 5.9].

Figure 15.19. Low-level Constellation definition layout, using rectilinear links and spatial position. (a) The base layout, with horizontal lines color-coded for link type. (b) Long-distance links are drawn between the master version of the word and all of its duplicated proxies. From [Munzner 00, Figure 5.10].

Each definition is drawn with all of its associated words in order to make it easy to read, so any word that appears in multiple definitions is duplicated. The master version of the word is the one on the most plausible path, and is drawn in black. All subsequent instances are proxies, which are drawn in gray and are connected to the master by a long slanted line mark, as shown in Figure 15.19(b).

Constellation is optimized for three different viewing levels: a global view for interpath relationships, a local view for reading individual definitions, and an intermediate view for associations within path segments. It uses a subtle form of semantic zooming to achieve this effect, where the amount of space devoted to different classes of words changes dynamically depending on the zoom level. Figure 15.20 shows three steps of a zoom animated transition sequence. In the first frame, the words at the top are given much more space than the rest; in the last frame, the allocation of space is nearly equal for all words.

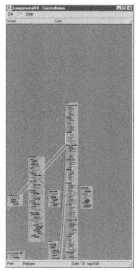  

Figure 15.20. Constellation uses a subtle version of the semantic zooming design choice, where the space allocated for the first word versus the rest of the definition changes according to the zoom level. From [Munzner 00, Figure 5.19].

System	Constellation
What: Data	Three-level network of paths, subgraphs (definitions), and nodes (word senses).
Why: Tasks	Discover/verify: browse and locate types of paths, identify and compare.
How: Encode	Containment and connection link marks, horizontal spatial position for plausibility attribute, vertical spatial position for order within path, color links by type.
How: Manipulate	Navigate: semantic zooming. Change: Animated transitions.
How: Reduce	Superimpose dynamic layers.
Scale	Paths: 10–50. Subgraphs: 1–30 per path. Nodes: several thousand.

15.9   Further Reading

Graph-Theoretic Scagnostics Scagnostics builds on ideas originally proposed by statisticians John and Paul Tukey [Wilkinson et al. 05, Wilkinson and Wills 08].

VisDB The VisDB system was an early proposal of dense displays for multidimensional tables [Keim and Kriegel 94].

Hierarchical Clustering Explorer Different aspects of the Hierarchical Clustering Explorer system are described in a series of papers [Seo and Shneiderman 02, Seo and Shneiderman 05].

PivotGraph The PivotGraph system visually encodes a different derived data abstraction than most network vis idioms [Wattenberg 06].

InterRing The InterRing system supports hierarchy exploration through focus+context interaction with geometric distortion and multiple foci. [Yang et al. 02].

Constellation The Constellation system supports browsing a complex multilevel network with a specialized layout and dynamic layering [Munzner et al. 99, Munzner 00].

Figure Credits

Any figures not listed here are released under the Creative Commons Attribution 4.0 International license (CC BY 4.0), to be credited as Tamara Munzner, with illustrations by Eamonn Maguire, *Visualization Analysis and Design*, A K Peters Visualization Series, CRC Press, Boca Raton, FL, 2014.

Figure 1.1   Copyright © 2013 by IEEE.

Figure 1.2   Reproduced under Creative Commons Attribution Non-Commercial license (CC BY-NC 2.0).

Figure 1.4   Copyright © 2007 by IEEE.

Figure 1.5   Courtesy of Miriah Meyer.

Figure 1.6   Michael J. McGuffin and Jean-Marc Robert, *Information Visualization* (9:2) pp. 115-140, copyright © 2010 by SAGE Publications. Reprinted by Permission of SAGE.

Figure 2.5   Courtesy of Miriah Meyer.

Figure 2.9   Courtesy of Miriah Meyer.

Figure 3.4   Copyright © 2008 by IEEE.

Figure 3.8(a)   Courtesy of Catherine Plaisant.

Figure 3.8(b)   [Munzner et al. 03] © 2003 Association for Computing Machinery, Inc. Reprinted by permission.

Figure 3.10   Courtesy of David Auber.

Figure 3.12   Copyright © 1998 by IEEE.

Figure 4.3   Copyright © 2008 by IEEE.

Figure 4.6   Copyright © 2005 by IEEE.

Figure 4.8   Copyright © 2006 by IEEE.

Figure 4.10   Copyright © 2005 by IEEE.

Figure 4.12   [McLachlan et al. 08] © 2008 Association for Computing Machinery, Inc. Reprinted by permission.

Figure 4.14   Springer, *Graph Drawing*, Lecture Notes in Computer Science, 2912, 2004, pages 425-436, "An Energy Model for Visual Graph Clustering," Andreas Noack, Figure 1, copyright © 2004 Springer. With kind permission from Springer Science and Business Media.

Original caption: Pseudo-random graph with intra-cluster edge probability 0.16 and inter-cluster edge probability 0.02; left: LinLog model.

Figure 4.16   [Heer et al. 09] © 2010 Association for Computing Machinery, Inc. Reprinted by permission.

Figure 5.8   [Heer and Bostock 10] © 2010 Association for Computing Machinery, Inc. Reprinted by permission.

Figure 5.9   Courtesy of TeleGeography, www.telegeography.com.

Figure 5.14   Courtesy of Edward H. Adelson. © 1995 Edward H. Adelson.

Figure 5.15   Courtesy of Dale Purves, http://www.purveslab.net/seeforyourself.

Figure 6.3   Copyright © 1996 by IEEE.

Figure 6.4   Courtesy of Stephen Few. An example of poor design, from http://perceptualedge.com/files/GraphDesignIQ.html.

Figure 6.5   Copyright © 1996 by IEEE.

Figure 6.6   Copyright © 2007 by IEEE.

Figure 6.7   Copyright © 1999 by IEEE.

Figure 6.8   Copyright © 2010 by IEEE.

Figure 6.9   Copyright © 2007 by IEEE.

Figure 7.2   Copyright © 2008 by IEEE.

Figure 7.3   "A layered grammar of graphics," Hadley Wickham, *Journal of Computational and Graphical Statistics* 19:1 (2010), 3-28. Reprinted by permission of the American Statistical Association (http://www.amstat.org).

Figure 7.5   Courtesy of Robert P. Bosch, Jr.

Figure 7.6   Copyright © 2008 by IEEE.

Figure 7.7   Copyright © 2008 by IEEE.

Figure 7.10   Copyright © 2006 by IEEE.

Figure 7.11   From http://en.wikipedia.org/wiki/File:Heatmap.png. Created by Miguel Andrade using the program Cluster from Michael Eisen, which is available from http://rana.lbl.gov/EisenSoftware.htm, with data extracted from the StemBase database of gene expression data.

Figure 7.13   "Hyperdimensional Data Analysis Using Parallel Coordinates," Edward J. Wegman, *Journal American Statistical Association* 85:411 (1990), 664–675. Reprinted by permission of the American Statistical Association (http://www.amstat.org).

Figure 7.14   Copyright © 1999 by IEEE.

Figure 7.15(a,b)   "A layered grammar of graphics," Hadley Wickham, *Journal of Computational and Graphical Statistics* 19:1 (2010), 3-28. Reprinted by permission of the American Statistical Association (http://www.amstat.org).

Figure 7.17   "A layered grammar of graphics," Hadley Wickham, *Journal of Computational and Graphical Statistics* 19:1 (2010), 3-28. Reprinted by permission of the American Statistical Association (http://www.amstat.org).

Figure 7.18   Courtesy of Michael Bostock, made with D3 [Bostock et al. 11]. From http://bl.ocks.org/mbostock/3887235, http://bl.ocks.org/mbostock/3886208, and http://bl.ocks.org/mbostock/3886394.

Figure 7.19   Copyright © 2012 John Wiley & Sons, Ltd.

Figure 7.20   Courtesy of John Stasko.

Figure 8.2   Courtesy of Michael Bostock, made with D3 [Bostock et al. 11]. From http://bl.ocks.org/mbostock/4060606.

Figure 8.3   Courtesy of Joe Kniss.

Figure 8.4   Courtesy of Land Information New Zealand Data Service (CC BY 3.0 NZ). From https://data.linz.govt.nz/layer/768-nz-mainland-contours-topo-150k.

Figure 8.5   Copyright © 2004 by IEEE.

Figure 8.6   Copyright © 2004 by IEEE.

Figure 8.7   Copyright © 2005 by IEEE.

Figure 8.8   Reprinted from *Computers and Graphics*, Vol. 26, No. 2, Xavier Tricoche, Thomas Wischgoll, Gerik Scheuermann, and Hans Hagen, "Topology tracking for the visualization of time-dependent two-dimensional flows," Pages 249–257, Copyright 2002, with permission from Elsevier.

Figure 8.9   Copyright © 2013 by IEEE.

Figure 8.10   Copyright © 2005 by IEEE.

Figure 8.11   Courtesy of Gordon Kindlmann. From http://www.cs.utah.edu/~gk/papers/vis99/ppt/slide03.html.

Figure 8.12   Copyright © 2004 by IEEE.

Figure 8.13   Copyright © 2004 by IEEE.

Figure 9.2(a)   Springer, *Graph Drawing*, Lecture Notes in Computer Graphics 2528, 2002, pages 344–353, "Improving Walkers Algorithm to Run in Linear Time," Christoph Buchheim, Michael Junger, and Sebastien Leipert, Figure 2d, copyright © 2002 Springer. With kind permission from Springer Science and Business Media.

Original caption: Extending the Reingold-Tilford algorithm to trees of unbounded degree.

Figure 9.2(b)   Courtesy of Michael Bostock, made with D3 [Bostock et al. 11]. From http://mbostock.github.com/d3/ex/tree.html.

Figure 9.3   Courtesy of David Auber, made with Tulip [Auber et al. 12].

Figure 9.4   Courtesy of Michael Bostock, made with D3 [Bostock et al. 11]. From http://bl.ocks.org/mbostock/4062045 and http://bl.ocks.org/1062288.

Figure 9.5   From "A Gallery of Large Graphs," JDG_Homologycis-n4c6, b14 and b4. Courtesy of Yifan Hu; see http://yifanhu.net/GALLERY/GRAPHS/citation.html.

Figure 9.6   Reprinted by permission from Macmillan Publishers Ltd: *Nature Methods* [Gehlenborg and Wong 12], copyright 2012.

Figure   9.7   Courtesy of Michael McGuffin, from http://www.michaelmcguffin.com/courses/vis/patternsInAdjacencyMatrix.png.

Figure   9.8   Courtesy of David Auber, made with Tulip [Auber et al. 12].

Figure   9.9   Michael J. McGuffin and Jean-Marc Robert, *Information Visualization* (9:2) pp. 115–140, copyright © 2010 by SAGE Publications. Reprinted by Permission of SAGE.

Figure   9.10   Copyright © 2008 by IEEE.

Figure   10.8   Reproduced under Creative Commons Attribution license (CC BY 2.0).

Figure   10.9   Copyright © 2012 by IEEE.

Figure   10.10 Copyright © 2012 by IEEE.

Figure   10.11 Copyright © 1998 by IEEE.

Figure   10.12 Copyright © 1995 by IEEE.

Figure   10.13 Courtesy of Gordon Kindlmann, from http://www.cs.utah.edu/~gk/lumFace.

Figure   11.2   Courtesy of Michael McGuffin, made using Tableau, http://tableausoftware.com.

Figure   11.3   Copyright © 2013 by IEEE.

Figure   11.4   Copyright © 2013 by IEEE.

Figure   11.5   Copyright © 2003 by IEEE.

Figure   11.6   Copyright © 2011 by IEEE.

Figure   11.7   [McLachlan et al. 08] © 2008 Association for Computing Machinery, Inc. Reprinted by permission.

Figure   11.8   © 2008 Christian Rieder, Felix Ritter, Matthias Raspe, and Heinz-Otto Peitgen. *Computer Graphics Forum* © 2008 The Eurographics Association and Blackwell Publishing Ltd.

Figure   11.9   Copyright © 1993 by IEEE.

Figure   12.2   Reproduced with permission from Graham Wills.

Figure   12.4   Copyright © 2003 by IEEE.

Figure   12.5   Copyright © 2008 by IEEE.

Figure   12.7   Reproduced under Creative Commons Attribution-ShareAlike 4.0 International license (CC BY-SA 4.0); created by Chris Weaver of The University of Oklahoma, from http://www.cs.ou.edu/~weaver/improvise/examples/census.

Figure   12.8   Courtesy of Michael Bostock, made with D3 [Bostock et al. 11]. From http://bl.ocks.org/mbostock/3887051, after http://bl.ocks.org/mbostock/4679202.

Figure   12.9   "The Visual Design and Control of Trellis Display," Ronald A. Becker, William S. Cleveland, and Ming-Jen Shyu, *Journal of Computational and Statistical Graphics* 5:2 (1996), 123–155. Reprinted by permission of the American Statistical Association (http://www.amstat.org).

Figure 12.10   "The Visual Design and Control of Trellis Display," Ronald A. Becker, William S. Cleveland, and Ming-Jen Shyu, *Journal of Computational and Statistical Graphics* 5:2 (1996), 123–155. Reprinted by permission of the American Statistical Association (http://www.amstat.org).

Figure 12.11   Copyright © 2009 by IEEE.

Figure 12.12   Copyright © 2009 by IEEE.

Figure 12.13   From [Stone 10], courtesy of Maureen Stone; original color image by National Park Service, http://www.nps.gov/pore/planyourvisit/upload/map_pore_areamap.pdf.

Figure 12.15   Copyright © 2010 by IEEE.

Figure 12.16   Copyright © 2006 by IEEE.

Figure 12.17   Reproduced under Creative Commons Attribution Non-Commercial license (CC BY-NC 2.0).

Figure 13.2   [Ahlberg and Shneiderman 94] © 1994 Association for Computing Machinery, Inc. Reprinted by permission. Courtesy of Human-Computer Interaction Lab, University of Maryland.

Figure 13.3   Copyright © 2007 by IEEE.

Figure 13.4   Copyright © 2003 by IEEE.

Figure 13.6   Copyright © 2008 by IEEE.

Figure 13.7   "40 years of boxplots," Hadley Wickham and Lisa Stryjewski, *The American Statistician*. Reprinted by permission of the American Statistical Association (http://www.amstat.org).

Figure 13.8   Copyright © 1998 by IEEE.

Figure 13.9   Copyright © 1999 by IEEE.

Figure 13.10   Courtesy of Adrienne Gruver, Penn State Geography.

Figure 13.11   Copyright © 2007 by IEEE.

Figure 13.12   Copyright © 2009 by IEEE.

Figure 14.2   Copyright © 2004 by IEEE.

Figure 14.3   [Bier et al. 93] © 1993 Association for Computing Machinery, Inc. Reprinted by permission.

Figure 14.4   Copyright © 1997 by IEEE.

Figure 14.5   Courtesy of David Auber, made with Tulip [Auber et al. 12].

Figure 14.6   Copyright © 1998 by IEEE.

Figure 14.7   [Munzner et al. 03] © 2003 Association for Computing Machinery, Inc. Reprinted by permission.

Figure 14.8   Copyright © 2006 by IEEE.

Figure 14.9   Copyright © 1998 by IEEE.

Figure 14.10   Copyright © 2010 by IEEE.

Figure 15.2   Copyright © 2005 by IEEE.

Figure 15.3   "Scagnostics Distributions," Leland Wilkinson and Graham Wills, *Journal of Computational and Graphical Statistics (JCGS)* 17:2 (2008), 473–491. Reprinted by permission of the American Statistical Association (http://www.amstat.org).

Figures 15.4 and 15.1(a)   Copyright © 2005 by IEEE.

Figure 15.5   Copyright © 1994 by IEEE.

Figures 15.6 and 15.1(b)   Copyright © 1994 by IEEE.

Figure 15.7   Copyright © 1994 by IEEE.

Figure 15.8   Copyright © 2002 by IEEE. Courtesy of Human-Computer Interaction Lab, University of Maryland.

Figures 15.9 and 15.1(c)   Copyright © 2005 by IEEE. Courtesy of Human-Computer Interaction Lab, University of Maryland.

Figure 15.10   Copyright © 2005 by IEEE. Courtesy of Human-Computer Interaction Lab, University of Maryland.

Figure 15.11   [Wattenberg 06] © 2006 Association for Computing Machinery, Inc. Reprinted by permission.

Figures 15.12 and 15.1(d)   [Wattenberg 06] © 2006 Association for Computing Machinery, Inc. Reprinted by permission.

Figures 15.13 and 15.1(e)   Copyright © 2002 by IEEE.

Figure 15.14–15.20 and 15.1(f)   From the PhD thesis of Tamara Munzner [Munzner 00].

Bibliography

[Ahlberg and Shneiderman 94] Chris Ahlberg and Ben Shneiderman. "Visual Information Seeking: Tight Coupling of Dynamic Query Filters with Starfield Displays." In *Proceedings of the SIGCHI Conference on Human Factors in Computing Systems (CHI)*, pp. 313–317. ACM, 1994. DOI 10.1145/259963.260390. *(pages 301, 302, 320, 373)*

[Aigner et al. 11] Wolfgang Aigner, Silvia Miksch, Heidrun Schumann, and Christian Tominski. *Visualization of Time-Oriented Data*. Springer, 2011. *(page 40)*

[Amar et al. 05] Robert Amar, James Eagan, and John Stasko. "Low-Level Components of Analytic Activity in Information Visualization." In *Proceedings of the IEEE Symposium on Information Visualization (InfoVis)*, pp. 111–117. IEEE Computer Society, 2005. *(page 64)*

[Andre and Wickens 95] Anthony D. Andre and Christopher D. Wickens. "When Users Want What's Not Best for Them." *Ergonomics in Design: The Quarterly of Human Factors Applications* 3:4 (1995), 10–14. *(page 129)*

[Andrews 08] Keith Andrews. "Evaluation Comes in Many Guises." AVI Workshop on BEyond time and errors: novel evaLuation methods for Information Visualization (BELIV) Position Paper, 2008. http://www.dis.uniroma1.it/beliv08/pospap/andrews.pdf. *(page 79)*

[Ankerst et al. 98] Michael Ankerst, Stefan Berchtold, and Daniel A. Keim. "Similarity Clustering of Dimensions for an Enhanced Visualization of Multidimensional Data." In *Proceedings of the IEEE Symposium on Information Visualization (InfoVis)*, pp. 52–60. IEEE Computer Society, 1998. *(pages 305, 321)*

[Anscombe 73] F.J. Anscombe. "Graphs in Statistical Analysis." *American Statistician* 27 (1973), 17–21. *(pages 7, 8, 19)*

[Archambault et al. 07a] Daniel Archambault, Tamara Munzner, and David Auber. "Grouse: Feature-Based, Steerable Graph Hierarchy Exploration." In *Proceedings of the Eurographics/IEEE VGTC Symposium on Visualization (EuroVis)*, pp. 67–74. Eurographics, 2007. *(page 10)*

[Archambault et al. 07b] Daniel Archambault, Tamara Munzner, and David Auber. "TopoLayout: Multilevel Graph Layout by Topological Features." *IEEE Transactions on Visualization and Computer Graphics* 13:2 (2007), 305–317. *(page 216)*

[Archambault et al. 08] Daniel Archambault, Tamara Munzner, and David Auber. "GrouseFlocks: Steerable Exploration of Graph Hierarchy Space." *IEEE Transactions on Visualization and Computer Graphics* 14:4 (2008), 900–913. *(page 215)*

[Auber et al. 12] David Auber, Daniel Archambault, Romain Bourqui, Antoine Lambert, Morgan Mathiaut, Patrick Mary, Maylis Delest, Jonathan Dubois, and Guy Melançon. "The Tulip 3 Framework: A Scalable Software Library for Information Visualization Applications Based on Relational Data." Technical report, INRIA Research Report 7860, 2012. *(pages 371, 372, 373)*

[Auber 02] David Auber. "Using Strahler Numbers for Real Time Visual Exploration of Huge Graphs." *Journal of WSCG (International Conference on Computer Vision and Graphics)* 10:1–3 (2002), 56–69. *(pages 61, 61, 65)*

[Bachthaler and Weiskopf 08] Sven Bachthaler and Daniel Weiskopf. "Continuous Scatterplots." *IEEE Transactions on Visualization and Computer Graphics (Proc. Vis 08)* 14:6 (2008), 1428–1435. *(pages 307, 308)*

[Baldonado et al. 00] Michelle Q. Wang Baldonado, Allison Woodruff, and Allan Kuchinsky. "Guidelines for Using Multiple Views in Information Visualizations." In *Proceedings of the International Working Conference on Advanced Visual Interfaces (AVI)*, pp. 110–119. ACM, 2000. *(page 296)*

[Barsky et al. 07] Aaron Barsky, Jennifer L. Gardy, Robert E. Hancock, and Tamara Munzner. "Cerebral: A Cytoscape Plugin for Layout of and Interaction with Biological Networks Using Subcellular Localization Annotation." *Bioinformatics* 23:8 (2007), 1040–1042. *(pages 5, 6, 295)*

[Barsky et al. 08] Aaron Barsky, Tamara Munzner, Jennifer Gardy, and Robert Kincaid. "Cerebral: Visualizing Multiple Experimental Conditions on a Graph with Biological Context." *IEEE Transactions on Visualization and Computer Graphics (Proc. InfoVis 08)* 14:6 (2008), 1253–1260. *(pages 274, 275)*

[Becker and Cleveland 87] Richard A. Becker and William S. Cleveland. "Brushing Scatterplots." *Technometrics* 29 (1987), 127–142. *(page 296)*

[Becker et al. 96] Ronald A. Becker, William S. Cleveland, and Ming-Jen Shyu. "The Visual Design and Control of Trellis Display." *Journal of Computational and Statistical Graphics* 5:2 (1996), 123–155. *(pages 155, 282, 283, 284)*

[Bederson and Hollan 94] Ben Bederson and James D Hollan. "Pad++: A Zooming Graphical Interface for Exploring Alternate Interface Physics." In *Proceedings of the Symposium on User Interface Software and Technology (UIST)*, pp. 17–26. ACM, 1994. *(page 262)*

[Bergman et al. 95] Lawrence D. Bergman, Bernice E. Rogowitz, and Lloyd A. Treinish. "A Rule-Based Tool for Assisting Colormap Selection." In *Proceedings of the IEEE Conference on Visualization (Vis)*, pp. 118–125. IEEE Computer Society, 1995. *(pages 232, 240)*

[Bertin 67] Jacques Bertin. *Sémiologie Graphique: Les diagrammes—Les réseaux—Les cartes.* Gauthier-Villard, 1967. Reissued by Editions de l'Ecole des Hautes Etudes en Sciences in 1999. *(pages 19, 114, 175)*

[Bier et al. 93] Eric A. Bier, Maureen C. Stone, Ken Pier, William Buxton, and Tony D. DeRose. "Toolglass and Magic Lenses: The See-Through Interface." In *Proceedings of the Annual Conference on Computer Graphics and Interactive Techniques (SIGGRAPH)*, pp. 73–80. ACM, 1993. DOI 10.1145/166117.166126. *(pages 326, 373)*

[Booshehrian et al. 11] Maryam Booshehrian, Torsten Möller, Randall M. Peterman, and Tamara Munzner. "Vismon: Facilitating Risk Assessment and Decision Making in Fisheries Management." Technical report, School of Computing Science, Simon Fraser University, Technical Report TR 2011-04, 2011. *(page 167)*

[Borgo et al. 13] Rita Borgo, Johannes Kehrer, David H.S. Chung, Eamonn Maguire, Robert S. Laramee, Helwig Hauser, Matthew Ward, and Min Chen. "Glyph-Based Visualization: Foundations, Design Guidelines, Techniques and Applications." In *Eurographics State of the Art Reports*, pp. 39–63. Eurographics, 2013. *(pages 115, 296)*

[Borland and Taylor 07] David Borland and Russell M. Taylor, III. "Rainbow Color Map (Still) Considered Harmful." *IEEE Computer Graphics and Applications* 27:2 (2007), 14–17. *(page 240)*

[Bosch 01] Robert P. Bosch, Jr. "Using Visualization to Understand the Behavior of Computer Systems." Ph.D. thesis, Stanford University Department of Computer Science, 2001. *(page 152)*

[Bostock et al. 11] Michael Bostock, Vadim Ogievetsky, and Jeffrey Heer. "D3: Data-Driven Documents." *IEEE Transactions on Visualization and Computer Graphics (Proc. InfoVis 11)* 17:12 (2011), 2301–2309. *(pages 371, 371, 371, 371, 372)*

[Brandes 01] Ulrik Brandes. "Chapter 4, Drawing on Physical Analogies." In *Drawing Graphs: Methods and Models*, Lecture Notes in Computer Science, 2025, edited by M. Kaufmann and D. Wagner, pp. 71–86. Springer, 2001. *(page 216)*

[Brehmer and Munzner 13] Matthew Brehmer and Tamara Munzner. "A Multi-Level Typology of Abstract Visualization Tasks." *IEEE Transactions on Visualization and Computer Graphics (Proc. InfoVis 13)* 19:12 (2013), 2376–2385. *(page 64)*

[Brewer 99] Cynthia A. Brewer. "Color Use Guidelines for Data Representation." In *Proceedings of the Section on Statistical Graphics*, pp. 55–60. American Statistical Association, 1999. *(pages 226, 240)*

[Buchheim et al. 02] Christoph Buchheim, Michael Jünger, and Sebastien Leipert. "Improving Walker's Algorithm to Run in Linear Time." In *Proceedings of the International Symposium on Graph Drawing (GD 02)*, Lecture Notes in Computer Science, 2528, pp. 344–353. Springer, 2002. *(pages 201, 202)*

[Byron and Wattenberg 08] Lee Byron and Martin Wattenberg. "Stacked Graphs Geometry & Aesthetics." *IEEE Transactions on Visualization and Computer Graphics (Proc. InfoVis 08)* 14:6 (2008), 1245–1252. *(pages 153, 153, 154, 175)*

[Cabral and Leedom 93] Brian Cabral and Leith Casey Leedom. "Imaging Vector Fields Using Line Integral Convolution." In *Proceedings of the Annual Conference on Computer Graphics and Interactive Techniques (SIGGRAPH)*, pp. 263–270. ACM, 1993. *(pages 193, 198)*

[Card and Mackinlay 97] Stuart K. Card and Jock Mackinlay. "The Structure of the Information Visualization Design Space." In *Proceedings of the IEEE Symposium on Information Visualization (InfoVis)*, pp. 92–99. IEEE Computer Society, 1997. *(page 40)*

[Card and Mackinlay 99] Stuart K. Card and Jock D. Mackinlay. "The Structure of the Information Visualization Design Space." In *Proceedings of the IEEE Symposium on Information Visualization (InfoVis)*, pp. 92–99. IEEE Computer Society, 1999. *(pages 175, 328)*

[Card et al. 91] Stuart Card, George Robertson, and Jock Mackinlay. "The Information Visualizer, an Information Workspace." In *Proceedings of the SIGCHI Conference on Human Factors in Computing Systems (CHI)*, pp. 181–186. ACM, 1991. *(pages 137, 142)*

[Card et al. 99] Stuart K. Card, Jock Mackinlay, and Ben Shneiderman. *Readings in Information Visualization: Using Vision to Think.* Morgan Kaufmann, 1999. *(pages xvi, 40, 65)*

[Carpendale et al. 95] M. Sheelagh T. Carpendale, David J. Cowperthwaite, and F. David Fracchia. "Three-Dimensional Pliable Surfaces: For Effective Presentation of Visual Information." In *Proceedings of the Symposium on User Interface Software and Technology (UIST)*, pp. 217–226. ACM, 1995. *(page 338)*

[Carpendale et al. 96] M. Sheelagh T. Carpendale, David J. Cowperthwaite, and F. David Fracchia. "Distortion Viewing Techniques for 3D Data." In *Proceedings of the IEEE Symposium on Information Visualization (InfoVis)*, pp. 46–53. IEEE Computer Society, 1996. *(pages 121, 338)*

[Carpendale 08] Sheelagh Carpendale. "Evaluating Information Visualizations." In *Information Visualization: Human-Centered Issues and Perspectives*, Lecture Notes in Computer Science, 4950, edited by Andreas Kerren, John T. Stasko, Jean-Daniel Fekete, and Chris North, pp. 19–45. Springer, 2008. *(page 92)*

[Carr et al. 04] Hamish Carr, Jack Snoeyink, and Michiel van de Panne. "Simplifying Flexible Isosurfaces Using Local Geometric Measures." In *Proceedings of the IEEE Conference on Visualization (Vis)*, pp. 497–504. IEEE Computer Society, 2004. *(pages 186, 197)*

[Chalmers 96] M. Chalmers. "A Linear Iteration Time Layout Algorithm for Visualising High Dimensional Data." In *Proceedings of the IEEE Conference on Visualization (Vis)*, pp. 127–132. IEEE Computer Society, 1996. *(page 321)*

[Chi and Riedl 98] Ed H. Chi and John T. Riedl. "An Operator Interaction Framework for Visualization Systems." In *Proceedings of the IEEE Symposium on Information Visualization (InfoVis)*, pp. 63–70. IEEE Computer Society, 1998. *(page 65)*

[Chuah 98] Mei C. Chuah. "Dynamic Aggregation with Circular Visual Designs." In *Proceedings of the IEEE Symposium on Information Visualization (InfoVis)*, pp. 35–43. IEEE Computer Society, 1998. *(pages 310, 311)*

[Cleveland and McGill 84a] William S. Cleveland and Robert McGill. "Graphical Perception: Theory, Experimentation, and Application to the Development of Graphical Methods." *Journal of the American Statistical Association* 79:387 (1984), 531–554. *(pages 104, 105, 113, 114, 155)*

[Cleveland and McGill 84b] William S. Cleveland and Robert McGill. "The Many Faces of a Scatterplot." *Journal of the American Statistical Association* 79:388 (1984), 807–822. *(page 19)*

[Cleveland et al. 88] William S. Cleveland, Marylyn E. McGill, and Robert McGill. "The Shape Parameter of a Two-Variable Graph." *Journal of the American Statistical Association* 83:402 (1988), 289–300. *(page 176)*

[Cleveland 93a] William S. Cleveland. "A Model for Studying Display Methods of Statistical Graphics (with Discussion)." *Journal of Computational and Statistical Graphics* 2:4 (1993), 323–364. *(page 114)*

[Cleveland 93b] William S. Cleveland. *Visualizing Data.* Hobart Press, 1993. *(pages 175, 176)*

[Cockburn and McKenzie 00] Andy Cockburn and Bruce McKenzie. "An Evaluation of Cone Trees." In *People and Computers XIV: Usability or Else. British Computer Society Conference on Human Computer Interaction*, pp. 425–436. Springer, 2000. *(pages 129, 141)*

[Cockburn and McKenzie 01] Andy Cockburn and Bruce McKenzie. "3D or Not 3D? Evaluating the Effect of the Third Dimension in a Document Management System." In *Proceedings of the SIGCHI Conference on Human Factors in Computing Systems (CHI)*, pp. 434–441. ACM, 2001. *(pages 129, 141)*

[Cockburn and McKenzie 04] Andy Cockburn and Bruce McKenzie. "Evaluating Spatial Memory in Two and Three Dimensions." *International Journal of Human-Computer Studies* 61:30 (2004), 359–373. *(page 141)*

[Cockburn et al. 08] Andy Cockburn, Amy Karlson, and Benjamin B. Bederson. "A Review of Overview+Detail, Zooming, and Focus+Context Interfaces." *Computing Surveys* 41:1 (2008), 1–31. *(pages 295, 337)*

[Cormen et al. 90] Thomas H. Cormen, Charles E. Leiserson, and Ronald L. Rivest. *Introduction to Algorithms*. MIT Press, 1990. *(page 92)*

[Craig and Kennedy 03] Paul Craig and Jessie Kennedy. "Coordinated Graph and Scatter-Plot Views for the Visual Exploration of Microarray Time-Series Data." In *Proceedings of the IEEE Symposium on Information Visualization (InfoVis)*, pp. 173–180. IEEE Computer Society, 2003. *(pages 271, 272)*

[Csikszentmihalyi 91] Mihaly Csikszentmihalyi. *Flow: The Psychology of Optimal Experience*. Harper, 1991. *(page 139)*

[Davidson et al. 01] George S. Davidson, Brian N. Wylie, and Kevin W. Boyack. "Cluster Stability and the Use of Noise in Interpretation of Clustering." In *Proceedings of the IEEE Symposium on Information Visualization (InfoVis)*, pp. 23–30. IEEE Computer Society, 2001. *(pages 52, 130)*

[Diehl et al. 10] Stephan Diehl, Fabian Beck, and Micheal Burch. "Uncovering Strengths and Weaknesses of Radial Visualizations—An Empirical Approach." *IEEE Transactions on Visualization and Computer Graphics (Proc. InfoVis 10)* 16:6 (2010), 935–942. *(pages 170, 176)*

[Dix and Ellis 98] A. Dix and G. Ellis. "Starting Simple—Adding Value to Static Visualisation Through Simple Interaction." In *Proceedings of the International Working Conference on Advanced Visual Interfaces (AVI)*, pp. 124–134. ACM, 1998. *(page 261)*

[Dow et al. 05] Steven Dow, Blair MacIntyre, Jaemin Lee, Christopher Oezbek, Jay David Bolter, and Maribeth Gandy. "Wizard of Oz Support Throughout an Iterative Design Process." *IEEE Pervasive Computing* 4:4 (2005), 18–26. *(page 77)*

[Draper et al. 09] Geoffrey M. Draper, Yarden Livnat, and Richard F. Riesenfeld. "A Survey of Radial Methods for Information Visualization." *IEEE Transactions on Visualization and Computer Graphics* 15:5 (2009), 759–776. *(page 176)*

[Drebin et al. 88] Robert A. Drebin, Loren C. Carpenter, and Pat Hanrahan. "Volume Rendering." *Computer Graphics (Proc. SIGGRAPH 88)* 22:4 (1988), 65–74. *(page 197)*

[Dykes and Brunsdon 07] Jason Dykes and Chris Brunsdon. "Geographically Weighted Visualization: Interactive Graphics for Scale-Varying Exploratory Analysis." *IEEE Transactions on Visualization and Computer Graphics (Proc. InfoVis 07)* 13:6 (2007), 1161–1168. *(pages 313, 314, 321)*

[Eick et al. 92] Stephen G. Eick, Joseph L. Steffen, and Eric E Sumner, Jr. "Seesoft—A Tool for Visualizing Line Oriented Software Statistics." *IEEE Transactions on Software Engineering* 18:11 (1992), 957–968. *(page 176)*

[Elmqvist and Fekete 10] Niklas Elmqvist and Jean-Daniel Fekete. "Hierarchical Aggregation for Information Visualization: Overview, Techniques and Design Guidelines." *IEEE Transactions on Visualization and Computer Graphics* 16:3 (2010), 439–454. *(page 321)*

[Emerson et al. 12] John W. Emerson, Walton A. Green, Barret Schloerke, Dianne Cook, Heike Hofmann, and Hadley Wickham. "The Generalized Pairs Plot." *Journal of Computational and Graphical Statistics* 22:1 (2012), 79–91. *(page 175)*

[Engel et al. 06] Klaus Engel, Markus Hadwiger, Joe Kniss, Christof Reza-Salama, and Daniel Weiskopf. *Real-Time Volume Graphics.* A K Peters, 2006. *(page 197)*

[Ferstay et al. 13] Joel A. Ferstay, Cydney B. Nielsen, and Tamara Munzner. "Variant View: Visualizing Sequence Variants in Their Gene Context." *IEEE Transactions on Visualization Computer Graphics (Proc. InfoVis 13)* 19:12 (2013), 2546–2555. *(page 4)*

[Few 07] Stephen Few. "Graph Design I.Q. Test." http://perceptualedge.com/files/GraphDesignIQ.html, 2007. *(page 122)*

[Few 12] Stephen Few. *Show Me the Numbers: Designing Tables and Graphs to Enlighten*, Second edition. Analytics Press, 2012. *(page xvii)*

[Field and Hole 03] Andy Field and Graham A. Hole. *How to Design and Report Experiments.* Sage, 2003. *(page 93)*

[Frick et al. 95] A. Frick, A. Ludwig, and H. Mehldau. "A Fast Adaptive Layout Algorithm for Undirected Graphs." In *Proceedings of the International Symposium on Graph Drawing (GD 94)*, Lecture Notes in Computer Science, 894, pp. 388–403. Springer, 1995. *(page 216)*

[Friendly 08] Michael Friendly. "A Brief History of Data Visualization." In *Handbook of Data Visualization, Computational Statistics*, edited by Antony Unwin, Chun-houh Chen, and Wolfgang K. Härdle, pp. 15–56. Springer, 2008. *(pages 175, 197)*

[Fua et al. 99] Ying-Huey Fua, Matthew O. Ward, and Elke A. Rundensteiner. "Hierarchical Parallel Coordinates for Exploration of Large Datasets." In *Proceedings of the IEEE Conference on Visualization (Vis)*, pp. 43–50. IEEE Computer Society, 1999. *(pages 165, 311, 312, 321)*

[Furnas 82] George W. Furnas. "The FISHEYE View: A New Look at Structured Files." Technical report, Bell Laboratories Technical Memorandum No. 82-11221-22, 1982. *(page 337)*

[Furnas 86] George W. Furnas. "Generalized Fisheye Views." In *Proceedings of the SIGCHI Conference on Human Factors in Computing Systems (CHI)*, pp. 16–23. ACM, 1986. *(pages 324, 337)*

[Furnas 06] George W. Furnas. "A Fisheye Follow-up: Further Reflection on Focus + Context." In *Proceedings of the SIGCHI Conference on Human Factors in Computing Systems (CHI)*, pp. 999–1008. ACM, 2006. *(pages 335, 338)*

[Gehlenborg and Wong 12] Nils Gehlenborg and Bang Wong. "Points of View: Networks." *Nature Methods* 9:2 (2012), Article no. 115. *(pages 209, 371)*

[Ghoniem et al. 05] Mohammad Ghoniem, Jean-Daniel Fekete, and Philippe Castagliola. "On the Readability of Graphs Using Node-Link and Matrix-Based Representations: A Controlled Experiment and Statistical Analysis." *Information Visualization* 4:2 (2005), 114–135. *(pages 212, 216)*

[Gleicher et al. 11] Michael Gleicher, Danielle Albers, Rick Walker, Ilir Jusufi, Charles D. Hansen, and Jonathan C. Roberts. "Visual Comparison for Information Visualization." *Information Visualization* 10:4 (2011), 289–309. *(page 296)*

[Gratzl et al. 13] Samuel Gratzl, Alexander Lex, Nils Gehlenborg, Hanspeter Pfister, and Marc Streit. "LineUp: Visual Analysis of Multi-Attribute Rankings." *IEEE Transactions on Visualization and Computer Graphics (Proc. InfoVis 13)* 19:12 (2013), 2277–2286. *(pages 246, 247)*

[Green 89] T. R. G. Green. "Cognitive Dimensions of Notations." In *People and Computers V*, edited by A. Sutcliffe and L. Macaulay, pp. 443–460. Cambridge University Press, 1989. *(page 69)*

[Grivet et al. 06] Sébastian Grivet, David Auber, Jean-Philippe Domenger, and Guy Melançon. "Bubble Tree Drawing Algorithm." In *Proceedings of the Conference on Computational Imaging and Vision, Computer Vision and Graphics*, pp. 633–641. Springer, 2006. *(page 202)*

[Grossman et al. 07] Tovi Grossman, Daniel Wigdor, and Ravin Balakrishnan. "Exploring and Reducing the Effects of Orientation on Text Readability in Volumetric Displays." In *Proceedings of the SIGCHI Conference on Human Factors in Computing Systems (CHI)*, pp. 483–492. ACM, 2007. *(page 124)*

[Hachul and Jünger 04] S. Hachul and M. Jünger. "Drawing Large Graphs with a Potential-Field-Based Multilevel Algorithm." In *Proceedings of the International Symposium on Graph Drawing (GD 04)*, Lecture Notes in Computer Science, 3383, pp. 285–295. Springer, 2004. *(page 216)*

[Hansen and Johnson 05] Charles C. Hansen and Christopher R. Johnson, editors. *The Visualization Handbook*. Elsevier, 2005. *(pages xvii, 40, 92)*

[Havre et al. 00] Susan Havre, Beth Hetzler, and Lucy Nowell. "ThemeRiver: Visualizing Theme Changes over Time." In *Proceedings of the IEEE Symposium on Information Visualization (InfoVis)*, pp. 9–20. IEEE Computer Society, 2000. *(page 175)*

[Healey 07] Christopher G. Healey. "Perception in Vision." http://www.csc.ncsu.edu/faculty/healey/PP, 2007. *(page 115)*

[Heer and Agrawala 06] Jeffrey Heer and Maneesh Agrawala. "Multi-Scale Banking to 45 Degrees." *IEEE Transactions on Visualization and Computer Graphics (Proc. InfoVis 06)* 12:5 (2006), 701–708. *(pages 158, 176)*

[Heer and Bostock 10] Jeffrey Heer and Michael Bostock. "Crowdsourcing Graphical Perception: Using Mechanical Turk to Assess Visualization Design." In *Proceedings of the SIGCHI Conference on Human Factors in Computing Systems (CHI)*, pp. 203–212. ACM, 2010. DOI 10.1145/1753326.1753357. *(pages 105, 105, 115, 370)*

[Heer and Card 04] Jeffrey Heer and Stuart K. Card. "DOITrees Revisited: Scalable, Space-Constrained Visualization of Hierarchical Data." In *Proceedings of the International Working Conference on Advanced Visual Interfaces (AVI)*, pp. 421–424. ACM, 2004. *(page 325)*

[Heer and Robertson 07] Jeffrey Heer and George Robertson. "Animated Transitions in Statistical Data Graphics." *IEEE Transactions on Visualization and Computer Graphics (Proc. InfoVis 07)* 13:6 (2007), 1240–1247. *(pages 249, 262)*

[Heer and Shneiderman 12] Jeffrey Heer and Ben Shneiderman. "Interactive Dynamics for Visual Analysis: A Taxonomy of Tools That Support the Fluent and Flexible Use of Visualizations." *Queue* 10:2 (2012), 30–55. *(pages 64, 175)*

[Heer et al. 08] Jeffrey Heer, Jock Mackinlay, Chris Stolte, and Maneesh Agrawala. "Graphical Histories for Visualization: Supporting Analysis, Communication, and Evaluation." *IEEE Transactions on Visualization Computer Graphics (Proc. InfoVis 08)* 14:6 (2008), 1189–1196. *(page 50, 50)*

[Heer et al. 09] Jeffrey Heer, Nicholas Kong, and Maneesh Agrawala. "Sizing the Horizon: The Effects of Chart Size and Layering on the Graphical Perception of Time Series Visualizations." In *Proceedings of the SIGCHI Conference on Human Factors in Computing Systems (CHI)*, pp. 1303–1312. ACM, 2009. DOI 10.1145/1518701.1518897. *(pages 90, 91, 370)*

[Henry and Fekete 06] Nathalie Henry and Jean-Daniel Fekete. "MatrixExplorer: A Dual-Representation System to Explore Social Networks." *IEEE Transactions on Visualization and Computer Graphics (Proc. InfoVis 06)* 12:5 (2006), 677–684. *(pages 83, 84, 85, 216)*

[Henry et al. 07] Nathalie Henry, Jean-Daniel Fekete, and Michael McGuffin. "NodeTrix: A Hybrid Visualization of Social Networks." *IEEE Transactions on Computer Graphics and Visualization (Proc. InfoVis 07)* 13:6 (2007), 1302–1309. *(page 216)*

[Henze 98] Chris Henze. "Feature Detection in Linked Derived Spaces." In *Proceedings of the IEEE Conference on Visualization (Vis)*, pp. 87–94. IEEE Computer Society, 1998. *(pages 62, 63, 65)*

[Herman et al. 00] Ivan Herman, Guy Melançon, and M. Scott Marshall. "Graph Visualisation in Information Visualisation: A Survey." *IEEE Transactions on Visualization and Computer Graphics (TVCG)* 6:1 (2000), 24–44. *(page 216)*

[Holten 06] Danny Holten. "Hierarchical Edge Bundles: Visualization of Adjacency Relations in Hierarchical Data." *IEEE Transactions on Visualization and Computer Graphics (Proc. InfoVis 06)* 12:5 (2006), 741–748. *(pages 292, 293)*

[Holtzblatt and Jones 93] K. Holtzblatt and S. Jones. "Contextual Inquiry: A Participatory Technique for System Design." In *Participatory Design: Principles and Practices*, edited by D. Schuler and A. Namioka, pp. 177–210. Lawrence Erlbaum Associates, 1993. *(pages 77, 92)*

[Hornbæk and Hertzum 11] Kaspar Hornbæk and Morten Hertzum. "The Notion of Overview in Information Visualization." *International Journal of Human-Computer Studies* 69:7–8 (2011), 509–525. *(page 142)*

[Hornbaek 13] Kaspar Hornbaek. "Some Whys and Hows of Experiments in Human–Computer Interaction." *Foundations and Trends in Human–Computer Interaction* 5:4. *(page 93)*

[Hu 05] Yifan Hu. "Efficient and High Quality Force-Directed Graph Drawing." *The Mathematica Journal* 10 (2005), 37–71. *(pages 207, 207, 216)*

[Hu 14] Yifan Hu. "A Gallery of Large Graphs." http://yifanhu.net/GALLERY/GRAPHS/, 2014. *(page 207)*

[Ingram et al. 09] Stephen Ingram, Tamara Munzner, and Marc Olano. "Glimmer: Multilevel MDS on the GPU." *IEEE Transactions on Visualization and Computer Graphics* 15:2 (2009), 249–261. *(pages 317, 318, 321)*

[Ingram et al. 10] Stephen Ingram, Tamara Munzner, Veronika Irvine, Melanie Tory, Steven Bergner, and Torsten Möller. "DimStiller: Workflows for Dimensional Analysis and Reduction." In *Proceedings of the IEEE Conference on Visual Analytics Software and Technologies (VAST)*, pp. 3–10. IEEE Computer Society, 2010. *(page 321)*

[Inselberg and Dimsdale 90] Alfred Inselberg and Bernard Dimsdale. "Parallel Coordinates: A Tool for Visualizing Multi-Dimensional Geometry." In *Proceedings of the IEEE Conference on Visualization (Vis)*. IEEE Computer Society, 1990. *(page 176)*

[Inselberg 09] Alfred Inselberg. *Parallel Coordinates: Visual Multidimensional Geometry and Its Applications*. Springer, 2009. *(page 176)*

[Javed and Elmqvist 12] Waqas Javed and Niklas Elmqvist. "Exploring the Design Space of Composite Visualization." In *Proceedings of the IEEE Symposium on Pacific Visualization (PacificVis)*, pp. 1–9. IEEE Computer Society, 2012. *(page 296)*

[Javed et al. 10] Waqas Javed, Bryan McDonnel, and Niklas Elmqvist. "Graphical Perception of Multiple Time Series." *IEEE Transactions on Visualization and Computer Graphics (Proc. InfoVis 10)* 16:6 (2010), 927–934. *(page 292)*

[Johnson and Shneiderman 91] Brian Johnson and Ben Shneiderman. "Treemaps: A Space-Filling Approach to the Visualization of Hierarchical Information." In *Proceedings of the IEEE Conference on Visualization (Vis)*, pp. 284–291. IEEE Computer Society, 1991. *(page 217)*

[Johnson 10] Jeff Johnson. *Designing with the Mind in Mind: Simple Guide to Understanding User Interface Design Rules*. Morgan Kaufmann, 2010. *(page 142)*

[Jones et al. 02] James A. Jones, Mary Jean Harrold, and John Stasko. "Visualization of Test Information to Assist Fault Localization." In *Proceedings of the International Conference on Software Engineering (ICSE)*, pp. 467–477. ACM, 2002. *(pages 172, 173, 176)*

[Kadmon and Shlomi 78] Naftali Kadmon and Eli Shlomi. "A Polyfocal Projection for Statistical Surfaces." *The Cartographic Journal* 15:1 (1978), 36–41. *(page 337)*

[Kaiser 96] Peter K. Kaiser. *The Joy of Visual Perception*. http://www.yorku.ca/eye, 1996. *(page 222)*

[Kaufman and Mueller 05] Arie Kaufman and Klaus Mueller. "Overview of Volume Rendering." In *The Visualization Handbook*, edited by Charles C. Hansen and Christopher R. Johnson, pp. 127–174. Elsevier, 2005. *(page 197)*

[Keahey and Robertson 97] T. Alan Keahey and Edward L. Robertson. "Nonlinear Magnification Fields." In *Proceedings of the IEEE Symposium on Information Visualization (InfoVis)*, pp. 51–58. IEEE Computer Society, 1997. *(page 338)*

[Keahey 98] T. Alan Keahey. "The Generalized Detail-in-Context Problem." In *Proceedings of the IEEE Symposium on Information Visualization (InfoVis)*, pp. 44–51. IEEE Computer Society, 1998. *(page 333)*

[Keim and Kriegel 94] Daniel A. Keim and Hans-Peter Kriegel. "VisDB: Database Exploration Using Multidimensional Visualization." *IEEE Computer Graphics and Applications* 14:5 (1994), 40–49. *(pages 340, 341, 347, 348, 349, 350, 367)*

[Keim 97] Daniel A. Keim. "Visual Techniques for Exploring Databases." KDD 1997 Tutorial Notes, 1997. http://www.dbs.informatik.uni-muenchen.de/~daniel/KDD97.pdf. *(page 175)*

[Keim 00] Daniel A. Keim. "Designing Pixel-Oriented Visualization Techniques: Theory and Applications." *IEEE Transactions on Visualization and Computer Graphics* 6:1 (2000), 59–78. *(page 176)*

[Kindlmann 02] Gordon Kindlmann. "Transfer Functions in Direct Volume Rendering: Design, Interface, Interaction." SIGGRAPH 2002 Course Notes, 2002. http://www.cs.utah.edu/~gk/papers/sig02-TF-notes.pdf. *(pages 233, 234)*

[Kindlmann 04] Gordon Kindlmann. "Superquadric Tensor Glyphs." In *Proceedings of the Eurographics/IEEE Conference on Visualization (VisSym)*, pp. 147–154. Eurographics, 2004. *(pages 195, 196, 196, 198)*

[Klippel et al. 09] Alexander Klippel, Frank Hardisty, Rui Li, and Chris Weaver. "Color Enhanced Star Plot Glyphs—Can Salient Shape Characteristics Be Overcome?" *Cartographica* 44:3 (2009), 217–231. *(page 296)*

[Kniss et al. 05] Joe Kniss, Gordon Kindlmann, and Charles Hansen. "Multidimensional Transfer Functions for Volume Rendering." In *The Visualization Handbook*, edited by Charles Hansen and Christopher Johnson, pp. 189–210. Elsevier, 2005. *(pages 187, 188, 197)*

[Kniss 02] Joe Kniss. "Interactive Volume Rendering Techniques." Master's thesis, University of Utah, Department of Computer Science, 2002. *(pages 182, 187, 197)*

[Kong et al. 10] Nicholas Kong, Jeffrey Heer, and Maneesh Agrawala. "Perceptual Guidelines for Creating Rectangular Treemaps." *IEEE Transactions on Visualization and Computer Graphics (Proc. InfoVis 10)* 16:6 (2010), 990–998. *(page 217)*

[Kosara et al. 03] Robert Kosara, Christopher G. Healey, Victoria Interrante, David H. Laidlaw, and Colin Ware. "Thoughts on User Studies: Why, How, and When." *IEEE Computer Graphics and Applications* 23:4 (2003), 20–25. *(page 92)*

[Kuniavsky 03] Mike Kuniavsky. *Observing the User Experience: A Practitioner's Guide to User Research.* Morgan Kaufmann, 2003. *(page 92)*

[Laidlaw et al. 05] David H. Laidlaw, Robert M. Kirby, Cullen D. Jackson, J. Scott Davidson, Timothy S. Miller, Marco Da Silva, William H. Warren, and Michael J. Tarr. "Comparing 2D Vector Field Visualization Methods: A User Study." *IEEE Transactions on Visualization and Computer Graphics (TVCG)* 11:1 (2005), 59–70. *(page 190, 190)*

[Lam and Munzner 10] Heidi Lam and Tamara Munzner. *A Guide to Visual Multi-Level Interface Design from Synthesis of Empirical Study Evidence.* Synthesis Lectures on Visualization Series, Morgan Claypool, 2010. *(pages 295, 335, 337)*

[Lam et al. 06] Heidi Lam, Ronald A. Rensink, and Tamara Munzner. "Effects of 2D Geometric Transformations on Visual Memory." In *Proceedings of the Symposium on Applied Perception in Graphics and Visualization (APGV)*, pp. 119–126. ACM, 2006. *(page 335)*

[Lam 08] Heidi Lam. "A Framework of Interaction Costs in Information Visualization." *IEEE Transactions on Visualization and Computer Graphics (Proc. InfoVis 08)* 14:6 (2008), 1149–1156. *(page 142)*

[Lambert et al. 10] Antoine Lambert, David Auber, and Guy Melançon. "Living Flows: Enhanced Exploration of Edge-Bundled Graphs Based on GPU-Intensive Edge Rendering." In *Proceedings of the International Conference on Information Visualisation (IV)*, pp. 523–530. IEEE Computer Society, 2010. *(pages 328, 335, 336)*

[Lamping et al. 95] John Lamping, Ramana Rao, and Peter Pirolli. "A Focus+Content Technique Based on Hyperbolic Geometry for Visualizing Large Hierarchies." In *Proceedings of the SIGCHI Conference on Human Factors in Computing Systems (CHI)*, pp. 401–408. ACM, 1995. *(page 338)*

[Laramee et al. 04] Robert S. Laramee, Helwig Hauser, Helmut Doleisch, Benjamin Vrolijk, Frits H. Post, and Daniel Weiskopf. "The State of the Art in Flow Visualization: Dense and Texture-Based Techniques." *Computer Graphics Forum (Proc. Eurographics 04)* 23:2 (2004), 203–221. *(page 198)*

[Larkin and Simon 87] Jill H. Larkin and Herbert A. Simon. "Why a Diagram Is (Sometimes) Worth Ten Thousand Words." *Cognitive Science* 11:1 (1987), 65–99. *(page 19)*

[Lasseter 87] John Lasseter. "Principles of Traditional Animation Applied to 3D Computer Animation." *Computer Graphics (Proc. SIGGRAPH 87)* 21:4 (1987), 35–44. *(page 141)*

[Lee et al. 06] Bongshin Lee, Catherine Plaisant, Cynthia Sims Parr, Jean-Daniel Fekete, and Nathalie Henry. "Task Taxonomy for Graph Visualization." In *Proceedings of the AVI Workshop on BEyond time and errors: novel evaLuation methods for Information Visualization (BELIV)*, Article no. 14. ACM, 2006. *(page 64)*

[Leung and Apperley 94] Ying K. Leung and Mark Apperley. "A Review and Taxonomy of Distortion-Oriented Presentation Techniques." *Transactions on Computer-Human Interaction (ToCHI)* 1:2 (1994), 126–160. *(page 337)*

[Levoy 88] Marc Levoy. "Display of Surfaces from Volume Data." *IEEE Computer Graphics and Applications* 8:3 (1988), 29–37. *(page 197)*

[Li and Shen 07] Liya Li and Han-Wei Shen. "Image-Based Streamline Generation and Rendering." *IEEE Transactions on Visualization and Computer Graphics (TVCG)* 13:3 (2007), 630–640. *(page 125, 125)*

[Liiv 10] Innar Liiv. "Seriation and Matrix Reordering Methods: An Historical Overview." *Journal of Statistical Analysis and Data Mining* 3:2 (2010), 70–91. *(page 176)*

[Lopez-Hernandez et al. 10] Roberto Lopez-Hernandez, David Guilmaine, Michael J. McGuffin, and Lee Barford. "A Layer-Oriented Interface for Visualizing Time-Series Data from Oscilloscopes." In *Proceedings of the IEEE Symposium on Pacific Visualization (PacificVis)*, pp. 41–48. IEEE Computer Society, 2010. *(page 128, 128)*

[Lorensen and Cline 87] William E. Lorensen and Harvey E. Cline. "Marching Cubes: A High Resolution 3D Surface Construction Algorithm." *Computer Graphics (Proc. SIGGRAPH 87)* 21:4 (1987), 163–169. *(page 197)*

[Maalej and Thurimella 13] Walid Maalej and Anil Kumar Thurimella. "An Introduction to Requirements Knowledge." In *Managing Requirements Knowledge*, edited by Walid Maalej and Anil Kumar Thurimella, pp. 1–22. Springer, 2013. *(page 92)*

[MacEachren 79] Alan M. MacEachren. "The Evolution of Thematic Cartography/A Research Methodology and Historical Review." *The Canadian Cartographer* 16:1 (1979), 17–33. *(page 197)*

[MacEachren 95] Alan M. MacEachren. *How Maps Work: Representation, Visualization, and Design.* Guilford Press, 1995. *(pages 115, 197)*

[Mackinlay et al. 90] Jock D. Mackinlay, Stuart K. Card, and George G. Robertson. "Rapid Controlled Movement Through a Virtual 3D Workspace." *Computer Graphics (Proc. SIGGRAPH 90)*, pp. 171–176. *(page 262)*

[Mackinlay et al. 91] Jock D. Mackinlay, George G. Robertson, and Stuart K. Card. "The Perspective Wall: Detail and Context Smoothly Integrated." In *Proceedings of the SIGCHI Conference on Human Factors in Computing Systems (CHI)*, pp. 173–179. ACM, 1991. *(page 338)*

[Mackinlay 86] Jock Mackinlay. "Automating the Design of Graphical Presentations of Relational Information." *Transactions on Graphics (TOG)* 5:2 (1986), 110–141. *(page 115, 115)*

[Maguire et al. 12] Eamonn Maguire, Philippe Rocca-Serra, Susanna-Assunta Sansone, Jim Davies, and Min Chen. "Taxonomy-Based Glyph Design—With a Case Study on Visualizing Workflows of Biological Experiments." *IEEE Transactions on Visualization and Computer Graphics (Proc. InfoVis 12)* 18:12 (2012), 2603–2612. *(pages 115, 230, 231, 296)*

[McGrath 94] J.E. McGrath. "Methodology Matters: Doing Research in the Behavioral and Social Sciences." In *Readings in Human-Computer Interaction: Toward the Year 2000*, edited by R.M. Baecker, J. Grudin, W. Buxton, and S. Greenberg, pp. 152–169. Morgan Kaufmann, 1994. *(page 91)*

[McGuffin and Balakrishnan 05] Michael J. McGuffin and Ravin Balakrishnan. "Interactive Visualization of Genealogical Graphs." In *Proceedings of the IEEE Symposium on Information Visualization (InfoVis)*, pp. 17–24. IEEE Computer Society, 2005. *(pages 81, 82, 83)*

[McGuffin and Robert 10] Michael J. McGuffin and Jean-Marc Robert. "Quantifying the Space-Efficiency of 2D Graphical Representations of Trees." *Information Visualization* 9:2 (2010), 115–140. *(pages 16, 175, 214, 217)*

[McGuffin 12] Michael J. McGuffin. "Simple Algorithms for Network Visualization: A Tutorial." *Tsinghua Science and Technology (Special Issue on Visualization and Computer Graphics)* 17:4 (2012), 383–398. *(pages 211, 212, 216)*

[McGuffin 14] Michael McGuffin. "Visualization Course Figures." http://www.michaelmcguffin.com/courses/vis, 2014. *(pages 163, 175)*

[McLachlan et al. 08] Peter McLachlan, Tamara Munzner, Eleftherios Koutsofios, and Stephen North. "LiveRAC—Interactive Visual Exploration of System Management Time-Series Data." In *Proceedings of the SIGCHI Conference on Human Factors in Computing Systems (CHI)*, pp. 1483–1492. ACM, 2008. DOI 10.1145/1357054.1357286. *(pages 87, 87, 88, 255, 256, 262, 369, 372)*

[McLoughlin et al. 13] Tony McLoughlin, Mark W. Jones, Robert S. Laramee, Rami Malki, Ian Masters, and Charles D. Hansen. "Similarity Measures for Enhancing Interactive Streamline Seeding." *IEEE Transactions on Visualization and Computer Graphics* 19:8 (2013), 1342–1353. *(page 192, 192)*

[McLouglin et al. 10] Tony McLouglin, Robert S. Laramee, Ronald Peikert, Frits H. Post, and Min Chen. "Over Two Decades of Integration-Based Geometric Flow Visualization." *Computer Graphics Forum (Proc. Eurographics 09, State of the Art Reports)* 6:29 (2010), 1807–1829. *(page 198)*

[Melançon 06] Guy Melançon. "Just How Dense Are Dense Graphs in the Real World?: A Methodological Note." In *Proceedings of the AVI Workshop BEyond time and errors: novel evaLuation methods for Information Visualization (BELIV)*. ACM, 2006. *(pages 210, 216)*

[Meyer et al. 09] Miriah Meyer, Tamara Munzner, and Hanspeter Pfister. "MizBee: A Multiscale Synteny Browser." *IEEE Transactions on Visualization and Computer Graphics (Proc. InfoVis 09)* 15:6 (2009), 897–904. *(pages 69, 70)*

[Meyer et al. 13] Miriah Meyer, Michael Sedlmair, P. Samuel Quinan, and Tamara Munzner. "The Nested Blocks and Guidelines Model." *Information Visualization.* Prepublished December 10, 2013, doi:10. 1177/1473871613510429. *(page 91)*

[Micallef et al. 12] Luanna Micallef, Pierre Dragicevic, and Jean-Daniel Fekete. "Assessing the Effect of Visualizations on Bayesian Reasoning Through Crowdsourcing." *IEEE Transactions on Visualization and Computer Graphics (Proc. InfoVis 12)* 18:12 (2012), 2536–2545. *(page 69)*

[Moscovich et al. 09] Tomer Moscovich, Fanny Chevalier, Nathalie Henry, Emmanuel Pietriga, and Jean-Daniel Fekete. "Topology-Aware Navigation in Large Networks." In *Proceedings of the SIGCHI Conference on Human Factors in Computing Systems (CHI)*, pp. 2319–2328. ACM, 2009. *(page 337)*

[Mukherjea et al. 96] Sougata Mukherjea, Kyoji Hirata, and Yoshinori Hara. "Visualizing the Results of Multimedia Web Search Engines." In *Proceedings of the IEEE Symposium on Information Visualization (InfoVis)*, pp. 64–65. IEEE Computer Society, 1996. *(page 122)*

[Munzner et al. 99] Tamara Munzner, François Guimbretière, and George Robertson. "Constellation: A Visualization Tool For Linguistic Queries from MindNet." In *Proceedings of the IEEE Symposium on Information Visualization (InfoVis)*, pp. 132–135. IEEE Computer Society, 1999. *(pages 341, 360, 367)*

[Munzner et al. 03] Tamara Munzner, François Guimbretière, Serdar Tasiran, Li Zhang, and Yunhong Zhou. "TreeJuxtaposer: Scalable Tree Comparison Using Focus+Context with Guaranteed Visibility." *Transactions on Graphics (Proc. SIGGRAPH 03)* 22:3 (2003), 453–462. DOI 10.1145/882262.882291. *(pages 59, 59, 65, 331, 332, 338, 369, 373)*

[Munzner 98] Tamara Munzner. "Exploring Large Graphs in 3D Hyperbolic Space." *IEEE Computer Graphics and Applications* 18:4 (1998), 18–23. *(pages 330, 331, 338)*

[Munzner 00] Tamara Munzner. "Constellation: Linguistic Semantic Networks (Chap. 5)." In *Interactive Visualization of Large Graphs and Networks (PhD thesis)*, pp. 105–122. Stanford University Department of Computer Science, 2000. *(pages 340, 341, 360, 361, 363, 364, 364, 365, 365, 366, 367, 374)*

[Munzner 09a] Tamara Munzner. "A Nested Model for Visualization Design and Validation." *IEEE Transactions on Visualization and Computer Graphics (Proc. InfoVis 09)* 15:6 (2009), 921–928. *(page 91)*

[Munzner 09b] Tamara Munzner. "Visualization." In *Fundamentals of Computer Graphics*, edited by Peter Shirley and Steve Marschner, Third edition, pp. 675–708. A K Peters, 2009. *(page xxi)*

[Newman and Yi 06] Timothy S. Newman and Hong Yi. "A Survey of the Marching Cubes Algorithm." *Computers & Graphics* 30:5 (2006), 854–879. *(page 197)*

[Noack 03] Andreas Noack. "An Energy Model for Visual Graph Clustering." In *Proceedings of the International Symposium on Graph Drawing (GD 03)*, Lecture Notes in Computer Science, 2912, pp. 425–436. Springer, 2003. *(pages 89, 89, 90)*

[Openshaw 84] Stan Openshaw. *The Modifiable Areal Unit Problem.* Number 38 in Concepts and Techniques in Modern Geography, Geo Books, 1984. *(page 321)*

[Peng et al. 04] Wei Peng, Matthew O. Ward, and Elke A. Rundensteiner. "Clutter Reduction in Multi-Dimensional Data Visualization Using Dimension Reordering." In *Proceedings of the IEEE Symposium on Information Visualization (InfoVis)*, pp. 89–96. IEEE Computer Society, 2004. *(page 321)*

[Phan et al. 05] Doantam Phan, Ling Xiao, Ron Yeh, Pat Hanrahan, and Terry Winograd. "Flow Map Layout." In *Proceedings of the IEEE Symposium on Information Visualization (InfoVis)*, pp. 219–224. IEEE Computer Society, 2005. *(pages 85, 86, 86)*

[Pirolli 07] Peter Pirolli. *Information Foraging Theory: Adaptive Interaction with Information.* Oxford University Press, 2007. *(pages 303, 320)*

[Plaisant et al. 02] Catherine Plaisant, Jesse Grosjean, and Ben Bederson. "SpaceTree: Supporting Exploration in Large Node Link Tree, Design Evolution and Empirical Evaluation." In *Proceedings of the IEEE Symposium on Information Visualization (InfoVis)*, pp. 57–64. IEEE Computer Society, 2002. *(pages 59, 59, 65)*

[Plaisant 04] Catherine Plaisant. "The Challenge of Information Visualization Evaluation." In *Proceedings of the International Working Conference on Advanced Visual Interfaces (AVI)*, pp. 109–116. ACM, 2004. *(page 92)*

[Plumlee and Ware 06] M. Plumlee and C. Ware. "Zooming versus Multiple Window Interfaces: Cognitive Costs of Visual Comparisons." *Transactions on Computer-Human Interaction (ToCHI)* 13:2 (2006), 179–209. *(page 295)*

[Post et al. 03] Frits H. Post, Benjamin Vrolijka, Helwig Hauser, Robert S. Laramee, and Helmut Doleisch. "The State of the Art in Flow Visualisation: Feature Extraction and Tracking." *Computer Graphics Forum (Proc. Eurographics 03)* 22:4 (2003), 1–17. *(page 198)*

[Pretorius and van Wijk 09] A. Johannes Pretorius and Jarke J. van Wijk. "What Does the User Want to See? What Do the Data Want to Be?" *Information Visualization* 8:3 (2009), 153–166. *(page 92)*

[Purchase 12] Helen Purchase. *Experimental Human-Computer Interaction: A Practical Guide with Visual Examples.* Cambridge University Press, 2012. *(page 93)*

[Rieder et al. 08] Christian Rieder, Felix Ritter, Matthias Raspe, and Heinz-Otto Peitgen. "Interactive Visualization of Multimodal Volume Data for Neurosurgical Tumor Treatment." *Computer Graphics Forum (Proc. EuroVis 08)* 27:3 (2008), 1055–1062. *(page 259)*

[Robbins 06] Naomi B. Robbins. "Dot Plots: A Useful Alternative to Bar Charts." http://www.perceptualedge.com/articles/b-eye/dot_plots.pdf, 2006. *(page 297)*

[Roberts 07] Jonathan C. Roberts. "State of the Art: Coordinated & Multiple Views in Exploratory Visualization." In *Proceedings of the Conference on Coordinated & Multiple Views in Exploratory Visualization (CMV)*, pp. 61–71. IEEE Computer Society, 2007. *(page 296)*

[Robertson et al. 91] George Robertson, Jock Mackinlay, and Stuart Card. "Cone Trees: Animated 3D Visualizations of Hierarchical Information." In *Proceedings of the SIGCHI Conference on Human Factors in Computing Systems (CHI)*, pp. 189–194. ACM, 1991. *(pages 327, 338)*

[Robertson et al. 98] George Robertson, Mary Czerwinski, Kevin Larson, Daniel C. Robbins, David Thiel, and Maarten Van Dantzich. "Data Mountain: Using Spatial Memory for Document Management." In *Proceedings of the Symposium on User Interface Software and Technology (UIST)*, pp. 153–162. ACM, 1998. *(page 129)*

[Robertson et al. 08] George Robertson, Roland Fernandez, Danyel Fisher, Bongshin Lee, and John Stasko. "Effectiveness of Animation in Trend Visualization." *IEEE Transactions on Visualization and Computer Graphics (Proc. InfoVis 08)* 14:6 (2008), 1325–1332. *(pages 142, 147)*

[Rogowitz and Treinish 96] Bernice E. Rogowitz and Lloyd A. Treinish. "How Not to Lie with Visualization." *Computers in Physics* 10:3 (1996), 268–273. *(page 240)*

[Rogowitz and Treinish 98] Bernice E. Rogowitz and Lloyd A. Treinish. "Data Visualization: The End of the Rainbow." *IEEE Spectrum* 35:12 (1998), 52–59. Alternate version published online as *Why Should Engineers and Scientists Be Worried about Color?*, http://www.research.ibm.com/people/l/lloydt/color/color.HTM. *(pages 233, 240)*

[Saraiya et al. 05] Purvi Saraiya, Chris North, and Karen Duca. "An Insight-Based Methodology for Evaluating Bioinformatics Visualizations." *IEEE Transactions on Visualization and Computer Graphics (TVCG)* 11:4 (2005), 443–456. *(page 78)*

[Scarr et al. 13] Joey Scarr, Andy Cockburn, and Carl Gutwin. "Supporting and Exploiting Spatial Memory in User Interfaces." *Foundations and Trends in HumanComputer Interaction* 6 (2013), Article no. 1. *(page 141)*

[Schroeder and Martin 05] William J. Schroeder and Kenneth M. Martin. "Overview of Visualization." In *The Visualization Handbook*, edited by Charles Hansen and Christopher Johnson, pp. 3–39. Elsevier, 2005. *(page 197)*

[Schroeder et al. 06] Will Schroeder, Ken Martin, and Bill Lorensen. *The Visualization Toolkit: An Object-Oriented Approach to 3D Graphics*, Fourth edition. Pearson, 2006. *(pages xvii, 40)*

[Schulz et al. 11] Hans-Jörg Schulz, Steffen Hadlak, and Heidrun Schumann. "The Design Space of Implicit Hierarchy Visualization: A Survey." *IEEE Transactions on Visualization and Computer Graphics* 17:4 (2011), 393–411. *(page 217)*

[Schulz 11] Hans-Jörg Schulz. "Treevis.net: A Tree Visualization Reference." *IEEE Computer Graphics and Applications* 31:6 (2011), 11–15. *(page 216)*

[Sedlmair et al. 12] Michael Sedlmair, Miriah Meyer, and Tamara Munzner. "Design Study Methodology: Reflections from the Trenches and the Stacks." *IEEE Transactions on Visualization and Computer Graphics (Proc. InfoVis 12)* 18:12 (2012), 2431–2440. *(pages 19, 92)*

[Sedlmair et al. 13] Michael Sedlmair, Tamara Munzner, and Melanie Tory. "Empirical Guidance on Scatterplot and Dimension Reduction Technique Choices." *IEEE Transactions on Visualization and Computer Graphics (Proc. InfoVis 13)* 19:12 (2013), 2634–2643. *(pages 320, 321)*

[Seo and Shneiderman 02] Jinwook Seo and Ben Shneiderman. "Interactively Exploring Hierarchical Clustering Results." *IEEE Computer* 35:7 (2002), 80–86. *(pages 341, 351, 352, 367)*

[Seo and Shneiderman 05] Jinwook Seo and Ben Shneiderman. "A Rank-by-Feature Framework for Interactive Exploration of Multidimensional Data." *Information Visualization* 4:2 (2005), 96–113. *(pages 340, 341, 351, 353, 354, 367)*

[Sharp et al. 07] Helen Sharp, Yvonne Rogers, and Jenny Preece. *Interaction Design: Beyond Human-Computer Interaction*. Wiley, 2007. *(page 92)*

[Shirley and Marschner 09] Peter Shirley and Steve Marschner. *Fundamentals of Computer Graphics*, Third edition. A K Peters, 2009. *(page xxi)*

[Shneiderman and Plaisant 06] Ben Shneiderman and Catherine Plaisant. "Strategies for Evaluating Information Visualization Tools: Multi-dimensional In-Depth Long-Term Case Studies." In *Proceedings of the AVI Workshop on BEyond time and errors: novel evaLuation methods for Information Visualization (BELIV)*, Article no. 6. ACM, 2006. *(page 92)*

[Shneiderman 96] Ben Shneiderman. "The Eyes Have It: A Task by Data Type Taxonomy for Information Visualizations." In *Proceedings of the IEEE Conference on Visual Languages*, pp. 336–343. IEEE Computer Society, 1996. *(pages 40, 135, 142)*

[Simons 00] Daniel J. Simons. "Current Approaches to Change Blindness." *Visual Cognition* 7:1/2/3 (2000), 1–15. *(pages 15, 19, 142)*

[Sinha and Meller 07] Amit Sinha and Jaroslaw Meller. "Cinteny: Flexible Analysis and Visualization of Synteny and Genome Rearrangements in Multiple Organisms." *BMC Bioinformatics* 8:1 (2007), 82. *(page 228)*

[Slack et al. 06] James Slack, Kristian Hildebrand, and Tamara Munzner. "PRISAD: Partitioned Rendering Infrastructure for Scalable Accordion Drawing (Extended Version)." *Information Visualization* 5:2 (2006), 137–151. *(pages 332, 332, 338)*

[Slingsby et al. 09] Adrian Slingsby, Jason Dykes, and Jo Wood. "Configuring Hierarchical Layouts to Address Research Questions." *IEEE Transactions on Visualization and Computer Graphics (Proc. InfoVis 09)* 15:6 (2009), 977–984. *(pages 286, 287, 296)*

[Slocum et al. 08] Terry A. Slocum, Robert B. McMaster, Fritz C. Kessler, and Hugh H. Howard. *Thematic Cartography and Geovisualization*, Third edition. Prentice Hall, 2008. *(page 197)*

[Spence and Apperley 82] Robert Spence and Mark Apperley. "Data Base Navigation: An Office Environment for the Professional." *Behaviour and Information Technology* 1:1 (1982), 43–54. *(page 337)*

[Spence 07] Robert Spence. *Information Visualization: Design for Interaction*, Second edition. Prentice Hall, 2007. *(page xvii)*

[Springmeyer et al. 92] Rebecca R. Springmeyer, Meera M. Blattner, and Nelson L. Max. "A Characterization of the Scientific Data Analysis Process." In *Proceedings of the IEEE Conference on Visualization (Vis)*, pp. 235–252. IEEE Computer Society, 1992. *(page 64)*

[St. John et al. 01] Mark St. John, Michael B. Cowen, Harvey S. Smallman, and Heather M. Oonk. "The Use of 2-D and 3-D Displays for Shape Understanding versus Relative Position Tasks." *Human Factors* 43:1 (2001), 79–98. *(pages 119, 119, 124, 129, 141)*

[Steinberger et al. 11] Markus Steinberger, Manuela Waldner, Marc Streit, Alexander Lex, and Dieter Schmalstieg. "Context-Preserving Visual Links." *IEEE Transactions on Visualization and Computer Graphics (Proc. InfoVis 11)* 17:12 (2011), 2249–2258. *(page 253, 253)*

[Stevens 46] S. S. Stevens. "On the Theory of Scales of Measurement." *Science* 103:2684 (1946), 677–680. *(pages 33, 40)*

[Stevens 57] S. S. Stevens. "On the Psychophysical Law." *Psychological Review* 64:3 (1957), 153–181. *(pages 115, 118)*

[Stevens 75] S. S. Stevens. *Psychophysics: Introduction to Its Perceptual, Neural, and Social Prospects.* Wiley, 1975. *(pages 103, 104, 115)*

[Stolte et al. 02] Chris Stolte, Diane Tang, and Pat Hanrahan. "Multiscale Visualization Using Data Cubes." In *Proceedings of the IEEE Symposium on Information Visualization (InfoVis)*, pp. 176–187. IEEE Computer Society, 2002. *(page 40)*

[Stone 03] Maureen Stone. *A Field Guide to Digital Color.* A K Peters, 2003. *(page 240)*

[Stone 06] Maureen Stone. "Color in Information Display." IEEE Visualization Course Notes, 2006. http://www.stonesc.com/Vis06. *(page 221)*

[Stone 10] Maureen Stone. "Get It Right in Black and White." *Functional Color*, http://www.stonesc.com/wordpress/2010/03/get-it-right-in-black-and-white, 2010. *(pages 140, 142, 240, 289, 290, 296, 373)*

[Telea 07] Alexandru Telea. *Data Visualization: Principles and Practice.* A K Peters, 2007. *(pages xvii, 40, 92)*

[Torgerson 52] W. S. Torgerson. "Multidimensional Scaling: I. Theory and Method." *Psychometrika* 17 (1952), 401–419. *(page 321)*

[Tory and Möller 04a] Melanie Tory and Torsten Möller. "Human Factors in Visualization Research." *IEEE Transactions on Visualization and Computer Graphics (TVCG)* 10:1 (2004), 72–84. *(page 40)*

[Tory and Möller 04b] Melanie Tory and Torsten Möller. "Rethinking Visualization: A High-Level Taxonomy." In *Proceedings of the IEEE Symposium on Information Visualization (InfoVis)*, pp. 151–158. IEEE Computer Society, 2004. *(page 65)*

[Tory and Möller 05] Melanie Tory and Torsten Möller. "Evaluating Visualizations: Do Expert Reviews Work?" *IEEE Computer Graphics and Applications* 25:5 (2005), 8–11. *(page 78)*

[Tory et al. 07] Melanie Tory, David W. Sprague, Fuqu Wu, Wing Yan So, and Tamara Munzner. "Spatialization Design: Comparing Points and Landscapes." *IEEE Transactions on Visualization and Computer Graphics (Proc. InfoVis 07)* 13:6 (2007), 1262–1269. *(pages 129, 130, 130)*

[Tory et al. 09] Melanie Tory, Colin Swindells, and Rebecca Dreezer. "Comparing Dot and Landscape Spatializations for Visual Memory Differences." *IEEE Transactions on Visualization and Computer Graphics (Proc. InfoVis 09)* 16:6 (2009), 1033–1040. *(page 130)*

[Treisman and Gormican 88] Anne Treisman and Stephen Gormican. "Feature Analysis in Early Vision: Evidence from Search Asymmetries." *Psychological Review* 95:1 (1988), 15–48. *(page 115)*

[Tricoche et al. 02] Xavier Tricoche, Thomas Wischgoll, Gerik Scheuermann, and Hans Hagen. "Topology Tracking for the Visualization of Time-Dependent Two-Dimensional Flows." *Computers & Graphics* 26:2 (2002), 249–257. *(page 189)*

[Tufte 83] Edward R. Tufte. *The Visual Display of Quantitative Information.* Graphics Press, 1983. *(pages xvi, 19)*

[Tufte 91] Edward Tufte. *Envisioning Information.* Graphics Press, 1991. *(page xvi, xvi)*

[Tufte 97] Edward R. Tufte. *Visual Explanations.* Graphics Press, 1997. *(page xvi)*

[Tukey 77] John W. Tukey. *Exploratory Data Analysis.* Addison-Wesley, 1977. *(page 320)*

[Tversky et al. 02] Barbara Tversky, Julie Morrison, and Mireille Betrancourt. "Animation: Can It Facilitate?" *International Journal of Human Computer Studies* 57:4 (2002), 247–262. *(page 141)*

[van Ham and Perer 09] Frank van Ham and Adam Perer. "Search, Show Context, Expand on Demand: Supporting Large Graph Exploration with Degree-of-Interest." *IEEE Transactions on Visualization and Computer Graphics (Proc. InfoVis 09)* 15:6 (2009), 953–960. *(page 137)*

[van Ham 03] Frank van Ham. "Using Multilevel Call Matrices in Large Software Projects." In *Proceedings of the IEEE Symposium on Information Visualization (InfoVis)*, pp. 227–232. IEEE Computer Society, 2003. *(page 249)*

[van Wijk and Nuij 03] Jarke J. van Wijk and Wim A. A. Nuij. "Smooth and Efficient Zooming and Panning." In *Proceedings of the IEEE Symposium on Information Visualization (InfoVis)*, pp. 15–22. IEEE Computer Society, 2003. *(page 262)*

[van Wijk and van Liere 93] Jarke J. van Wijk and Robert van Liere. "HyperSlice: Visualization of Scalar Functions of Many Variables." In *Proceedings of the IEEE Conference on Visualization (Vis)*, pp. 119–125. IEEE Computer Society, 1993. *(pages 259, 260)*

[van Wijk and van Selow 99] Jarke J. van Wijk and Edward R. van Selow. "Cluster and Calendar Based Visualization of Time Series Data." In *Proceedings of the IEEE Symposium on Information Visualization (InfoVis)*, pp. 4–9. IEEE Computer Society, 1999. *(pages 125, 126)*

[van Wijk 06] Jarke J. van Wijk. "Bridging the Gaps." *IEEE Computer Graphics & Applications* 26:6 (2006), 6–9. *(page 65)*

[Velleman and Wilkinson 93] Paul F. Velleman and Leland Wilkinson. "Nominal, Ordinal, Interval, and Ratio Typologies Are Misleading." *The American Statistician* 47:1 (1993), 65–72. *(page 65)*

[Vilanova et al. 06] A. Vilanova, S. Zhang, G. Kindlmann, and D. Laidlaw. "An Introduction to Visualization of Diffusion Tensor Imaging and Its Applications." In *Visualization and Processing of Tensor Fields*, pp. 121–153. Springer, 2006. *(page 198)*

[von Landesberger et al. 11] Tatiana von Landesberger, Arjan Kuijper, Tobias Schreck, Jörn Kohlhammer, Jarke J. van Wijk, Jean-Daniel Fekete, and Dieter W. Fellner. "Visual Analysis of Large Graphs: State-of-the-Art and Future Research Challenges." *Computer Graphics Forum* 30:6 (2011), 1719–1749. *(page 216)*

[Wainer and Francolini 80] Howard Wainer and Carl M. Francolini. "An Empirical Inquiry Concerning Human Understanding of Two-Variable Color Maps." *The American Statistician* 34:2 (1980), 81–93. *(pages 235, 240)*

[Ward et al. 10] Matthew O. Ward, Georges Grinstein, and Daniel Keim. *Interactive Data Visualization: Foundations, Techniques, and Applications*. A K Peters, 2010. *(pages xvii, 40, 92)*

[Ward 02] Matthew O. Ward. "A Taxonomy of Glyph Placement Strategies for Multidimensional Data Visualization." *Information Visualization* 1:3-4 (2002), 194–210. *(page 296)*

[Ward 08] Matthew O. Ward. "Multivariate Data Glyphs: Principles and Practice." In *Handbook of Data Visualization, Computational Statistics*, edited by Antony Unwin, Chun-houh Chen, and Wolfgang K. Härdle, pp. 179–198. Springer, 2008. *(page 296)*

[Ware and Bobrow 04] Colin Ware and Robert Bobrow. "Motion to Support Rapid Interactive Queries on Node–Link Diagrams." *Transactions on Applied Perception (TAP)* 1:1 (2004), 3–18. *(pages 241, 252)*

[Ware 01] Colin Ware. "Designing with a 2 1/2 D Attitude." *Information Design Journal* 10:3 (2001), 255–262. *(page 125)*

[Ware 08] Colin Ware. *Visual Thinking for Design.* Morgan Kaufmann, 2008. *(pages xvi, 115, 119, 119, 141)*

[Ware 13] Colin Ware. *Information Visualization: Perception for Design*, Third edition. Morgan Kaufmann, 2013. *(pages xvi, 19, 108, 115, 115, 141, 141, 223, 223, 223, 240, 241, 296)*

[Wattenberg and Viegas 08] Martin Wattenberg and Fernanda B. Viegas. "The Word Tree, an Interactive Visual Concordance." *IEEE Transactions on Visualization and Computer Graphics (Proc. InfoVis 08)* 14:6 (2008), 1221–1228. *(pages 71, 72)*

[Wattenberg 05] Martin Wattenberg. "Baby Names, Visualization, and Social Data Analysis." In *Proceedings of the IEEE Symposium on Information Visualization (InfoVis)*, pp. 1–7. IEEE Computer Society, 2005. *(pages 48, 49)*

[Wattenberg 06] Martin Wattenberg. "Visual Exploration of Multivariate Graphs." In *Proceedings of the SIGCHI Conference on Human Factors in Computing Systems (CHI)*, pp. 811–819. ACM, 2006. DOI 10.1145/1124772.1124891. *(pages 340, 341, 355, 356, 357, 367, 374, 374)*

[Weaver 04] Chris Weaver. "Building Highly-Coordinated Visualizations in Improvise." In *Proceedings of the IEEE Symposium on Information Visualization (InfoVis)*, pp. 159–166. IEEE Computer Society, 2004. *(pages 277, 296)*

[Weaver 10] Chris Weaver. "Cross-Filtered Views for Multidimensional Visual Analysis." *IEEE Transactions on Visualization and Computer Graphics* 16:2 (2010), 192–204. *(page 296)*

[Wegman 90] Edward J. Wegman. "Hyperdimensional Data Analysis Using Parallel Coordinates." *Journal of the American Statistical Association (JASA)* 85:411 (1990), 664–675. *(pages 164, 176)*

[Weickert and Hagen 06] Joachim Weickert and Hans Hagen, editors. *Visualization and Processing of Tensor Fields.* Springer, 2006. *(page 198)*

[Weiskopf and Erlebacher 05] Daniel Weiskopf and Gordon Erlebacher. "Overview of Flow Visualization." In *The Visualization Handbook*, edited by Charles Hansen and Christopher Johnson, pp. 261–278. Elsevier, 2005. *(page 198)*

[Wickham and Hofmann 11] Hadley Wickham and Heike Hofmann. "Product Plots." *IEEE Transactions on Visualization and Computer Graphics (Proc. InfoVis 11)* 17:12 (2011), 2223–2230. *(page 175)*

[Wickham and Stryjewski 12] Hadley Wickham and Lisa Stryjewski. "40 Years of Boxplots." Technical report, had.co.nz, 2012. *(pages 309, 320)*

[Wickham et al. 12] Hadley Wickham, Heike Hofmann, Charlotte Wickham, and Diane Cook. "Glyph-Maps for Visually Exploring Temporal Patterns in Climate Data and Models." *Environmetrics* 23:5 (2012), 382–393. *(pages 170, 171)*

[Wickham 10] Hadley Wickham. "A Layered Grammar of Graphics." *Journal of Computational and Graphical Statistics* 19:1 (2010), 3–28. *(pages 148, 167, 168)*

[Wilkinson and Friendly 09] Leland Wilkinson and Michael Friendly. "The History of the Cluster Heat Map." *The American Statistician* 63:2 (2009), 179–184. *(page 176)*

[Wilkinson and Wills 08] Leland Wilkinson and Graham Wills. "Scagnostics Distributions." *Journal of Computational and Graphical Statistics (JCGS)* 17:2 (2008), 473–491. *(pages 345, 366)*

[Wilkinson et al. 05] Leland Wilkinson, Anushka Anand, and Robert Grossman. "Graph-Theoretic Scagnostics." In *Proceedings of the IEEE Symposium on Information Visualization (InfoVis)*, pp. 157–164. IEEE Computer Society, 2005. *(pages 340, 341, 342, 343, 346, 366)*

[Wilkinson et al. 06] Leland Wilkinson, Anushka Anand, and Robert Grossman. "High-Dimensional Visual Analytics: Interactive Exploration Guided by Pairwise Views of Point Distributions." *IEEE Transactions on Visualization and Computer Graphics* 12:6 (2006), 1363–1372. *(pages 341, 342)*

[Wilkinson 99] Leland Wilkinson. "Dot Plots." *The American Statistician* 53:3 (1999), 276–281. *(page 155)*

[Wilkinson 05] Leland Wilkinson. *The Grammar of Graphics*, Second edition. Springer, 2005. *(pages xvii, 40, 175)*

[Willett et al. 07] Wesley Willett, Jeffrey Heer, and Maneesh Agrawala. "Scented Widgets: Improving Navigation Cues with Embedded Visualizations." *IEEE Transactions on Visualization and Computer Graphics (Proc. InfoVis 07)* 13:6 (2007), 1129–1136. *(pages 303, 303, 320)*

[Williams 08] Robin Williams. *The Non-Designer's Design Book*, Third edition. Peachpit Press, 2008. *(page 142)*

[Wills 95] Graham J. Wills. "Visual Exploration of Large Structured Datasets." In *Proceedings of New Techniques and Trends in Statistics (NTTS)*, pp. 237–246. IOS Press, 1995. *(page 268, 268, 268)*

[Wills 96] Graham J. Wills. "Selection: 524,288 Ways to Say 'This Is Interesting'." In *Proceedings of the IEEE Symposium on Information Visualization (InfoVis)*, pp. 54–61. IEEE Computer Society, 1996. *(page 262)*

[Wills 08] Graham J. Wills. "Linked Data Views." In *Handbook of Data Visualization, Computational Statistics*, edited by Antony Unwin, Chun-houh Chen, and Wolfgang K. Härdle, pp. 216–241. Springer, 2008. *(page 296)*

[Wise et al. 95] J. A. Wise, J.J. Thomas, K. Pennock, D. Lantrip, M. Pottier, A. Schur, and V. Crow. "Visualizing the Non-Visual: Spatial Analysis and Interaction with Information from Text Documents." In *Proceedings of the IEEE Symposium on Information Visualization (InfoVis)*, pp. 51–58. IEEE Computer Society, 1995. *(page 130)*

[Wong 09] David Wong. "The Modifiable Areal Unit Problem (MAUP)." In *The SAGE Handbook of Spatial Analysis*, edited by A. Stewart Fotheringham and Peter A. Rogerson, pp. 105–123. Sage, 2009. *(page 321)*

[Wood and Dykes 08] Jo Wood and Jason Dykes. "Spatially Ordered Treemaps." *IEEE Transactions on Visualization and Computer Graphics (Proc. InfoVis 08)* 14:6 (2008), 1348–1355. *(pages 288, 296)*

[Yang et al. 02] Jing Yang, Matthew O. Ward, and Elke A. Rundensteiner. "InterRing: An Interactive Tool for Visually Navigating and Manipulating Hierarchical Structures." In *Proceedings of the IEEE Symposium on Information Visualization (InfoVis)*, pp. 77–84. IEEE Computer Society, 2002. *(pages 340, 341, 358, 359, 367)*

[Yang et al. 03a] Jing Yang, Wei Peng, Matthew O. Ward, and Elke A. Rundensteiner. "Interactive Hierarchical Dimension Ordering, Spacing and Filtering for Exploration of High Dimensional Datasets." In *Proceedings of the IEEE Symposium on Information Visualization (InfoVis)*, pp. 105–112. IEEE Computer Society, 2003. *(pages 304, 304, 321)*

[Yang et al. 03b] Jing Yang, Matthew O. Ward, Elke A. Rundensteiner, and Shiping Huang. "Visual Hierarchical Dimension Reduction for Exploration of High Dimensional Datasets." In *Proceedings of the Eurographics/IEEE Symposium on Visualization (VisSym)*, pp. 19–28. Eurographics, 2003. *(page 321)*

[Yang et al. 04] Jing Yang, Anilkumar Patro, Shiping Huang, Nishant Mehta, Matthew O. Ward, and Elke A. Rundensteiner. "Value and Relation Display for Interactive Exploration of High Dimensional Datasets." In *Proceedings of the IEEE Symposium on Information Visualization (InfoVis)*, pp. 73–80. IEEE Computer Society, 2004. *(page 321)*

[Yi et al. 07] Ji Soo Yi, Youn Ah Kang, John T. Stasko, and Julie A. Jacko. "Toward a Deeper Understanding of the Role of Interaction in Information Visualization." *IEEE Transactions on Visualization and Computer Graphics (Proc. InfoVis 07)* 13:6 (2007), 1224–1231. *(page 142)*

[Young and Householder 38] G. Young and A. S. Householder. "Discussion of a Set of Points in Terms of Their Mutual Distances." *Psychometrika* 3:1. *(page 321)*

[Zacks and Tversky 99] Jeff Zacks and Barbara Tversky. "Bars and Lines: A Study of Graphic Communication." *Memory and Cognition* 27:6 (1999), 1073–1079. *(pages 156, 157, 175)*

[Zacks and Tversky 03] Jeffrey M. Zacks and Barbara Tversky. "Structuring Information Interfaces for Procedural Learning." *Journal of Experimental Psychology: Applied* 9:2 (2003), 88–100. *(page 141)*

[Zhang and Norman 95] Jiajie Zhang and Donald A. Norman. "A Representational Analysis of Numeration Systems." *Cognition* 57 (1995), 271–295. *(page 19)*

[Zhang 97] Jiajie Zhang. "The Nature of External Representations in Problem Solving." *Cognitive Science* 21:2 (1997), 179–217. *(page 19)*

[Zuk et al. 08] Torre Zuk, Lothar Schlesier, Petra Neumann, Mark S. Hancock, and Sheelagh Carpendale. "Heuristics for Information Visualization Evaluation." In *Proceedings of the AVI Workshop on BEyond time and errors: novel evaLuation methods for Information Visualization (BELIV)*, Article no. 9. ACM, 2008. *(page 78)*

Idiom and System Examples Index

Concept Index